Poets, Prophets,
and Revolutionaries

Poets, Prophets, and Revolutionaries

THE LITERARY AVANT-GARDE FROM RIMBAUD THROUGH POSTMODERNISM

Charles Russell

New York   Oxford

OXFORD UNIVERSITY PRESS

1985

Oxford University Press

London   New York   Toronto
Delhi   Bombay   Calcutta   Madras   Karachi
Kuala Lumpur   Singapore   Hong Kong   Tokyo
Nairobi   Dar es Salaam   Cape Town
Melbourne   Auckland

and associated companies in
Beirut   Berlin   Ibadan   Mexico City   Nicosia

Copyright © 1985 by Oxford University Press, Inc.

Published by Oxford University Press, Inc.,
200 Madison Avenue, New York, New York 10016

Printing (last digit):   9 8 7 6 5 4 3 2 1

Printed in the United States of America

Preface

For more than a century now, the term "avant-garde" has been part of popular parlance, literary and artistic debate, and academic discourse in Europe and the Americas. It has been used to describe fields of social activity as diverse as political activism, successive waves of clothing fashions, even hair styles, and the numerous innovations in the "high" and "low" arts, from architecture to popular music. The variety of uses of the term is significant in itself, for it calls our attention to the values and expectations of a society apparently obsessed with constant change, with the promise—or threat—that the future holds, and with the sensed inadequacy or irrelevance of the past and even the present moment. Thus, if we wish to use the word "avant-garde" as a meaningful term for the works and theories of a number of modern writers and artists—either to define a particular movement called "the" avant-garde or to illuminate a significant aesthetic sensibility shared by a diverse group of writers and artists—we have first to take into account that the term avant-garde, like many popular terms, is so loosely defined and indiscriminately used that we must provide a working definition appropriate to the particular arts we study.

Presently, in the literary and art worlds, "avant-garde" occurs most frequently in the popular media and the organs of the culture industry, particularly in journalistic criticism of the literary and art scenes.

Here it is rather promiscuously applied to whichever movement, individual, or work is said to represent the most recent trend—or fad—
in any number of popular and "serious" arts. Depending on the critic's tastes or allegiances, the new avant-garde might signal either a
commodity or idea to be possessed and consumed for fashion and social status, a potential financial investment, or the latest installment
in a long-standing tradition of bohemian, aesthetic rebellion against
bourgeois taste—hence something to criticize, laud, or merely analyze
in print. Even among writers and artists, who are more likely to use
the term seriously, the concept of the avant-garde frequently lacks
precision and appears to depend on the vicissitudes of social history
and aesthetic fashion. For example, writers and artists of some periods (such as the nineteen-twenties) have enthusiastically adopted the
term to announce their social disaffiliation and their aesthetic and
political radicalism; at other times it is the collectors, investors, and
publicists who seem to govern the dispensation of the title independently of the writers' and artists' intentions. In the literary and art
worlds the term itself goes in and out of fashion erratically. Thus,
for example, artists of a decade such as the nineteen-sixties might
confidently declare all stylistic innovations "avant-garde," while during another period, such as the nineteen-seventies and early eighties,
writers, artists, and critics seem almost embarrassed to use the word,
even though significant innovations continue to occur.

One might assume that academic writers would be more serious
about their terminology and less profligate in their tendency to label
writers and artists avant-garde. Yet there are significant disagree-
ments about the meaning and use of the term avant-garde in the
academy, especially among British and American critics. Some treat
it as a period term; for others it distinguishes a particular aesthetic
sensibility manifested in stylistic innovation; for still others the
avant-garde is a more or less coherent movement of writers and artists distinct from many of the major writers and artists of the modern period. Indeed, there is even less consensus about who is "avant-
garde." For some critics any self-conscious literary innovator merits
the name: Proust, Pound, Marinetti, Joyce, Stein, Tzara, Eliot,
Woolf, Breton, and Beckett have all been called avant-garde. Other
critics declare that the differences among these writers are so great
that no one term is adequate. Similarly, some literary historians apply the term only to the writers' aesthetic activities, while others assert that the true avant-garde links aesthetic innovation with social
activism. In addition, there is sharp disagreement about when the
avant-garde first appeared. Its origins have been located in the Ro-

mantic period, in the mid- and late nineteenth century, and during
the first three decades of the twentieth century. Finally, much critical debate centers upon whether there is—or even can be—an avant-
garde today.

Part of the confusion originates in the problem of establishing any
coherent terminology for aesthetic periods. Who or what is deemed
avant-garde depends on which specific characteristics a critic accents,
what antecedents and what aesthetic and social contexts he or she describes. Frequently, the critic's perspective is restricted by his or her
participation in a critical tradition that does not usually inquire into
the social aspirations or political context of the literary work. And
part of the difficulty lies in the fact that the avant-garde actively challenges the aesthetic values and political assumptions of the scholars
and critics who are attempting to define the avant-garde.

A primary example of this confusion of perspective and terminology is the various uses of the words "modernism" and "avant-garde"
in critical discourse today. When academic critics have referred to
the patterns of formal innovation in the arts of the past century, they
rarely have clearly distinguished between the two terms. For example, Renato Poggioli's important book, *The Theory of the Avant-
Garde,* uses the concept of the avant-garde to define the basic aesthetic
sensibility of the modern period. To Poggioli, all major formally
innovative writers—Rimbaud and Eliot, Marinetti and Pound, Apollinaire and Joyce, the surrealists and Proust—are avant-garde. Alter-
natively, Malcolm Bradbury and James MacFarlane adopt the term
"modernism" for the title of their comprehensive collection of essays on the international movement of innovative literature, while
slighting the term "avant-garde." Much more frequently, however,
academic critics speak of the avant-garde and modernism interchange-
ably, treating the two terms as synonyms.

In tracing the history of the literary avant-garde and discussing the
works of particular avant-garde writers and movements, I necessarily
enter into this terminological debate. I believe it valuable to distinguish among the various aesthetic strategies of modern writers, and
one way of doing this is to use the two terms modernism and the
avant-garde as categories that delineate distinct forms of aesthetic behavior and vision. Although this book is not primarily an essay on
terminology, it suggests that discriminations can be made among
writers that will allow an analysis of the avant-garde as an important,
if subsidiary, phenomenon in modern culture.

My primary assumption is that while many modern writers share
the need to create self-consciously innovative works, there are signifi-

cant differences between the aesthetic visions of such representative writers of the past century as, on the one hand, Eliot, Woolf, Pound, Proust, and Pirandello, and, on the other hand, Rimbaud, Tzara, Marinetti, Breton, and Brecht. I distinguish between modernism and the avant-garde initially by discussing the explicit temporal references of these terms and then by grouping the different aesthetic programs of modern writers according to the types of behavior that can be associated with the two terms. Certainly, both modernism and the avant-garde point to the modern writer's awareness of the compulsive aspects of the past century's experience of time, especially of a sense of inescapable "modernity" and of a society threatened, or driven, by a vision of convulsive history. In this context, I use "modernism" to suggest many writers' efforts to create in the context of—and often in spite of—an ambivalent sense of cultural modernity. Modernism signals the writers' and artists' heightened sensation of the new and constantly changing social and aesthetic visions of their societies. Thus, I believe that modernism can be used as a comprehensive period term though I use it most frequently to refer to individual writers or groups of writers deeply concerned with the most problematic aspects of their time's modernity, individuals who have been, not incidentally, among the most significant writers of the past century. I believe the term avant-garde can be profitably used to distinguish writers and artists who believe not only that the world they inhabit is essentially modern and that they need to find an aesthetic language to express this newness, but also that they are in some manner in advance of a future state of art and society which their innovative works will help bring into existence.

Thus, exemplary "modernist" writers, such as Proust, Eliot, Pound, Woolf, and Joyce, may have created dramatically innovative works, works which have influenced later generations of innovative writers. But generally, their sensed alienation from modern culture and their fear for the loss of the traditional bases of art led them to seek—even within their innovations—to sustain a tradition of high art that would transcend or devalue the apparently disruptive social and historical change that heightened the sensation of their modernity. The avant-garde, on the other hand, has been represented by writers and movements such as Rimbaud, Italian and Russian futurism, dada, surrealism, and Brecht, writers who were much more prone to find the tradition of high art and culture excessively restrictive in their desire to declare themselves "en avant"—in advance of a radically new culture. The adoption of this military-political term is an expression of the writers' self-conscious extremism, an extremism meant to accelerate the disruption of aesthetic and social traditions in order to thrust art and society further and faster into the future.

Both modernism and the avant-garde may be seen as activist movements, for both create new literary forms to express new personal and collective realities. But in every case, avant-garde writers and artists are more extreme, more radical in their behavior and in their aesthetic and ultimately political vision than are the modernists. The avant-garde writers are more nihilistic in their rejection of the social values and aesthetic practices of their predecessors and contemporaries; they are more extreme in their belief that a new art and a new society can emerge from aesthetic and social activism. In effect, avant-garde writers expressly seek to alter the nature and social function of literature in order to go beyond the generally hermetic aesthetic boundaries that the modernists assign themselves. Avant-garde writers at all points attempt to act in and on social reality, both through literary creation and personal behavior. At times this activism takes the form of extreme bohemian behavior, at others, it is seen in their identification with the radical politics of the left or the right; at still other times, it takes the form of their appropriation of the language of scientific experimentation and technological advances to justify their aesthetic innovations and social utopianism. But for all avant-garde writers, the basis of personal and collective vision and the agent of social change is the aesthetic activism of literary innovation.

This book represents, in part, an exercise in analytic and classificatory criticism. I group writers and artists within the classification "avant-garde" by identifying patterns of aesthetic and social assumptions and behavior evident in the works of a diverse group of writers who express an activist stance towards art, society, and the future. The particular characteristics of avant-garde behavior are varied and are shared, in different combinations and to different degrees, by a significant number of writers and artists of the past one hundred and twenty-five years. Thus, when I discuss "the avant-garde," I am speaking less of an explicit, coherent literary movement than of the striking recurrence of a number of aesthetic assumptions and strategies consciously adopted by writers which distinguish them from most of their contemporaries. Yet it is fair to say that an avant-garde "movement" has emerged as generations of writers and artists have exhibited similar attitudes towards their work and culture. Many of the writers I discuss were both aware of and referred explicitly to the work of other similarly innovative creators. Many of them self-consciously adopted the label "avant-garde" or declared themselves to be "in advance" of their true audience of the future. Some of these writers and artists, however, neither called themselves avant-garde nor would have been comfortable with the name, though their works and their vision of the role and future of art clearly ally them with the interests of the other writers of the avant-garde. Finally, there are even some writers whom I discuss, such as Apollinaire, whose work in many of its aspects even contradicted some of what I hold to be the basic tenets of avant-garde writing. Nevertheless, they exemplify the essential concerns of a tradition of writers who believed themselves to be participating in the creation of a new world and art.

Thus, in this book, I argue that distinctions can and should be drawn among avant-garde and modernist writers, that there is a particular avant-garde sensibility, and, in fact, that a movement and a tradition of avant-garde creation have existed in Europe and the Americas for the past one hundred years. This study focuses, then, on what I consider to be representative avant-garde writers and movements and, more specifically, on the aesthetic and behavioral aspects of these writers' critiques of the aesthetic, social, and political values of their society. I also examine their assumptions about the nature and significance of activist literary innovation—an innovation which attempts to alter the practice of writing, yet also intends to change consciousness, personal and collective behavior, and social and political reality as well. Yet this book is not primarily a study of the writers' political visions; nor does it analyze the works of the avowedly marxist writers who attempted to create a socially activist literature by adopting the naturalist heritage of socialist realism. The writers I identify as avant-garde tend to dismiss the activist claims of socialist realism in their belief that in order for society truly to change, art must free itself from the nineteenth century bourgeois tradition of realism upon which socialist realism is based and discover instead radically innovative forms of perception, expression, and action. In effect, although I insist on the differences between the avant-garde and modernism, the avant-garde is finally more closely related to the modernist tradition of individual aesthetic innovation than to the more programmatic political action of the engaged writers with whom the avant-garde's social radicalism has frequently brought the avant-garde writers into temporary alliances.

Although the writers and movements I have chosen to discuss are representative of what I have defined as the avant-garde sensibility, this book does not claim to be comprehensive. Clearly, other writers, such as several of the German expressionists as well as the American beats, exhibit many aesthetic and social tendencies that conform to what I classify as avant-garde; furthermore, there have been a myriad of smaller and more ephemeral avant-garde movements throughout the century. And although the avant-garde tends to be a group phenomenon, I have chosen to discuss certain individual writers, such as Rimbaud, Apollinaire, and Brecht, because they believed themselves and their art to be in advance of a qualitatively different future culture and because they asserted that the formal innovations of their works contributed actively to its emergence.

The individual chapters which discuss these writers and movements emphasize particular aspects of what seems most essential about the avant-garde sensibility in the writers' works. As a consequence, what I accent in one chapter—such as the writers' attitudes toward modernity and the technological future in the Apollinaire and Italian futurism chapter—may also characterize the works of other writers, but in the chapters devoted to those writers I emphasize other attributes of avant-garde activism. My intention has not been to present radically new interpretations of the writers' individual works or careers, but rather to see what is often familiar about an individual's or movement's career within a framework of an ill-perceived and misunderstood tradition of aesthetic activism that makes up the record of the avant-garde. Taken together, these studies should provide both an analysis of the phenomenology of the avant-garde aesthetic venture and an overview of the history of the avant-garde. Since each avant-garde initiative is a product of the historical situation of its creator, the works and theories of the individual writers and movements are seen in terms of their historical contexts; therefore, the avant-garde is described as a phenomenon constantly modified by individual temperament and social-historical situation. Ultimately, this leads us to the question of the relevance of the idea of the avant-garde in the contemporary period—this age of the postmodern. Thus, while I begin this book with a general discussion of the theory and history of the avant-garde, I conclude it with an inquiry into the state of the avant-garde today.

Swarthmore, Pennsylvania   C.R.
August 1984

Acknowledgments

In the process of writing this book, I have benefited from the examples of other writers' works and from many conversations with artists, writers, colleagues, and students about my ideas as they were being formulated. My debts are widespread and diverse. A chance conversation in a photocopying center with a colleague, a student's question in class, a late night dinner conversation with a former mentor, editorial discussions with my fellow editors on *The American Book Review,* and the fortuitous participation in a week-long international symposium on cultural innovation and renovation, all have contributed to this work. This book is offered with gratitude to the many friends and colleagues I have known and worked with in the past and to those who will continue the discussion with me in the future.

These ideas have been made public in a series of academic conferences, visiting lectures, here and abroad, in classes, and in print. Sections of chapter eight appeared in different form in *Chicago Review* and *Sub-stance.* I thank their editors for their early support and permission to use the material again.

I received financial support from the National Endowment for the Humanities' Summer Fellowship program and from a Rutgers University FASP grant, as well as from the Rutgers University Research Council, and for this I am grateful.

For her constant personal support and assistance in revising, and for being a model of a scholar and writer, I am indebted beyond words:

Mary Poovey

Contents

Chapter I   The Theory of the Avant-garde   3

Chapter II   The Poet as Seer: Rimbaud   39

Chapter III   The Poets of Time: Apollinaire and the Ital-
                 ian Futurists   62

Chapter IV   Negation, Scandal, and Purification: The
                 Dada Movements   97

Chapter V   The Revolutionary Unconscious: Surrealism   122

Chapter VI   The Avant-garde and Political Revolution:
                 Mayakovsky and Russian Futurism   165

Chapter VII   Literature, Politics, and the Critical Spirit:
                 Brecht   206

Chapter VIII   Postmodernism and the Neo-avant-garde   236

                 Notes   271

                 Selected Bibliography   285

                 Index   297

Poets, Prophets,
and Revolutionaries

The Theory of the Avant-garde

In 1871, Arthur Rimbaud, describing the new type of poetry that he believed must be created for his age, declared: "the poet would define the amount of the unknown awakening in his time in the universal soul: he would give more—than the formulation of his thought, than the annotation *of his march toward Progress!* Enormity becoming normal, absorbed by all, he would really be *a multiplier of progress! . . .* Poetry . . . *will be in advance.*"[1]

Fifty years later, the Futurist painters declaimed "there can be no modern painting without the starting point of an absolutely modern sensation. . . . If our paintings are Futurist, it is because they are the result of absolutely Futurist conceptions, ethical, aesthetic, political, social."[2]

In our own period, similar voices, though muted, insist that the mission of vanguard writing and art is to challenge outdated and restrictive aesthetic traditions in order to open up new possibilities of expression and vision, both aesthetic and ideological. Charles Bernstein of the L=A=N=G=U=A=G=E group has stated: "people can begin to take control of the language. . . . The world exists in the ways we create it and we can learn how to see the world in different ways and a lot of cracks in that system by beginning to explore alternative methods of writing and thinking and talking."[3]

Thus for more than a century now, a significant number of writers and artists of Europe and the Americas have envisioned themselves at the leading edge of the modern moment, poised on the brink of an era of discovery and change, as, in fact, the creative agents of new manners of perceiving, creating, and acting. Generation after generation, avant-garde writers, painters, sculptors, dancers, musicians, and dramatists have invoked and striven to shape the "unknown awakening" in their age. These vanguard writers and artists have struggled to find innovative literary and artistic forms both to articulate their sense of the distinctly new world in which they lived and to stimulate even further change in their art and society.

During the past one hundred years, there have been numerous avant-garde movements and many writers and artists who have called themselves, or have been called, avant-garde. Their works and aesthetic programs might appear to have little in common, their historical contexts differ, and the degree of their artistic accomplishment and reception varies. But common to all writers and artists who make up the avant-garde movement are four basic assumptions about their times, their culture, their work, and the aesthetic imagination: (1) the avant-garde perceives itself to be part of a self-consciously modern culture subject to constant socio-historical change; (2) the avant-garde adopts an explicitly critical attitude toward, and asserts its distance from, the dominant values of that culture; (3) each avant-garde movement reflects the writers' and artists' desire that art and the artist may find or create a new role within society and may ally themselves with other existing progressive or revolutionary forces to transform society; (4) but most essentially, the avant-garde explores through aesthetic disruption and innovation the possibilities of creating new art forms and languages which will bring forth new modes of perceiving, expressing, and acting—which will, in effect, proclaim the avant-garde writers as poets, prophets, and revolutionaries.

These modes of aesthetic activism are especially evident in the works of the individual writers and movements which are the subject of this book: Rimbaud, Apollinaire, the Italian futurists, the dadaists, and surrealists, Mayakovsky and the Russian futurists, Brecht, and many of the innovative writers of the postmodern period. Out of their shared assumptions concerning their writing and their role in society emerges the fundamental vision of the avant-garde, its aesthetic programs, and social vision, as well as its internal contradictions, paradoxes, and limits.

The Arts of Modernity

The origins of the avant-garde, indeed of all serious modern literature, lie in the modern writer's recognition of the deeply problematic
relationship between the writer and modern society. The writer is at
once inextricably part of the culture, driven to speak the visions
and values of the times, yet senses at the same time that the dominant
values of the society are often antagonistic or inadequate to the primary needs of the aesthetic experience. Since the mid-nineteenth
century in France, the late nineteenth century in England, and the
early twentieth century in much of the rest of Europe and the Americas, writers have been faced with three general alternatives for the
social role of literature: (1) to be the largely uncritical voice of society's primary values; (2) to articulate an ethical, spiritual, or aesthetic vision perhaps at odds with the current direction of social
thought, but in the interests of adding or recapturing a significant
dimension to that existing culture; (3) to attempt to imagine and
possibly provoke a radical change in society by their work. The first
option has led to the creation of kitsch and the popular arts of mass
culture, in addition to the lingering tradition of academic writing
and art. The second is the impulse of most serious—or "high"—art,
particularly that of the modernist movement. The third suggests the
path of the avant-garde, as well as the various movements of specifically political art.

For the dual—and often overlapping—traditions of modernism and
the avant-garde, the writers' most intimate attitudes toward the process of creation, the literary work, and the audience have all been
shaped, if not distorted, by a sense of a profound alienation from the
generally secular and materialistic focus of the society of which they
are a part. A pervasive and frequently unconscious, though at times
sharply delineated antagonism between the writer and society has resulted in anguished and paradoxical efforts to define an aesthetics appropriate to the modern age. Recognizing that he or she is necessarily a creation of modern culture, even if in rebellion against it,
the writer has had to question all aspects of the literary work and its
creation. What is the relation of the individual writer's vision to the
thoughts and values of society at large, a society apparently made up
of a myriad of isolated individuals? What is the connection between
the values and pleasures implicit in the literary and artistic work and
the general concerns and pleasures of an obsessively materialist, secular culture? How can a sense of aesthetic continuity, if not literary
tradition, be sustained in a culture which seems to privilege the ideal

of constant innovation and the denial of the past? All of these questions concern the possibility of the individual creator finding the basis for creating a work which speaks to or brings into focus the shared and affirmed positive values of modern culture. On this depends the strength of the literary or art work and the sense of personal authenticity for the artist and the audience. One critic of modern, bourgeois culture, Lucien Goldmann, has argued that major artistic and literary creations exist only:

> where there is an aspiration to surpass the individual and a search for qualitative trans-individual values. . . . Man will only be authentic to the extent that he conceives of himself or feels himself part of an evolving group and situates himself within a trans-historical or transcendent dimension.[4]

The challenge for the modern writer is to discover such a trans-historical or transcendent dimension which would link the writer and the literary work to a recognized audience. However, for most of the writers of the modernist and avant-garde traditions, a commonly assumed collective vision has not been possible since the Romantic period. In fact, to the modernist and avant-garde writers, the Romantic period marks a sort of a watershed, the conclusion to the eighteenth-century Enlightenment faith in a confluence of aesthetic vision and the progressive potentiality of bourgeois culture. The literature of the middle and late eighteenth century was an expression of the shared belief of writer and populace that human action in history could lead to the moral, political, spiritual, and aesthetic advance of the culture as a whole. In Goldmann's terms, the trans-personal was to be found in history, the temporal dimension in which individuals were joined as members of an evolving group, just as the transcendent dimension, which was formerly identified with spirituality or religion, became identified with the secular ideal of a future that human action would create. But as the promise of unending human development in history shifted from the moral and political idealism of the Enlightenment to the economic, materialist focus of the nineteenth century, and as the rising bourgeoisie's social vision of expanding human liberties appeared to be contradicted by the strident class conflict which emerged in the nineteenth century, history lost a significant teleological dimension and seemed instead to become mere ceaseless, directionless change. For the post-Romantic writers, a faith in the progress of human history was difficult, if not impossible to sustain; even in the case of avant-garde writers and artists who continued to envision the promise of the future, it could only be done from an awareness of their radical alienation from the contemporary values of their society.

Throughout this book, I refer to the separate, if historically parallel, traditions of the avant-garde and modernism. What primarily distinguishes them are their aesthetic responses to alienation from the dominant values of modern culture. Most immediately, we shall note that how a writer sustains the sense of the trans-personal and transcendent dimensions in his or her work may be seen as the basis for classifying the writer as modernist or avant-garde. Briefly stated, modernist writers, who represent the main tradition of modern writing, despair of finding in secular, social history a significant ethical, spiritual, or aesthetic dimension. The works of such exemplary modernists as Proust, Pound, Joyce, Woolf, Gide, and Hemingway all deny the possibility of discerning within the flow of modern history anything but the record of meaningless chaos or evident cultural decline. The avant-garde—represented by Rimbaud, Apollinaire, the dadaists, surrealists, and futurists, as well as Brecht and many of the postmodernists—attempts to sustain a belief in the progressive union of writer and society acting within history, but although this implies an allegiance to a Romantic vision, they are little more able than the modernists, their contemporaries, to find in modern, bourgeois society hope for either art or humanity. And if they wish to remain true to a Romantic belief in the prophetic and activist role of the writer, this must be done with full awareness of the gulf that exists between them and the audience to whom they would speak. What differentiates modernists from the avant-garde are their social and aesthetic assumptions about their cultural placement; what unites them, or makes them contemporaneous traditions, is their common awareness of the most problematic aspects of cultural modernity, a modernity which seems to rip them free of both past and future historical continuity.

The beginnings of both movements lie in mid-nineteenth-century France. In fact, they may be seen to share a common progenitor— Baudelaire. Many of Baudelaire's writings express a late-Romantic search for a visionary beauty and proclaim the necessity of thrusting oneself into the unknown in search of a transforming vision not to be found in ordinary reality. This Romantic desire and his portrayal of the poet as passionate seer directly inspired Rimbaud, the surrealists, and many avant-garde writers of the twentieth century. Baudelaire's work, however, also dramatizes the despair and frustration that make the Romantic quest necessary; and perhaps even more frequently than he depicted the search for an as yet unknown beauty,

Baudelaire seemed content to adopt the impersonal, stoic, and ironic mask of the alienated artist. Championing Gautier's ideal of hermetic aestheticism, Baudelaire developed his mystique of the absolute and self-sufficient beauty of the artwork which so influenced the great modernist poets, Mallarmé, Yeats, Valéry, and Eliot.

Ultimately, Baudelaire's writing is closer to the modernist tradition that followed him than to the avant-garde. For finally, as with his contemporary Flaubert, personal irony and a glorification of the refuge found in the artwork govern his aesthetic venture. Both this irony and aestheticism were for Baudelaire (and Flaubert) enabling strategies to live and create in bourgeois society, and especially to endure the pressures of cultural modernity. Indeed, Baudelaire's essays and poems reflect an obsession with the sensation of forced modernity. His work, especially his art criticism, returns repeatedly to the chaotic dynamism of the changing society around him and the pettiness of his culture which inordinately valued every new fashion or style that spun out of this dynamism. Baudelaire was even more aware, however, of the inherent stolidity of the new bourgeois culture, its ethical narrowness and philosophical reductiveness, its lack of spiritual vision or inspired aesthetic ideal, and worst of all, its intolerable smugness.

Nevertheless, Baudelaire recognized that it is from this world that the modern artist must create beauty. The writer's and artist's mission is to uncover the beauty that exists within their society, even if that society is dominated by a bourgeoisie which seems antithetical to it. Since all ages must have their particular forms of beauty, Baudelaire argues rather desperately, so must the modern era. But it is precisely in the concept of modernity that his problem lies. Baudelaire recognizes that all past ages had their particular sense of modernity, and it was this uniqueness that distinguished their vision of beauty from that of other periods. However, in all preceding eras, the sense of modernity had been linked to a accepted aesthetic tradition and belief in a transcendent dimension that gave the modern element both continuity and distinctiveness. "Modernity: it is the transitory, the fugitive, the contingent—one half of art, of which the other half is the eternal and the immutable."[5] The particular difficulty that the modern artist faces, Baudelaire recognized, is that neither the nature of the beauty characteristic of the new era nor the form of "the eternal and the immutable" which should be revealed within that contingent beauty may be evident to a world dominated by a narrow and disruptive sense of historical change.

Baudelaire was one of the first writers to fully realize the destructive effects of the modern age's glorification of history as the terrain upon which human promise would be displayed. Certainly, since the aesthetic "quarrel of the ancients and the moderns" during the late seventeenth century, writers and artists had generally favored the merits of the new over the authority of past aesthetic practices. By Baudelaire's time, however, modernity had become as much a threat to aesthetic production as a stimulus to it, for social modernity effectively undermined the bases upon which aesthetic traditions had rested. Baudelaire and the artists and writers who followed him were placed in the contradictory position of attempting to be true to the vision of their times and to assert some form of transcendent or transpersonal dimension in their art which their culture appeared to deny.

When, echoing Baudelaire, Rimbaud declared in 1873, *"Il faut être absolument moderne,"*[6] he stated the challenge and the compulsion that all major modern writers and artists have had to face. When, a half century later, Pound's dictum "Make it new!" articulated the demands felt by all serious writers, modernist and avant-garde alike, few could have been entirely unaware of the social anxiety implied by the corollary threat that Pound enunciated: "No good poetry is ever written in a manner twenty years old."[7] The particular tension felt by Pound and his colleagues is that the writer's need to create a new style appropriate to the present moment both tends to disrupt the sense of a coherent literary tradition and emphasizes that the value and significance of the literary work are in some essential manner determined by constantly changing extra-aesthetic social conditions, conditions over which the writer has practically no control. For the modernist writers especially, the primary aesthetic challenge is to find an appropriately modern style, yet one which enables them to assert a degree of literary and personal freedom from the world they must depict. Because literary modernism is the main tradition of serious writing in our century, a tradition against which the avant-garde is defined, even as it shares many of the same concerns, it will be of value here to discuss briefly the general modernist response to its culture.

To most of the great modernist writers, the dominant materialist concerns of bourgeois society have proven to be particularly alien to the aesthetic vision necessary for significant creation. Common social behavior and ideology are seen to be either inadequate or hostile to what writers as diverse as Rilke, Hemingway, and Proust regard as personally necessary spiritual, ethical, or aesthetic fulfillment. Nor does the economic, political, and scientific history of modern society promise significant change in the conditions of personal and collective life. In fact, modernist writers generally agree with E. M. Forster that social history is "amoral" and merely reveals the record of a disorder which only in retrospect seems to have meaning. As a consequence, the majority of modernist writers either avoid or dismiss the social context in their literary works (as frequently did Mallarmé, Trakl, Valéry, Gide, H. D., Stevens, and Beckett), or they chronicle the failure of society to provide an adequate dimension for the development of individual spirit (as did Proust, Eliot, Musil, Lawrence, Hemingway, and Joyce). In effect, most modernists, no matter what their personal political affiliations, are to some degree in accord with Mallarmé, who declared himself *"en grève"* against society.

Not surprisingly, the political positions of many modernist writers have been generally conservative, if not reactionary. Both modernist and avant-garde writers criticize the bourgeois society of which they are a part, but modernists as a group tend to dismiss the idea that further social and political change would benefit their interests. Each step into the unknown future would increase their separation from the ethical, aesthestic, and spiritual values of the classical culture upon which the tradition of serious art is based. Nor have they been able to find in the proletariat, which Marxists champion and the avant-garde frequently courts, an aesthetic sensibility that would give them cause to hope. In essence, modernists prize order—both aesthetic and political. And throughout the late nineteenth and twentieth centuries, they have often placed their social, and occasionally their literary, hopes in monarchist, fascist, and elitist political movements that seem to value order and authority, and thus retard further disruptive social change.

Commenting on the ironical situation of a society which emerged declaring the promise of history but rapidly translated the idea of cultural dynamism into the narrowest of terms, Goldmann has argued

> bourgeois thought, which like bourgeois society is tied to the existence of economic activity, is the first thought in history to be at the same time radically profane and ahistoric; the first mode of thought which tends to deny everything sacred, whether that entails the celestial sacred of transcendental religions, or the immanent sacred of the historical future. This is the fundamental reason, it seems to me, why bourgeois society has created the first expression of a radically non-aesthetic consciousness.[8]

To the extent that this is true, the modernist rejection of the sociohistoric dimension can be seen to be a fairly direct expression of its culture. Nevertheless, the writers of the late nineteenth and twentieth century who rebel against their confinement in a restrictive historical framework, seek other temporal perspectives. They deny the value of both an ahistorical and a progressive historical attitude; instead, they appeal to a transcendent, if not explicitly sacred, dimension of experience. They seek to ground their aesthetic—and social—vision in a religious, natural, anthropological, or psychological domain. Whether it be to the racial myths or mystical vision of Yeats, the religious nostalgia of Eliot, the invocation of a generative life-force of Lawrence or Miller, the cosmic longings and awe of Rilke, or Mallarmé's ideal of an absolute and hermetic book, modernist writers as a group appeal to a presumed reality beyond mere society and its history. Their search is carried on in the name of both that society, which apparently ignores such a dimension of experience, and the literary work which needs an informing structure. However, as modernist works become increasingly self-reflexive—falling back as they often do from the complex demands of a world which seems to exceed them—aesthetic allegiance appears greater than social concern, for modernist authors seem more interested in adopting an ahistorical perspective by which they can *depict* an order to the individual's experience of modern life than in asserting that such a transcendent perspective may have actual reality. Thus Eliot, for example, despite his own growing faith in a spiritual realm to which society and the writer could appeal, found in Joyce's use of myth in *Ulysses* a formal model for modern aesthetic practice. This use, he stated,

> is simply a way of controlling, of ordering, of giving a shape and a significance to the immense panorama of futility and anarchy which is contemporary history. It is a method already adumbrated by Mr. Yeats, and of the need for which I believe Mr. Yeats to have been the first contemporary to be conscious. It is a method for which the horoscope is auspicious. Psychology, . . . ethnology, and *The Golden Bough* have concurred to make possible what was impossible even a few years ago. Instead of narrative method, we may now use the mythical method. It is, I believe, a step toward making the modern world possible for art, toward . . . order and form.[9]

Eliot makes clear that the primary enemies of the modern writer and the literary work are the anarchy and futility—the chaos and meaninglessness—of modern social reality. But against this chaos, which defeats in advance the search for a unified audience or stable aesthetic tradition, all transcendent or aesthetic orders which the modernist writers project seem inevitably to reveal their own individualistic and tenuous foundations. And almost invariably, the major modernist writers are well aware of this groundlessness. Richard Gilman, discussing the self-consciousness of "modernists" such as "Joyce, Proust, Mann, Eliot, Kafka, Yeats, Stevens, Faulkner, Rilke" in terms of the "newly prophetic and quasi-religious function of literature," stated

> they understood . . . that these new worlds would remain inventions, imaginative increments . . . or surrogate visions . . . all of which arose from the most intimate connections with the world of physical events, moral questions and issues of power . . . but would leave all those things intact.[10]

In fact, no matter how coherent or encompassing its totalizing vision, the modernist work necessarily testifies to the individual sensibility which generates it. For example, the efforts of the modernists to determine the shape and unity of the personal experience of time are legion, from the intuited duration of Proustian time, to Gide's celebration of unconnected moments of passionate intensity, to Valéry's arbitrary and ironically willful assertion of order despite the impersonal discontinuity of existence.[11] Perhaps even more frequently than it invokes order in the "immense panorama" of social existence, the literary work focuses both thematically and formally on the struggle of the isolated and fragmentary consciousness to give meaning and continuity to its existence. Thematically, modernist novels present characters who constantly confront a disruptive and perhaps meaningless environment, as do Hemingway's, Woolf's, Musil's, and Beckett's, with nothing to fall back upon other than personal heroism, brute sensation, or endangered consciousness. Since the work, like the literary character, also responds aesthetically to this disturbing environment, the self-conscious literary text is torn between faithfully describing the conflicting aspects of individual experience and the desire to transcend that experience. Formally, then, the modernist work generally represents an effort either to portray the nature and quality of personal experience in modern culture, or to achieve an impersonal, hermetic voice and perspective. The first alternative highlights the processes of one's conscious or unconscious response to the environment and encompasses such techniques as stream of consciousness (Joyce, Woolf), the analytic—if fragmentary—reflections of an alienated mind (Musil), the lyric though perhaps distraught sensibility of a figure ruled by subconscious drives (Eliot, Gide), and the sensual impressionism of a passive and often victimized character (Proust, Kafka). On the other hand, the efforts of writers such as

Mallarmé, Yeats, Valéry, and the later Rilke and Stein to create a pure language, an ironic voice, an impersonal mask, or self-reflexive artwork signal an anti-Romantic and anti-expressive intention to free the literary work not only from the social referent, but also from an excessive dependence on the individual perspective and voice at the base of all modern works.

These two impulses—the personal and the impersonal—testify to a basic paradox of modernist literature. Modernist writers on the whole have reacted against the individualist, expressionist, and socially activist tendencies of the Romantic movement. However, these modernist aesthetic strategies are direct legacies of literary Romanticism, for even if the modernist vision is decidedly more private and self-contained than the Romantic, these strategies sustain the Romantic belief in the unique attributes of the literary work and the special capabilities of the poet to apprehend and articulate a realm of significant value and meaning, freed from the debasing contingency of modern bourgeois life. Throughout the modern era, writers and critics have seen in this effort an heroic, if doomed striving, for now being more than the "unacknowledged legislators of the World," as Shelley had proclaimed them, poets are called upon to serve as ersatz priests, substituting the powers of art for the religion that no longer dominates our culture. In fact, according to Lionel Trilling, the work and its creator not only provide the audience with a vision of potential authenticity; they become the self-reflexive model of its discovery. Even if the middle-class audience initially resists the poet's vision, the integrity of the aesthetic work establishes a value which the audience is invited to share.

> The work of art is authentic by reason of its entire self-definition: it is understood to exist wholly by the laws of its own being, which include the right to embody painful, ignoble, or socially inacceptable subject-matters. Similarly the artist seeks his personal authenticity in his entire autonomousness—his goal is to be as self-defining as the art-object he creates. As for the audience, its expectation is that through its communication with the work of art, which may be resistant, unpleasant, even hostile, it acquires the authenticity of which the object itself is the model and the artist the personal example.[12]

In effect, the modernist writers' aesthetic strategies announce the putative primacy of the creative consciousness and the literary work over the social domain. The work and its language thus not only create an apparently autonomous domain from which one critically views modern society, but also claim to offer new knowledge and a sense of authentic being not attainable in daily life. At every turn, modernist writers foster strategies of inwardness and aesthetic privilege which purportedly give strength and validity to private experience and perception in opposition to—but in the ultimate interests of—their society, while, in fact, they are direct expressions of that society.

Thus while the modernist work may represent a protest against its governing social conditions, and while the semi-autonomous space of the aesthetic artifice may allow a glimpse of a fragmented consciousness momentarily freed from the contingency of daily life, the literary text inevitably reveals its submission to the world against which it protests. In fact, the entire history of modernism is one of increasing internal contradictions and limitations in the modernist aesthetic. Whether the writer's ideal be the absolute, self-contained linguistic artifice of which Flaubert, Mallarmé, and Valéry dreamed, or the individual's self-possession in the midst of temporal flux which haunts the works of Woolf, Gide, Hemingway, or, instead, the totalizing perspective by which the threatened individual might glimpse a vision of essential meaning that was sought by Musil, Joyce, and Lawrence, the literary work itself only testifies to the strength of the writer's desire, not to the ideal's fulfillment. For if the literary work is meant to transcend and provide a refuge from modern society, for the past one hundred years modernist writers have struggled with the fact that the work remains a vulnerable artifact; it is the product of an individual's alienation and of his or her effort to impose personal will on a hostile or indifferent world in order to overcome or deny that alienation. The history of modernist writing—from Flaubert's clinical observation of his deluded and frustrated characters, to Beckett's obsessive and beleaguered, fragmentary voices—reveals that that alienation has not decreased; on the contrary, it has increased dramatically. However, the efficacy of personal will and the aesthetic artifice have diminished correspondingly. The social realm has expanded its dominion over individual consciousness, and social discourse has undermined the supposed autonomy and qualitative distinctiveness of aesthetic language.

Throughout its history, the avant-garde has faced the same social and aesthetic challenges. It has struggled to posit the distinctiveness of activist aesthetic behavior against the threatening social realm, only to continuously confront its increasing marginalization in its culture. For both the modernist and avant-garde traditions, this struggle is centered in the writers' assumption that they can, indeed have to, create new forms and justifications for art in their society. Thus,

even though the particular aesthetic strategies vary significantly between the two movements, several perceptive critics have argued that
they should be considered one and the same movement. For example,
Renato Poggioli, Octavio Paz, and George T. Noszlopy have called
all forms of modern literary innovation "avant-garde." Noszlopy, in
particular, has suggested, that even the seemingly major differences
between the Parnassian impulse (which I associate with modernist
"hermeticism") and socio-political activism (which I argue is one
form of avant-garde behavior) are both aspects of a single phenomenon.

> Socio-political Activism and ivory-tower Parnassism are only phenome-
> nal characteristics of the avant-garde concept of art. It is the idea of
> commitment as an aesthetic attitude affecting all aspects of the creative
> act, which is the cause and the basis of any avant-garde notion of art.
> At a psychological level, there was little difference between the socio-
> political and the aestheticist commitment.[13]

Noszlopy is correct in noting the common psychological orientation of all serious modern writers and artists whose commitment to
the primacy of the aesthetic act is born out of their awareness of the
social ambiguity of art in modern culture. However, it need be
stressed that when hermeticism and socio-political activism move beyond the mere recognition of a problem and the initial turn toward
the creative act, the artists' expectations of the effects of their commitment differ qualitatively. It is here, in the writer's or artist's attitude toward art, the artwork, the creative act itself, and toward the
audience and society, that significant psychological differences are
evident between writers and artists in the avant-garde and modernist
camps.

To a great extent, the difference between the avant-garde and modernism is the degree of the former's protest against both the values of
its culture and its encapsulation within that culture. In avant-garde
writing, modernism's social antagonism approaches nihilism, formal
innovation becomes strident experimentalism, and the desire for a
transcendent dimension to art and society is transformed into an
invocation of the writer's visionary powers. But these quantitative
differences are reinforced by a qualitative difference: avant-garde
writers' aesthetic activism has an entirely different purpose. The avant-
garde writer attempts to break free of the self-imposed restrictions
of the largely reactive and defensive postures of modernist writing.
Avant-garde extremism and militancy are directed toward changing the institution of art and the social conditions that place litera-

ture and art in such a problematic position. The avant-garde wants to be more than a merely *modern*ist art, one that reflects its contemporary society; rather, it intends to be a *vanguard* art, in advance of, and the cause of, significant social change.

For avant-garde writers and artists, the notion of social change is very broadly defined. At times it is explicitly political, at times spiritual, and at still others it signifies a transformation of solely personal, often erotic, behavior. Always, however, the social changes the avant-garde seeks would affect the nature and role of art in society. Thus, the avant-garde movement is neither purely aesthetic, nor narrowly political. Certainly, many of the writers I list as modernists have been formally innovative and have held definite political opinions, whether of the left or the right, but rarely did they link aesthetic innovation and political, or even social practice. In all cases, however, the avant-garde writers and movements discussed in this book have expressed the belief that innovations in the form and language of art have social significance, either by their independent effects on the individual's or group's perception, knowledge, and behavior, or in association with the work of other activist members of society. Furthermore, in every case the notion of being a member of a vanguard places the writer in an explicit social context and calls the attention of the writer and audience to the inherent social dynamics of their culture, whether those dynamics be represented by other visionaries, scientists, political activists, or even apparently abstract and impersonal forces with which the writer identifies.

In France, where avant-garde aesthetic activism first developed, the vision of the activist union of the artist with other progressive figures of the society was articulated during the first half of the nineteenth century in the writings of the utopian socialists, particularly by the thinkers associated with Saint-Simon and Fourier. The term "avant-garde" had already entered modern usage, however, appearing shortly after the French Revolution in the pro-Jacobin military journal *L'Avant-garde de l'armée des Pyrennées orientales*.[14] The military avant-garde were the special troops who advanced before the main body of their army into enemy lines, serving as shock troops to disrupt the enemy's forces, and, usually with great loss to themselves, insuring the success of those who followed. The idea that the artist would advance into the terrain of society's future was adopted several decades later by the utopian socialists. But the socialists' theories lacked the aggressive aspects of the military metaphor, for the socialists did not focus on the enemy to be vanquished, but instead invoked the organic evolution of the new society.

For Saint-Simon and his followers, the visionary artist, along with the scientist and industrialist, led the way into the future. Artists—"men of imagination"—were to "present images of the new prosperity" which all members of the future society would enjoy. They would help fulfill the change that the scientists, industrialists, and socialists initiated by articulating the "blessings of civilization."[15] Saint-Simon's disciple Olinde Rodrigues was the first to use the term avant-garde in this sense in an 1825 dialogue entitled "L'Artiste, le savant et l'industriel," which elaborated upon the artist's function of propagating the ruling ideas of the socialists.

> It is we, the artists, that will serve as your avant-garde, the power of the arts is indeed the most immediate and the fastest. We have weapons of all sorts: when we want to spread new ideas among people, we carve them in marble or paint them on canvas; we popularize them by means of poetry and music; . . . We address ourselves to the imagination and feelings of people: we are therefore supposed to achieve the most vivid and decisive kind of action; and if today we seem to play no role or at best a very secondary one, that has been the result of the arts' lacking a common drive and a general idea, which are essential to their energy and success.[16]

As Matei Calinescu has pointed out, the artist's role here is primarily that of a translator of received ideas.[17] The artwork is, in effect, determined by the common drives that impel socialist development. The artist creates no independent images separate from those implicit in the socialist program; but, then again, for the political theorist who wrote this dialogue, there was no reason for the artist to think of the artwork as independent of the organic unity of the developing society that gave the artist a privileged and integrated role. And, as we shall see, this has been the tendency of most political theorists to the present day, a tendency against which the avant-garde has had continuously to struggle.

The idea of the organic struggle of society in which artists had an integral role was itself a product of the French Revolution,[18] and, during the first decades of the nineteenth century, the idealism of socialist thought combined with the Romantic movement in the arts to foster the model of a positive, activist advance guard art. It would remain for later writers and artists who no longer felt the imminence of such a social integration to take up the more aggressive aspects of the military metaphor and declare that the artist must first battle against the enemy of cultural conservatism before the utopic integration of artist and society could become a reality.

Few of the writers discussed in this book trace their aesthetic programs back to the ideas of Saint-Simon or Fourier. But these socialists and their disciples initiated a tradition of a political role for the artist in revolutionary movements and made the term avant-garde popular in literary and artistic circles by the mid-nineteenth century. The idea of the self-proclaimed avant-garde artist was current enough by 1860 for Baudelaire to comment derisively in his journals about "les littérateurs d'avant-garde," who, by brandishing a military term to describe their aesthetic role, only signalled that they were "esprits, non pas militants, mais faits pour la discipline, c'est-à-dire pour la conformité."[19] A decade later, art critics were using the term to denote the formal innovations of the impressionist painters, and Rimbaud was delineating the socially activist side of the visionary avant-garde when he wrote that poetry "sera en avant."[20] Finally, by the first three decades of the twentieth century, the concept of the avant-garde had become a standard by which a succession of innovative writers and artist groups would measure their aesthetic innovations and social posture.

It is particularly important to note in this brief chronology that even though the idea of the advance guard and the socially activist artist originates in the Romantic period, the major avant-garde writers and artists do not appear until the late nineteenth and early twentieth centuries. One prominent theorist of the avant-garde, Peter Bürger, has asserted that the avant-garde could develop only after the emergence in early mid-century France of the late-Romantic—although essentially anti-Romantic—"art for art's sake movement," associated with Théophile Gautier.[21] The aggressive aestheticism of this movement, which foreshadowed the hermetic tendency evident in most later modernisms, signalled the writers' rejection of a utilitarian model of art which they felt implicit in both the bourgeoisie's popular and academic arts and the programmatic vision of the utopian socialists and the Romantic writers associated with them. Against the reduction of art to a form of mere entertainment or its submission to a socially ameliorative program, the aestheticist poets proclaimed the absolute independence of the artwork and the integrity of the aesthetic form. It is from this position of assumed autonomy and privileged perspective that all modernist and avant-garde creations emerge; it is on this basis that the writers and artists justify their freedom to create radically innovative works. But it is here that Baudelaire's and the subsequent modernist and avant-garde writers' ambivalent attitude toward their work and society is born. For the autonomy they assert is the obverse of the alienation that they endure, and though many of the writers may have believed they were freeing themselves from the Romantic poets' naive messianism and social vulnerability, they merely carried into their aesthetic vision the social and aesthetic tensions already emerging in the Romantic period. As a consequence, much of the aesthetic strategies that distinguish the avant-garde from modernism are explicit responses to a dilemma only implicit in the Romantic period. For example, Shelley, whose social and poetic vision has been compared to the ideas of Saint-Simon,[22] may have expressed a belief that later writers considered naive—or envied—when he declared in "A Defence of Poetry" that "Poets are the unacknowledged legislators of the World."[23] But we may also read in these words, as has Raymond Williams, an implicit helplessness in the word "unacknowledged" which severely qualifies the noble calling of "legislator of the World."[24] Commenting on the ambivalent effects of the Romantics' glorification of imagination and of art as a specialized form of social action, Williams also argues that

> the positive consequence of the idea of art as a superior reality was that it offered an immediate basis for an important criticism of industrialism. The negative consequence was that it tended, as both the situation and the opposition hardened, to isolate art, to specialize the imaginative faculty to this one kind of activity, and thus to weaken the dynamic function which Shelley proposed for it.[25]

The central paradox of avant-garde and modernist creation is that what is perceived by the writers and artists of the modern period as a positive expression of their creative powers can also be seen as a negative consequence of a problematic social situation. Nowhere is this more evident than in modern writers' and critics' explorations of the aesthetic imagination, which establishes a critical distance upon which most modern theories of aesthetics are based and against which those theories often implicitly struggle.

The Paradoxes of the Critical Imagination

The arts of modernity are riven by paradoxes which emerge from their historical origins and theoretical underpinnings, paradoxes which shape the aesthetic program and literary works of both the modernists and the avant-garde. The self-conscious questioning of the particular nature of the creative process, the artwork, and the social position of the artist that generates much of modern creation and criticism frequently focuses on the special attributes and role of the "autonomous" imagination.

In the writers' and artists' assertion of the autonomy of the imagination it is possible to see an expression of the age-old belief that the imagination of the artist opens out unto another order of experience beyond common reality; certainly, we can also recognize a more modern theory that the imagination is an expression of a constant rebellion of the unconscious against the reality principle. But the constant demand of the modern arts that reality be more than, or indeed that it be different than, what is commonly experienced results from a specific historical situation of social alienation and aesthetic protest which has shaped all modern theories of art, whether elaborated by writers, artists, or critics and aestheticians. As Noszlopy has noted, whether that protest take the form of pure aestheticism or socio-political activism, the modern artist's first allegiance is to the authority of the artwork itself. But as Williams has observed, the writer's assertion of the seeming superiority of realms of imaginative experience both reflects and reinforces the fragmentation and alienation which those realms are meant to overcome. Thus, while the central impulse of modern aesthetics is to champion the special privileges of the aesthetic imagination, the premises upon which those privileges are asserted undermine the very goals of the creative act. The central drama of modern art is this struggle to overcome both its regretted handicaps and its valued attributes. Out of alienation and fragmentation of perspective comes a call for personal and aesthetic authenticity; from an aesthetics of distance and critical disruption emerges a claim to unified, integrated vision; and on the basis of the presumed autonomy of the aesthetic realm is built an ideal of the artist's essential social mission.

The origins of these conflicting visions lie in the attempt to translate the experience of personal alienation into a presumed artistic autonomy. In different arguments, Peter Bürger, Raymond Williams, and Fredric Jameson have enjoined us to see the simultaneous truth and falsehood in this premise. To focus almost exclusively on— to "specialize"—the apparent freedom of the imaginative faculty is to call attention to art's implicit protest against the values of modern society, but specialization is itself a direct expression of the fragmentation. Indeed, it is the specialization of labor and consciousness so central to the social system being criticized. An alternative vision is established, yes, but in spite of its immediate intensity it may be seen as a particularly delusive and encapsulated experience. This is the necessary expression, Jameson argues, of the reification so endemic to modern, capitalist society.

Reification may be seen as a fragmentation of the psyche and of its world that opens up the semiautonomous and henceforth compartmentalized spaces of lived time over against clock time, bodily or perceptual experience over against rational or instrumental consciousness, a realm of "originary" or creative language over against the daily practice of a degraded practical speech, the space of sexual and the archaic over against the reality and performance principles of *"le serieux"* and of adult life. . . . Modernism not only reflects and reinforces such fragmentation and commodification of the psyche as its basic precondition, but . . . the various modernisms all seek to overcome that reification as well, by the explorations of a new Utopian and libidinal experience of the various sealed realms or psychic compartments to which they are condemned, but which they also reinvent.[26]

The sealed aesthetic realm appears to exist entirely "by the laws of its own being" and thus, as Trilling pointed out above, gives rise to the feeling of aesthetic and personal authenticity. This feeling is the basis of the modernist writers' "parnassian commitment" to the self-reflexive artwork of which Noszlopy spoke. It is also a sensation that avant-garde writers alternately glorify and struggle against in their effort to critique and change their culture and to assert their independence from its restrictive values.

Whether the sealed realm of art reveals the artist's alienation or autonomy, almost all writers, artists, and critics of the modern period assert that the special power of the aesthetic imagination is its tendency to negate ordinary perception and thus to see—and to image—the world differently. The imagination is commonly described as a critical agent, necessarily demystifying quotidian reality in order to create a vision of another order of possibility. For example, the philosophical and aesthetic concepts of defamiliarization, de-humanization, *Priem Ostrannenija,* phenomenological bracketing, *entfremdung,* demystification, disruption, and deconstruction that appear in the writings of the Russian formalists, the Prague School, the New Critics, the phenomenologists, the Frankfurt School, and the post-structuralists all represent versions of this modern belief that the aesthetic and social function of the imagination is to establish a critical distance from the world and common discourse to discover the possibility of new patterns of creative order.

These analyses of aesthetic activity all assign to the imagination a critical function closely related to that of critical reason which underlies modern rationalist thought. No matter how irrational or visionary individual artworks are, especially those of the avant-garde, modern aesthetics express a critical spirit which questions all inherited beliefs to determine the grounds of action and value. Critical reason—whether philosophic, scientific, political, or aesthetic—both distances itself from what it analyzes and, by implicitly devaluing the authority of the subject analyzed, necessarily emphasizes the primacy of the analytic consciousness. But this premise also condemns the modern writer and artist to constant disruption of vision and thought. In effect, the basis of modern aesthetics works against artistic closure. The origin of each creation is negation; the emergence of a new artwork rends the tradition of art; and thus, as Adrian Marino has argued, "the whole meaning of the modern mind and spirit heads toward the establishment and validation—in a continuous, systematic and aggressive sense—of rupture."[27] What is so frightening to many modernist writers, in particular, is the obsessive, even demonic nature of the critical spirit represented by the apparently paradoxical phrase the systematic *establishment* of *rupture*. Ultimately, the critical imagination, which struggles against the conditions of social modernity, both accentuates the sensation of that modernity and undermines itself. Octavio Paz has stated that

> critical reason, our ruling principle, . . . acts as self critic. It governs in so far as it unfolds and sets itself up as the object of analysis, doubt and negation. . . . Critical reason, by its very rigor, accentuates temporality. Nothing is permanent; reason becomes identified with change and otherness.[28]

It may be argued that this emphasis on the critical aspect of the aesthetic imagination developed especially during the Enlightenment and the Romantic period when artists and intellectuals in general identified with the progressive values of the rising bourgeoisie, based as they were on the principles of critical reason. And it may be held that one aspect of the modern writer's alienation is a willingness to sustain such a critical attitude toward the world even though modern society seems more intent on consolidating its material gains and on limiting its self-critical vision. For example, Noszlopy has commented on the paradoxical situation of artists who, though often deeply regretting the pressures of modernity which destroy the basis of any sustained aesthetic tradition, feel compelled to create in constantly new ways, even though large segments of the supposedly anti-traditional society of which they are a part desire an art that is inherently nonprogressive, one that validates society's legitimacy by means of traditional aesthetic conventions.[29]

What is most significant about Paz's observations on the critical spirit, however, is that as long as the aesthetic imagination defines itself in terms of a critical attitude, it cannot overcome the compulsion to be modern. For critical reason, "nothing is permanent," since everything is subject to questioning. According to Paz, the modernity of our civilization is itself the expression of this critical passion, one result of which is that our culture unconsciously grounds itself not in the past but in the everchanging present moment. The apparent oxymoron "the modern tradition," which is so common to discussion of the modern arts, is just one sign of this temporal unrest.

> It is a criticism of the past, and it is an attempt, repeated several times throughout the past two centuries, to found a tradition on the only principle immune to criticism, because it is the condition and the consequence of criticism: change, history.[30]

But the ground of this "tradition" is always slipping out from under the writers' and artists' feet. Each new creation redefines the tradition, and in spite of the efforts of such major modernist poets as Pound and Eliot to achieve a literary historical perspective which could encompass, in fact guide, the constant reshaping of tradition, the experience of most modern writers has been of participating in the process of ceaseless literary disruption. For many modernists these aesthetics are more oppressive than liberating; they demand that the creator recognize that not only is the aesthetic tradition undermined by his or her actions, but so is the work being created since it can no longer stand above time, only be embraced by a very tenuous tradition.

Nevertheless, in order to sustain a belief in the special mission of their art, modern writers and artists, both modernist and avant-garde, continue to fall back upon the privileged nature of the aesthetic realm. Breton speaks for the modern tradition, for example, when he states: "art . . . is summoned to the realization that its quality resides in imagination alone, independently of the exterior object that brought it to birth. Namely, that *everything depends on the freedom with which this imagination manages to express and assert itself and to portray only itself.*"[31] Furthermore, despite the disclaimers of a number of avant-garde writers, most modern writers and critics share a belief in the special attributes of aesthetic language. In distinct opposition to the social languages of positivism, functionalism, political rhetoric, and everyday discourse, which they hold to be reductive and distortive languages, literary discourse is proclaimed, here usually by the modernists, to have a density, richness—and ambiguity—which make the literary artifice a unique form of non-instrumental, self-sufficient articulation. This is particularly evident in the New Criticism school of literary theory which is a direct extension of the aesthetic principles of modernist poets such as Eliot and Pound. However, while both modernists and the avant-garde believe that the mission of art is to offer its creator and audience a unique experience of order and knowledge, the avant-garde usually argues that the special attributes of imaginative language are what make it a particularly powerful form of instrumental discourse. All avant-garde writers proclaim in some form a belief in what Rimbaud called the "alchemy of the word," a belief in the magical powers of a language that can make us see the world differently and act to transform it.

The avant-garde vision takes three related, but increasingly utopic forms: most avant-garde writers and artists desire that the activist artwork have an actual effect not only on the practice of art, but on individual and collective perception and behavior, and on the quality, if not the structures of social life. But many also demand that art, in some essential way, merge with life, that the separation between the aesthetic or imaginative realm and real life be overcome. And finally, many avant-garde writers concurrently assert that life may come to be guided by and embody the fullness of imaginative experience. This essentially utopian impulse envisions the transformation of reality, but most immediately, it challenges the entire tradition of art, for it redefines both the practice and function of art.

This confusing conflation of the desired goals for art and life often results in an abruptly shifting focus both by the avant-garde writers and within their works. They tend to move from addressing specific aesthetic and social concerns to projecting utopic resolutions to fundamental human problems, yet they then drop back unexpectedly to self-conscious play within the apparently hermetic domain of pure art. This shifting between the specific and the utopic is particularly apparent among the three common domains of avant-garde activism—the aesthetic, behavioral, and political. For example, the works and programs of avant-garde writers may oscillate between assaulting specific conventions of academic or modernist art and their role in bourgeois society, to demanding that the entire ontology of art in the Western tradition be changed, as for example, by denying any special value or essence to art. Similarly, the avant-garde writer may protest against common behavior in modern society, such as the valorization of the benefits of rationality in opposition to the irrational or the suggestive states of dream experience; but then the writer may, as did the surrealists, suddenly call for the transformation of consciousness by the merging of subconscious and conscious life in a state of surreality which would manifest itself in all aspects of social life. Furthermore, an avant-garde writer's response to a specific historical event, such as the dadaist Huelsenbeck's to World War I, may suddenly escalate into a demand for the total restructuring of the political organization of society.

Even more significant, however, than these oscillations between a focus on social reality or art is the belief, held by many avant-garde writers, that the aesthetic, behavioral, and political dimensions are not separate, and that action in one necessarily affects the conditions of the others. Thus, for example, the Italian futurists' disruption of syntax in their "words-in-freedom" poems was, in their minds, absolutely linked to the technological transformation of the modern spirit and to Italian political and military destiny. Dada's derisive dismissal of bourgeois sensibility was expressed in these artists' nonsense poems and performances at the Cabaret Voltaire, yet these performances signalled to Hugo Ball the uncovering of a primitive-religious spirit that might presage the emergence of a "new man" and a new spiritual reality. And Rimbaud's demand that the artist willfully derange himself by submitting to extreme mental and physical experiences was the first step in the creation of a seer who would be able to perceive and communicate realms of absolute, universal beauty that contained the future of humanity. The utopic leaning of particular avant-garde works and writers is best summed up by Breton's statement: " 'Transform the world,' Marx said; 'change life,' Rimbaud said. These two watchwords are one for us."[32]

The Activist Imagination

Their enthusiasm and shifting vision of the means of transforming the world and changing life testify to the essentially unprogrammatic nature of the avant-garde. Although individual writers or movements advance particular versions of personal and collective transformation, taken as a general movement, when avant-garde writers invoke imaginative action beyond the realm of art, they envision many forms of fulfillment. At times, avant-garde writers assert the relative primacy of a political bias, but the transformation of life that Rimbaud, Apollinaire, the dadaists, surrealists, and Mayakovsky desired also encompassed the poetic, spiritual, ethical, and sexual liberation of humankind. Accordingly, the programs of avant-garde aesthetic and behavioral activism demand the union of the subconscious and consciousness (surrealism), the discovery of a realm of absolute being in which humanity is at home (Rimbaud, Hugo Ball,

Apollinaire) or, perhaps, an absolute realm in which human aspirations are chastened by their insignificance (Arp, Richter), the achievement of a state of free playfulness and gratuitousness (dada, postmodernism), or, most simply—but uncompromisingly—the attainment of satisfying love (Apollinaire, Mayakovsky, the surrealists). These goals represent the utopic impulse of the avant-garde. They reveal that although avant-garde art seeks to act in the present moment to effect change, it will probably find the fulfillment of the imagination's desires only in the distant future.

Yet even if that future appears to recede from view at times, the avant-garde nevertheless proclaims its mission as an activist force of the present moment struggling to create the future. And even though the avant-garde movement projects visions of personal and social transformation that tend to accent the special province of art to imagine—and create—the future, almost all avant-garde writers and artists look for other forms of vanguard activity within their society which appear to challenge social complacency and presage radical changes in individual and collective consciousness. Invariably, avant-garde writers turn toward the examples of science and radical politics to find support for their activist aesthetics. Just as invariably, however, the particular demands of avant-garde art prove inherently incompatible with the goals and methods of science and politics. This identification signals the writers' efforts to overcome alienation and aesthetic hermeticism by asserting an activist social role that would challenge the prevailing ideas about the nature and role of both the imagination and social behavior. But the result is an unresolvable confusion of realms that afflicts all avant-garde works. Avant-garde artists judge social reality by the standards of aesthetic desire, but in seeking to make reality conform to that desire, their works are judged in turn, and found wanting, according to the standards of current political praxis or scientific and philosophic positivism by the members of the society they critique. Nevertheless, without the informing models of scientific or political activism, the avant-garde's aesthetic vision would be impoverished. Like the avant-garde, science and radical politics are based on the critical spirit. They each imply that the present state of human consciousness and behavior is potentially subject to alteration, and furthermore, that that state of consciousness, particularly the standard patterns of perception and conceptualization, is not to be trusted uncritically. Nor, for that matter, should the given conditions of social and physical reality be naively accepted.

To the avant-garde, for example, the rapid development of scientific thought and technology during the past one hundred years indicates a process of remarkable change in humanity's understanding of its world and in the actual nature and quality of daily life. Each avant-garde movement, at some point, seizes on the process or products of science to support some aspect of its aesthetic vision or pattern of "experimental" innovation. The sudden transformation of the physical environment by the forces of technology at the turn of the twentieth century, for instance, inspired Apollinaire and the Italian and Russian futurist movements, just as the vision of a potential techno-arcadian future attracts many postmodern innovative thinkers. In addition, theoretical physics' radical alteration of the concepts of space and time early in this century had a strong effect on some of the dada poets, and Freud's explorations of the unconscious provided a "scientific" basis for much of expressionist and surrealist poetics.

More important to the avant-garde, however, is the apparent support that the scientific model lends to the belief that there is an integral relationship among the discovery of new data, the development of new perceptual orientations, the creation of new languages or linguistic possibilities, and the expansion of consciousness. The discoveries of the natural and social sciences of the nineteenth and twentieth centuries also support a belief that the laws governing human behavior and thought can be determined, and that as new discoveries are made, new perceptions, conceptual patterns, and finally new modes of thought will result. This implies to the avant-garde that analogous artistic experimentation and innovation in perception and language will lead to new discoveries and modes of behavior.

A stronger, and more utopic, attraction science holds for the avant-garde is its invocation of the unknown—the yet undiscovered—rather than the actual rationalism of scientific methodology. The apparent open-endedness of the scientific vision, and especially the residual power of the scientific theory that first influenced the avant-garde—evolution—support an avant-garde faith in the constant development and expansion of knowledge, behavior, and consciousness. Ultimately, the avant-garde desires that evolution may become self-conscious, that the imagination will be able to seize possession of itself and of the conditions that determine it, and direct its own evolutionary development. This combination of the will toward the future and the anticipation of the unknown discoveries it will reveal constitutes what Herbert Read has called the avant-garde's "speculative volition."[33]

The visionary dimension of avant-garde scientism also supports the movement's social antagonism. Avant-garde nihilism and extremism are spurred on by the disruptive effect new discoveries potentially have on the complacency and the secular, materialist concerns of the bourgeoisie. Expressionism's and surrealism's probing of the unconscious and the irrational, dada's mock-tragic invocation of a galactic perspective, post-structuralism's deconstruction of discourse, all claim to threaten the solidity of the social construct. However, the impact of many of these scientific analogies is to undermine any theory of social value and action, including the radical leftist ideas of other avant-garde writers. Indeed, the avant-garde often adopts scientific ideas to reassert a metaphysical and cosmic perspective in modern literature and art. By providing a model of investigation and discovery of both cosmic and microscopic realms, science may cause a radical reorientation of human self-consciousness and position in the universe. For the avant-garde, science thus joins the inquiring imagination and the natural realm. It fosters a sense of ultimate connection with the universe that can be called religious. In effect, avant-garde art seeks the return of a metaphysical dimension to consciousness. It wants to reveal a transcendent reality by which human life is given an extra-social perspective.[34] Here, supposedly grounded in the rationalism of scientific thought, the visionary and irrational dimension of avant-garde desire is once again revealed.

The basic tension evident throughout the history of the avant-garde is the conflict of its rationalism and irrationalism. It manifests itself in all political, scientific, and aesthetic expressions of avant-garde theory. The first visionary metaphor of the avant-garde, one which provides not only the program of an individual poet but a pattern for succeeding generations, is Rimbaud's "raisonné dérèglement de tous les sens."[35] The faith that the human imagination can transform itself, can identify its needs and weaknesses, and direct itself by a program of specific action, is eminently rational. It is ultimately a faith in the critical spirit that informs every avant-garde use of scientific imagery. But simultaneously, the belief that rationalism itself, along with a life of ordered analysis and action, restrains imaginative fulfillment, and that consequently one must thrust oneself beyond rationality is a Romantic desire. Each generation of the avant-garde takes up Rimbaud's banner and glorifies the irrational in the name of the rational. Each movement thrusts itself off from the past toward a future unknown.

The inherent conflict between the rational and the irrational, the pragmatic and utopic impulses of avant-garde desire is most evident in the avant-garde's association with radical political movements.

Each avant-garde writer has claimed a political extension of his or her aesthetic efforts. For Rimbaud, this political extension was the Commune of 1871; for the Italian futurists it was the Fascist party; for Apollinaire, anarchist thinking; for several dadaists, surrealists, Mayakovsky, and Brecht, it was the Communist Party; and for many of the writers of the fifties and sixties, a generally anarchistic countercultural upheaval provided the political framework of aesthetic innovation. Generally, in societies in which significant revolutionary activity occurs, the avant-garde tends to develop a more rigorous political dimension, as was the case with the post-World War I German dadaists, or with the surrealists, Russian futurists, and Brecht, who responded to the ideology of post-revolutionary Russian communism. At other times, the avant-garde is more prone to merely allude to political movements or assert its essentially metaphoric connection with the forces of revolutionary change. This is the example, for instance, of Rimbaud, Apollinaire, and many of the postmodernists.

The actual results of the avant-garde writers' efforts to ally themselves with political movements, however, has been uneven at best. In general, when avant-garde writers and artists have addressed specific political movements, they have declared themselves to be autonomous workers and creators of a new social reality, allies of the political movements, but independent nonetheless, since the avant-garde's primary province is held to be the autonomous critical imagination. Immediately after the revolution, for example, the Russian futurists asserted there had been three roads to the revolution—the economic, the political, and the spiritual—and that all were necessary, but independent of each other. Their own creative efforts could serve the spiritual revolution without direct intervention of the Communist Party, and would work in the interests of the two other revolutions. Similarly, even while attempting to ally the "surrealist revolution" with the French Communist Party, the surrealists insisted on their ability to advance both the political and the poetic revolutions through independent poetic practice. Furthermore, their poetic program drew from extra-aesthetic sources—Freud and Marx—lessons first for aesthetic, then for social change, but accepted the authority of the disciples of neither man to determine the course of that change.

Nevertheless, once the poetic revolution perceives itself in terms of a social or political revolution, the practices and products of poetic activism are invariably judged by non-aesthetic standards. The avant-garde poet may proclaim his or her autonomy, but he or she will find that a significant part of the poetic program will be spent justifying the relationship of poetics to politics. For from this position of autonomous but analogous action, it is but one step to active participation in the political revolution. The late surrealist call to place the movement "at the service of" the social revolution was one attempt to unite the two domains; however, it failed largely because their communist "allies" couldn't imagine how one could be a surrealist and a revolutionary at the same time. More successful, though short-lived, was Mayakovsky's effort to present his post-revolutionary political writing and poetry as significant labor guided by the specific needs of the revolution. And although he always maintained a personal and poetic distance from the most narrow, if pressing, demands of the Party and the proletarian writers' movements, he consciously "stepped on the throat" of his lyric capabilities in order to write didactic and satiric verse for very specific and often mundane purposes. The Italian futurists' glorification of the military, industrial, and financial interests, and ultimately the Fascist Party, explicitly identified the greater powers which they believed furthered the values and goals they had championed in their art. Furthermore, Brecht's activist aesthetics were often specifically developed to address and teach the working-class revolutionary audience, although the works themselves rarely pleased the Communist Party members.

Each of these efforts to place the avant-garde "at the service of the revolution" was an individual writer's or movement's initiative to identify poetic action with existent political movements. All of these writers quickly discovered, however, that their initiatives either were not welcomed or were distrusted by the political theorists and activists of these movements. The writers soon learned that if they expected to ally themselves with political parties, they had to follow the dictates of those parties; even aesthetic concerns were to be shaped and evaluated by the political theorists, not by the writers and artists themselves. As Mayakovsky and the surrealists were informed, for example, the theories concerning aesthetic production and the role of art in society that were promulgated by the Communist Party in the nineteen twenties and thirties insisted that the aesthetic imagination did not operate independently of immediate social reality. Rather, the forms and values implicit in imaginative creations were held to be direct products of the economic and political bases of society; for art to be revolutionary, or even socially progressive, it had to be directed by the scientific and political forces which were directly engaged in transforming the social base.

According to the communist ideologues, the avant-garde writer clearly is not more perceptive than the revolutionary activist. Insofar as the imagination is intuitive, they maintain, it is limited; it cannot sustain a critical analysis of its own social basis. This can only be done from the "scientific" position of the political theorist. As a consequence, the communists argue, the writer's responsibility is to follow the directives of the Party, both in terms of aesthetic conventions and the political, thematic content. Many avant-garde writers and artists attempted to follow the Party's aesthetic doctrines as they developed during the twenties and thirties, but few were able to subordinate their works and desires to the particularly narrow aesthetic doctrines that came to dominate Party thinking. The writers and artists who did accept the Party's analysis—the Berlin dadaists John Heartfield and his brother Wieland Herzfelde, the surrealists Louis Aragon and Paul Eluard, and Amiri Baraka in the nineteen seventies—altered their literary styles significantly and played down the significance of formal innovation as they concentrated more on social themes and the vocabulary of the Party ideology. In effect, their successful alliances with communist ideology came at the expense of their identification with the avant-garde movement.

The avant-garde is faced with the ironical situation that it is invariably accepted—even honored—by the bourgeois society against which it rebels, but it is rejected by the revolutionary societies that it seeks to advance. The irony is intensified, yet explained, by the fact that the avant-garde's claim to social significance has been dismissed by the bourgeois culture that embraces it, even invests in it, while both communist and fascist governments agree that the avant-garde and art in general should be taken seriously. These regimes believe that art, as ideology, is too serious a matter to be left to the artists alone, and especially not to the avant-garde and modernist artists and writers. For communist Russia, as well as fascist Germany, any art that appeared to disrupt or question the officially accepted—and enforced—formal and thematic conventions of art, or that did not pay homage to the dominant ideology, was subversive, even if the artist was a committed party member or sympathizer. Particularly threatening to the political theorists, and therefore scorned by them, was the common avant-garde belief that an individual writer or artist was able to initiate significant innovations in collective language and vision, innovations whose value was primarily judged by the standards of the artist and not the politician. Thus, in effect, the avant-garde aesthetic and social program was most validated by those who most actively sought to suppress it.

To the extent that bourgeois culture has taken the avant-garde seriously, it has recognized that formal innovations by themselves do not pose significant threats to modern society. When avant-garde writers have identified potentially disruptive tensions, contradictions, or desires within their society, the generally irrational and individualistic aspects of avant-garde writings have been either readily absorbed in a pluralistic culture that admits many strains of private rebellion and accommodation, or in a few instances suppressed.[36] Usually, however, the art of protest has been viewed solely as an aesthetic concern and has been consigned to the support system of art history and marketing—the galleries, museums, universities, and mass media.

The primary points of contention between the avant-garde and bourgeois society are the avant-garde's positing of the social and aesthetic significance of formal innovation and the aesthetic imagination's utopic projection of either irrational states of personal immediacy or future states of absolute personal and social fulfillment. From the point of view of most avant-garde writers, few political movements remain faithful to, or even recognize the utopic goals implicit in radical politics. They are more concerned with the immediate problems of social reorganization. The avant-garde writers' impatience with Marxist movements, for example, undescores that the writers identify with more than the economic critique of capitalism in Marxist thought; they embrace the utopic spirit, even the religious or "magic" impulse of revolutionary desire that projects a vision of a world beyond alienation and reification. Yet it is precisely this utopic dimension that seems to be the first to be discarded in the interests of revolutionary praxis, to have been the first victim of the pragmatic struggles of the Bolshevik or Communist Parties.

The avant-garde desire that there be a link between the present moment and the utopic future shifts the focus of their activism from political programs to aesthetic innovation, for the artwork, as imaginative creation, at least provides a partial but immediate experience of imaginative pleasure, and sensed possibility. Commenting on the romantic and avant-garde desire to find in poetic inspiration a merger of art and life, Octavio Paz has noted that "neither philosophers nor revolutionaries can patiently tolerate the ambivalence of poets who see in magic and revolution two parallel but not mutually exclusive methods of changing the world."[37] Political revolutionaries recognize that avant-garde writing attempts to articulate a form of being beyond the constraints of present reality, an ideal realm of vision and experience which the slow workings of social history and the restricted focus of the rational, critical method of political theory cannot offer.[38] The avant-garde poetic strategies of disruption, absurdity, chance play, invocation of the subconscious or the cosmic, and the intoxication of the poet are all means toward a "magical" end, the immediate and partially—if temporarily—satisfying experience of a future state of being that poetic activism, if not political praxis, will bring about.

Both the visionary and activist dimensions of avant-garde thought, then, enable avant-garde writers to sustain a Romantic faith in spite of all the aesthetic contradictions of modernity and their complex relations to bourgeois and revolutionary societies, because both dimensions are justified by the writers' faith in the future resolution of those contradictions. The avant-garde is true to its defining metaphor. It lives by its belief that it is in advance of aesthetic and social success. While modernists may search for a principle of transcendence or autonomy within their contemporary context, avant-garde writers and artists seek strategies of utopic potentiality. If modernists are conscious of the implicit demystification of any transcendent vision by their own critical stance, the avant-garde is safe in its knowledge that the future cannot be totally undermined precisely because it is the realm of promise, not reality. The only aspects of the avant-garde venture that are threatened by critical judgment—whether aesthetic or political—are their particular strategies for reaching and creating the future. And even though the various forms of avant-garde activism that we shall study in the following chapters are constantly criticized by other writers, critics, and political activists of all persuasions, the avant-garde is usually able to reject these criticisms. For even the strategies of avant-garde social and aesthetic innovation can claim that they are to be judged only by a future state of existence, and that the present state of aesthetic and social thought provides inadequate standards of judgment. As a result, all avant-garde writers and movements can be seen—in fact, may recognize themselves—to be products of the modern society against which they rebel, yet they have been able to sustain a faith in their programs and their future for more than a century.

The Aesthetic Activism of the Avant-garde

The tensions that give rise to the avant-garde's troubled association with the political domain originate in the writers' and artists' efforts to overcome the implicit hermeticism of much of modern art. Yet not being fully willing to give up their presumption that aesthetic behavior is autonomous of the social realm, the formal innovations of avant-garde works can tend to be as self-reflexive and idealistic as any of the creations of the modernists. Torn between the conflicting demands of the purely aesthetic and the social in their effort to radically change the form and function of art in modern culture, the works of avant-garde writers and artists struggle to contain within themselves opposing tendencies and allegiances: between reason and the irrational; revolutionary praxis and utopic desire; present reality and the imagined future; negation and creation.

At the heart of avant-garde aesthetic activity is the dynamic tension between the poles of negation and creation, between the assault on the given world and its aesthetic tradition and the search for the basis of a new culture and its art. The famed absurdity of many avant-garde activities—their nihilism, gratuitousness, irrationality, and humourousness—is caused by its rejection of any dependence on, or respect for, prior standards of aesthetic and behavioral judgment, and by its willingness to seek the unknown, the surprising, and the patently irrational as alternatives to given reality. However, since the future is unknown and often unimaginable, the nihilistic impulse in the avant-garde artwork is often the most dramatic expression of avant-garde desire.

Avant-garde writers programmatically deny the authority of any aesthetic convention, social value, or political ideology which would restrict their creative freedom. Freedom represents, in fact, the only absolute value shared by all avant-garde writers. Since they have, at best, a tenuous commitment to specific political programs of historical development, the concept of self-liberation—aesthetic, personal, and political—is both the generative principle of the specific avant-garde work and the goal toward which the work struggles. As a consequence, avant-garde writers tend to judge their creations by the distance the works achieve from prior art forms and social values. For the dadaists and futurists especially, the success of avant-garde bohemian behavior was often measured by the outraged reaction of their audience; the uniqueness of their poetic contribution was a function of their disruption of the literary conventions accepted or held onto by the previous avant-garde movement. In effect, the avant-garde frequently "advances" more by pushing away from the known than by identifying a distinct goal toward which it moves.

In this process, one of the main concerns of the avant-garde work is to disorient the audience's perception of the world and their aesthetic expectations so that they will be freed from restrictive literary conventions. The experience of disorientation may in itself provide the desired perceptual and conceptual freedom if the writer believes, as did many of the dadaists, that there are no adequate grounds upon which to build an alternative system of art. More frequently, however, literary disruption is seen as a necessary expression of an affir-mative modernity, and disorientation is felt to free the audience to perceive things of previously unimagined beauty, or experience states of abruptly expanded consciousness. According to Apollinaire, for example, "poets will be charged finally with giving by means of lyric teleologies and arch-lyric alchemies a constantly purer meaning to the idea of divinity, which is so alive within us, which is perpetual re-newal of ourselves, that eternal creation, that endless rebirth by which we live."[39]

The embrace of the new (which for Apollinaire was essentially an endless renewal of imaginative possibility) has been, of course, a lit-erary compulsion since at least the time of Baudelaire, and modern-ist and avant-garde writers alike have hoped to find in the element of discovery—of surprise—a new form of beauty which would enliven the modern world. Baudelaire's declaration "the beautiful is *always* surprising" became the aesthetic credo of the modern period.[40] And though he continued by saying "it would be absurd to assume that the surprising is *always* beautiful," numerous avant-garde writers and artists have valued the moment of discovery and surprise as the dis-tinctive goal of aesthetic action. Writers such as Rimbaud, Apolli-naire, the Italian futurists, Hugo Ball, Jean Arp, and the surrealists have especially privileged this sensation of unexpected experience. They have favored the "new," the "surprising," "convulsive beauty," the "marvelous," the unknown, and the "intoxicating" experience created by their artworks. For some of these writers, and certainly for the more politically inclined such as Mayakovsky and Brecht, this disorientation was the initial stage of the demystification of quotidian reality, after which one could create an alternative world and poetry.

The primary expression of the positive impulse within avant-garde aesthetic activity is the creation of a new poetic language capable of expressing these new states of consciousness and discovering others for which ordinary language and literary conventions are inadequate. Rimbaud proclaimed that a new language must be found, a language which would enable the poet to "define the amount of the unknown awakening in his time."[41] All subsequent avant-garde writers take up the challenge to become experimenters and innovators in language and literary tradition. Like Apollinaire's invocation of "lyric teleologies and arch-lyric alchemies," their works echo Rimbaud's belief in the potent "alchemy of the word." The various avant-gardes seek this new language in states of personal derangement (Rimbaud), traditional poetic inspiration (Apollinaire), games of chance (dada), subconscious automatism (surrealists), or scientific analysis of linguistic elements (Russian futurists, the postmodern L=A=N=G=U=A=G=E group).

Like each general avant-garde program, these new poetic languages embody both negative and positive elements, though it is frequently difficult to distinguish them from one another. Since the avant-garde rejects in general the values and systems of thought of its society, it also rejects the literary conventions of representing that world. It rebels against unself-conscious referentiality and any implicit theological or philosophic system of belief upon which aesthetic realism is based. But since avant-garde literary works are constructed out of words which bear many semantic associations, the avant-garde writer is not as free as the visual artist to freely play with his or her medium. There is an ultimate limit to the creation of abstract or "antirealistic" works. As a consequence, the avant-garde writer frequently explores the limits of the creator's freedom to disrupt syntax and to use new patterns of linguistic association. On the one hand, the writer rips words free from their customary metaphoric and symbolic contexts (Rimbaud, the surrealists, L=A=N=G=U=A=G=E), disrupts syntax (Italian futurism), or reduces words to phonemes and brute sounds (the Russian futurists, dada), and on the other hand, the writer places these words or word elements in surprising juxtapositions with other words to create outrageous or startling new metaphors or to evoke scenes (Rimbaud, Lautréamont, Apollinaire, the surrealists, and dadaists), or makes graphic designs out of them (Italian futurists, dadaists, concrete poets).

This aesthetic activism often results in difficult, and sometimes incomprehensible works. It is hard to know if their apparently absurd language is meant to disrupt our understanding and thus represent the process of derangement or negation, or if the confusing language signifies the unfolding of new states of consciousness with which we are not yet familiar.[42] This, for example, is the source of ambiguity in some of Rimbaud's *Illuminations* and dada sound poems. Often, avant-garde works are understood only by their creators, or by members of the writer's coterie. For as products of individualistic or group action on the most collective of phenomena—language—avant-garde literary works frequently become private languages, even if they are intended to reform the language, hence the consciousness, of the audience. The fact that only a few people can understand the new language may signify to the writers that they are truly in advance of their time, but it also condemns the avant-garde to a perpetually limited audience.

The avant-garde tendency to determine or validate its futurist vision by relying on the negation of a particular past aesthetic style or social ideology, and by its rapid and often incomplete adoption of political or scientific concepts, often results in a severe narrowing of focus and a strongly dogmatic aesthetic vision. While declaring its desire for an expansive sensibility, the avant-garde often falls into patterns of behavior dominated by a single and narrow principle, such as the primacy of the subconscious (surrealism), technology (Italian futurism), or linguistic analysis (Russian futurists, and many postmodernists or post-structuralists). It is frequently a reductivist art, presenting a "problem" that is then "solved" by creating a "new reality." Methodological concerns can overshadow total vision. This is particularly the case with the socio-political perspective. The self-reflexive activity of self-creation often seems to have more importance than the work's reception, though this itself is one result of the modern artist's and audience's turning to the artwork for their sensation of authenticity.

In fact, avant-garde writers insist that even this self-reflexiveness has social significance. The tension between the aesthetic and social dimensions of the literary work are particularly evident in the projected image of the avant-garde writer who is to perform a new function in a changing society. Just as the avant-garde work seeks to invoke a future ideal and to provide the means of attaining that ideal, the avant-garde poet claims to be both a prophet who unveils the future and a paradigmatic creative revolutionary. The writer as activist explores several scientific and political models of social criticism and methods of self-liberation. These models and methods then shape the creative process, just as in turn, the writers frequently extend aesthetic experiments in their personal lives. The writer's life thus becomes the explicit focus and testing ground of the dream of merging art and life. Rimbaud, Apollinaire, Marinetti, and Mayakovsky all proclaim the special heroism of the writer, who by his or her example leads others into states of freedom and realms of potential beauty. But they are all aware, as are most other avant-garde writers, of the personal price they must pay. For no matter what the promise the avant-garde venture holds, each call for a new language increases the possibility that the writer will not be understood; each denial of ordered social behavior, each willed submission to the irrational, the subconscious, drugs, sensual derangement, or brute chance entails a loss of control over oneself and the forces in one's environment; each step toward the future increases one's alienation from the present. Indeed, since total liberation and transformation can only be achieved in the future, the present moment can only be suffered as a personal sacrifice. Even if the writer claims to find in immediate, anarchic, and poetic intoxication an experience of the desired ideal, he or she is condemned to return to the real world and time of unfulfilled existence once that intoxication is over.

For the avant-garde writer there is no escaping this situation. It is the necessary result of the writer's adoption of a temporally defined, activist role. If imagination is to join with reality and if the artwork is to act upon the present to bring about a transformed future world, no avant-garde writer can hope to be entirely successful or satisfied in the present moment, and no individual work can claim to be self-sufficient and complete. The avant-garde writer inevitably suffers from what Renato Poggioli has termed the agonist dilemma.[43] Caught between the opposing impulses of negation and creation and between a denial of the present and a desire for the future, each avant-garde writer recognizes to some extent that he or she is trapped within the present that is to be negated and that, consequently, the writer must be sacrificed to the future that will follow from that sacrifice. Similarly, each avant-garde movement foresees its own obsolescence and at the same time engenders its own successors who will be committed to negating not only its contemporary bourgeois world, but the previous avant-garde as well.

Just as each avant-garde writer and movement projects both an heroic and a doomed self-image, the particular avant-garde work both seeks to transform art and undermines itself in the process. By definition, no avant-garde artwork can be totally successful. If it is to be activist, it must lead beyond itself. It must be judged by a context other than the merely aesthetic. In effect, the avant-garde must deny the greatest attribute of traditional art—the apparent self-sufficiency, the atemporal completeness of the aesthetic work seemingly freed from the passing of time and from the pragmatic demands of material life. While the great modernists, such as Proust, Mann, and Joyce, struggled to create literary masterpieces by which an individual aesthetic vision transcended the pressures of modernity, the avant-garde cries out, with Artaud, "No more masterpieces!"[44] The work, like the avant-garde poet, assumes prophetic and revolutionary roles to announce and create an art and a culture it will never see.

Chapter
II
The Poet as Seer: Rimbaud

In the brief poetic career of Rimbaud we encounter many of the poetic roles that characterize the avant-garde tradition: the poet as seer, discoverer of realms of beauty, mystery, and significance heretofore inaccessible to humankind; the poet as innovator, inventor of a language which articulates the poet's new vision and generates further discovery; the poet as prophet, spokesman of aesthetic, spiritual, and social progress, champion of the necessary advancement of consciousness and spirit; the poet as bohemian, disgruntled product of the middle or lower-middle classes, flamboyant rejector of bourgeois life and seeker of an alternative, if alienated, style of life; the poet as nihilist, denier of existing social and aesthetic values, demanding radical destruction as prelude to redemptive creation; and the poet as social visionary or "revolutionary," identifying with and speaking for both the oppressed classes in particular, and the good of a future society in general. However, we also recognize in Rimbaud's art the fundamental conflicts, contradictions, and basic patterns of failure that have plagued so many subsequent avant-garde writers and movements: the discovery of the limits of innovative language; the general alienation of the poet from the working class or any force of potential change in society; the necessary solitude of the poet who declares himself "in advance" of the rest of the culture; the inherent solipsism and hermeticism of the modern poetic tradition; and the essentially religious or idealist basis of the revolutionary aesthetic vision.

Consequently, Rimbaud stands as an important figure for most avant-garde groups, as well as for many modernists. The expressionists, dada, the surrealists, the Russian futurists, Brecht, Henry Miller, the beat writers of the nineteen-fifties, and the radicals of the sixties, for example, all have found in Rimbaud's life and works an inspiration and a challenge to their own efforts. To varying degrees, all have seen in his poetic manifestoes—the *lettres du voyant*—and in his dense but extremely evocative texts supports for their own programs of social critique and artistic innovation. But at the same time, Rimbaud remains a figure of mystery. Beyond overcoming the difficulty of interpreting his visionary, often confusing and incoherent poems, writers and critics have had to provide for his spite, irony, flamboyant posturing, evident contradictions, bitter self-parody, self-mystification, and his silence. Especially, his silence. From a few straightforward declarations of intent, many obscure works, pitiably sparse letters, and undependable recollections of friends and family, they—and we—struggle to find some coherence in the poet's life and work. We can trace the general impulse of his work from the *lettres du voyant*, but the poems themselves, even his famous self-analysis "Une Saison en Enfer" (1873), are so frequently ambiguous, complex, and impenetrable, that all interpretation entails creative speculation.

As a result, there are many Rimbauds—all the creations of the premises and desires of his critics. Complex poems such as "Une Saison en Enfer," because of their shifting tone and perspective, their spiteful voice and vacillations between self-recrimination and justification, defy consistent interpretation. Many of the poems in *Illuminations* hint at states of order and significance, but offer no obvious key to their presumed unity. And then, how do we interpret even such an apparently simple poem as "Solde," which seems to speak directly to us in a single, unchanging tone? Do we read it as a joyous proclamation of the promises of poetry, one which playfully adopts the metaphors of a sales barker? (Rick Osmond); as an admission of failure, a "going out of business sale?" (W. Frohock); as a lament that ours is a society which would attempt to sell everything, even its most intangible and spiritual values? (J. P. Houston); as the sarcastic taunt of a poet speaking down to an audience whom he considers incapable of attaining his vision without discount? (Robert Greer Cohn). Or do we read it as a statement of the process of freeing oneself from all earthly ties and desires as a prelude to achieving a mystical state? (W. Fowlie).[1] Each of these interpretations evokes a shadowy emanation called Arthur Rimbaud, who is little more than a creation of the critic's alchemy. I also present my version of Arthur Rimbaud, but rather than seeking an integral interpretation of all his works to determine the uniqueness of Rimbaud's poetic venture, I prefer to single out ideas and tendencies in his works which contribute to the developing tradition of the avant-garde. For finally, his behavior, desires and failures, admittedly so personal, are not unique. Nevertheless, we need briefly to note certain facts of his biography, if only to identify those elements which, while extreme in his case, prove to be so common to other avant-garde writers and artists. Primary among these are his social background and his youth.

Rimbaud's petit bourgeois, provincial background is one of the sources of his ambivalent and frequently aggressive attitude toward French middle-class life. Grandson of a farmer who managed to rise into the lower middle class, son of a mother whose two brothers disgracefully failed to sustain this achievement by falling back to lower-class jobs—a mother who, in the wake of her husband's desertion, bore the burden of family propriety and pride and demanded that her two sons uphold their fragile bourgeois status—brother to one who emulated his uncles' fall by working as a station drayman, Rimbaud was expected to insure the family's respectability and financial security by leading an exemplary bourgeois life.[2] And while his mother may not have been the monster that Rimbaud and most critics make her out to be, it is clear that she strongly impressed upon her sons the virtues of a Christian life and economic stability. These were, of course, exactly what he—for a while—refused to accept. Whether it was against his mother's overbearing insistence on propriety, or against the narrowmindedness of the church, the sincerity but naïveté of his lycée teachers, the pathetic exhibitions of local and national patriotism during the Franco-Prussian War, the brutality of the Versailles forces against the Commune, or even the petty concerns of his fellow poets, Rimbaud's rebellion, like that of so many bohemians before and after him, signified a violent, if temporary, rejection of the total bourgeois order.

The struggle of Rimbaud and the bohemian elements of the avant-garde is, in essence, the action of self-declared declassés who search within their society for supportive images of social antagonism and project onto future social orders dreams of social integration. The working class, the exploited populace, the blacks or "third world" people, all are seen not only as oppressed figures but as outsiders with whom the alienated poets can identify. If the proletariat ends by not actually offering clear models for social change or aesthetic vision, it serves at least to refute the authority of the bourgeois order and might become an audience for whom the poet could speak, as well.

During Rimbaud's temporary rejection of his bourgeois destiny, he
found support for his rebellion in the victims and rebels of his society: the poor, the communards and the workers. However, this identification, as several critics have noted, was not without ambivalence.
For Rimbaud was fully conscious of the drudgery of the workers'
lives and of the weakness and submissiveness exhibited by so many
of the poor, which disgusted him. Nevertheless, a strain of compas-
sion and pity for the victims of his society runs through many of his
poems, and there are moments when he explicitly associates his work
as a poet with the workers and the fighters of the Commune.[3] It is
doubtful whether we will ever sufficiently settle the question of
whether Rimbaud participated in the Commune of 1871 (most evidence points against the possibility, even though Verlaine and Demeny indicated that he probably told them he did), but it is clear that
he supported the workers and socialists in their struggle and that he
was sickened by the bourgeoisie's repression of the Commune. Furthermore, he was briefly associated with the exiled socialists in London
in 1872 and 1873, and some critics find in his poems an "illuminisme
social," a faith in a transformed future created by workers, socialists,
and artists.[4] His early poems of satire and sarcasm against his society
and its war effort—"Morts de Quatre-vingt-douze," "Le Mal," "Rages
de Césars," "L'Éclatante Victoire de Sarrebruck"—culminate in the
Commune poems of exaltation and anger—"Chant de guerre parisien," "L'Orgie parisienne," "Les Mains de Jeanne-Marie"—and lead
beyond to that poem of apocalyptic rage, "Qu'est-ce pour nous?"

> Qu'est-ce pour nous, mon coeur, que les nappes de sang
> Et de braise, et milles meurtres, et les longs cris
> De rage, sanglots de tout enfer renversant
> Tout ordre; et l'Aquilon encor sur les débris;
>
> Et toute vengeance? Rien! . . . —Mais si, toute encor,
> Nous la voulons! Industriels, princes, sénats:
> Périssez! puissance, justice, histoire: à bas!
> Ça nous est dû. Le sang! le sang! la flamme d'or!
>
> Tout à la guerre, à la vengeance, à la terreur,
> Mon esprit! Tournons dans la morsure; Ah! passez,
> Républiques de ce monde! Des empereurs,
> Des régiments, des colons, des peuples, assez!
>
> *What does it matter for us, my heart, the sheets of blood*
> *And coals, and a thousand murders, and the long cries*

Of rage, sobs from every hell upsetting
Every order; and the north wind still over the debris;

And all vengeance? Nothing! . . . But yes, still,
We want it! Industrialists, princes, senates:
Perish! Power, justice, history: down with you!
That is our due. Blood! blood! golden flame!

All to war, to vengeance and to terror,
My spirit! Let us turn about in the biting jaws. Ah! vanish,
Republics of this world! Of emperors,
Regiments, colonists, peoples—enough![5]

In this poem, what begins as a rebellion against the power structure of his society rapidly escalates into a call against all order, against
the world itself. Here, we see the anarchistic impulse of Rimbaud
which is similar to that of many later avant-garde writers. This anarchism may originally have socialist overtones, but it is finally an expression of the poet's self-conscious isolation within his society and
his tendency to fall back upon himself to call up visions of radical
destruction and change. Even more significant, the last line of this
poem signals the troubling recognition of the insubstantial nature of
the personal vision. It is a recognition that will constantly haunt his
later poetic efforts: "Ce n'est rien; j'y suis! j'y suis toujours (Bernard,
p. 172). ("*It is nothing; I am here; I am still here,*" Fowlie, p. 127.)

Rimbaud's rebellion, in fact, was always primarily a personal
drama. He provoked and mocked the bourgeoisie of his town, of
Paris, and of the poetic cenacles by his outrageous behavior. His radical *encrapulement,* his self-degradation and dissipation, however,
seemed more directed against the bourgeois in himself than those
around him. Whatever positive, poetic benefit he believed this de-
basement to have, it represented at least a holding action against the
necessity of entering as a mature adult into the social order dominant
in his society. Indeed, the youthfulness of his rebellion is the source
of much of his idealism and extremism.

Rimbaud's struggle and poetic achievement occurred between his
seventeenth and twenty-first years. Yet even though his experience
was remarkable in its intensity and productivity, this represents a
period only a few years earlier in life than that of most avant-garde
writers' creative moments. The avant-garde, in fact, is generally a
youthful, if not adolescent, phenomenon. It frequently entails the efforts by young individuals and groups to establish an independent
identity against the authority of whatever social values or aesthetic

school—academic, or prior avant-garde—is reigning at the time. Poets, such as Mayakovsky, will flaunt their youth and strength against the society they challenge—"I shake the world with the might of my voice, / and walk—handsome, / twentytwoyearold."—and whole movements, such as the Italian futurists, will declaim in their manifestoes the necessary rebellion of the sons against the fathers—"The oldest of us is thirty: so we have at least a decade for finishing our work. When we are forty, other younger and stronger men will probably throw us in the wastebasket like useless manuscripts—we want it to happen!"[6] The extremism of the avant-garde's position denies the possibility of compromise, refuses to admit the necessity of bowing to the established social order, and insists on the absoluteness and sanctity of their desire and vision.

This youthfulness also accounts, especially in Rimbaud's case, for the frequent images of lost purity, innocence, or some state of an ideal past in avant-garde works, which claim to be always looking toward the future. Many times, their projections of a utopian future seem to be but displaced appeals to a childhood experience of mystical union with the world. "Jadis, si je me souviens bien, ma vie était un festin où s'ouvraient tous les coeurs, où tous les vins coulaient" ("Une Saison en Enfer," Bernard, p. 211). ("*Long ago, if my memory serves me, my life was a banquet where everyone's heart was generous, and where all wines flowed,*" Fowlie, p. 173.) The adult world which is so threatening to the child is, consequently, to be transformed by either the private vision of the poet or the collective action of the avant-garde group, each intent on regaining some privileged state of the past, whether it be a childhood memory or the "younger" ages of civilization. Here, the avant-garde often represents a resurgence of the Romantics' dream of the idealized past, be it Greek, medieval, or Renaissance. And here too, as Rimbaud himself would realize only too well, is a reworking of the ever-present dynamics of the Judeo-Christian nostalgia for some lost Eden.

For Rimbaud, the ideal world seems to be a pastiche of the late-Romantic vision of the Parnassian poets (especially their love of ancient Greece), a longing for a childhood fullness of experience, as well as popular images of Eastern or non-European mysteries, ideas of socialist utopianism, and finally, some version of mystical experience grounded in a search for the lost Eden. Even though Rimbaud's style changed so radically in a short period, certain elements of this invocation of an ideal world remain constant throughout his career. In particular, his poems repeat specific images, the configuration of these images, and the perspective of the poetic voice. For example, his early poem "Soleil et Chair," derivative as are its Parnassian clichés, nevertheless suggests Rimbaud's constant desires.

The theme of the poem is the fall of man; the mood, a nostalgia for lost innocence and strength; the vision, a hope for their recovery. The fall that Rimbaud depicts, however, is into Christianity and reason, the two gods of the modern West. The pre-Christian world is presented as a culture of fertility, passion, youth—*antique jeunesse*—and strength. A place where "tout croît, et tout monte," it sustains a humanity fully at home with nature, the source of all life and love. But while it is a world of evident passion, it is curiously calm and stately, even elegant. It is above all a world of inherent luxury. (One is reminded of Baudelaire's "L'Invitation au Voyage": "Là, tout n'est qu'ordre et beauté, / Luxe, calme et volupté.") But humanity has been exiled from this ideal by denying the vitality of the natural world and its own innate divinity. Humanity has substituted instead a distorted vision of its "god-like" powers.

> Misère! Maintenant il dit: Je sais les choses,
> Et va, les yeux fermés et les oreilles closes.
> —Et pourtant, plus de dieux! plus de dieux! l'Homme est Roi,
> L'Homme est Dieu!
>
> (Bernard, p. 41)

> *Woe! Now he says: I comprehend things,*
> *And goes off, with eyes closed and ears closed.*
> *—And yet, no more gods! no more gods! Man is King!*
> *Man is God!*
>
> (Fowlie, pp. 27, 29)

Demanding a reawakening of humanity and culture, the poet yearns for and foresees a future return to the past ideal.

> Il ressuscitera, libre de tous ses Dieux,
> Et, comme il est du ciel, il scrutera les cieux!
> L'Idéal, la pensée invincible, éternelle,
> Tout; le dieu qui vit, sous son argile charnelle,
> Montera, montera, brûlera sous son front!
>
> (Bernard, p. 42)

> *He will revive, free of all his gods,*
> *And as he is of heaven, he will scan the skies!*
> *The Ideal, the invincible eternal thought.*

Everything; the god who lives, under his clay of flesh,
Will rise, will rise, and burn under his brow!

(Fowlie, p. 29)

Evoking this desired future, "Soleil et Chair" closes with a panorama
of the ancient gods and humans in familiar poses—Ariadne and The-
seus, Zeus the bull and Europa, Zeus the swan and Leda, Cypris, Her-
cules, the Dryad, Selene and Endymion, Eros. The final passage offers an image of ideal beauty, suggestive in many respects of the more
original images in Rimbaud's later poetry. The luxurious world of
prolific yet stately nature is inhabited by beings at peace with each
other and their environment. It is a landscape of energy, but all is
viewed as if in stasis. The world offers itself as a series of distinct tab-
leaux, each frozen pose revealing the essence and fulfillment of humanity and the gods.

Many of the most beautiful—if opaque—of Rimbaud's later poems
similarly appear to be descriptions of ideal landscapes, or of theatrical scenes that exhibit these same qualities. "Bruxelles," "Scènes,"
"Fleurs," "Marine," "Fête d'hiver," "Les Ponts," "Promontoire,"
"Mystique," and "Véillées" offer us images of luxurious nature, elegant crowds, and noble civilizations or of an unfallen world of youth
and vigor. Rarely is there any sense of narrative. Rather, any motion
described is singularly static, the action passive. Nor is there any evident connection among the images themselves. Instead, a panorama
or a frieze seems to be created out of discrete parts all of which combine to suggest, but not make explicit, an order and harmony. As in
the latter part of "Soleil et Chair," the poems verge on being lists of
things seen by some sympathetic, yet external and passive spectator.
As has been frequently noted, for example, images of the theater
dominate the *Illuminations*. It is not the idea of drama, however,
that makes theater a primary metaphor for Rimbaud, but the stage
and its scenery. For example, the poem "Scènes" tells us of scenes and
plays being performed, but only their setting, not their content is
mentioned.

Scènes

L'ancienne Comédie poursuit ses accords et divise ses
Idylles:

    . . . .

Des scènes lyriques accompagnées de flûte et de tambour
s'inclinent dans des réduits ménagés sous les plafonds, autour des
salons de clubs modernes ou des salles de l'Orient ancien.

La féerie manoeuvre au sommet d'un amphithéâtre couronné
par les taillis, —ou s'agite et module pour les Béotiens, dans
l'ombre des futaies mouvantes sur l'arête des cultures.
   L'opéra-comique se divise sur notre scène à l'arête d'inter-
section de dix cloisons dressées de la galerie aux feux.

(Bernard, p. 300)

*Ancient Comedy continues its harmonies and divides up in
idylls:*

. . . .

*Lyric scenes, accompanied by flute and drum,
bow gracefully in corners, under the ceilings round
modern club rooms or ancient Oriental halls.*
   *The fairy-play takes place at the top of an amphitheatre crowned
with foliage—or is performed in a modulated key for Boetians, in
the darkness of moving trees or the crest of fields.*
   The opéra-comique *is divided on our stage at the line of intersec-
tion of ten partitions placed between the gallery and the footlights.*

(Fowlie, pp. 227, 229)

There is little *action* in these poems; rather we sense the presence
of a *force,* an animating spirit reaching out to include the poet-
spectator. In "Une Saison en Enfer," Rimbaud informs us: "l'action
n'est pas la vie, mais une façon de gâcher quelque force, un énerve-
ment" (Barnard, p. 233). Even in a poem entitled "Mouvement,"
there is little evidence of motion. The poem evokes sea journeys and
voyages of discovery, but in the first stanza, an incomplete sentence,
there is no verb. Voyagers are seen, aspects of their journey described.
From what is said about their setting we are supposed to be able to
see "Eux chassés dans l'extase harmonique, / Et l'héroïsme de la dé-
couverte" (Bernard, p. 304). ("*Themselves driven into harmonic ecstasy, / And the heroism of discovery,*" Fowlie, p. 253.) It is as if the
ideal that we are to strive for offers, in its fullness and passion, a stable, if violent harmoniousness.
   Harmony and discovery: these are the two primary themes of Rimbaud's poetry. The poet is always in search of harmony—either that
of the past, or the future, or that which is present but not perceived
by the mass of humanity. The discovery of this harmony and its presentation to the debased world which it will redeem is the mission of
the seer, Rimbaud's ideal of the poet.
   This ideal is most clearly elucidated in the *lettres du voyant* (13
and 15 May, 1871). Here, we are told that the seer's duty is to awaken

himself, and subsequently humanity, to the presence of the "universal intelligence," or soul, that exists around us, to teach humanity the origin of their spirit and of the ideas which heretofore they believed to be their own creations.

> Universal intelligence has always thrown out its ideas naturally; men picked up a part of these fruits of the mind; people acted through them and wrote books about them. Things continued thus: man not working on himself, not yet being awake, or not yet in the fulness of the great dream. Civil servants, writers: author, creator, poet, that man never existed!
>
> (Fowlie, p. 307)

According to Rimbaud, the new poet, only able to come into existence now in the nineteenth century, would provide the voice which "would define the amount of the unknown awakening in his time in the universal soul (p. 309). Rimbaud's assumption is that his writings will suggest the essential harmony of this "unknown." "Always filled with *Number* and *Harmony,* these poems will be made to endure. —Fundamentally, it would be Greek poetry again in a way" (p. 309). Harmony and Number are to be the bases of what promises to be a new, architectonic poetry. But the poet, awakening unto this universal order from which his poetry will emerge, can claim neither to be the author of the poem or order, nor even to comprehend them. As a visionary, he is merely a discoverer and transmitter. "If what he brings back from *down there* has form, he gives form; if it is formless, he gives formlessness" (p. 309).

This form or formlessness demands a new language; for how can one express in everyday language or traditional poetic discourse this new profusion and harmony? "A language must be found. Moreover, every word being an idea, the time of a universal language will come! . . . This language will be of the soul for the soul, containing everything, smells, sounds, colors, thought holding onto thought and pulling. . . . let us ask the *poet* for the *new*—ideas and forms. . . . Inventions of the unknown call for new forms" (pp. 309, 311). Here begins the avant-garde search for an innovative language that would allow words to say more than they usually say, and thus its effort to distort, extend, and liberate customary language from its explicitly referential function. Rimbaud initiates the avant-garde tradition of a willfully irrational, hallucinatory language whose supposed origin lies beyond the individual poet and poetic tradition. Later avant-garde poets will create this new, impersonal language through formal disruption of words and syntax (the Russian futurists), through chance operations (dada), and through free play of the subconscious (surrealism).

Much of Rimbaud's poetry, however, merely seems to start from familiar Romantic metaphors and to proceed both by making them more extreme and by breaking them out of their traditional contexts. He piles image upon image, creating a profusion, and a confusion, of images, as in "Voyelles."

> A, noir corset velu des mouches éclatantes
> Qui bombinent autour des puanteurs cruelles,
>
> Golfes d'ombre; E, candeurs des vapeurs et des tentes,
> Lances des glaciers fiers, rois blancs, frissons d'ombelles;
>
> I, pourpres, sang craché, rire des lèvres belles
> Dans la colère ou les ivresses pénitentes
>
> (Bernard, p. 110)

> *A, black hairy corset of shining flies*
> *Which buzz around cruel stench,*
>
> *Gulfs of darkness; E, whiteness of vapors and tents,*
> *Lances of proud glaciers, white kings, quivering of flowers;*
>
> *I, purples, spit blood, laughter of beautiful lips*
> *In anger or penitent drunkenness*
>
> (Fowlie, p. 121)

Occasionally, he will construct singular metaphors out of radically disparate elements (though not nearly so frequently or in such an extreme manner as Lautréamont and the surrealists). The power of Rimbaud's works comes rather from the rapid accumulation of disjunctive images which seem to suggest causal relationships, but instead constantly shift the reader's focus—"thought holding onto thought and pulling"—and never coalesce into a clearly defined picture. "Villes I" is exemplary.

> Des groupes de beffrois chantent les idées des peuples. Des châteaux bâtis en os sort la musique inconnue. Toutes les légendes évoluent et les élans se ruent dans les bourgs. Le paradis des orages s'effondre. Les sauvages dansent sans cesse la fête de la nuit. Et une heure je suis descendu dans le mouvement d'un boulevard de Bagdad où des compagnies ont chanté la joie du travail nouveau, sous une brise épaisse, circulant sans pouvoir éluder les fabuleux fantômes des monts où l'on a dû se retrouver.

Quels bons bras, quelle belle heure me rendront cette région
d'où viennent mes sommeils et mes moindres mouvements?
(Bernard, pp. 276–277)

*Groups of belfries intone the ideas of the people. Unfamiliar
music comes from castles built of bones. All legends gyrate and
the impulses of the living hurl themselves about in the villages.
The paradise of storms comes to its end. The savages dance
ceaselessly in the celebration of night. And for one hour, I went
down into the animated Baghdad boulevard where groups sang
of the joy of new work, in a sluggish breeze, moving about without eluding the fabulous phantoms of mountains where people
had to find themselves again.*

*What good arms, what precious hour will give me back that place
from whence come my sleep and my slightest movements?*
(Fowlie, p. 241)

The "travail nouveau" of Rimbaud's poetry is the effort to unveil
these regions of generative force, of movement and plenitude. As he
states in "Une Saison en Enfer," hallucination and the willingness to
imagine the constant transformation of the ordinary into the potential and the fabulous lie at the origin of these creations. Certainly,
some are drug-induced; others are products of an imagination trying
to liberate itself from its dependence on the given world. "A chaque
être, plusieurs *autres* vies me semblaient dues. Ce monsieur ne sait ce
qu'il fait: il est un ange. Cette famille est une nichée de chiens. Devant plusieurs hommes, je causai tout haut avec un moment d'une
de leurs autres vies.—Ainsi, j'ai aimé un porc" (Bernard, p. 233).
("*To each being it seemed to me that several other lives were due.
This gentleman does not know what he is doing. He is an angel. This
family is a litter of dogs. In front of several men, I talked out loud
with one moment of one of their other lives.—In that way, I loved a
pig,*" Fowlie, p. 201.)
As this last reference to Verlaine indicates, the poet may perceive
the potential of other people's lives, even though they may not live
up to it, or may not even recognize what they are. Rimbaud suggests
here, however, as many avant-garde writers will later, that a new poetic language may reveal both the process and the promise of the
transformation of everyday life. Many of the poems of *Illuminations*,
for example, may be read as instances of such transformations rather
than as invocations of purely imaginary realms. The just quoted section of "Villes I" might be the result of re-seeing an ordinary street

scene of Paris or London. Because it is described by a poet who, under the influence of poetic inspiration or drugs, chooses to imagine alternate festive and mysterious lives for each entity found in this chance unity of disparate elements, the busy street becomes a scene of magical profusion and harmony. At work here is a combination of poetic action (the transformation of objects) and poetic passivity (the refusal to give or find a pre-established order in the original subject, or explicitly in the resulting poem).

Many of the unique qualities and difficulties of Rimbaud's poetic venture lie in this precarious balance of personal activism and impersonal and passive vision. For if the ideal he seeks is an impersonal and universal harmony, that ideal is attainable only through the specific actions of a special creature—the poet-seer, whose actions thrust him beyond personal identity to make him merely an instrument for the expression of the universal harmony speaking through him. "If brass wakes up a trumpet, it is not its fault. . . . I am present at this birth of my thought: I watch it and listen to it." Similarly, in his letter to Izambard, Rimbaud writes: "It is wrong to say: I think. One ought to say: People think me [*On me pense*] . . . I is someone else" (Fowlie 305; 303, 305). While this description may suggest a new image of an individual possessed by the muse of poetry, from this stance emerges Rimbaud's demand for an impersonal poetry, an "objective poetry."

This depersonalization of the poetic process is an anti-romantic gesture, asserting that we are the initiators of neither our ideas nor language. It is also related to the modernist—and to a certain extent, the avant-garde—rejection of the excesses of the Romantic conception of the poet as privileged visionary. At the same time, however, the image of the seer suggests that what Rimbaud desired was a version of Romantic inspiration. For it is ironic, and for Rimbaud probably tragic, that such possession by the universal soul is only attained by a radical self-involvement. Rimbaud's goal was to deny the importance of the self—to willfully reject the primacy of the ego so basic to bourgeois society and its poetic tradition. He attempted to destroy the self, to root out the bourgeois, the provincial, the religious, the modern, finally, the Western in himself, and in the process, to forcibly awaken himself to the other life that was due him. Yet, paradoxically, his first step was to investigate himself and to intensify his sensations and desires. "The first study of the man who wants to be a poet is the knowledge of himself, complete. He looks for his soul, inspects it, tests it, learns it. As soon as he knows it, he must cultivate it!" (Fowlie, p. 307). Rimbaud's means of cultivation was to live a life of extremes, to thrust himself by means of bohemianism, dissipation, drugs, absinthe, and sexual activity beyond the proper style of life for which he had been groomed.

> The Poet makes himself a *seer* by a long, gigantic and rational *derangement* of *all the senses*. All forms of love, suffering and madness. He searches himself. He exhausts all poisons in himself and keeps only their quintessences. Unspeakable torture where he needs all his faith, all his superhuman strength, where he becomes among all men the great patient [*invalid*], the great criminal, the one accursed—and the supreme Scholar!—Because he reaches the unknown!
>
> (Fowlie, p. 307)

Rimbaud fully realized that when he freed himself from social restraint, he flung himself into an apparent chaos, an unknown that he hoped would sustain whatever remained of the self that he so deranged. The poet, responsible for humanity, must, at a certain point, give up responsibility for himself, his actions, and his words. His first responsibility is solely to reach the unknown in order to glimpse the *new* and to become the depersonalized voice of what he sees, whether he understands it or not. The implicit paradox in this poetic venture is that the passionate derangement of self should lead to a vision of an impersonal harmony. Chaos should suddenly uncover order. The ideal echoes the end of "Soleil et Chair"; the poet achieves a state of being and vision in which passion and chaos are transformed into a fulfilled and unchanging balance of energy and plenitude.

Here, at the center of Rimbaud's poetic quest is the creative relationship of reason and unreason. Rimbaud made much of the "rational *derangement* of *all the senses*," but perhaps it is the word *rational* that ought to be stressed. Rimbaud and the whole tradition of the avant-garde present a rational apology for the irrational. Reason, investigating itself and its place in culture, discovers itself to be inadequate to the truest needs of humanity. Its answer is a programmatic anti-rationalism. But the goal, finally, is a form of super-rationalism, a universal intelligence and harmony which redeem the poet and his culture. From a restrictive and narrow rationality, the poet is thrust through chaos toward an absolute reason. It is perhaps such a reason that is invoked in "À une raison," a universal by which human life will be transformed.

> Un coup de ton doigt sur le tambour décharge tous les sons
> et commence la nouvelle harmonie.

Un pas de toi c'est la levée des nouveaux hommes et leur
en marche.
Ta tête se détourne: le nouvel amour! Ta tête se retourne:
—le nouvel amour!
. . . .
Arrivée de toujours, qui t'en iras partout.

(Bernard, p. 268)

*A tap with your finger on the drum releases all sounds
and begins the new harmony.
One step of yours, and the new men rise up
and march.
Your head turns aside: new love! Your head turns back—
new love!*
. . . .
You will go everywhere, since you have come from all time.

(Fowlie, p. 247)

The problem that the poet and the reader face, however, is that
this harmonious ideal may be only intermittently glimpsed, and even
then it may not be understood. The harmony of many of the *Illuminations,* for example, is disorienting. The poems purport to be the
expression of a fullness of experience far surpassing the narrowed
perspective that characterizes personal and collective life in modern
society. The poet, as spectator and participant, moves amid these visions of totality, singing from within or above. But he is only a part
of a whole over which he has no control, and usually only imperfect
comprehension. Each image, indeed each poem, is like a note within
a chord and a melody which it suggests, but does not know fully. As
several writers and critics have pointed out, the experience of Rimbaud's poetry is primarily sensual. The unity and the effect of the
poems seem to emerge from the visual evocativeness of the images
and the sounds of the words, and not from explicit argument or logical relationships among images. As Valéry noted, Rimbaud's poetry
is a poetry of an "incoherence harmonique."[7]
    If the poet does lose control of himself, his language, and his vision
to enter a realm of experience so much greater than himself, it is difficult then to know at what point the chaos of derangement leaves off
and the profusion of the universal order reveals itself. At which point
does the irrational become the super-rational? For the poet, evi-

dently, the knowledge is personal and immediate. For the reader, however, it is not so easily achieved. In fact, we encounter here two problems that mark every avant-garde movement which searches for a new language and basis of its vision. First, the reader is confronted with the challenge of distinguishing what is primarily an expression of revolt in the poet's language—a distortion of traditional language and the means toward a new awareness—and what claims to be the new, ideal language of poetic expression.[8] In Rimbaud's case, for example, it is not always evident which works are reflections of his *"encrapulement"* or of the derangement of his senses and which speak the nascent universal language of our time. Second, and more problematic, is that the avant-garde's experiment in language and consciousness involves a conflict between individual action and collective expectation. The works of Rimbaud and other avant-garde writers are the products of individual acts of derangement or hallucination, but their goal is to get beyond the heightened alienation of the individual in order to find some transcendent, interpersonal realm. Ironically, the poet must first increase the distance between himself and his audience in order to attain a language or a vision which ideally will provide the basis for a new type of communication and communion with his society. This conflict is usually most evident in the poem's language, where the limits of an individual's freedom to distort what is essentially a collective phenomenon are soon apparent.

Rimbaud declares the poet to be separated from the reigning language and values of his time by his works, works which introduce a presently unknown reality that will bring about change in his society. The poet "would give more—than the formulation of his thought, than the annotation *of his march toward Progress!* Enormity becoming normal, absorbed by all, he would really be *a multiplier of progress!* . . . Eternal art would have its functions, since poets are citizens. Poetry will not lend its rhythm to action, it *will be in advance"* (Fowlie, p. 309). Thus the poet speaks for historical progress and is an agent of change, but he speaks from what he assumes to be the eternal perspective of a universal reality. Consequently, his works are not to be equated with actions. ("L'action n'est pas la vie, mais une façon de gâcher quelque force.") They are in advance of a world that will arrive at what he has already discovered in his solitude.

Nevertheless, the poet can be completely confident neither of the success of his poetic venture, nor that he will survive its demands. In fact, part of the romance of the seer is that the derangement *and* the

unknown exact their toll on the poet. Having given up his ties to the
social world, he may find himself without support in the realm he
seeks, and instead of harmony, strength, and luxury, he may experience only an annihilating chaos. "He reaches the unknown, and
when, bewildered, he ends by losing the intelligence of his visions,
he has seen them. Let him die as he leaps through unheard of and
unnamable things: other horrible workers will come; they will begin
from the horizons where the other one collapsed" (Fowlie, p. 307).

With characteristic avant-garde agonism, Rimbaud's program pre-
dicts its own collapse; the heroics of *voyance* envision their necessary
fall back to earth and "l'ancienne ("Matinée d'Ivresse). In fact, many
of Rimbaud's poems, including "Matinée d'Ivresse," indicate that if
the harmonious vision is to be glimpsed, it is only for a moment. If
many of his poems present scenes of luxury and stability, a significant
number describe the passionate search and fall of the poet. They
reveal the violence directed against the bourgeois world, the derangement of self, and the dissipation that is felt during the return from
the voyage after a brief moment of success. If the first group of poems
offer little narrative development, these others, on the contrary, are
primarily descriptions of the stages of *voyance*. Poems such as "Le
Bateau ivre," "Les Poëtes de sept ans," and "Matinée d'Ivresse" invoke or describe the voyage, whether the voyage succeeds or fails.
Other poems such as "Conte," "Aube," and "Départ" suggest narratives whose meaning may be obscure, but which follow the pattern
of the poetic quest: departure from or rejection of a particular state
of being; passionate undertaking of some quest; achieved moment of
peace or accomplishment; and return to self-consciousness. Still others,
"Après de déluge," "Villes I," "Qu'est-ce pour nous?", illuminate
only parts of this journey.

In general, Rimbaud's works affirm the rewards of the seer's adventure, as well as the price the poet pays. "Matinée d'Ivresse" is perhaps
the most powerful evocation of the effort entailed.

Cela commença sous les rires des enfants, cela finira par eux. Ce poison
va rester dans toutes nos veines même quand, la fanfare tournant, nous
serons rendu à l'ancienne inharmonie. O maintenant, nous si digne de
ces tortures! rassemblons fervemment cette promesse surhumaine faite
à notre corps et à notre âme créés: cette promesse, cette démence!
L'élégance, la science, la violence! . . . Cela commença par quelques
dégoûts et cela finit, —ne pouvant nous saisir sur-le-champ de cette
éternité, —cela finit part une débandade de parfums. . . .
Petite veille d'ivresse, sainte! quand ce ne serait que pour le masque

dont tu nous as gratifié. Nous t'affirmons, méthode! Nous n'oublions
pas que tu as glorifié hier chacun de nos âges. Nous avons foi au poison.
Nous savons donner notre vie tout entière tous les jours.

(Bernard, p. 269)

*It all began with the laughter of children, and will end there. This
poison will still be in my veins even when the fanfare dies away and I
return to the earlier discord. And now that I am so worthy of this tor-
ture, let me fervently gather in the superhuman promise made to my
created body and soul. This promise, this madness! Elegance, science,
violence! . . . It all began with feelings of disgust and it ended—since
I would not seize its eternity on the spot—it ended with a riot of per-
fumes. . . . Brief night of intoxication, holy night! even if it was only
for the mask you bequeathed to us. We assert you, method! I am not
forgetting that yesterday you glorified each of our ages. I believe in that
poison. I can give all of my existence each day.*

(Fowlie, p. 233)

Even within this bombast, however, there is a sense of the unavoid-
able repetitiousness of this venture. Three times the poet uses the
phrase "it began"; three times he states "it ended." Three times the
poisons proved effective, but each time the poet realized that eternity,
his ideal of elegance, science, and violence, could never be seized, only
glimpsed. He will have to begin again, and again. To a certain extent, this is not only a function of the conflict between individual
temporality and eternity, but also a consequence of the avant-garde
poet's essential isolation. He is *in advance*. The ideal he glimpses
will only much later be evident to society. The life and people he returns to after each voyage have no knowledge of the world he has
seen. With each return, the gap between the real and the ideal is
ever more clear.

For Rimbaud, it seems, the constant oscillation between these two
states finally became too much. What is already sensed in his early
poem, "Le Bateau ivre" (1871), culminates in "Une Saison en Enfer"
(1873). "Le Bateau ivre" begins as a joyous affirmation of freedom
and the visionary experience only to end with the drunken boat missing its place of origin, Europe. The boat proves too weak for the
venture, but more pitifully, also too weak to reconcile itself to the
world to which it has returned.

> Si je désire une eau d'Europe, c'est la flache
> Noire et froide où vers le crépuscule embaumé
> Un enfant accroupi plein de tristesses, lâche
> Un bateau frêle comme un papillon de mai.

Je ne puis plus, baigné de vos langueurs, ô lames
Enlever leur sillage aux porteurs de cotons,
Ni traverser l'orgueil des drapeaux et des flammes,
Ni nager sous les yeux horribles des pontons.

(Bernard, p. 131)

If I want a water of Europe, it is the black
Cold puddle where in the sweet-smelling twilight
A squatting child full of sadness releases
A boat as fragile as a May butterfly.

No longer can I, bathed in your langour, O waves,
Follow in the wake of the cotton boats,
Nor cross through the pride of flags and flames,
Nor swim under the terrible eyes of prison ships.

(Fowlie, p. 121)

Whether we interpret the last lines to mean that the speaker cannot
bear or accept the guidance of commercial and military Europe, or
whether they suggest instead that he cannot assert his independence
from them, these lines clearly express a disaffection from his society.
But the pathos of the image of the child of sadness, having only a
dream, an imaginary voyage, makes us acutely aware of the vulnerability and the tenousness of the poet's private venture.

By the summer of 1872, when Rimbaud wrote "Une Saison en
Enfer," little faith in the liberating voyage must have remained. This
poem is marked by a strong sense of solitude, of radical alienation
from those around him, from society, from his past work, and from
his image of himself as a seer. It is a poem given over to bitter self-
judgment, recrimination, and fitful justification. Yet there seems to
be no stable perspective from which Rimbaud—or the reader—can
establish a coherent view. He constantly shifts his voice and tone. At
one point he condemns his actions, at another he justifies them, and
at still others, he even seems to reaffirm his idealism. Furthermore,
he appears to accept the power of the church to judge him, only then
to reject it completely.

The poem is primarily an analysis of his aesthetic program of *voyance,* and a farewell to it. It is probably not, however, a farewell to
poetry, since there is too much evidence that he continued to write
for at least a year after completing "Une Saison en Enfer." But given
the emotionalism of his rejection of his role as a seer, there is little
here that could long sustain innovative poetic creation. As a rejection
of *voyance,* it is a dismissal of an activist, avant-garde role for the

poet. Throughout, Rimbaud reveals the tension and pain of his isolation, his idealism, and his vision of remaking society and poetry.
Certainly, though he could not have realized it, he was successful in
the latter effort. But the former, the social role of art, proved to be a
failure. Caught up in the passion and ideas of his time, drawn toward
the socialists, believing in the possibility of historical change, Rimbaud once assumed that the poet's heroism and visionary qualities
would be part of a larger movement and would inspire others by the
combined spirit of nihilism and progressivism. We can only specu-
late that, instead, Rimbaud found the failure of the Commune, the
desultory life of the exiles in London, the condemnation of his and
Verlaine's love and bohemianism, and Verlaine's own limits to be
too great a reality against which to struggle. Rimbaud's life after giving up poetry proved that he could bear solitude and reject Europe,
but what is central to "Une Saison en Enfer" and evident during the
remainder of his life is that he could not sustain his idealism.

Dominating the poem is Rimbaud's sense of his personal weakness
and the resulting bitterness over his awareness that he is able neither
to escape his culture nor to change it. Particularly distressing to him
is that his desire to transform life, far from denying the established
culture, only serves to pay homage to it. For when he is forced to
confront the nature of his idealism, he recognizes its religious dimension. Similarly, his nihilism is itself defined by what he would reject,
so that each action of denial is an implicit testament to its subject. As
many other modern poets—especially Baudelaire and Lautréamont—
have discovered, an obsession with denying morality and glorifying
the debased, the fallen and the cruel, all in the name of freedom
from social values, is but an ineffectual rebellion against the church
and society felt within themselves. "Les gens d'Église diront: C'est
compris. Mais vous voulez parler de l'Éden. Rien pour vous dans
l'histoire des peuples orientaux. —C'est vrai; c'est à l'Éden que je
songeais!" (Bernard, p. 236). (*"Churchmen will say: It is agreed. But
you mean Eden. Nothing for you in the history of Oriental peoples.—
It is true; I was thinking of Eden!"* Fowlie, p. 203.)

Rimbaud may truly reject, or, at least, despise his society and
dream of committing a crime "que je tombe au néant de par la loi
humaine" (Bernard, p. 220), but he cannot escape the church's power
over him so easily. For the core of his desire is spiritual. He seeks
salvation, either personal or collective, and the recognition of his
failure causes him to question his methods. "Une Saison en Enfer"
is dominated by religious imagery; even to imagine his life a hell is
to validate Christian thinking. "Je me crois en enfer, donc j'y suis.

C'est l'exécution du catéchisme. Je suis esclave de mon baptême"
(Bernard, p. 220). ("*I think I am in hell, and therefore I am. It is a
result of the catechism. I am a slave to my baptism,*" Fowlie, p. 183.)
In this poem of defeat, Rimbaud sees that his past actions, his derangement, his attempt to declare himself a pagan—a savage, a Scandinavian, a Greek, a non-Western primitive—were childish illusions.
His idealization of strength, the future vigor invoked in "Le Bateau
ivre," "Génie," "Matinée d'Ivresse," the *lettres du voyant,* were all
appeals to a power he desired more than experienced. No, he is not a
Scandinavian, only a Gaul—a spiteful, pitiably weak pagan destined
to fall under the power of the church and modern, "scientific" bourgeois society. There are no ancestors who will aid him; he must create himself *ex nihilo,* and this is precisely what neither he nor any
subsequent avant-garde writer can do.

Consequently, "Une Saison en Enfer" is a poem of dejection and
self-denigration, a poem that recognizes the power of his adversaries,
especially the church. But it is not totally a work of submission. To
the end of the poem, even admitting the Christian source of his
ideal, he declares that he was right to reject the church and his culture.

J'ai eu raison de mépriser ces bonshommes qui ne perdraient pas
l'occasion d'une caresse, parasites de la propreté et de la santé de nos
femmes, aujourd'hui qu'elles sont si peu d'accord avec nous. . . .
"sommes-nous assez de damnés ici-bas! Moi, j'ai tant de temps déjà
dans leur troupe! Je les connais tous. Nous nous reconnaissons toujours;
nous nous dégoûtons. La charité nous est inconnue. Mais nous sommes
polis; nos relations avec le monde sont très-convenables." Est-ce
étonnant? Le monde! les marchands, les naïfs!

(Bernard, p. 235)

*I was right to despise those fellows who never lost the chance of a
caress, parasites of the cleanliness and health of our women today when
they are so little in agreement with us . . .
"Aren't there enough of us who are damned here below? Already I have
been so long in their troop! I know them all. We always recognize one
another. Each of us disgusts the other. Charity is unknown to us. But
we are polite. Our relationship with the world is very correct." Is this
surprising? The world! merchants, simple souls!*

(Fowlie, p. 203)

This fallen world is all very correct, but damned. There are no elect;
there are only the "faux élus." If the idea of the church remains

strong, it only serves to confirm how poor life on earth is. The fate of humanity is to struggle, as Rimbaud has, without any promise from above of the amelioration of their pain. "Le combat spirituel est aussi brutal que la bataille d'hommes; mais la vision de la justice est le plaisir de Dieu seul" (Bernard, p. 241). (*"A spiritual battle is as brutal as a battle of men; but the vision of justice is the pleasure of God alone,"* Fowlie, p. 209.)

Ultimately, however, this poem of self-judgment remains a poem of self-justification. Whether his ideal was based on Eden or not, he declares that he never desired to take leave of this world or to deny its reality; rather, he sought to transform it. That desire remains alive in the poem, and certainly his awareness of the miserable inadequacy of modern life is still strong. However, his options are narrowed. Rimbaud has no faith in politics, or in the church, or in *voyance,* or in poetry, and "la science est trop lente" (Bernard, p. 238). Change may be taking place, but Rimbaud will not experience its fruits. The poet has only rough reality and the modern world to accept, and to live in.

Moi! moi qui me suis dit mage ou ange, dispensé de toute morale, je suis rendu au sol, avec un devoir à chercher, et la réalité rugueuse à étreindre! Paysan . . .
Il faut être absolument moderne.

(Bernard, p. 240, 241)

I who called myself magus or angel, exempt from all morality, I am thrown back to the earth, with a duty to find, and rough reality to embrace! Peasant! . . .
We must be absolutely modern.

(Fowlie, p. 209)

Saying this, the poet takes leave of hell, of his past derangement, and of his rebellion against society and the church. But in doing this, he also frees himself (until his deathbed) of the church. And it *is* a harsh reality that he enters. While we might detect a bit of residual romanticism in Rimbaud's departure from Europe for Africa to live as a low-level functionary of economic imperialism, all the evidence we have indicates that he became everything he once abhorred. The few tantalizing suggestions in "Une Saison en Enfer" that once he freed himself from his torment, some aspect of the old ideals might remain viable, quickly proved ephemeral.

Or, tout dernièrement m'étant trouvé sur le point de faire le dernier *couac!* j'ai songé à rechercher la clef du festin ancien, où je reprendrais peut-être appétit.

(Bernard, p. 211)

But recently, on the verge of giving my last croak, I thought of looking for the key to the ancient banquet where I might possibly recover my appetite.

(Fowlie, p. 173)

Cependant c'est la veille. Recevons tous les influx de vigueur et de tendresse réelle. Et à l'aurore, armés d'une ardente patience, nous entrerons aux splendides villes.

(Bernard, p. 241)

However this is the vigil. Let us welcome all the influxes of vigor and real tenderness. And, at dawn, armed with ardent patience, we will enter magnificent cities.

(Fowlie, p. 209)

To the end of "Une Saison en Enfer," Rimbaud appeals to an ideal of vigor, and dreams of entering magnificent cities, but in Africa, all he found was further decay and desolation. Perhaps this last desire allowed him to compose some of the last *Illuminations,* but as he predicted, he was only to fall back to earth, bewildered, having lost the intelligence of his visions. He was not wrong, however, in also predicting that others would take up where he had collapsed, as each successive generation of avant-garde writers proved.

Chapter
III
The Poets of Time:
Apollinaire
and the Italian Futurists

The creative ferment and rapid succession of aesthetic movements during the first three decades of the twentieth century signal the high point of modernism and the avant-garde. The writers and artists of this era displayed a heightened awareness of the radically new aspects of their culture—especially the dramatic changes in daily life that resulted from the scientific, technological, economic, and political developments in European culture during the period surrounding the First World War. In response to these developments, writers and artists, individually or as part of particular aesthetic movements, strove to create a literature and art appropriate to their times. What united such diverse, but representative post-symbolist and anti-naturalist writers as Yeats, Trakl, Rilke, Pound, Eliot, Musil, Joyce, Apollinaire, Mayakovsky, and Brecht, as well as the artists associated with fauvism, expressionism, *die Brücke, Blaue Reiter,* cubism, futurism, dada, surrealism, constructivism, and *de stijl,* was the knowledge that, whether artists regretted it or not, the social position and aesthetic traditions of literature and art had been radically altered. Consequently, their own creations had to define a new social role for art and to establish the artists' place within a disrupted and problematic aesthetic tradition. Whatever their individual response to modernity, these writers and artists explicitly had to accept the possibilities—and responsibilities—of innovation.

Whereas the major modernist writers revealed a general doubt about the positive aspects of this new situation, on the whole, the visual artists of the period threw themselves with greater zeal into the dynamics of formal innovation, especially in the era prior to the First World War. The pre-war years—the "banquet years" as Roger Shattuck has called them—were a time of relatively little social unrest, particularly in France. Consequently, with the exception of German expressionism, Italian futurism, and a few writers such as Apollinaire, the innovative artists of this period rarely addressed the question of the social and political implications of art. Movements like *die Brücke, Blaue Reiter,* fauvism, cubism, and orphism seemed most concerned with the epistemological, conceptual, and spiritual significance of their stylistic innovations and with purely formal problems of perspective, color, materials, and composition. Even the artists and writers who did investigate the political and social dimensions of their work—most notably Apollinaire and Marinetti—were swept along in a general enthusiasm for the positive and creative possibilities of modernity.

For Apollinaire and the Italian futurists, art was an expression of change, change most specifically within the traditional conventions of art, but also in society as a whole. For them, art responded directly to the inherent dynamism of society, and by its own constant transformation, participated in and augmented that social energy.

While there are important differences between Apollinaire and the futurists, their common enthusiasm for modern culture, fascination with the idea of constant social change, and emphasis on the future in their aesthetic innovations represent the spirit of the avant-garde in this early modernist era. Both were strongly affected by the recent scientific discoveries and the inventions of the technological industries of modern mass culture. The radical changes in the quality of daily life which had characterized the preceding few decades, particularly in recently industrialized northern Italy, and the promise of new discoveries and changes in the future seemed to announce both humanity's potential mastery of nature and the re-creation of the phenomenal world by their societies' newly developed powers. The electric light—electricity, itself—the gas turbine engine, the airplane, x-rays, modern steel construction, as well as the automobile, cinema, and the phonograph, all touched people's lives intimately and created a significantly new universe for art to depict.

Modern science and technology represented to these writers benign powers with which the individual could wholeheartedly identify. Unlike a significant number of modernist writers, neither Apollinaire nor the futurists expressed any anxiety about the increasing dominance of the scientific spirit in modern culture. Rather than representing a threat to the aesthetic imagination, science spurred these writers' poetic inspiration, even to the point that all of them found the energy and technological aspects of modern war something to marvel at. Furthermore, since science represented to them the spirit of the new age, they were able to avoid the social alienation that so many avant-garde writers experienced. Rather than basing their visions of a new society upon metaphors and programs of political activists, these early-twentieth-century avant-garde artists identified institutions that already existed in their societies as the agencies of the developments they desired. As a result, these writers exhibit little of the personal antagonism and nihilism that characterize so much of the later avant-garde. Any negativism that did exist was directed toward those people who did not recognize or who opposed what appeared to them to be inevitable change.

For Apollinaire and the futurists, the poet's responsibility and challenge was to equal the promise of science and to participate in the new spirit of their time. Inspired by the potentiality of the future, they formulated a new social role for the artist, one which would awaken those elements of society as yet unaware of the inherent dynamism of their culture, combat those forces which actively retarded change, and create an art that would provide new images and poetic forms appropriate to humanity's future. Once again, the artist was declared to be *in advance* of culture. The poet was to be both a popularizer of the new spirit already at work in society and a prophet of what was to come.

The "epic vision" which Apollinaire recognized in Marinetti's work as early as 1908[1] characterizes, to a certain extent, both these writers' works. For despite their differences, both attempted to express the effects of science, technology, and the "new spirit" of their times on the whole of life. They were particularly interested in the idea of a new audience, the creation of mass culture. The "industrialized" arts of the masses, particularly the cinema, phonograph, and variety theater, represented the dynamism and the popularity that they hoped to attain. But at the same time, their literary experiments were destined to speak more to the "new man" of the future than the masses of their day. Throughout the works of both, the poet and artist figured as inventors, discoverers, and prophets. As inventor, the poet was to create new means of expression and vision. As discoverer, he or she would lay bare the eternally new life as it emerged in the culture. As a prophet, the poet would sing of the possible—the future—world to come.

But in spite of their similar interests and experiments, there are also radical differences between Apollinaire and the Italian futurists, which illuminate some of the complexities of modernism and the avant-garde of this early period. Their aesthetic and personal sensibilities differ dramatically. Apollinaire is clearly the most personable and intimate, the most self-conscious and self-questioning, the most subtle, sensitive, and finally humane of these writers. And while the futurists' program appears simplistic in its narrow dogmatism, Apollinaire's statements often reveal a richness and suggestiveness born of personal ambiguity and confusion. But these differences provide more than just a basis for judgment: indeed, a comparison of Apollinaire and the Italian futurists allows us to study some of the inherent tensions of avant-garde thought. In particular, these artists highlight the ambiguities of the modernist and avant-garde concepts of time and the complex interactions of the individual consciousness and collective experience.

I

Some of the ambiguities of the avant-garde emerge most clearly in the wrenching conflicts and contradictions of Apollinaire's personality and poetry; yet part of the beauty of his poetry also originates in these very same conflicts. For Apollinaire's work displays two opposing tendencies which he tried to balance but could never fully reconcile: a tendency toward expanding his personal perspective to take in the totality of his society and its historical moment; and one toward focusing on the most private of experiences. Neither tendency is dominant, neither alone is fully adequate to his needs, and each presents a significant threat to his personal vision and poetics.

One example of this persistent conflict is Apollinaire's attitude toward aesthetic tradition. For, on the one hand, Apollinaire was a particularly vigorous spokesman for modernity and innovation in the arts; on the other hand, he was also inherently conservative and cautioned against too radical a break with the past. Like many modernist writers and painters, he was a man with sensibilities divided among the past, present, and future, attempting to reconcile antagonistic impulses and loyalties in an art that paid homage to the efficacy of earlier poetic conventions while asserting the need to establish new techniques to articulate a new spirit. Thus, his own work was alternately a testament to the accepted traditions of poetics and the most innovative and influential experimental writing of his time; from each new innovation that would provide future poetic movements with new techniques and ideas, Apollinaire turned, yet again, to stress his commitment to tradition.

Apollinaire was similarly divided between emphasizing the personal and the collective dimensions of poetry and experience. He was a complex man, given, on the one hand, to personal glorification and egocentric myth-making, and, on the other, to expressions of an absolutely intimate and vulnerable sensibility. He envisioned himself as an archetypal poet-seer, singer of an epic vision and of the heroic potential in the modern individual and society. Yet many of his most moving and accomplished works are intensely personal songs of individual loss and regret. As a consequence, his poems are marked by alternating passages of exuberance and quietude, idealistic expansiveness and melancholy retreat. For to expand his vision in space and in time, to identify with the vitality and complexity of modern society, and to look fervently to its unfolding future threatened Apollinaire with the loss of a cherished sense of personal intimacy, even as he gained from this expansion a much desired public role. Yet to withdraw into private experience made him all the more aware of the intense vulnerability of the isolated self in an expansive world of rapid change.[2] Apollinaire's poetry is obsessed with the experience of time; in many of his poems the poet stands alone observing the erosion of his past experiences by the flow of time, fully aware that even the present moment is destined to fade. Thus, his identification with his culture's surge into the future seemed to promise an entirely different structure and dynamism to his personal sense of time; the excitement of the new experiences and self that the future brought offset the slow but incessant loss of self to the past.

Both tendencies—the visionary and the melancholic, whether expressed in terms of innovation and tradition or personal expansion and contraction—are intensely lyrical. Indeed, Apollinaire's entire poetic and personal venture is rooted in the conflict between the promise and danger of the modern lyric moment. The promise of this moment is the increased intensity of transcending the boundaries of individual personality and immediate place and time. The danger is that in the absence of any shared notion of the essential unity of the external world, time, values, or even personal identity, each lyric moment that seems to offer a merger of self with something external to that self also threatens the identity of that individual. Thus, for example, Apollinaire describes himself in "Merveilles de la Guerre" as a poet able to identify with all the horror and excitement that war offers.

> Je lègue à l'avenir l'histoire de Guillaume Apollinaire
> Qui fut à la guerre et sut être partout
> Dans les villes heureuses de l'arrière
> Dans tout le reste de l'univers
> Dans ceux qui meurent en piétinant dans le barbelé

> *I bequeath to the future the story of Guillaume Apollinaire*
> *Who was in the war and could be everywhere*
> *In happy villages behind the lines*
> *In all the rest of the universe*
> *In those who died tangled in the barbed wire*[3]

However, even though he believes himself heroically expansive, he also knows himself to be essentially isolated. The lyric merger with experience was a notoriously one-sided affair.

> Et ce serait sans doute bien plus beau
> Si je pouvais supposer que toutes ces choses dans lesquelles
>   je suis partout
> Pouvaient m'occuper aussi
> Mais dans ce sens il n'y a rien de fait
> Car si je suis partout à cette heure il n'y a cependant que
>   moi qui suis en moi
>
>   (Adéma and Décaudin, p. 272)

> *And without doubt it would be more beautiful*
> *If I could suppose that all the things everywhere in which*
>   *I reside*
> *Could be also in me*
> *But there is nothing so made in this respect*
> *For if I am everywhere right now there is still only I who*
>   *can be in me*
>
>   (Shattuck, p. 185)

In other poems, even this isolated self-possession is questioned, for the poet does not always achieve a synthesizing perspective capable of unifying the disparate aspects of his expansive experience. More often, he experiences lyric moments successively in time. Each moment that he extends himself, he also loses that new part of himself as the experience fades into the past. Thus, to reconstitute his identity, he must find himself in retrospect. For example, in "Cortège," the poet asks if he can come to know just who he is.[4]

Un jour je m'attendais moi-même
Je me disais Guillaume il est temps que tu viennes
Et d'un lyrique pas s'avançaient ceux que j'aime
Parmi lesquels je n'étais pas
. . . . .
Le cortège passait et j'y cherchais mon corps
Tous ceux qui survenaient et n'étaient pas moi-même
Amenaient un à un les morceaux de moi-même
On me batît peu à peu comme on élève une tour
Les peuples s'entassaient et je parus moi-même
Qu'ont formé tous les corps at les choses humaines
                              (Adéma and Décaudin, pp. 75–76)

One day I was waiting for myself
I said to myself Guillaume it's time that you came
And with a lyric step all those that I love came forward
And I was not among them
. . . .
The procession passed and I looked in it for my body
All these turned up and were not myself
Brought one by one the pieces of myself
They built me little by little as a tower is raised
The people heaped themselves up and I appeared myself
Who was formed of all bodies and all human things
                              (Shattuck, pp. 77, 79)

Potentially, then, the lyric personality enjoys only a series of discrete moments of identification with the world, but each moment of self-expansion may also be the beginning of personal disintegration. If the traditional lyric poet might find personal unity and significance in memory and the poem, for the self-consciously modern writer, both memory and the literary work seem to be agents of self-disintegration and inauthenticity since they pull one away from the reality of the ever-new present moment.

Apollinaire knew only too well the nature of his divided loyalties and the conflicts of the lyric vision. Indeed, they became the subjects of many of his poems and essays. He frequently referred to the interminable battles between past and future, tradition and innovation, order and liberty, self and external experience, and he knew his own stakes within these conflicts. Yet he sought an ideal reconciliation between these sets of opposing pairs. In fact, most of Apollinaire's poetry is the expression of his attempt to find a unifying principle of personal and collective life in the idea of cultural modernity. He sought to reach out and embrace life and love, whether they were present or had fled. His eroticism, his universal acceptance of life, his love of the quotidian, and his promiscuous consumption of all his epoch had to offer—urbanism, science, and war, especially war—reveal him as a man whose spirit "will permit life to be exalted in whatever form it occurs."[5]

Apollinaire's description of the "new spirit" of his age provides a portrait of himself as a new poet dedicated "to explore truth, to search for it, as much in the ethic domain . . . as in that of the imagination" (p. 227). The concepts of the new spirit and the new poet represent the visionary side of the avant-garde; they foresee the resolution of the essential alienation of the individual in modern culture through a projected union of the poet with the defining spirit and reality of the age. But even in his important essay, "The New Spirit and the Poets" (1918), which claimed to perceive such a union, all the problematic elements of his work are apparent.

This essay is, in many ways, an exemplary avant-garde manifesto. In "The New Spirit and the Poets," as in Apollinaire's most expansive poems such as "Cortège," "Les Fenêtres," "Les Collines," or "Mervcilles de Guerre," we are at first made aware of the poet's positive response to the discovery of the new, his recognition of the modernity of his culture and the attraction of the future. In these works, the future is a realm of surprise, vitality, and necessity. The essay argues that since the individual is a product of his or her times, and since one's most essential life, in particular the imagination, is shaped by the physical environment, he or she must live within the flow of time and embrace that culture which so constantly moves toward its future. For to do otherwise—to cling to tradition and reject the new world and its innovations—would be to live an *inauthentic* life. We would be separating ourselves from the spirit of our culture, thus consigning ourselves to memory, the past, and death.

Apollinaire suggests that these imperatives are most strongly felt by the poet. The contemporary era, Apollinaire declares, provides a multitude of new subjects and perspectives for poetry. In addition to new sights, objects, inventions, and physical environments, the poet

will be able to explore realms of experience formerly excluded from
the poetic sphere—the grotesque, the base, the horrible, and the absurd, for example. To do justice to these new subjects, the poet will
have to create appropriate forms, images, and conventions—in short,
a new language. For as part inventor, the poet will also of necessity
be an experimenter, a searcher for new possibilities of expression.
And, as all avant-garde writers agree, this new language will by itself
lead to further discoveries of poetic potential. "The investigations of
form have subsequently assumed a great importance. Is it not under-
standable? How could the poet not be interested in these investigations which can lead to new discoveries in thought and lyricism?"
(p. 227).

Of special significance is that Apollinaire believed that these poetic
explorations are not isolated concerns. They are part of a general
cultural ferment throughout modern society, characterized by constant discovery, invention, and creation in the sciences and the other
arts. Thus, poetry has an integral role in that society's development.
In fact, for Apollinaire, all creators are to be called poets. "Only that
man can be called poet who invents, who creates insofar as a man can
create. . . . One can be a poet in any field: it is enough that one be
adventuresome and pursue any new discovery" (p. 234).

Apollinaire's emphasis here is on adventure, for the discovery of
the new demands a determined exploration of the unknown—of what
has as yet not even been imagined. This activity, as Rimbaud and
countless avant-garde writers inform us, requires a special heroism
and strength in solitude. Apollinaire wrote,

> the poet, by the very nature of his explorations, is isolated in the new
> world into which he enters the first, and the only consolation which is
> left to him is that, since men must live in the end by truths in spite of
> the falsehoods with which they pad them, the poet alone sustains the
> life whereby humanity finds these truths. This is why modern poets are
> above all singers of a constantly new truth. And their task is infinite;
> they have surprised you and will surprise you again. . . . They will
> carry you, living and awake, into a nocturnal world sealed with dreams.
> Into universes which tremble ineffably above our heads (p. 235).

To thrust himself into the unknown means that the poet must be
willing to give up all connections with the given world, with poetic
convention, and with the past. He must accept his necessary solitude.
Ultimately, he must even give up all that he has been and what he
has known. Apollinaire's earlier poem "Toujours" challenges the
poet and all modern explorers to accept this quest:

Et tant d'univers s'oublient
Quels sont les grands oublieurs
Qui donc saura nous faire oublier telle ou telle partie du monde
Où est le Christophe Colomb à qui l'on devra l'oubli d'un
    continent
                Perdre
Mais perdre vraiment
Pour laisser place à la trouvaille
                Perdre
La vie pour trouver la Victoire
                (Adéma and Décaudin, p. 237)

And so many of the universe forget themselves
Who are the great forgetters
Who will know just how to make us forget such and such a part
    of the world
Where is Christopher Columbus to whom is owed the forgetting
    of a continent
                To lose
But to lose genuinely
In order to make room for discovery
                To lose
Life in order to find Victory
                (Shattuck, p. 177)

The poet who discovers these truths necessary for life is a seer creating for humanity's benefit images of its deepest desires. And from these dreams, visions of humanity's future will emerge. At his most exuberant, Apollinaire declared that the poet is not only the discoverer of the unknown and the "divine" that exists within and around us, but a creator and prophet of the future as well. He suggested, for example, that just as the poet's dream of flight in the legend of Icarus served for thousands of years as an unconscious stimulus until it was realized in the invention of the airplane, the dreams of contemporary poets would provide the realities of the future. Apollinaire even asserted, at times, that he and other poet-seers had direct vision into the immediate future and could thus serve as active agents in humanity's development. In the remarkable and complex poem "Les Collines," from *Calligrammes*, Apollinaire writes:

        Certains hommes sont des collines
        Qui s'élèvent d'entre les hommes

Et voient au loin tout l'avenir
Mieux que s'il était le présent
Plus net que s'il était passé
. . . .
Profondeurs de la conscience
On vous explorera demain
Et qui sait quels êtres vivants
Seront tirés de ces abîmes
Avec des univers entiers

Voici s'élever des prophètes
Comme au loin des collines bleues
Ils sauront des choses précises
Comme croient savoir les savants
Et nous transporteront partout
                              (Adéma and Décaudin, p. 172)

Certain men stand out like hills
Rising above their fellow men
To see the future from afar
Better than they see today
Clearer than if it were the past
. . . .
Depths of consciousness
You will be explored tomorrow
And who knows what living beings
Will be pulled from these depths
Along wth entire universes

Now the prophets arise
Like those blue hills in the distance
They will know exact things
As scientists believe themselves to know
And will carry us everywhere[6]

   But the idealization of the poet's role that we find in poems such as "Les Collines" and "Toujours," as well as in "The New Spirit and the Poets," is not sustained without significant difficulties and self-doubt. Tellingly, there is little actual prophesy—few "choses pre-cises"—in "Les Collines." Rather, Apollinaire presents us only meta-phors of an awareness of time and our constant movement into the future. The poet illuminates this movement, not its specific goal—the promise, not the achievement.

L'esclave tient une épée nue
Semblable aux sources et aux fleuves
Et chaque fois qu'elle s'abaisse
Un univers est éventré
Dont il sort des mondes nouveaux

Le chauffeur se tient au volant
Et chaque fois que sur la route
Il corne en passant le tournant
Il paraît à perte de vue
Un univers encore vierge

Et le tiers nombre c'est la dame
Elle monte dans l'ascenseur
Elle monte monte toujours
Et la lumière se déploie
Et ces clartés la transfigurent
                    (Adéma and Décaudin, pp. 176–177)

The slave holds up a naked sword
Quite similar to springs and streams
And every time it is brought down
A universe is disembowelled
From which new worlds are born again

The driver grips the steering wheel
And every time along the road
He blows the horn rounding a curve
There appears on the horizon's rim
A universe as yet unknown

The third one is the lady who
Is taking the elevator up
She keeps on going up and up
And light seems to unfold itself
In brilliance which transfigures her
                    (Shattuck, pp. 149, 151)

Apollinaire's emphasis here on the dynamics of discovery, rather than on the nature of the "univers encore vierge," illustrates a general avant-garde tendency to focus on the primacy and intensity of the moment of creation; moreover, it exemplifies what proves to be the blind faith of most avant-garde writers in a future about which they are rarely specific.

But if Apollinaire invokes the promise of a new time and a new poetics, he also reveals the pain of the poet's calling more than most avant-garde writers. For Apollinaire, the poet as an individual is intensely aware that if he is drawn toward the public role of seer, it is at the expense of his personal life. He sees within himself a constant struggle between what he has been and what he will be, between what he has loved and his love itself, which will always seek new loves. "Les Collines" opens with an image of this battle taking place under the eyes of the *eternal* sun. Out of this combat, however, a new moment—the present—emerges, which will give the poet powers of prediction.

> Au-dessus de Paris un jour
> Combattaient deux grands avions
> L'un était rouge et l'autre noir
> Tandis qu'au zénith flamboyait
> L'éternel avion solaire
>
> L'un était toute ma jeunesse
> Et l'autre c'était l'avenir
> Il se combattaient avec rage
>
> . . . .
>
> Où donc est tombée ma jeunesse
> Tu vois que flambe l'avenir
> Sache que je parle aujourd'hui
> Pour annoncer au monde entier
> Qu'enfin est né l'art de prédire
>   (Adéma and Décaudin, p. 171)

> *High above Paris roofs one day*
> *Two airplanes struggled in the sky*
> *The one was red and the other black*
> *While at the zenith timelessly*
> *The airplane-sun flamed in its track*
>
> *One of them was my long youth*
> *The other held the future's hate*
> *Each fought with the ferocity*
>
> . . . .
>
> *When did my youth fall from so high*
> *See how the future flames as well*

Know that I raise my voice today
To tell the peoples of the world
Prediction is at last an art

(Shattuck, p. 145)

At the beginning of the poem, the public persona of the poet appears to transcend the personal struggle that gives it birth. The poem ends, however, with a return to self, with a renewed recognition of the pain and loss suffered in the struggle of his past and future. The seer may have assumed that he had achieved the transcendent perspective of the eternal sun—which, evidently, he had laughed at—but he inevitably discovers that he also must fall back into time.

Mais pleure pleure et repleurons
Et soit que la lune soit pleine
Ou soit qu'elle n'ait qu'un croissant
Ah! pleure pleure et repleurons
Nous avons tant ri au soleil

Des bras d'or supportent la vie
Pénétrez le secret doré
Tout n'est qu'une flamme rapide
Que fleurit la rose adorable
Et d'où monte un parfum exquis

(Adéma and Décaudin, p. 177)

But weep and weep and weep again
And though the moon wax to its full
Or be it but a crescent moon
Ah! weep and weep and weep again
For we have laughed long at the sun

Golden arms sustain life
Penetrate its secret gold
All is but a fleeting flame
Which the adorable rose adorns
Shedding rises an exquisite perfume

(Shattuck, p. 151)

Like Rimbaud's seer, this poet, who enters new worlds before the others of his era, is not only isolated from them, but discovers the personal price of his role. In spite of his profession of faith in the future, his deepest regret is over the incessant passage of time. For if we are rushing into the future, everything that we are, that we have, or that we might gain is condemned to be nothing *"qu'une flamme rapide."* And the poet, testifying to that part of himself which enters the unknown first, is all too aware of his loss of another part of himself—his past—and of his eventual loss of even this newly gained moment. Contrary to his ideal image of himself, Apollinaire reveals that he cannot be the *"grand oublieur."*

These are conditions that most avant-garde writers accept, but Apollinaire could not reconcile himself to them. Whereas the futurists and the dadaists, for example, met the challenge by asserting that they welcomed their eventual irrelevancy and negation, Apollinaire could not let go of his own past, or the past of others he loved. And whereas other avant-garde writers would, by the vehemence of their announced hatred for the past and their sense of the inadequacy of the present, thrust themselves forward into an unknown which would not yet reveal what their future world or selves would be like, Apollinaire could deny neither the world in which he lived nor his own present identity. For a lyric sensibility such as Apollinaire's to be satisfied, it must achieve an actual identification with immediate experience, and not merely be content with its promise. Unlike Rimbaud, Apollinaire could not declare that "real life is absent." Nor would "real life" be found in the future. For the future is never experienced as such. It doesn't exist; it is only a dream, a projection of the present's desires. And for Apollinaire, that dream, in spite of his occasional attempts to image it, is blank. Only the past and the present are known, and thus alive to feeling.

> Temps passés Trépassés Les dieux qui me formâtes
> Je ne vis que passant ainsi que vous passâtes
> Et détournant mes yeux de ce vide avenir
> En moi-même je vois tout le passé grandir
>
> Rien n'est mort que ce qui n'existe pas encore
> Près du passé luisant demain est incolore
> Il est informe aussi près de ce qui parfait
> Présente tout ensemble et l'effort et l'effet
>
> ("Cortège," Adéma and Décaudin, p. 76)

> *The past the Dead The gods who created me*
> *I live to move on as you yourselves have lived*
> *And turning from the future's emptiness*
> *I watch within me all the past arise*

Nothing is dead but what has never been
The colored past outshines tomorrow's grey
Besides whose formlessness it can display
The sequence of the effort and effect

(Shattuck, p. 79)

In keeping with this tenacious affection for the present, some of Apollinaire's most beautiful poems evoke the beauty of this *passé luisant*. Even recognizing the pressure to move on with time, the poet will sing of what is being lost. "Passons passons puisque tout passe / Je me retournerai souvent / Les souvenirs sont cors de chasse / Dont meurt le bruit parmi le vent" ("Cors de Chasse"; Adema and Décaudin, p. 148). "On on since all must pass / I'll frequently turn back / Memories are hunting horns / Whose sound dies out along the wind" (Shattuck, p. 131). In "Le Pont Mirabeau" the poet stands caught in the flow of time, watching his love and the river drift away from him. Here, time is not *"une flamme rapide";* rather, it is painfully slow. And yet, if he is impotent before this passing while the feeling of loss lies heavily upon him, ironically, his only hope is with the future—"La joie venait toujours après la peine." Thus, the haunting refrain invokes the full awareness of time. It locates the poet standing still in the present moment, watching the past while calling up the future.

L'amour s'en va comme cette eau courante
L'amour s'en va
Comme la vie est lente
Et comme l'Espérance est violente

Vienne la nuit sonne l'heure
Les jours s'en vont je demeure

Passent les jours et passent les semaines
Ni temps passé
Ni les amours reviennent
Sous le pont Mirabeau coule la Seine

Vienne la nuit sonne l'heure
Les jours s'en vont je demeure

(Adéma and Décaudin, p. 45)

Love leaves us like this flowing stream
Love flows away

How slow life is and mild
And oh how hope can suddenly run wild

May night come and the hours ring
The days go by and I remain

May the long days and the weeks go by
Neither the past
Nor former loves return
Under the pont Mirabeau flows the Seine

May night come and the hours ring
The days go by and I remain

(Shattuck, p. 65)

Thus, throughout Apollinaire's poetry, he views the past with both nostalgia and a recognition that it must depart, and the future with both resignation and hope. Both are exhilarating and frightening, for each threatens to deny that part of himself which feels its allegiance to the opposing sense of time.

As a consequence of this dual vision, Apollinaire was ever anxious to achieve some balance between past and future within himself and his era. With the exception of his sole aggressive manifesto, "L'Anti-tradition futuriste," which he wrote only one week after harsh reviews of his *Alcools,* Apollinaire's works attempt to reconcile the spirit of innovation and liberty with that of tradition. Nowhere is this more apparent than in his oft-quoted poetic testament "La Jolie Rousse."

Je sais d'ancien et de nouveau autant qu'un homme seul
    pourrait des deux savoir
Et sans m'inquiéter aujourd'hui de cette guerre
Entre nous et pour nous mes amis
Je juge cette longue querelle de la tradition et de l'invention
    De l'Ordre et de l'Aventure

Vous dont la bouche est faite à l'image de celle de Dieu
Bouche qui est l'ordre même
Soyez indulgents quand vous nous comparez
A ceux qui furent la perfection de l'ordre
Nous qui quêtons partout l'aventure

Nous ne sommes pas vos ennemis
Nous voulons vous donner de vastes et d'étranges domaines
Où le mystère en fleurs s'offre à qui veut le cueillir

Il y a là des feux nouveaux des couleurs jamais vues
Mille phantasmes impondérables
Auxquels il faut donner de la réalité
Nous voulons explorer la bonté contrée énorme où tout se tait
Il y a aussi le temps qu'on peut chasser ou faire revenir
Pitié pour nous qui combattons toujours aux frontières
De l'illimité et de l'avenir

> (Adéma and Décaudin, pp. 313–314)

I know of the old and of the new as much as one man alone
   can know of them
And without being uneasy today about this war
Between us and for us my friends
I pronounce judgement on this long quarrel of tradition and
   innovation
      Of Order and Adventure

You whose mouths are made in the image of God's
Mouths which are order itself
Be indulgent when you compare us
To those who have been the perfection of order
We who seek everywhere for adventure

We are not your enemies
We wish to offer you vast and strange domains
Where flowering mystery offers itself to whoever wishes to
   pick it
There are new fires there and colors never yet seen
A thousand imponderable phantasms
To which reality must be given
We would explore goodness a vast country where everything
   is silent
There is also time which one can banish or call back
Pity us who fight always in the front lines
Of the limitless and of the future

> (Shattuck, p. 195)

Ever mindful of the authority of the past and anxiously poised before the blankness of this "contrée énorme où tout se tait," Apollinaire sought in the present moment a resolution of the old and the new, order and liberty, and his past and potential selves. Unlike most avant-garde writers, Apollinaire did not think it necessary to destroy the past in order to champion the future. Throughout his writings, both public and private, he reiterated his claim that the new adventurers were not the enemies of the traditionalists. All that Apollinaire sought was the chance to increase the opportunities for artistic expression in his time. In 1918, writing to André Billy, for example, Apollinaire stated: "I have never destroyed, on the contrary I have tried to construct. . . . Neither have I destroyed anything in the arts while trying to support the new schools, and never to the detriment of past schools. . . . God is my witness that I have only wanted to add new domains to the arts and letters in general, without disowning the merits of the true masterpieces of the past or the present."[7]

If, in this respect, Apollinaire was conservative by avant-garde standards, he did contribute important innovative works to the avant-garde tradition: in drama, *Les Mamelles de Tirésias* (1917); in prose, *Le Poète Assassiné* (1916) and "Oneirocriticism" (1908); and in poetry, many of his *Calligrammes*. These works were to have a significant effect on dada and surrealism, and to open up new directions for subsequent literary production. For Apollinaire, their innovations represent an effort to achieve through formal experimentation a vision of the fullness of the present moment which would resolve the thematic conflict of past and future time. These are not visionary works; there is no prophesy in them. And in the poems, it is not a Rimbauldian hallucinatory imaging of ideal worlds that we encounter, but rather surprising, occasionally obscure, efforts to describe the world the poet inhabited. As Georges Schmits has pointed out, most of Apollinaire's images are based in rather ordinary scenes of daily life.[8] It is his stylistic innovations—his disjunctive verse, his collage and "conversation" poems, his abandonment of punctuation, and his *idéogrammes lyriques*—which serve primarily to disorient our perception of the customary world so that it may be experienced in a new manner.

Apollinaire found a model for these innovations in the contemporary visual arts. A professional art critic and friend of many painters, Apollinaire was especially interested in new formal techniques to represent the full complexity of time caught in an image of simultaneity. He was particularly drawn to the innovative work of futurism, cubism, and the orphism of Robert Delaunay. Although Apollinaire generally disassociated himself from the futurists and always tempered their inflated claims, he was one of the first critics in France to recognize their importance. And while he was more drawn to the formal accomplishments and analytic spirit of cubism and discerned futurism's indebtedness to the cubists (which they were always quick to deny), he was sympathetic to the futurist effort to depict the sense of increased motion in the modern environment. He was especially intrigued by Marinetti's concepts of "words in liberty" and the "imagination without strings" which broke words free from normal syntactical relationships and from traditional logic. These techniques (which Apollinaire claimed were only extensions of the work of Rimbaud and Mallarmé) opened up new means of poetic description and liberated the perceiving mind from an excessive concern with division and particularity in the world it experienced. Ideally, these techniques would resolve a feeling of personal and social fragmentation by promoting a sense of the simultaneity of the disparate sensations of modern experience. Apollinaire faulted the futurists, however, for being too tied to the particular subjects they described, and for not achieving the state of simultaneity, since they focused instead on successive, subjective perceptions.[9]

Apollinaire was personally closer to Picasso and the cubists, and saw in their work none of the limitations that he found in futurist creations. The cubist focus on geometric and abstract form distanced the painter and the viewer from both the subject and the emotions it evoked. According to Apollinaire, the cubists thus painted not what people saw, but what they imagined, and in doing so, they opened up an entirely new dimension for art—the fourth dimension. This dimension in cubist paintings suggested the unity of space and time. "It represents the immensity of space eternalized in all directions at a given moment. It is space itself, or the dimension of infinity."[10] Like Rimbaud and many other avant-garde visionary writers, Apollinaire sought to capture the eternal and the infinite in the momentary and the particular, as he believed the cubists to have done.

Temperamentally, Apollinaire was drawn even more to Delaunay than to the cubists. Delaunay's work combined the formal abstraction of cubism with a sensual, vibrant interaction of color. His works were both sensual and intellectual and seemed to promise the highest experience of simultaneity, successfully capturing in a single work and moment of perception the unity of time and space toward which Apollinaire strove. Writing about Delaunay's works and writings (which he quoted at length), Apollinaire stated: "Simultaneity is life itself, and in whatever order the elements of a work succeed each other, it leads to an ineluctable end, which is death; but the creator knows only eternity. Artists have for too long strained toward death by assembling the sterile elements of art, and it is time they attained fecundity, trinity, simultaneity."[11]

Apollinaire attempted to present in his writing the same experience of simultaneity which these visual artists introduced to painting.

His innovations sought both to revitalize the techniques of description and to locate the writer and reader more intensely in "life itself." His earliest departure from poetic convention, the removal of all punctuation from his poems, seems like a minor gesture of revolt against tradition, but it does serve to create the impression of an uninterrupted flow of images as well as to confuse, but perhaps make more suggestive, the relationships among semantic elements of the poem. In his subsequent innovative works—his *idéogrammes lyriques,* as he first called the *Calligrammes*—Apollinaire depicted the literal subject graphically through the arrangement of the words on the page. These poems represent Apollinaire's efforts to create a visual poetry. (It is significant that when planning a small album of these works in 1914, he intended to give them the subtitle, *Et moi aussi je suis peintre.*) But they may also be seen as one effort to create a type of literature that would overcome the handicap that separates music and writing from the visual arts, that is, the necessity of experiencing the parts of a literary work successively. "In literature and in music, everything is successive, and one cannot return to certain words or sounds at random."[12] He sought in these works to present everything at once, freed from the sensation of passing time.

Apollinaire's other innovations also reveal his efforts to free literature—and the writer—from the trap of temporal succession. His "conversation poems," such as "Lundi rue Christine," are composed of random sentences or phrases overheard by the poet and presented as an integral poem. They represent the aural equivalent of cubism, the presentation of a three-dimensional perspective—here, one merely of sounds—in a two-dimensional format, the page of the printed poem. They also lack a narrative, represent an experience of simultaneity, and may be entered and read randomly. Poems such as "Liens," "Les Fenêtres," "Arbre," or "Visée" are poems in which all or part of the work is composed of similarly random, or apparently random, images. They are collages in which the organizing principle, be it the narrative voice, temperament, or situation, is obscure. In "Visée," for example, the eleven individual lines have no direct relationship to each other, but are implicitly unified by the lyric sensibility of a soldier at war. Furthermore, each generative element is then transformed by the poet into an image of mystery and beauty in its own right.

> Chevaux couleur cerise limite des Zélandes
> Des mitrailleuses d'or coassent les légendes
> Je t'aime liberté qui veilles dans les hypogées

> Harpe aux cordes d'argent ô pluie ô ma musique
> L'invisible ennemi plaie d'argent au soleil
>
> . . . .
>
> (Adéma and Décaudin, p. 224)

> *Cherry colored horses boundary of the Zealanders*
> *Machine guns made of gold croak legends*
> *I love you liberty who hide in basement rooms*
> *Silver stringed harp O rain O my music*
> *The invisible enemy a silver wound in the sun*
>
> . . . .
>
> (Shattuck, p. 172)

In this poem, the informing presence of Apollinaire, the lover of war, is extremely strong. He finds beauty or surprising revelation in widely disparate objects and elements of experience—machine guns, the enemy, rain, the incoming artillery shell, even, at the end, a dead child. He alters them and unites them, suggesting at once both a coherent personal vision and an extensive sensibility which embraces a reality that normally would appear chaotic.

In other poems, however, especially "Arbre," the unifying principle is not at all clear. Neither the subject matter, the person or object addressed, the identity of the poetic voice, the grammatical coherence, the mood of the poet, the relationship among the verb tenses used, nor the structural principle of the various stanzas can be clearly determined. The individual parts of the poem, sometimes only images or a few lines, suggest a sustained mood or thematic concern, only to come rapidly into conflict with other elements or groupings that deny the proposed interpretation.[13] If "Arbre" is an expression of a state of simultaneity that has achieved the "fourth dimension," that achievement is so private as to be impenetrable. Apollinaire might have achieved here such a totally lyrical moment that the unity of time, space, and the poet was the expression of a solipsistic projection, but in doing this, he undermined his public role of the seer. Apollinaire was probably very conscious of such a danger. Throughout his career, he continued to write traditional lyrics, and rarely are his innovative works as difficult as "Arbre."

As Apollinaire sought to achieve a balance between poetic tradition and poetic innovation, he was also torn between an avant-garde faith in the future and a desire to hold onto the world he already had experienced. He had both to assert his identification with the processes of discovery and the unfolding of the new in which the creative poet participated and to reject the basic avant-garde belief in the inevitability of significant change in human life, specifically, the ideal of progress. Thus, he accepted the role of the poet as prophet, but finally, in place of a committed avant-gardism, Apollinaire exhibited an extreme—if essentially affirmative—modernism. Thus, in "The New Spirit and the Poets," he dismisses the compulsive faith in endless progress. He shudders before "an eternal becoming, a sort of messianism as appalling as the fable of Tantalus, Sisyphus and the Danaidae," and asserts that "what is new exists without being progress. Everything is in the effect of surprise. The new spirit depends equally on surprise, on what is most vital and new in it. *Surprise is the greatest source of what is new*" (p. 233). Surprise represents the revitalization of perception and spirit—the sudden expansion of vision caused by the shock of disorientation, so that what is new is not only a different world created by changing times, but a different perspective on what already exists or what has already passed.

Nevertheless, this concept of surprise does not of itself fully resolve the problems associated with passing time. For just as Apollinaire knew that the present moment would become part of the past, each sensation of shock would grow old. His only recourse was to turn toward the next moment of surprise. Apollinaire's focus was on the present, then, but it was on the leading edge of that present. He identified with the futurist aspects of poetry and experience because he needed to encounter the future at the very moment it became the present. Nevertheless, even within this feverish passing of time, Apollinaire believed that a basic stability existed which united the separate moments of perception and creation, even if it could not be continuously experienced itself. This stability—his ideal—differed from a traditional conception of the Ideal invoked by art, an Ideal of changeless truth or value that art could represent through allegory. In 1914, Apollinaire wrote that truth and eternity could only be found in the successive moments of creation and surprise.

> My ideal of art: my feelings and my imagination, not at all an ideal, but the always new truth. . . .
> No ideal: but everything that exists: myself, my feelings, my imagination; others, their feelings, their imagination; things, their appearance, their properties; the surprises, the beings they engender and that they modify.
> No ideal: surprise, invention, that is, good sense, always surprising, always unexpected, that is, truth. . . .
> Surprise: truth, eternity.[14]

Elsewhere, Apollinaire went even further and suggested that art, even though it has constantly to change with time, is an expression of something changeless in humankind, and that consequently its essence—the sublime—is also constant. Just as there is no real progress in time and human life, but only ceaseless change, the sublime of one period differs from that of another only in the way in which it manifests itself.

> [The sublime] never changes, since it constitutes the very essence of man's art, and in order for there to be a different kind of sublime, it would be necessary for man to be entirely different than he is. The modern sublime is identical to the sublime of past centuries and the sublime for future artists will be no different from what it is today.

Thus, just beyond the sensation of the incessant unfolding of life in time is an awareness of a fourth dimension—the eternal in art— which unites our past, present, and future. And just as individuals can awaken to the eternal in themselves, even if they are ruled by time, the artist must seek to sing both the eternal and the ever-new forms of experience. But for Apollinaire, however much he might desire a vision of the absolute, the poetic focus must always be on the primary sensations of temporal movement. For his essays suggest that truth is not abstract; it resides in the immediate and changing world. It can be known only in its constantly new aspects, just as the human spirit, he believed, is alive only when it is discovering, or creating, itself anew.

> Poets will be charged finally with giving by means of lyric teleologies and arch-lyric alchemies a constantly purer meaning to the idea of divinity, which is so alive within us, which is perpetual renewal of ourselves, that eternal creation, that endless rebirth by which we live.
>
> ("The New Spirit and the Poets," p. 235)

Apollinaire should be called the poet of time. His entire poetic venture is a record of his successful effort to participate in the dynamism of self-conscious modernity. Stimulated by a sense of the adventure of the new age, looking forward to further developments in his time, he expressed an avant-garde faith in the future and projected an image of the poet as explorer and prophet who would change the lives and dreams of humankind. But Apollinaire's sensitivity, sentimentality, and personal honesty prevented him from avoiding the complexities of such a vanguard attitude, complexities which

numerous avant-garde writers and artists would ignore. For he realized that an avant-garde invocation of the future resulted in a heightened sensation of the passing of time, of each moment passing in
succession into the past. And, for Apollinaire, succession necessarily
leads to death. The nether side of avant-garde futurism is nihilism,
the destruction of everything past and present. In essence, Apollinaire rejected the avant-garde gambit of agonism, the simultaneous
yearning for the future and undermining of the present. If the agonist posture is to embrace death and creation in the self-same moment, Apollinaire sought a mode of experiencing the present, one
that contained *and* overcame the dynamics of time. In doing so, his
work both complements the avant-garde and makes explicit what is
latent in other avant-garde writers' works. Just as Rimbaud sought
to use chaos to break through to a realm of absolute order, and the
futurists claimed that their stimulation of motion and "lines of
force" would uncover what Boccioni called a "physical transcendentalism," Apollinaire sought in the experience of simultaneity a momentary lyric vision that united the poet with his environment and
that encompassed his past, present, and future states of being.
Similarly, he sought in the sensation of surprise the always-new face
of eternal truth, in the process of continuous self-creation the divinity
of humanity, and in contemporary beauty the unchanging sublime.
Like the avant-garde, Apollinaire offers a poetry of prophesy, but
what he is come to announce is an ideal only manifest in the present
moment.

II

Sharing with Apollinaire both an historical moment and a set of aesthetic dilemmas, the Italian futurists also responded positively to
technological modern society and its opportunities for literary and
artistic experimentation. But the essential values and artworks of the
Italians were radically different from Apollinaire's poems. The futurists were far more successful in their projection of a consistent social
vision and more comfortable in their social identities than was Apollinaire, but by most standards they were less interesting and accomplished as artists than he was. For if what we find engaging in Apollinaire's poetry is the fruitful, if troubled, interaction between the
heroic self-projection of the poet of modernity and the vulnerable
poet of intimate joy and sorrow, the futurists offer, on the other hand,
a bombastic, but extremely impersonal and finally lifeless art. The
futurists' manifestoes and artworks do unceasingly assert the genius

of their creators, and the writers' and artists' public displays were dramatic exercises in self-promotion: indeed, the futurist manifestoes constantly praise the heroism of the individual futurists. But these men—Marinetti, Balla, Boccioni, Russolo, Severini—seem to have identified so completely with their role as the "new men" of their culture that they remain merely that—roles, constructed personae. There is little evidence in their writings of any complex or problematic personal response to their venture and their times. In adopting these roles they espoused the avant-garde belief in the poet as activist, prophet, and worker much more unambiguously than most other avant-garde movements, and certainly more than Apollinaire.

This energy and simplicity of vision accounts for much of the marked influence the futurists had on other literary and artistic movements throughout Europe during the second and third decades of this century. The futurists first announced the creation of their movement in 1909 with the publication of Marinetti's "The Founding and Manifesto of Futurism" in the Paris newspaper *Le Figaro*. This was followed, during the next four years, by a constant stream of manifestoes covering all forms of artistic production: painting (1910, by Boccioni, Carra, Russolo, Balla, Severini); music (1910, by Pratella); photography (1911, by Bragaglia); sculpture (1912, by Boccioni); cinema (1912, by Corra); music (1913, by Russolo); and by Marinetti's manifestoes "Destruction of Syntax—Imagination without Strings—Words in Freedom" (1913) and "The Variety Theatre" (1913), to name just a few. In addition, manifestoes on all forms of social behavior—lust, feminism, clothing, marriage, the family, war ("the world's only hygiene"), the "reign of the machine" and the "morality of speed"—projected the extension of the futurist spirit throughout modern society.

In this manner, even though they were roughly concurrent with the high point of German expressionism (1910–1922), the Italian futurists became the first fully formed avant-garde movement that sought to effect through their art the simultaneous transformation of art, social behavior, and politics. They were the first movement, for example, to participate in political action, such as supporting the Italian Irredentist movement which wished to wrest back from Austria regions with large populations of Italian-speaking residents. Similarly, their unrelenting chauvinism boisterously championed the Italian campaign in Tripoli, their nation's entrance into World War I, and eventually the rise to power of the fascists under Mussolini, "a marvelous Futurist temperament."[15] Each of these political sorties was an effort to glorify the strength, heroism, and aggressiveness of a modern Italy which they urged to free itself from both its ties to past history and its present state of weakness in Europe.

Even though they were intensely nationalistic, however, the Italian futurists also formed the first truly international avant-garde movement. Through Marinetti's and the other futurists' active self-promotion in Italy, France, England, Belgium, Germany, and Russia, futurism not only spread its own particular social and aesthetic vision, but also established a pattern of personal and artistic behavior that would shape many contemporary and subsequent avant-garde and modernist movements, most notably, Russian futurism, dada, surrealism, and vorticism. Their aggressive self-flaunting, declamatory manifestoes, public proclamations, attacks on their audiences, occasionally absurd dress and behavior, nonsensical or outrageous poetry, theater, and music, all became models for twentieth-century avant-garde activities.

Futurism thus holds an attraction for us far beyond its actual achievements because it so clearly embodied the fundamental desires of avant-garde activism. Its manifestoes constantly declaim ideals that appear again and again in other avant-garde movements. Most basic to the shared vision among the groups is, perhaps, the glorification of the dynamism of both the modern culture and the heroic and activist artist. These themes are reiterated in countless futurist writings, but nowhere so succinctly as in the founding manifesto.

1. We intend to sing the love of danger, the habit of energy and fearlessness.
2. Courage, audacity and revolt will be essential elements of our poetry.
3. Up to now literature has exalted a pensive immobility, ecstasy, and sleep. We intend to exalt aggressive action, a feverish insomnia, the racer's stride, the mortal leap, the punch and the slap.
4. We affirm that the world's magnificence has been enriched by a new beauty: the beauty of speed. A racing car whose hood is adorned with great pipes, like serpents of explosive breath—a roaring car that seems to ride on grapeshot is more beautiful than the *Victory of Samothrace*.
. . . .
7. Except in struggle, there is no more beauty. No work without an aggressive character can be a masterpiece. Poetry must be conceived as a violent attack on unknown forces, to reduce and prostrate them before man.
8. We stand on the last promontory of the centuries! . . . Why should we look back, when what we want is to break down the mysterious doors of the Impossible? Time and Space died yesterday. We al-

ready live in the absolute, because we have created eternal, omnipresent speed.
9. We will glorify war—the world's only hygiene—militarism, patriotism, the destructive gesture of freedom-bringers, beautiful ideas
   worth dying for, and scorn for women.
10. We will destroy the museums, libraries, academies of every kind,
    will fight moralism, feminism, every oportunistic or utilitarian
    cowardice.[16]

This glorification of speed, audacity, and violence was part bombast, part accurate description of the futurist sensibility. Worshippers
of force "in whatever form it occurs," they defined their activities in
extreme forms. Their targets, and the victims of this tirade, were individuals or institutions which represented the culture's ties to the
past: the *passeists,* the church, the monarchy, the bourgeoisie, the
schools and art establishment, passivists, and women. Their rejection
of these "reactionary" enemies was, in fact, more vicious than that of
any other avant-garde movement, with the possible exception of
dada. In effect, for the futurists, the world was simply divided into
two camps: the futurists and the *passeists*—the heroic individuals who
worked to ensure the progressive dynamism of the age, and those
who retarded change. There was no in-between state, no ambiguous
position.
     Most frequently, their opponents were other writers, artists, and
critics, as well as the bourgeois public enamoured of traditional art;
and the terrain of futurist combat was generally the fields of art.
Nonetheless, the aggressive aesthetic posturing was extremely important to the futurists, and it did have significant implications for their
political vision. The particular delight the futurists found in insulting their audiences and their ability, if not need, to provoke fights in
their theaters proved to them the power of their ideas. These fights
seemed to confirm their belief that their art and their behavior were
socially effective agents of change. And furthermore, the fights validated to them their professed role as activist poets, even if the wars
they fought were at first comedies of rotten fruit and insults.

the showers of potatoes, oranges and bunches of fennel became in-
fernal. Suddenly he [Marinetti] cried, "Damn!" slapping his hand to
his eye. We ran to help him; many in the public who had seen the
missiles land protested indignantly against the bestial cowardice, and,
with what we shouted from the stage, the place became a ghetto market where things are said that cannot be repeated, much less written.

I see Russolo again with saliva running from his mouth; I hear Carra
roaring, "Throw an idea instead of potatoes, idiots!"[17]

In retrospect, there is something charming about these battles.
Like other avant-garde confrontations of artists and audiences—those,
for example, of Russian futurism, dada, surrealism, Happenings and
street theater of the sixties—most of the conflicts were fought within
and about the separate space of art, even if they represented an effort
to change the nature of that space, to merge art and life. Insults were
traded, a few teeth were lost, but the bombast now seems all out of
proportion to the stakes contested. The futurists did take their battles out onto the streets (as did subsequent avant-garde groups), both
for literary and political campaigns, but even though they occasionally encountered potential danger, mostly they merely established a
pattern for avant-garde street theater. In fact, while the futurists presented themselves as major challengers to their society, they were not
really threatened by their "enemies," the *passeists*. Their antagonism
was, in effect, mostly theatrical, because with the exception of their
efforts to get Italy into a series of wars, most of their non-artistic campaigns did not espouse a significant change in the power relationships
of their society.

Although the futurists at first attacked two institutions of substantial power, the monarchy and the church, and though they initially
scorned the participation of industrialists, bankers, and fascists in
their revitalization of society, they came to accept the permanence of
the church and even to exalt the real powers that emerged by the
end of the world war: the military, the industrialists, the bankers,
and the businessmen. As early as 1913, in "The Futurist Manifesto
of Lust," these men were depicted as modern conquerors who embodied a life force capable of manipulating great masses of people
and sweeping the entire society to higher states of energy. Marinetti
also expressed great faith in the working class and in the petit bourgeoisie, but revealed his fascist mentality when he argued that these
men would have to be led by their natural superiors within each
group, as well as by other men of vision and the artists of their society—whom he called, amazingly, the "proletariat of gifted men."[18]
Even before the fascist victory in 1922, then, the futurists, far from
feeling alienated from their society, glorified the *de facto* powers in
it. After 1922, futurism tended to become the new academy and continued to sing the praises of these institutional powers.

In essence, futurist art did not attempt to change society or alter
consciousness, but only to increase and accent what already existed.

To the futurists, the future was neither a threatening blankness nor an alluring unknown. Rather, it was already emergent in the new environment.

> We will sing of great crowds excited by work, by pleasure, and by riot; . . . we will sing of the vibrant nightly fervour of arsenals and shipyards blazing with violent electric moons; greedy railway stations that devour smoke-plumed serpents; factories hung on clouds by crooked lines of their smoke; bridges that stride the rivers like giant gymnasts . . . adventurous steamers that sniff the horizon . . .[19]

This vision of the art of the future is constructed entirely of images of the present. In fact, in spite of the movement's name this is, in their own terms, an expression of extreme "modernolatry." Contrary to most avant-garde programs, that of the futurists does not appeal to a radically transformed future. If the futurists claimed to be in advance of their culture, it was merely by the degree of their passionate participation in the new—the modern—forces that structured their environment. The future would be measured by quantifiable development. It promised more of the same, only speeded up and intensified.

Nonetheless, in their effort to disrupt the reigning aesthetic tradition, to introduce new subject matter, to find a style appropriate to the age, and to accent the social role of their art, the futurists were avant-garde, even if their eyes were focused on the present. At the heart of their venture is an attempt to establish a new epic vision, one which would portray the inherent dynamism of their culture and its effect on the individual. Many of their works, however, are not particularly innovative, especially Marinetti's allegorical epics, *Le Momie sanglante, Roi Bombance, The Untamables,* or *Mafarka le Futuriste,* and, in fact, actual images of the new technological culture do not dominate their paintings. Instead, the primary focus is on the individual, on the emotional effects of living in modern culture, on the person's "states of mind." Many of the futurist theater pieces, for example Mario Carli's *Stati d'Animo (States of Mind),* Remo Chiti's *Parole (Words),* or Mario Dessy's *La Pazzia (Madness),*[20] as well as futurist paintings—Boccioni's "The Forces of a Street," "The City Rising," and his "States of Mind" series of 1911; Carra's "Theatre Exit"; and Balla's "Dynamic Depths"—attempt to express emotional and energized states of being among individuals or crowds within closed situations. Rather than an epic dimension, we are offered a new lyricism. For the futurists, such an art pointed to the heightened dynamism of the modern world. "I now declare that lyricism is the

exquisite faculty of intoxicating oneself with life, of filling life with
the inebriation of oneself. . . . I proposed . . . a swift, brutal, and
immediate lyricism, a lyricism that must seem anti-poetic to all our
predecessors, a telegraphic lyricism with no taste of the book about it
but, rather, as much as possible of the taste of life."[21] Futurist poetry,
theater, music, and art, as well as the manifestoes, sought to communicate, and provoke, this intoxication as directly as possible.

The principal innovations of futurist writing—"words in freedom"
and the "imagination without strings," or "wireless imagination"—
are specific attempts to heighten the emotionalism communicated, increase the speed of communication, and force the reader or listener
to recognize the complexity and disparity of environmental forces
acting on him or her at any single moment. Imagination without
strings, for instance, is a version of the radical juxtaposition and collage of disparate images prevalent in many avant-garde and modernist works. For Marinetti, the freedom offered by the new form expressed a love of the union of distant and seemingly hostile things in
the environment and had the effect upon the reader of constant surprise. "Poetry should be an uninterrupted sequence of new images,
or it is mere anemia and green-sickness. The broader their affinities,
the longer will images keep their power to amaze."[22] Similarly, "words
in freedom" have a plosive energy and directness of communication.
Here, there is no attempt to transform language in order to alter consciousness, as is common in avant-garde experimentation; rather, the
words are freed from normal syntax merely to act as supposedly more
efficient, that is, rapid and exciting communicators. Describing a hy-
pothetical account of some intense experience, Marinetti declared
that the speaker "will begin by brutally destroying the syntax . . .
vibration of his being. . . . Between poet and audience . . . essential *free* words."[23] The ideal of this art is a union between speaker
and audience based on immediate and intuitive comprehension. It is
an expression of the futurist perception of the essential union of individuals within environmental fields of force and passion. Their art
sought to portray and champion the dynamics of this interaction.
The more interesting visual works of Balla and Boccioni, as well as
the "words in freedom" poems of Marinetti, *Zang-tumb-tumb,* sought
to portray the "lines of Force" between an individual or object and
that environment which was conceived to be a web of interpene-
trating forces, each acting upon the other. In Boccioni's manifesto
"Absolute Motion + Relative Motion = Dynamism," he states that
futurists are interested in portraying "primordial psychology"—the
"psychology" of animate and inanimate objects, the forces with which

they are endowed. He distinguishes between two types of energy within an object and its environment. Relative energy is associated with the object's—or person's—movement in space. This is the most obvious energy, and, in the futurists' efforts to portray it, as in Balla's "Dynamism of a Dog on a Leash," the most comical. Absolute Motion, on the other hand, is the particular energy latent in any object or being, its primordial power over other objects. The sum of the interaction of the Absolute Motion of various objects acting on each other creates the dynamism of an environment.[24] What emerges from these ideas is a theory of the nature of a person's ties to the world. The individual, for example, is constantly acted upon by forces originating in the most powerful elements of his or her environment. In turn, that individual exerts a force upon others and on the environment in general.

To a certain extent this union of the individual with the environment is a solution to the avant-garde desire to achieve personal harmony with the external quotidian world. It also suggests, as Joshua C. Taylor has pointed out, a transcendental ideal of union with an abstract and absolute reality that frees one from the apparent chaos of daily life. "In spite of their constant threat of chaos, at the core of each of their compositions, at the climax of every action, they sought an intuitive intimation of an ideal order." The futurists themselves spoke of a "Marvellous spiritual world" which they were forced to depict by references to the physical world so that their audience would understand, and stated that "all objects, in accordance with what the painter Boccioni happily terms *physical transcendentalism,* tend to the infinite by their *force-lines,* the continuity of which is measured by our intuition."[25]

We see here the union of two apparently opposed dynamic states of being which are frequently present in avant-garde thought. These states involve, on the one hand, a will towards an abstract dimension, a search for a transcendent sublime, and, on the other, a primitivism and anti-intellectualism. The futurists themselves noted the opposition. "Our art will probably be accused of tormented and decadent cerebralism. But we shall merely answer that we are, on the contrary, the primitives of a new sensitiveness, multiplied hundredfold, and that our art is intoxicated with spontaneity and power."[26] The constant reference to states of intoxication accents the love of force that is their central concern. They are right in calling themselves new primitives, for their ideal is the complete merger of the individual with his or her surroundings, the subsuming of oneself into the states of energy and power that encompass the individual. But this willful abandonment of self to powers greater than oneself was not merely an abstract ideal, another expression of avant-garde or modernist cerebralism. The immediate ideal they proposed was not otherwordly; it certainly was not sublime. Nor did it envision entry into a realm qualitatively different from what already existed. Rather, it included the very real manifestations of force within the present society that the futurists worshipped and with which they urged the individual's active and conscious identification. The power of the corporations, the banks, the army, and eventually the Fascist Party became for these activists the forces to which one should give oneself up. Their ideal was achieved in that union of primitivism and technology, of passion and order characteristic of fascism.

By these means the futurist program was temporarily able to resolve the basic tensions of this early period of the avant-garde. Unlike Apollinaire, for example, they could envision a satisfying union of the individual with the social structure and with progressive history. Similarly, by worshipping the modern and anticipating a future not radically different from it, they were able to be in advance and yet not fundamentally in conflict with the social and political powers generating historical change. Their particular solution certainly seems extreme, but it is latent in all avant-gardes. For at the heart of the avant-garde is a desire to transcend alienation, to rediscover a union with society through identification of the forces which will change culture.

But as the other avant-garde movements rapidly discovered, and the futurists eventually saw, a successful alliance between political activists and aesthetic visionaries is bound to be elusive. German dada, for example, believed its program analogous to the communist movement, but found little support for its members' activities among the communists as long as they were still dadaists. Even more dramatically, the Russian futurists, especially Mayakovsky, and later the surrealists, proved themselves unable peacefully to resolve the conflict between the demand that they unquestioningly echo, or merely illustrate, the Communist Party line in their literary and art works, and their desire to remain true to the disruptive and utopic aspects of the avant-garde aesthetic and social vision. A third possibility, that they restrict their work to purely aesthetic activities, in short, give up the radical dimension of the avant-garde impulse, was neither possible in post-revolutionary Russia, nor acceptable to these activist artists.

Ironically, it was just this third option that the Italian futurists adopted, and which helped cause their decline. Already severely weakened by the loss of several important members during the world war which they had so joyously joined, the futurists discovered after the war the substantial difference between the excitement of being on the outside of power and thus able to attack the establishment in the name of some absolute ideal, and the compromising aspects of being allied with the reigning political party which concerned itself with pragmatic reality. Though they never admitted it—if they recognized it—they made clear that the avant-garde thrives on the spirit of negation, as well as on the vision of utopia. And neither can be sustained in the world of day-to-day governance. Having followed Mussolini's lead grudgingly, Marinetti and the futurists made their peace with the monarchy and the church; but they withdrew from the Fascist Party and political involvement completely by 1924, declaring that the futurists were "mystics of action," who desired to "intervene in political contests only in hours of great danger for the Nation."[27] Marinetti contented himself with attempting to sustain the futurist movement by making it a quasi-official academy—the *passeists* of the fascist society. But little of the original spirit remained, and none of the works produced after the early twenties comes close to the brute verve of the early futurist productions. The bombast remains only in a few invocations of national glory—like the pitiable salute to Mussolini on his fortieth birthday penned by Marinetti.[28]

Chapter
IV
Negation, Scandal, and Purification: The Dada Movements

Marcel Janco, one of the founding members of the dada movement in Zurich, distinguished between two impulses, or what he called "two speeds," of dada. The first, the negative speed, he described as a "spiritual violence," a "purifying and scandalous force to consume the past and open up a new creative route." This new route announced the second, or positive, speed of dada which, through "pure, childlike, direct [and] primal" actions, allowed a return to the "Promised Land of creativity." By these two speeds, Janco stated, dada was to establish "a new meaning for art in society."[1]

These two impulses were especially evident in dada, but they are also appropriate descriptions of—even prescriptions for—most avant-garde art movements, because for each avant-garde writer and movement, an explicit negation of traditional social and aesthetic practices and values is a necessary prelude to creation. For an activist art, situating itself in time, there is no advance into the future without a denial both of the past and of the present moment's ties with that past. All avant-garde art, whatever its "positive speed," thus displays a fundamental negativism, if not a nihilism, that declares itself a liberating force of creation.

This force is, as Janco noted, both scandalous and purifying. Scandal marks the social dimension of the avant-garde artwork, since by the outraged response of the audience, the artist may recognize his or her success in challenging received opinions and behavior. Whether or not mere scandal is effective social praxis is a question not often fully confronted by the avant-garde, but the movement nonetheless thrives on that public reaction which acknowledges the artists' difference, be that difference the product of simple bohemianism or the sign of truly threatening radicalism. Invariably, the purifying force of negation strives to go beyond merely shocking the audience to attempt to cleanse them, the artist, and ultimately the culture, to open the way toward a potent and untainted future. In doing so, the purifying impulse merges with the positive speed of the avant-garde as the artist, in the guise of the visionary, child, primitive, hero, or savior, offers up visions of an idealized future to provoke the audience's imaginations and stimulate their own process of self-purification. But in extreme cases—and dada seems to be the most extreme—the purifying force may fail to get beyond its negative impulse of mere disruption, and the purity sought in the childlike or the primitive creative act may not be achieved. The rebel or primitive can easily fail to become the seer and, instead, act only to undermine both the inherited values and the possibility of finding adequate grounds for the creation of the new. In no avant-garde movement is the negative or nihilist impulse so radical or all-encompassing as in dada. Dada's famed buffoonery, absurdity, primitivism, gratuitousness, and antagonism signalled the most significant non-political attack on the role and practice of art in modern society, and in the process dada questioned the traditional bases of bourgeois aesthetic, philosophic, and social values.

Dada's nihilism was directed at its society's smug and myopic attachment to the purely material satisfactions of labor, production, consumption, and ownership, and was a response to the catastrophically destructive effects, in particular, of World War I and class conflict. Dada demanded that modern individuals view themselves from a perspective outside the materialist bias of their culture, and from that perspective that they recognize the insignificance and inadequacy of their lives. Most avant-garde and modernist artists express similar concerns, but what distinguishes dada, beyond the extremism of their actions and demands, is that most of the dadaists refused to put on the mantle of priest, prophet, or political activist that avant-garde writers and artists usually adopt. Many of the dada painters and poets did demand a political assessment of their culture or sought to inspire a spiritual awareness in their audience, but dada artworks and manifestoes provided scant religious comfort, or legitimation of the historically determined social world. Finally, the spiritual perspective they did offer only announced the absolute insignificance of the human endeavor—dada included. Unlike other avant-garde and modernist writers, dadaists, for the most part, presumed no basis for a positive or alternative vision to bourgeois culture, or, for that matter, for human action in general. And while all dadaists did not share the same need to push the negative speed this far, few dadaists managed to escape the incapacitating implications of their initial nihilism.

The extremism of Picabia's "Manifeste Cannibale Dada" of 1920,[2] for example, turns the dada spirit against the entirety of its culture, and in doing so turns it against itself. Art, including dada, is of no more or less value than any cultural institution or ideal; they are all worthless.

[Dada]	is like your hopes:	nothing
It	is like your paradise:	nothing
It	is like your idols:	nothing
It	is like your politicians:	nothing
It	is like your heroes:	nothing
It	is like your artists:	nothing

This dada is bitter, mocking, and spiteful. It is also liberating, however, for it justifies a declaration of absolute freedom. But that freedom, of itself, has little value because it too is nothing. Thus the extreme nihilism of dada will not permit it to escape a vicious circle of denial.

Nevertheless, most of the dada painters and poets attempted at one time or another to move beyond this nihilism. They believed, with Janco, that negativity could mark the beginning point for the positive speed, the creative principle. Negation signified the denial of the false significance of the human order, but it also brought one into contact with a primal reality, an elemental life force, or a primitiveness in nature and the human being which was both humbling and invigorating. Scandal destroyed cultural systems while purification renewed creative desire, and though the universe that humans inhabit was seen to be senseless in absolute terms, most dadaists affirmed the beginnings of a new humanity and a new social world emerging out of underlying reality.

The complexity and difficulty of dada lie in its apparently contradictory, but simultaneous notions of destruction and creation, absurdity and seriousness, anger and joy, despair and playfulness found in the freedom of meaninglessness and philosophic pessimism. There were many dadas, perhaps as many versions as individual dadaists. It was an international movement, and in each major locale that it developed—Zurich, Paris, Berlin, New York—it assumed different aims and tactics. Yet all dadaists shared to some extent Janco's hope for a new social role for art. They all engaged the dual negative and positive impulses that lay at the heart of their buffoonery, spontaneousness, randomness, playfulness, and primitivism. Out of their negativity, five generally positive speeds developed.

(1) Dada was political. It recognized its relationship with contemporary anarchist and communist political movements. Attacking the political and social values of the bourgeois world, it desired the demolition of the established political order. Furthermore, its rebellion against the traditional practice of art sought to undermine the cultural legitimacy of its society. For some, such as Berlin dada and the *Das neue leben* group in Zurich, the creation of a revolutionary, socialist society seemed to promise a new and positive social role for art.

(2) Dada was self-conscious play. Believing that all human culture is a willful but deluded imposition of desire on indifferent reality, dada asserted that the only justifiable action was ironic, self-conscious, hence self-justifying *and* self-demystifying playfulness. Dada creations such as those of Duchamp and Picabia became "games of wisdom and clairvoyance,"[3] undermining their very foundation, while simultaneously attacking the premises of art and culture.

(3) Dada was the unmediated expression of pure chance. Believing that no aesthetic or social structure could ultimately be justified, dada declared that the most absolutely free and depersonalized, hence "pure," work would be the product of chance. For Arp, Schwitters, Tzara, and Duchamp, art and behavior were no longer the products of will and desire, but the undirected interactions of the artist with random and meaningless materials and events.

(4) Dada was the expression of underlying primitive, spontaneous, and/or unconscious human nature. Attempting to bypass one's will and intentionality, the dada of Janco, Ball, and Huelsenbeck appealed to the irrational and unconscious out of which might perhaps grow a "new man" freed of the restrictions inherent in bourgeois identity.

(5) Dada was a spiritual activity. Ball and Arp believed that through dada's primitiveness, playfulness, and chance creations the artist might be brought into contact with some essential principles of universal, natural, and human reality, ultimately to develop a new spiritual, perhaps religious, awareness.

The various patterns of social and aesthetic behavior and aspiration that made up this phenomenology of scandal, purification, and creation were largely the result of the differences among individual temperaments and social contexts. At no point could, or did, the dada writers and artists claim that dada was a clearly defined movement. Rather, it was the product of the collective, if frequently conflicting, actions and desires of individuals united by a common rebelliousness and desire for individual freedom. This is true, of course, of many avant-garde movements, but dada is a special case because the artists could not, and chose not to try to, design a coherent theory and practice for their movement.

Like all art movements, however, dada was not solely the product of the artists' desires. It and they were shaped by their historical situation. As they themselves recognized and proclaimed, dada was a protest against their culture, and the nature of that protest differed according to the specific political, economic, and cultural context in which the artists found themselves. The actions of an individual such as Huelsenbeck, for example, had much different significance in neutral Zurich during World War I than in defeated and potentially revolutionary Germany after the war. Thus any discussion of dada must acknowledge not only the differences among the individual artists, but also those among the specific places in which dada grew.

Dada activities appeared in many cities and countries since the various artists who were attracted to dada travelled widely, but the focal points were Zurich, Germany—especially Berlin—and Paris. In Zurich, during World War I, the dada spirit was the expression of a group of artists with highly individual personalities and visions, each of whom found in the others and in the brief flowering of dada a stimulus for a private dream of individual liberation and expression. In Germany, this individualistic spirit identified itself with the pressing needs and demands of masses of people severely affected by the war and post-war chaos. German dada attempted to develop a political dimension and to merge individual and ultimately anarchistic desires with collective actions. And in Paris, dada's critique of bourgeois culture found itself restricted within a purely aesthetic and idealist dimension, attacking the grounds upon which art was created, but unable to make of the art process anything but a self-contradictory gesture of criticism and perceptual privilege.

Zurich: 1916–1920

Each of the five writers and artists who formed the core group of dada in Zurich in 1916—Tristan Tzara, Hugo Ball, Richard Huelsen-

beck, Jean Arp, and Marcel Janco—came from a significantly different background and had his own particular interests in art. They
shared, however, a common enthusiasm for modern, innovative art
and displayed in their cabaret and in the eclectic journal *Cabaret
Voltaire* an appreciation of the various international forms of experimentation which were the bases for their own dada activities. Ball
and Huelsenbeck, for example, were initially influenced by expressionism and stimulated by the energy of Italian futurism. Janco was
attracted to cubism, Arp to the developing strains of pure abstrac-
tionism, while Tzara began by writing *fin de siècle* romantic poetry,
but soon envisioned himself the prime mover of an international artistic avant-garde. They came together as artists, all ready to experiment and change the practice and conventions of art, but also seeking
through their art a means of personal and perhaps social change.
Their experimentation led them beyond mere investigation of the
forms or materials of art to the more basic questions of the ends and
the very justification of art and the artist's activities. For what united
them even more than their interest in modernist or avant-garde innovation was their deep personal opposition to the world war that
was raging around them.

Prior to their incarnation as dadaists, they had all fled their homes
in the warring nations to take up residence in neutral Switzerland. In
Zurich, the international society of aliens, exiles, and resident bourgeoisie provided a unique locus for dada's artistic and social rebellion. Going beyond the limited criticism of the war that characterized
the pacifism of the exiled expressionists, the dadaists declared their
hatred of the entire bourgeois society that caused the war, whether it
was the bourgeoisie of the warring nations or the smug Swiss middle
class whose liberalism they profited from even while they attacked it.
Ball's personal outrage against this culture and its war was expressed
in some of the most emotional writings of the Zurich dadaists.

People act as if nothing had happened. The slaughter increases, and
they cling to the prestige of European glory. They are trying to make
the impossible possible and pass off the betrayal of man, the exploitation of the body and soul of the people, and all this civilized carnage as
a triumph of European intelligence. . . . They cannot persuade us to
enjoy eating the rotten pie of human flesh that they present to us. They
cannot force our quivering nostrils to admire the smell of corpses. They
cannot expect us to confuse the increasingly disastrous apathy and
coldheartedness with heroism. One day they will have to admit that we
acted very politely, even movingly. The most strident pamphlets did

not manage to pour enough contempt and scorn on the universally prevalent hypocrisy.[4]

The outrageous antics of the dada performances at the Cabaret Voltaire from 1916 to 1918 represented both a scornful dismissal of bourgeois life and a youthful declaration of anarchic play. The unintelligible cacophony produced by their simultaneous readings of poems or their improvised "music," their performance of meaningless poems and chants, their absurd behavior, dances, and skits, their insults of the audience, and their solemn and parodic declaration of their numerous manifestoes were all aimed at defeating their audience's and their own aesthetic expectations and at stimulating potentially new modes of perception and expression. Certainly much of their activity was inherited—or lifted—from Italian futurist provocation, but in dada there was no intention to awaken a populace from its lethargy in order to praise and stimulate the essential vitality of their society; nor was there a brute glorification of violence for its own sake. And finally, in dada there was no futurist effort to transform this world in order to bring into existence an ideal society. Rather, dada disruption and primitivism used art to discredit art, the artist, and the audience, and, ultimately, to undermine the basis of any bourgeois value system. Arp, in characteristic dada language, described some of these tactics (and their limits).

> The Dadaist thought up tricks to rob the bourgeois of his sleep. . . . The Dadaist gave the bourgeois a sense of confusion and distant, yet mighty rumbling, so that his bells began to buzz, his safes frowned, and his honors broke out in spots. "The Eggboard," a game for the upper ten thousand, in which the participants leave the arena covered with egg yolk from top to toe; "The Navel Bottle," a monstrous home furnishing in which the bicycle, whale, brassière, and absinthe spoon are combined; "The Glove," which can be worn in place of the old-fashioned head—were devised to show the bourgeois the unreality of his world, the nullity of his endeavors, even of his extremely profitable patrioteerings. This of course was a naive undertaking on our part, since actually the bourgeois has less imagination than a worm, and in place of a heart has an over-life-size corn which twitches in times of approaching storm—on the stock exchange.[5]

Striking out at the bourgeois world, dada invoked an anti-humanist perspective which reduced the presumptions of modern society, indeed, all human culture, to naught. "Measured by the scale of eternity, all activity is vain—(if we allow thought to engage in an adventure the result of which would be infinitely grotesque and add significantly to our knowledge of human impotence)."[6] According to dada, the modern materialist world does not address the "scale of eternity" except by the stale and pious repetitions of a dying religious tradition. Later in his life, Huelsenbeck stated that he and the dadaists were, therefore, the first existentialists because they declared that in a meaningless universe the only order and meaning humans lived by were generally unconscious products of their own desires, and that dada was the first art movement to demand that both the processes of the creation of those value systems and their ultimate lack of validity be made explicit.[7]

Of the founding members of dada, Tzara was the most uncompromising in his scorn for these systems of social meaning.

> If I cry out:
> *Ideal, ideal, ideal,*
> *Knowledge, knowledge, knowledge,*
> *Boomboom, boomboom, boomboom,*
> I have given a pretty faithful vision of progress, law, morality, and all other fine qualities that various highly intelligent men have discussed in so many books, only to conclude that after all everyone dances to his own personal boomboom.[8]

This reduction of all cultural creations to "personal boomboom" typified the negative speed of dada and justified all the absurd personal antics of the dadaists as well. For if no action could be declared more valid than any other, neither could dada claim to have any meaning. Picabia's assertion held true for all the dada painters and poets: dada, like its culture, was nothing. Dada recognized this and announced itself an art of self-evident contradiction. If it admitted it had no meaning (and it did this joyfully), nevertheless, there was a method—and a message—in their madness. For not only did they implicitly hold that consciousness of the groundlessness of all meaning was, relatively speaking, meaningful; but they stated that once all pretence to significant order was destroyed, an optimal state of demystified self-consciousness and an unmediated union with brute reality could be achieved.

> Let each man proclaim: there is a great negative work of destruction to be accomplished. We must sweep and clean. Affirm the cleanliness of the individual after the state of madness, aggressive complete madness of a world abandoned to the hands of bandits, who rend one another and destroy the centuries. Without aim or design, without organization: indomitable madness, decomposition.[9]

Thus, like Rimbaud, Tzara proposed a programmatic, if not rational, process of derangement in order to thrust the artist and the audience into a state of irrational reality. An ideal is stated: out of destruction ("without aim or design") comes purification, a goal in spite of itself. The newly cleansed individual will thus be free to live and create spontaneously. This new freedom represents an absolute condition for Tzara. In this purified state the individual will know no restriction, no necessity except maintaining that freedom. To a certain extent, this is a goal implicit in all avant-garde work. The totally unencumbered imagination is ontologically idealist, yet dramatically effective in its aesthetic and social program. For Tzara, however, the ideal of freedom is not only self-sufficient, it is self-limiting. All it permits, finally, is a glorification of the underlying chaos of existence which human culture and individual identity have always striven to transcend or control in order to survive. Tzara's dada would not allow the avant-garde to claim any privileged role except to serve as an acolyte to that chaos.

> *Dada; absolute and unquestionable faith in every god that is the immediate product of spontaneity:* Dada; elegant and unprejudiced leap from a harmony to the other sphere; trajectory of a word tossed like a screeching phonograph record; to respect all individuals in their folly of the moment: whether it be serious, fearful, timid, ardent, vigorous, determined, enthusiastic. . . . Freedom: Dada Dada Dada, a roaring of tense colors, and interlacing of opposites and of all contradictions, grotesque, inconsistencies: LIFE.[10]

If the futurists declared themselves primitives of a new order, Tzara's vision of dada came much closer to brute primitivism, for it had no faith in a new technological world arising from the ruins of the old. Indeed, unlike most avant-garde artists, the Tzara of Zurich (and Paris) dada looks forward to no future other than a series of actions that would thrust him continuously into the "folly of the moment." Tzara best represents the negative speed of dada because once he achieved the "tabula rasa" of art and personality, he could envision no premises upon which to build an alternate system of logic or value. Thus his poems, manifestoes, and performances could be only an unbroken succession of discrete moments of simultaneous destructiveness and play. They were both the means of breaking free of established conventions and the direct experience of illogical "LIFE." Childlike and joyful, but supremely disdainful of all cultural values, Tzara's works were not emulated by many other artists for long, for they undermined all aesthetic practice and hope. They asserted that only the immediate moment had value, that the artwork could not point beyond itself to any referential or abstract realm of significance, that, in fact, it had no meaning after the moment of its creation, and that even in the moment of its coming into existence, it was only a piece of folly. Finally, even the great negative spirit of dada must recognize its own irrelevance.

> But supposing life to be a poor farce, without aim or initial parturi- tion, and because we think it our duty to extricate ourselves as fresh and clean as washed chrysanthemums, we have proclaimed as the sole basis for agreement: art. It is not as important as we, mercenaries of the spirit, have been proclaiming for centuries. Art afflicts no one and those who manage to take an interest in it will harvest caresses and a fine opportunity to populate the country with their conversation. Art is a private affair, the artist produces it for himself.[11]

Tzara's poetry certainly seems private. It is almost completely im- penetrable, perhaps because it claims to have no depth, only a spon- taneous, surface existence. Rarely do his poems lend themselves to coherent explication, either because they are examples of his cut-up newspaper collages—in which the poems are "written" or "found" by the chance piecing together of words randomly cut out of a news- paper—or because they are products of an apparently irrational pro- cess of composition. If these latter poems have meaning, Tzara stated, that meaning is only accessible to the intuition.[12] Thus, he implied that subsurface meaning might be possible, but it was not the result of rational control or intention. This possibility would later provide the basis for his tenuous association with programmatic surrealism, but it represented a threat to dada's insistence on gratuitous purity. For not only had the dada writer to rebel against the traditional prac- tice and assumptions of literature, he had to make sure that his own unconscious determinism did not compromise his search for absolute freedom.

As extreme as Tzara's vision was, it was not significantly different from that of the other members of the dada group in Zurich. In fact, they all shared the same configuration of aesthetic activism: a disgust with the given conditions of their culture, a deconstructive and scorn- ful aesthetic program, and an invocation of a primitive, irrational realm of purity. What distinguished them from one another were their particular ideas about the nature and significance of that primi- tive realm.

Despite Arp's quiet mien and apparent gentleness, for instance, the negative spirit that lay at the origin of his art was as radical as any dada nihilism. Arp's poised and beautiful abstract constructions and his lyric, if obscure, poems belie the extremism of his rejection of bourgeois culture and its aesthetic assumptions. We have already noted Arp's scorn for the bourgeois world, but while his initial disgust was directed against the "slaughter-houses of the world war,"[13] his attack on the "nullity of bourgeois endeavors" rapidly expanded to include all of modern culture since the Renaissance, and then even further to assert that all human achievement—since the cavemen!— was a sign of gross perversion.

> The Renaissance taught men the haughty exaltation of their reason. Modern times, with their science and technology, turned men towards megalomania. The confusion of our epoch results from this overestimation of reason.[14]

> Man owes it to his incongruously developed reason that he is grotesque and ugly. He has broken away from nature. He thinks that he dominates nature. . . . Since the days of the caves, man has been painting still-lives, landscapes, nudes. Since the days of the caves, man has glorified and deified himself, and has brought about human catastrophes by his monstrous vanity. Art has collaborated in his false development. To me the conception of art that has upheld the vanity of man is sickening.[15]

An escalating indictment of human history is not uncommon among avant-garde writers. As we have already seen with Rimbaud, a particular critique of the writer's culture which generates avant-garde activity often has a definite social and historical context, but the inherent utopianism of the avant-garde imagination may soon demand a radical transformation of human nature, even if that demand contradicts the basis of the initial critique. For example, dadaists scorned the ethnocentricism of modern bourgeois society, but were guilty of it themselves. On the one hand, dada's social and political focus was extremely narrow. Dadaists assumed that the historical conditions governing their world were expressions of human culture in general and that, therefore, no alternative political, spiritual, or aesthetic system could be legitimately established. On the other hand, they frequently criticized the bourgeoisie's inflated self-image, but they constantly assumed the duty and ability to chastize their society from the perspective of cosmic and eternal reality. As a result, this art which denied its importance also proposed to cure the modern world of its ills.

This tendency is especially evident in Arp's work. Quite simply— and awesomely—Arp proposed through his art to "cure human beings of the raging madness of genius and return them modestly to their rightful place in nature."[16] Human beings were to be cured of the megalomania that resulted from their overestimation of reason. Consequently, Arp prized, and created according to, a vision of universal unreason. The cosmos was without sense; it was senseless (*gegensin-nig*) as opposed to being nonsense (*unsinnig*). Humankind was incorrect in believing it to be nonsense, just as it was wrong in believing that it had created sense in it. Arp's art declared itself to be an expression of the essential reality of life. Instead of representing and giving meaning, it saw itself as a pure creation of a reality equal to any other natural creation—no transcendence, just mere life.

> Dada aimed to destroy the reasonable deceptions of man and recover the natural and unreasonable order. Dada wanted to replace the logical nonsense of the men of today by the illogically senseless. . . . Dada is for the senseless, which does not mean nonsense. Dada is senseless like nature. Dada is for nature and against art. Dada is direct like nature. Dada is for infinite sense and definite means.[17]

Arp considered his abstract art concrete. It did not represent anything, did not abstract from particular objects, did not communicate non-objective spiritual or theosophic reality. Rather, it merely took its place among other natural objects. His works were "Realities, pure and independent with no meaning or cerebral intention. We rejected all mimesis and descriptions, giving free rein to the Elementary and the Spontaneous."[18]

Arp's specific means were to create his work largely according to the actions of chance. Like Janco, Schwitters, Tzara, Richter, and Duchamp, Arp suggested that the artist's relinquishing absolute control over the artwork would reduce human self-delusion and open up new forms and visions heretofore unperceived by man. By spontaneously cutting distinctly biomorphic shapes out of paper and dropping them randomly onto the floor—thus allowing gravity and chance to influence the construction of his collages—Arp insured that his own choice, hence intentionality, would be limited. The artwork could claim a purity of being—a natural status—with no other aim or meaning than its very existence. Created independently (or nearly so) of human will or direction, the works absolved the artist of responsibility for their form and also revealed a world of being and vision that was senseless, natural, and previously denied him—yet they were products of his action as well. Nevertheless, Arp's choice of biomorphic forms lent a suggestive natural beauty to the artworks, a beauty not found in other dada random works, which often used—as

did those of Kurt Schwitters—only the detritus of the urban environment. In his visual works, Arp clearly sought to escape entrapment
within the modern social realm in order to invoke the universal perspective he idealized. According to Arp, the goal of the artist would
be to share his or her creation with the universal reality of the senseless and the random, and in so doing be brought into contact with a
reality which had been denied by an anthropomorphic perception.
Implicit in Arp's nihilism, then, is a positive speed, a search for that
promised land of creativity that Janco invoked. Unlike Duchamp's
ironic gravity piece, *Trois Stoppages—Etalon,* which made a primarily negative comment on the significance of personal artistic creation,
Arp's artworks were meant to "restore the balance between heaven
and hell."[19]

The spiritual dimension invoked here was important to several of
the original dadaists, as it has been for much of the avant-garde in
general. It was especially the concern of Hugo Ball, the true origina-
tor of the dada group, the founder and prime mover behind the
Cabaret Voltaire. Yet perhaps to no other dadaist was dada's inability
to satisfy spiritual needs so apparent.

Ball, the actor, musician, poet, and cabaret performer, saw art as a
direct means of expressing his substantial disaffection with the modern world. His dada performances of nonsense poetry and quasi-
religious chanting while wearing one of Janco's "cubist" masks signalled his rejection of technology, materialism, pragmatism, and
rationality. Dada served two functions for him: its absurdity mocked
the pretensions of the seemingly rational bourgeois culture; and at
the same time dada supposedly brought the artist into contact with
a primitive, and largely subconscious, self which he felt to be the
source of a desired spiritual reality. Ball's interest in the spirit of
negation was intense, but short-lived:

> Perfect skepticism makes perfect freedom possible. . . . One can al-
> most say that when belief in an object or a cause comes to an end, this
> object or cause returns to chaos and becomes common property. But
> perhaps it is necessary to have resolutely, forcibly produced chaos and
> thus a complete withdrawal of faith before an entirely new edifice can
> be built up on a changed basis of belief.[20]

Just what this new basis of belief would be, Ball could not determine.
He hated the gross materialism of his age and the idolatry of technology (hence his dismissal of the futurists, even though he admired
their identification with the energy of the modern world). He did
not, however, retreat into a skeptical and solely aesthetic posture. He

yearned for a socialist future, and for several years worked for a political newspaper. But this was after he had left the dada movement, and even though his journal from the dada years reveals that he thought about the political problems of his age and was attracted to a leftist perspective, he saw no possibility of joining his dada activities with political praxis. Dada might have produced a few strident pamphlets, he realized, but mere scorn for the bourgeoisie was not significant political action.

During his dada days, Ball sought something else from art. For Ball, dada, like all art, found its roots in the subconscious, in humanity's purest and unmediated desires. Art, but especially dada, which attacked the equation of the adult with the rational world, returned the artist and audience to the spiritual resources of the unconscious, ordinarily known through dream and dimly recalled in childhood experiences. The artist dreamed of the liberation of man, but it was a spiritual and emotional liberation, not specifically a political one. Consequently, his involvement with dada represented his attempt to recover not only the lost dreams of humanity, but also more intensely the buried child in each human being.

> All dreams of childhood are unselfish and deal with the well-being and liberation of mankind. Men are all born as saviors and kings. But only very few are able to hold their own or, once they have lost themselves, to find themselves again. Anyone who wants to liberate life must liberate dreams.[21]

A similar fascination with childhood images of well-being, and with the well-being to be found in a return to a childlike vision, appears in the works of Rimbaud, Arp, Tzara, and many later avant-garde writers, especially the surrealists. For Ball, however, the particular attraction of the childhood state was its association with a religious sensibility. His dada performances, especially his recitations of the "sound poems" "gadji beri bimba," "Labadas Gesang an die Wolken," and "elefantenkarawane," provided him with an experience of both spiritual and primitive passion and confirmed his belief that art might set humanity dreaming again.

> I noticed that my voice had no choice but to take on the ancient cadence of priestly lamentation, that style of liturgical singing that wails in all the Catholic churches of East and West.
>
> I do not know what gave me the idea of this music, but I began to chant my vowel sequences in a church style like a recitative, and tried not only to look serious but to force myself to be serious. For a moment

it seemed as if there were a pale, bewildered face in my cubist mask, that half-frightened, half-curious face of a ten-year-old boy, trembling and hanging avidly on the priest's words in the requiems and high masses in his home parish. Then the lights went out, as I had ordered, and bathed in sweat, I was carried down off the stage like a magical bishop.[22]

As powerful as this experience may have been, however, it is also apparent that Ball came to feel that art, in and of itself, was inadequate to his primary needs. Its skeptical voice could make a new freedom possible; its dream-like spirit could invoke a yearned-for liberation. But it could not be made an end in itself. Ball's growing antagonism to Tzara developed out of his suspicion that Tzara was interested in turning dada into just the latest of a series of modern art movements, with himself at its head. In opposition to him, Ball expressed the essential avant-garde desire that art transcend art, that it lead beyond itself, even if that necessarily meant denying itself.

It can probably be said that for us art is not an end in itself—more pure naïveté is necessary for that—but it is an opportunity for true perception and criticism of the times we live in, both of which are essential for an unstriking but characteristic style. . . . Our debates are a burning search, more blatant every day, for the specific rhythm and the buried face of this age—for its foundation and essence; for the possibility of its being stirred, its awakening. Art is only an occasion for that, a method.[23]

What could emerge from this method Ball finally did not know. Personal liberation, personal salvation were ever on his mind, and his dada performances helped temporarily to stimulate the dreamer in him. But after a short time, this did not suffice. His first dada manifesto, read on July 14, 1916, was already an anouncement of his imminent withdrawal from the group. Then, having left the movement in 1916 for a few months, he returned in 1917 only finally to break with it later that same year. For the next two or three years, he turned his attention to politics, writing for the radical paper *Die Freie Zeitung,* and pondering Marxist and anarchist thought. Eventually, in 1920, he lost interest in politics and returned to writing the fantastic novel that had occupied him during his dada days. For, one must assume, he remained troubled by the antimony between art and politics which he had already recognized in 1917.

I can find no compromise between socalism and art. Where is the path that links dream to reality, and the most outlandish dream to the most banal reality? Where is the path of social productivity for this art? An application of its principles that would be more than applied art? My artistic and political studies seem to be at variance with each other, and yet my only concern is to find the bridge. I suffer from a split personality, yet I still believe that a single flash of lightning can fuse it together; but I cannot accept society as I see it and as I am supposed to believe it, and there is no other. And so I play socialism off against art and art against moralism and perhaps I will remain just a romantic.[24]

In this moment of self-awareness, Ball sums up the central problem of almost the entire avant-garde enterprise. Although the avant-garde was always drawn strongly toward political involvement, rarely could its members find the bridge between socialism and art. The need to find a connection became much more pressing during and immediately after the First World War. Whereas pre-war avant-garde writers and artists, such as Apollinaire and the Italian futurists, were able to project a social role for art that did not bring it into substantial conflict with the established political structure of their society, this was not the case for writers whose aesthetic and social visions were shaped during and after the war. After the widespread disruption the world war caused in the lives, economies, and politics of Europeans, and after the concurrent success of the Russian Revolution, most writers and artists could hardly avoid the political and social implications of their work. Indeed, most of the major developments in the avant-garde—dada, surrealism, Russian futurism and constructivism, and Brecht's dramatic theories—resulted directly from the war and its aftermath. Ball himself, only three months after this note, commented on the irony that Lenin was living in exile on the opposite side of the same street as the Cabaret Voltaire during the time of the dada performances, and asked,

. . . is dadaism as sign and gesture the opposite of Bolshevism? Does it contrast the completely quixotic, inexpedient, and incomprehensible side of the world with destruction and consummate calculation? It will be interesting to observe what happens here and there.[25]

For the next three years Ball did observe the events in Switzerland and the Soviet Union, but it would be up to other dadaists, particularly those in Germany, to answer whether dada and Bolshevism were truly opposite.

In 1920, Ball found his flash of lightning; his personality was fused, but by then he had drifted away from both art and politics. He continued to seek the dream of liberation and found it by a return to childhood—or, more specifically, to the Catholic faith of his childhood. Ball reconverted to his former religion and dedicated the rest of his life to studying religious thought, history, and spiritual matters, even writing a book on Herman Hesse. But his original search for a fusion of art and politics in the development of a passionate and unified new personality was sustained—for a while at least—in the life and works of his close friend, Richard Huelsenbeck.

Huelsenbeck shared Ball's dream—indeed the dream of all avant-garde artists—of finding the "specific rhythm and the buried face of [their] age" in order to stir it and awaken themselves and their society. For most of the dadaists the accent was purely on the awakening. Of what they were stirring up, what would emerge, they had little notion. What matter most was the promise of individual liberation, and only secondarily social transformation. Huelsenbeck's vision, however, had a political dimension because, unlike Ball, and more in tune with Tzara, the new man he envisioned was not spiritual per se, but psychological, anarchic, and rooted in the material and social world. What he sought was a fundamental revitalization of personality and an assertion of individual freedom which would be manifest on the most basic existential and political levels, as well as on the spiritual. Huelsenbeck was dada's drummer, the performer of nonsense poems, the shouter of personal and collective boomboom, the antagonist of the audience. Performance, personal display and spontaneous creation was his forte, and at the heart of his performance was a demand for a new dimension of personal—and collective—existence. For Huelsenbeck, and later the German dadaists, art was a means of creating a new behavioral mode, an action constantly leading beyond itself. Art had to become more than merely an aesthetic concern; it had to be an activist paradigm for creative, rebellious, and transformative experience.

Speaking of his art, which began in Zurich but only fully developed in Berlin, Huelsenbeck wrote:

> My dada, which I introduced in Berlin, was a philosophy that went beyond art into life itself, as Gauguin and Rimbaud had done before us. . . . Dada, as I understood it, was an over-all reaction, a response of the entire personality to the indefinable challenge of our era, and not just a rationalistic and aesthetic reaction. . . .

> The artist's position in our time has greatly preoccupied me, since I thought of dada as an assessment and possibly a reassessment of the artist. Dada contained a protest against the sentimental overestimation of the artist in our time, plus a protest against the concomitant underestimation.[26]

This protest marks all avant-garde work. For art to be effectively critical and activist, it must attack the bourgeois idolatry of art, the uncritical assumption that art embodies and legitimizes a culture's vision. For the dadaist, just as the society must be undermined, so must art. For art, as Picabia proclaimed, is like society's ideals—*nothing*. But, if a new humanity is being born, if, in fact, the avant-garde presumes to lay the base for a new culture or to take part in the emergence of a new society, then the true calling of the artist must not be underestimated. The constant dream of the avant-garde is thus to make the absolutely essential social role of the artist evident.

But the dadaists in Zurich found, like so many avant-garde artists after them, that while their message was radical and their art and behavior outrageous, they had little effect on the audience, other than mild agitation and amusement. The works and behavior that sought to liberate failed to inspire those who had little appreciation of their need to be liberated. Neutral, bourgeois Switzerland provided a liberal environment in which dada manifestoes blossomed, but the populace was not especially threatened by dada. This was even more evident when Janco and Hans Richter, who had joined the Zurich group as it began to break up (Ball having left for personal and political reasons, Huelsenbeck having travelled to Berlin in 1917), formed a political group of "revolutionary" artists called *Das Neue Leben,* only to meet with little response from the Swiss, and even less from their fellow dadaists. They discovered what all avant-garde movements must confront at some time: unless the material conditions in society are receptive to fundamental change, the avant-garde's calls for personal and social transformation remain little more than idealist dreams.

Dada in Zurich—and later, Paris—was the expression of individual searches for personal liberation which at times projected images of social change, but its defining characteristic was the dadaists' nihilism. And in the absence of nascent political rebellion in Switzerland and, later, France, which might have forced the artists beyond their negativism and individualism, this nihilism, this "negative speed," only served to undercut any positive or collective vision of the new world they hoped for. It remained for Huelsenbeck to serve as the carrier seed to take the spirit of dada to Germany in 1917. There, significantly different social conditions enabled dada's call for a new life to be a serious, even threatening concept.

Germany: 1918–1921

I felt as though I had left a smug fat idyll for a street full of electric signs, shouting hawkers, and auto horns. In Zurich the international profiteers sat in the restaurants with well-filled wallets and rosy cheeks, ate with their knives, and smacked their lips in a merry hurrah for the countries that were bashing each other's skulls in. Berlin was the city of tightened stomachs, of mounting, thundering hunger, where hidden rage was transformed into a boundless money lust, and men's minds were concentrating more and more on questions of naked existence. Here we would have to proceed with entirely different methods, if we wanted to say something to the people. Here we would have to discard our patent-leather pumps and tie our Byronic cravats to the doorpost.[27]

As grotesque as it may sound, in Berlin we projected our resentment into politics, but we were never really political. We remained eternal revolutionaries. We projected into art as well, but since there was more politics than art in Berlin, art got the worse end of the bargain. There is a difference between sitting quietly in Switzerland and bedding down on a volcano, as we did in Berlin.[28]

The first statement by Huelsenbeck is from his *En avant-Dada,* which he wrote in 1921. The second is from his revisionist memoirs, *Mit Witz, Licht und Grütze,* published when he was an emigré psychiatrist living in New York during the post-McCarthy period. His latter position echoes the statements of a number of dadaists associated with the Berlin movement, such as Hannah Höch and George Grosz, who insisted in retrospect that their involvement was not political. Grosz, for example, wrote in his 1946 autobiography:

We simply mocked everything. That was Dadaism. Nothing was holy to us. Our movement was neither mystical, communistic, nor anarchistic. All of these movements had some sort of program, but ours was completely nihilistic. We spat on everything, including ourselves. Our symbol was nothingness, a vacuum, a void. To what extent we were the expression of a despair that knew no salvation, I cannot say.[29]

These reflections cannot change the fact, however, that Berlin dada was a significantly different movement from the one in Zurich—and the difference lay in the political situation and aspirations of the artists. Whether or not individual dadaists like Huelsenbeck or Grosz grew distant from their earlier political feelings (and several, such as the Herzfelde brothers, did not), for a while at least Berlin dada represented a concerted effort on the part of a group of writers and artists to transform a nihilistic impulse into a revolutionary cause, and specifically to associate their works with the briefly burgeoning Communist Party. Their major problem, however, was that although the dadaists identified with a collective political movement in which the positive speed of this dada might develop, dada activities were never free of anarchic and individualistic tendencies. And as the statements by Huelsenbeck and Grosz reveal, the essential negativism and love of destruction that motivated all of dada finally condemned dada to be as limited in its political projections as in its aesthetic. The difficulties of a politicized dada, and the ultimate dissolution of the movement, however, were not solely the fault of the artists. Berlin dada was as much a product of its time as was Zurich dada, and its growth and fate were affected by the particular social and material realities of its environment.

Huelsenbeck brought to Berlin an art that called for a strident rejection of bourgeois culture, an art that envisioned the growth of a new man and the demolition of the boundaries between art and life. But his audience was not one which, secure in its bourgeois comforts, could afford to be offended or merely amused. Rather, he and the artists who were drawn to dada—Grosz, Höch, Raoul Hausmann, John Heartfield and his brother Wieland Herzfelde—spoke out in a society already rent by severe economic and political conflicts. In this context, dada could no longer be content with mere personal primitivism or spiritual awakening in its effort to merge art and personal life. Instead, the life art sought to join was necessarily social and explicitly political, and dada found itself not merely acting on that life, but being a product of it. Grosz, in his still radical days of 1925, wrote:

> The artist, whether he likes it or not, lives in continual correlation to the public, to society, and he cannot withdraw from its laws of evolution, even when, as today, they include class conflict. Anyone maintaining a sophisticated stance above or outside of things is also taking sides, for such indifference and aloofness is automatically a support of the class currently in power—in Germany, the Middle Class. . . .

> Let us summarize: the meaning, nature, and history of art are directly related to the meaning, nature, and history of society. The prerequisite for the perception and evaluation of contemporary art is an intellect directed at the knowledge of facts and of correlations with real life and all its convulsions and tensions.[30]

The German dadaists, continuing the demystification of art begun in Zurich, condemned the use of art to legitimize any residual pretense of the values of bourgeois and elitist culture after the war. It was "the height of fraud to pretend art created spiritual values," Grosz declared.[31] Instead, art had to unmask itself and acknowledge that whether it created masterpieces or merely blustered, the shooting, profiteering, lying, and hunger would still go on. In this atmosphere—with this knowledge—dada saw that it had to address social problems if it were to have meaning, even as a negative force. The primarily aesthetic and spiritual leanings of Zurich dada were judged to be regressive and bourgeois, and the consequences of the desired connections between art and life more substantial and complex than had heretofore been presumed.

The Berlin dada movement grew during the particularly violent years of 1918 and 1919, years which saw the spread of the German Socialist Party and its struggle with the sparticist movement, the abortive revolution, and finally the murderous repression of Rosa Luxembourg and the sparticist leaders. It was during this time that the Berlin dadaists turned their backs on Tzara's assertion that "dada means nothing" to insist that dada's absurd antics, nonsense poems, simultaneous readings, scathing satires, and insults did, indeed, have a meaning, a meaning sympathetic to the programs of the Communist Party. Hausmann's and Huelsenback's dada program deserves to be quoted at length, for it exemplifies dada's serio-comic vision of a political and aesthetic union.

1. *Dadaism demands:*
    a. The international revolutionary union of all creative and intellectual men and women on the basis of a radical Communism.
    b. The introduction of progressive unemployment through comprehensive mechanization of every field of activity. Only by unemployment does it become possible for the individual to achieve certainty as to the truth of life and finally become accustomed to experience.
    c. The immediate expropriation of property (socialization) and the communal feeding of all; further, the erection of cities of light, and gardens which will belong to society as a whole and prepare man for a state of freedom.
2. *The Central Council demands:*
    . . . .
    b. Compulsory adherence of all clergymen and teachers to the Dadaist articles of faith; . . .
    e. Introduction of the simultaneist poem as a Communist state prayer;
    f. Requisition of churches for the performance of bruitism, simultaneist and Dadaist poems;

   g. Establishment of a Dadaist advisory council for the remodelling of life in every city of over 50,000 inhabitants;

   h. Immediate organization of a large scale Dadaist propaganda campaign with 150 circuses for the enlightenment of the proletariat; . . .

   j. Immediate regulation of all sexual relations according to the views of international Dadaism through establishment of a Dadaist sexual center.[32]

"Dada is German bolshevism," Huelsenbeck later stated. (There is no record of any bolshevist declaring that bolshevism is political dadaism, however.)

The role Berlin dada claimed for itself in the revolutionary society was not the governance of material conditions, but the overseeing of the quality of social, spiritual, and aesthetic life. The particular demands of the dada "Central Council" display a typical dadaist love of the absurd, but the contemporary development of artists' councils in the Soviet Union, and the early support the avant-garde there received from the new government, suggested to the dadaists the possibility that art, however utopic, might find a definite role in a new culture.

This moment of idealism passed, however, in both Germany and the Soviet Union. With the decline of revolutionary conditions in Germany, the vision of a revolutionary art movement also faded. Dada was still active in 1920, with the performance and polemical tour of Germany and Czechoslovakia by Huelsenbeck, Hausmann, and Baader, and later the famous Berlin dada exhibit at which the new soviet art was praised with banners proclaiming "Art is Dead. Long Live the mechanical art of Tatlin." But the mounting economic crisis in Germany and the dramatic growth of a politically reactionary mood made the deeds and demands of dada even more absurd and utopic than before. Most of the dadaists gave up on creating an explicitly political art; some, like Huelsenbeck, who became a journalist and a doctor, simply left the movement and art altogether.

Not all dadaists became apolitical, however. For Heartfield, Herzfelde, and Grosz (at least until 1925), bolshevism remained a viable political movement to which an artist could contribute significant art and energy. These men continued to challenge the conventions and function of art in bourgeois society and worked to create an innovative art of political provocation. If, as in most political art, the message of the work took prominence over the form, Grosz's prints and Heartfield's photomontages nevertheless utilized aesthetic techniques and theories drawn from both avant-garde and modernist art. Radically different from the then popular but traditional imagery and style of the political woodcuts of Kathe Köllwitz or the lithographs of Heinrich Zelle, these works succeeded in introducing a new aesthetic vocabulary into the political art of this century, particularly in the socialist countries. Grosz was finally to reject a political stand, but Heartfield and Herzfelde remained in the Communist Party and continued to contribute innovative and accomplished works, though they did not consider themselves dadaists for long. It would have been hard for them to do so, for the dada movement in Berlin had collapsed by the end of 1921, and the dada movements that developed in Hannover and Cologne, where Arp, Schwitters, Ernst, and even the communist Baargeld had congregated, all separated aesthetic from political concerns.

Political dada died as a movement because it was unable to submit or ally itself to the long-term, practical demands of a political movement once the general social fervor of a chaotic era had significantly diminished. As Hugo Ball had foreseen, the essentially quixotic and inexpedient spirit of dada's anarchism had little in common with the Communist Party's political program. Dada could flower in the midst of social disruption and declare its negative impulse as a corollary to a positive activism that originated outside the aesthetic realm, but it could not create or sustain such an activist vision itself. At most, it expressed an idealistic desire for a spiritual rebirth or an anarchic demand for a state of absolute freedom, but without a supportive socio-political context—either that of Zurich during the war, or Berlin after it—dada was limited to disruptive aesthetic and personal behavior. This also proved to be the case, in fact, in Paris, where dada blossomed and choked itself within a closed artistic milieu.

Paris: 1919–1922

The dada movement in Paris was short-lived, existing fitfully from briefly before Tzara's arrival in 1920 through the moment he declared dada dead in 1922. After this, only sporadic fragments of dada activity and conflicts remained until the formal anouncement of surrealism in 1924. In fact, dada in Paris may be seen as little more than a prelude to surrealism. For even though Tzara entered Paris in triumph, coming to claim the role of avant-garde leader he so evidently covetted and joining Arp and Janco and many other important artists—Duchamp, Picabia, Ernst, Breton, Man Ray, Eluard, Ribemont-

Dessaignes, and Cocteau—the dada movement in Paris was scarcely able to define itself before it fell apart in acrimony and boredom.

The central problem of Paris dada was that its negative speed was not given an external dimension by a convulsive social or political conflict. Nor could the second generation dadaists comfortably embrace that negativism's all-encompassing rejection of culture and aesthetic values. Whereas Tzara and the Zurich dadaists had come to their radicalism in the midst of the outrage of the war and had demanded an individual self-consciousness and liberation which admitted no social or idealist support, the French used dada's negativity largely as a means to break free from their ties to the past in their search for the new. None of the French, however, would be able to state, after eight years of dada activity, as Tzara did in 1924, that

> the acts of life have no beginning or end. Everything happens in a completely idiotic way. That is why everything is alike. Simplicity is called Dada. . . . As Dada marches it continuously destroys, not in extension but in itself. From all these disgusts, may I add, it draws no conclusion, no pride, no benefit. It has even stopped combatting anything, in the realization that it's no use, that all this doesn't matter. What interests a Dadaist is his own mode of life.[33]

Nevertheless, the lure of the negative was strong, at least at the beginning of the Paris dada movement. The interest of Breton, Soupault, and Eluard in the Zurich movement, and their publication of Tzara's works in their journal *Littérature,* beginning in 1919, signalled their desire to effect a revolution in literature as meaningful as the one that had dominated the visual arts during the first two decades of the century. Indeed, the *Littérature* group had already declared its dissatisfaction with the standard tradition of letters and had sought to construct an alternative tradition, one based on Nerval, Baudelaire, Rimbaud, Lautréamont, Jarry, and Apollinaire. In this context the absurdity and negativity of dada promised the stimulus necessary for generating a new avant-garde movement. Dada's love of scandal and its call for the purification of art and culture were adopted by the French as statements of their own public disaffiliation from the French academic cultural tradition.

For a brief period dada flourished in Paris. Breton and the French were excited by its zaniness, its rebelliousness, and its radical subversiveness. In turn, Tzara and other dada figures, such as Duchamp and Picabia, were pleased to carry their work of the past five years to new surroundings and audiences. The most public of the dada events was a series of performances strongly influenced by Tzara, in which all the earlier forms of Zurich dada behavior were repeated. The new dadaists harangued, insulted, and entertained their audiences with shouted manifestoes, nonsense and sound poetry, simultaneous readings, written and improvised plays, skits and random actions, and original "musical" compositions frequently indistinguishable from mere noise.

Yet by the early 1920's dada had given birth to no more than another form of strident bohemianism. For with the exception of Tzara and Picabia, who had developed their attitudes long before the Paris venture, the Parisian dadaists were not prepared to proclaim the negation of all art, especially their own. Almost immediately conflicts arose among the dadaists. Some were over questions of personality. There was an inevitable struggle between Tzara and Breton for leadership of the movement; Picabia developed an antagonism toward Tzara; sides were taken; manifestoes and counter-manifestoes appeared. Dada's negativity unavoidably fed on its own practitioners; in effect, it fed on itself. For dada had reached a logical dead end. Since it had undermined all attempts to establish positive goals or principles of action, dada could only sustain itself by acting as a tool of endless negation. But this meant the ceaseless repetition of the same activities, the same absurdity, the same jokes. Nihilism and play finally proved merely boring.

The Parisians, under the leadership of Breton, became particularly dissatisfied with dada's inability to move beyond its negative speed. They were willing to use dada to attack their culture and its established literary tradition, but sought a positive alternative aesthetic principle by which they could judge and refute those they perceived as their enemies—whether they be the post-symbolist and modernist writers, the late naturalists and bourgeois realists, or even the numerous other avant-garde groups. But to assert such a principle contradicted the premises of dada which privileged dadaists, according to Tzara, only because they knew their work to be meaningless, in opposition to traditional writers, who believed their work to be serious. Consequently, when Breton wanted to try Maurice Barrès before a literary tribunal for being false to his earlier writing and for having betrayed the creative spirit, Picabia, for one, rejected the idea completely, and Tzara protested that they could not accept the role of judge without establishing an implicit value system that they could not justify.

In spite of this opposition, Breton insisted that Paris dada continue to move toward some positive program. But by seeking this principle, the dada movement could not separate itself from its radical past and essential nihilism without tearing itself apart. The climactic point came with Breton's efforts in 1922 to convene the "International Congress of Paris" in order to "establish directives for the modern spirit and defend it." This effort to direct change, to value the modern over any other time, and to defend their actions, was completely counter to the dada spirit. Undermined by Tzara, the conference was never convened, but the disputes over it broke the dada movement into irreconcilable opposing camps. Dada disintegrated, allowing Breton to assume leadership of his own developing movement which was, to a large extent, founded on the positive impulse which he had identified in dada. This positive impulse—or speed—became surrealism, whose activist aesthetic program was grounded in dada's glorification of primitivism, spontaneity, gratuitousness, the irrational, and the subconscious. Made programmatic, they were more than agents of destruction and demystification; rather, they were the basis of the surrealist creation of a utopic vision of society, life, and art.

Chapter
V
The Revolutionary Unconscious: Surrealism

" 'Transform the world,' Marx said; 'change life,' Rimbaud said. These two watchwords are one for us."[1] The surrealist movement represented the most extensive development of the avant-garde venture. More than any other avant-garde writers, the surrealists developed a programmatic aesthetic and social vision linking poetic discovery and creation with political and scientific praxis in order to provide the imaginative bases for a new style of life. Specifically, the surrealists sought to expand the possibilities of personal and collective behavior by breaking down what they felt to be the repressive barriers between the unconscious and the conscious, between the irrational and the rational, and between imagination and reason. From the resulting reconciliation of these polarities, new forms of perception and behavior were to emerge which would allow individuals to overcome their extreme alienation from their environment and other people. In effect, the surrealist goal was an erotics of daily life, an erotics based on the imaginative and sensual play between internal desire and external reality, between the individual and the social and phenomenal world. Furthermore, the desired liberation of imagination, perception, and behavior was believed to be consistent with the social goals and practice of the primary revolutionary movement of the age, the Communist Party, with which the surrealists tried to ally themselves. Thus, the surrealists looked to the conjunction of a

poet—Rimbaud—and a revolutionary thinker—Marx—as the symbol
of their poetic and social vision, but, significantly, their own work
made evident the inherent contradictions between the poetic and political realms represented by these two men.

The extensiveness of the surrealist vision is, in part, explained by
their historical position—both socially and aesthetically. Emerging
during the period immediately following World War I and the Russian Revolution, the surrealists were strongly influenced by the social
upheaval that also affected other avant-garde movements of the time.
Their situation in victorious, and generally stable, France, however,
spared them the dramatic and frequently destructive challenges to
the avant-garde social programs that the Berlin dadaists, Mayakovsky and the Russian futurists, and Brecht all experienced. Even so,
the attempt by many surrealists to unite the surrealist poetic "revolution" with the socialist revolution dominated by the Soviet leadership through its arm, the French Communist Party, resulted in severe internal disruptions within the surrealist movement. On the one
hand, although some of the surrealists were later critical of Stalin's
purges of the soviet leadership, they conducted their own purges of
insufficiently political writers and artists. Yet on the other hand,
some members, who considered the core of the movement centered
around André Breton politically naive, left the movement to become
Communist Party members and proceeded to condemn surrealist
idealism. These internal conflicts were, of course, only one expression of the volatile alliances of European avant-garde writers and
movements with radical political parties in the two decades between
the wars, but perhaps because the French Communist Party could
not directly control the aesthetic and social programs of the surrealists, the inherent political ambiguities of avant-garde activism were
most dramatically highlighted over an extended period of time.

In addition to the socio-historical position of the surrealists, their
relationship to the by then noticeable tradition of avant-garde writing significantly affected surrealist theory and practice. Emerging out
of the dada movement, taking their name from a neologism of Apollinaire, aware first of the Italian futurists, then later of Mayakovsky
and the Russian futurists, and, furthermore, looking back to the poetic and personal examples of Rimbaud, Lautréamont, and Jarry,
the surrealists pictured themselves as disruptors of established literary tradition and practice just as their predecessors were. But precisely because they recognized so many antecedent and contemporary allies, they understood, perhaps more than any other avant-garde
group, that they constituted an alternative aesthetic tradition, a tra-

dition the idea of which contradicted the very notion of the avant-garde. Whereas the poetic example of the dadaists, Apollinaire, Rimbaud, Lautréamont, and before them of Baudelaire and Nerval, provided the surrealists' linguistic innovations with an authoritative historic, aesthetic precedence, the evident limitations, failures, and betrayals of the romantic, visionary quests by these earlier writers represented a threat to the surrealists' own claims to the revolutionary potential of their works. As a consequence, the surrealists were torn between affirming and denying their ties to the past avant-garde.

In fact, the surrealists were never able to overcome either the social or poetic conflicts within their movement. The poles of social activism, represented by Marx, and aesthetic activism, represented by prior avant-garde writers, thus serve to put into perspective the particular nature and contradictions of the surrealists' contribution to the history of the avant-garde.

Surrealism and the Prior Avant-garde

The surrealist movement, which was officially born in 1924 with the first "Manifeste du surréalisme," had its roots in the previous decade's literary experiments and innovations of Apollinaire, dada, and the writings of the young Breton, Louis Aragon, Philippe Soupault, and Paul Éluard. Breton and Aragon were particularly attracted to the Parisian literary world during the war years. They gravitated toward the innovators of the older generation and published their poems in the modernist journals *Sic* (which also printed Apollinaire's and Pierre Reverdy's works) and *Nord-Sud,* edited by Reverdy. Breton and Aragon, joined by Soupault, soon followed in their literary mentor's footsteps by founding the journal *Littérature* in March, 1919. This journal, whose name was meant to be taken ironically to indicate the editors' disaffection from the prevailing literary tradition, attracted the contributions of new and established modernist and avant-garde writers: Apollinaire, Valéry, Gide, and the young writers who would later make up the surrealist movement. In addition, previously unpublished works by the writers who suggested an alternative literary tradition—Rimbaud, Lautréamont, and de Sade—were printed. Yet the journal did not radically depart from contemporary aesthetic tradition, even though its main emphasis was on formal innovations. As Maurice Nadeau has pointed out, the editors were still under the influence of the poets associated with the cubist, modernist movement that sought new ways of representing perceptions and experiences, but which generally did not suggest that new patterns of perception could affect one's behavior in and conceptual orientation toward the world.[2]

The liberating agent that would bring a new dimension to literary experimentation was the Zurich dada movement, especially its ambassador Tristan Tzara. Having been introduced to Tzara's journal, *Dada,* in 1919, by Apollinaire, Breton was well aware of Tzara and the dada movement. Tzara's poems were published in *Littérature* frequently, and Breton opened the journal's pages to Tzara to reply to French critics of dadaism. But Tzara was at first only one literary figure among many in the journal, and throughout 1919, the *Littérature* group—Breton, Soupault, Aragon, and Éluard—were pursuing their own direction by exploring automatic writing, independent of any dada influence. However, when Tzara arrived in Paris in January, 1920, he quickly galvanized the literary scene and drew the young experimental writers—and especially Breton—to him. Tzara continued to publish *Dada* in Paris and, for a brief time, Breton and the *Littérature* editors called themselves dadaists and delighted in playfully shocking their audiences as previous dadaists in Zurich and Berlin had done. Nevertheless, the Paris dada movement was short-lived. Breton and Tzara struggled for leadership of the literary scene, and Tzara was eventually expelled (or quit, depending on one's perspective) from the centralized avant-garde forces until 1929, when he joined the then active surrealists.

In spite of the brief and chaotic career of Tzara and Paris dada, they served two important functions for Breton and his group. Initially, the nihilistic aspects of Tzara's aesthetics provided the necessary stimulus for Breton to sever the bonds of dependency on his literary mentors, Apollinaire and Reverdy. Similarly, his attacks on logic, bourgeois ethics, and self-control provoked feelings of absolute freedom, a freedom that originated in the denial of any *a priori* principle of order or value. Tzara's 1918 declaration, "there is a great negative work of destruction to be accomplished. We must sweep and clean. Affirm the cleanliness of the individual after the state of madness," became the guiding spirit of the early Parisian dada activities.[3]

Beyond the purely destructive spirit of this madness, however, Tzara and dada brought to the young French writers a positive faith in spontaneity, irrationality, and playful absurdity, which complemented their own previous experiments with automatic writing. Earlier influenced by the work of Freud, and to an extent by the theories of Pierre Janet (as Anna Balakian has argued),[4] Breton had been fascinated by the idea of the subconscious, by irrational behavior, and by their relationship to both ordinary life and poetry. And even though Tzara had not claimed for the unconscious the inherent significance that Hugo Ball and Huelsenbeck had argued for it in Zurich, he did champion the "anti-objective" impulse against the order of logic.[5] This spirit was taken up enthusiastically by Breton, who in the first of his 'Deux manifestes Dada" announced: "DADA, recognizing only instinct, condemns *a priori* all meaning. According to DADA, we must give up all control over ourselves. There can no longer be any question of the dogmas of morality and taste."[6]

However, whereas for Tzara instinct was privileged only because it undermined the authority of reason and any aesthetic, philosophic, or moral order, for Breton and the proto-surrealists the disruptiveness and passion they were exposed to while submitting to subconscious impulses seemed to promise an entirely new manner of perceiving and experiencing the world. Soon, they were dissatisfied with Tzara's contentment to merely repeat the playful litanies of destruction and arbitrariness that generated the dada artworks. Rather, they preferred to follow their newfound creative freedom to more productive ends.

Even in his essay *"Pour Dada"* (1920), Breton, while defending dada's illogic, was establishing the principles of the future surrealist movement. In fact, he introduces Apollinaire's use of the term *surrealist* to indicate the process of spontaneous creation which is customarily called inspiration and which is, for Breton, the result of the poets' abandoning themselves "to the inclination of their spirit." In this context, Breton enigmatically states, there has been talk of a "systematic exploration of the unconscious," and then claims that dada is wrongly interpreted as the mere "application" of the system of Freudian psychoanalysis. That application, which for Breton was clearly not a part of dada's activities, is, however, promised as a future activity of the article's author.[7]

As a consequence, when Breton states in his dada manifestoes that one must give up control over the self, his goal is not a simple, gratuitous disorder, but a descent into another form of control, the control of the subconscious order from which the poet can learn and create. It is apparent that Breton, while looking for a means to get beyond the literary practice of the "cubist" poets of Apollinaire's generation, had already come across that method in the principle of automatic writing with which he and Soupault had already experimented. Their collaborative work *Les Champs magnétiques,* which began to appear in *Littérature* in 1919 and was published as a complete text in 1920, is, to a certain extent, similar to dada's experiments with spontaneous creation. For Breton and Soupault, however, the process of writing these texts thrust the writers into a dream-like creative state (already prefigured in Apollinaire's "Oneirocriticism"). More important, they believed that a systematic exploration of this dream state could reveal the sources of literary creation.

This eventual association of systematic discovery with the loss of rational, critical intervention during the process of creation suggests surrealism's indebtedness to Rimbaud, even more than to dada. For in Breton's work, once again, we see the essential avant-garde paradox of rational derangement of the senses. The dream or hallucinatory state is given a function; the irrational, a rational role: the transformation of consciousness and poetry. Breton's and Soupault's early texts thus provided what was to become the basis of surrealist poetics. At the same time, these texts were seen by their creators as extensions of Rimbaud's concept of the "alchemy of the word." Throughout his career Breton—indeed, most of the surrealists—referred constantly to the example of Rimbaud's effort to transform poetic language and the creative consciousness, and, by extension, the world of daily experience.

For Breton and Soupault, the suspension of self-control and critical reflection during the creative process resulted in a euphoric state in which the poet could state, as did Rimbaud, "I is an other." But unlike Rimbaud, the surrealists did not seek an impersonal voice of "universal reason" in this "other" that spoke through the poet. Rather, they sought another aspect of the self—the subconscious and repressed self. The systematic orientation of the early surrealists led them to seize upon the theories of Freud and Janet to locate the source and significance of the "magical *dictation*"[8] in a latent self. Because the surrealists' idea of the derangement of the senses largely meant relinquishing their reliance on rationality in order to uncover the source of the poetic process, there is not as much anguish and self-destructiveness associated with their experiments as with Rimbaud's creations. Nor did Breton, at least, think it necessary to make oneself "monstrous" through the extreme use of drugs and alcohol, as did Rimbaud. Furthermore, in the surrealists' writings there is little of the desperation evident in Rimbaud's desire to liberate himself from the world around him. For even though Breton's statement at the end of the first surrealist manifesto, "Existence is elsewhere,"[9] echoes Rimbaud's statement in *Une Saison en Enfer,* "Real life is absent,"[10] in Breton's works there is a sense that real life is actually present, that it underlies all experience and needs only to be noticed and indulged. Thus, Breton does not state that one must thrust oneself on a romantic quest "any where out of the world,"[11] but looks toward the world, toward daily life for inspiration and satisfaction.

This particular attitude of the surrealists was nourished by their more immediate relationship with another figure of the avant-garde, Apollinaire. Clearly, the Apollinaire who championed all expressions of the modern spirit in poetry and society gave the young Breton personal support as Breton was just beginning to write, and Apollinaire's own experiments with automatic writing and his play *Les Mamelles de Tirésias* were stylistically similar to the works later produced by the surrealists. But it was also the Apollinaire who called himself the "flâneur des deux rives" (stroller of the two banks) who provided a living example of surrealist behavior and aesthetics. The surrealists, like Apollinaire, enjoyed directionless walks through the streets of Paris, leaving themselves open to chance occurrences and inspiration, attempting to find moments of unexpected beauty and instinctive connection with the physical, urban environment. Just as Apollinaire suggested that with beauty "everything is in the effect of surprise,"[12] Breton echoed "the marvelous is always beautiful, anything marvelous is beautiful, in fact only the marvelous is beautiful."[13] Like Apollinaire's poems, the poetry of surrealism sought to transform the mundane aspects of daily life into moments of marvel. Here, both Apollinaire and the surrealists recall Rimbaud's belief that "to each being . . . several *other* lives were due."[14] But, again, for the later writers, these lives apparently were much closer to reality and depended less on the frenzied alteration of the perceiver's mind than Rimbaud had believed.

Finally, the surrealists also recognized, if not their indebtedness, then their similarity to other avant-garde movements of their day, particularly Italian futurism. The surrealists declared that theirs was a time of significant poetic experiment, and although Breton, for one, felt little sympathy for the Italian futurists, he argued that the three most important modern movements (prior to surrealism) were cubism, futurism, and dada.[15] Implicit in futurism, beyond the transformation of poetic language and style, was a faith in the latent power of the physical environment, a power the poet had the responsibility to uncover and glorify. But in contrast to the futurists, the surrealists held that the power that resulted in convulsive beauty lay not in the object seen, but in the perceiver's sensibility. The surrealists did not wish to submit to the environment, but to be stimulated by it. Nor was it brute energy that they sought in the phenomenal world, but mystery. Hence, the works of the Italian Giorgio de Chirico, rather than those of the futurists, earned their greatest admiration. Nevertheless, the program of surrealist poetics ultimately profited from the example of the Italian futurists, just as its roots lay in the avant-garde vision and works of Rimbaud, Apollinaire, and dada.

Surrealist Poetics

I believe in the future resolution of these two states, dream and reality, which are seemingly so contradictory, into a kind of absolute reality, a *surreality,* if one may so speak. It is in quest of this surreality that I am going, certain not to find it but too unmindful of my death not to calculate to some slight degree the joys of its possession.[16]

The surrealist movement, as it is presented in this, Breton's first manifesto, represents—like other avant-garde movements—a quest for an absolute state of being, a state admittedly unattainable, but one by which ordinary life and art are judged and found wanting. As with all avant-garde writers and movements, the surrealists began with a sense of personal and collective limitation, then sought some form of imaginative action to overcome that limitation. For the surrealists, the awareness of personal limitation was most profound in the individual's alienation from him- or herself, in the feeling of imaginative and sensual impoverishment, and in the sensation of personal discontinuity.

In the eloquent opening pages of the first manifesto, Breton describes the quiet desperation that resignation to this impoverished condition brings to the individual of his time. But Breton is also aware that this resignation is uneasy and that people are unable to repress completely their desire for something different, or their memories that once, at least, life *felt* different. The adult, living a lusterless life, can "turn back toward his childhood which, however his guides and mentors may have botched it, still strikes him as somehow charming. There, the absence of any known restrictions allows him the perspective of several lives lived at once" (p. 3). Like Rimbaud, the surrealists found in childhood a haunting model of alternative existence and a troubling reminder of their loss. To the surrealists, the child, who is not burdened by the need to suppress the intensity of desire and sensation in order to achieve practical goals, inhabits a world of immediacy, imaginative freedom, and unrestricted possibility. But having been threatened, cajoled, and educated to accept the restrictive norms of personal behavior, the adult either gives up desires that cannot be assuaged in the material world or fulfilled by narrowly defined social relationships, or he or she lives uneasily with unaccommodated memories and desires. This is especially difficult, the surrealists argued, since the feeling of personal fullness and potential that the child once experienced is available to adults every night in their dreams. And each morning, the dutiful adult must repeat the betrayal of his or her childhood naturalness and psychic integration by acquiescing to a personal fragmentation that relegates the dream state to inconsequential status. Dreams and the dreaming self are thus "reduced to a mere parenthesis, as is the night" (p. 11), in the individual's only real and significant life.

For the surrealists, the essential element of both dream and the child's world was the free imagination. The imagination gives vitality and a sense of unlimited possibility to both, and it is what is most threatened—if not destroyed—by the adult, waking life. Therefore, it must be defended by the activist writer and artist.

> To reduce the imagination to a state of slavery . . . —is to betray all sense of absolute justice within oneself. Imagination alone offers me some intimation of what *can be,* and this is enough to remove to some slight degree the terrible injunction; enough, too, to allow me to devote myself to it without fear of making a mistake (as though it were possible to make a bigger mistake). (pp. 4–5)

The entire surrealist program in art and literature, in their personal behavior, and in their political activism was determined by this dedication to the health and expansion of the "beloved imagination" (p. 4).

Since the imagination was the heart of poetic inspiration and creation for the surrealists, the activist poet had a pivotal role in reawakening imagination in modern life. To fulfill this role, the surrealists believed it necessary to alter radically the theory and practice of an art which had too easily accommodated itself to the repressive demands of modern society. Their glorification of imagination and inspiration placed the surrealists in an explicitly romantic tradition of poetry, a tradition rejected by most of the writers of their age, yet kept alive in the writings of the visionaries and rebels to whom they turned—Nerval, Rimbaud, Lautréamont, and Jarry. Later in their careers, some of the surrealists would also look back to Shelley and Blake for support for the activist imagination.

The surrealists insisted, however, that their efforts were validated by more than just a poetic tradition. They found in the contemporary period more significant support in the theories of Freud. Even though they held the "reign of logic" and "absolute rationalism" in modern society to be deadly to the imagination, they appealed to the scientific theories of the psychologists to justify their explorations of the irrational elements of art and imagination. They perceived no contradiction in this, in part because their enemy was a particularly narrow conception of rationality which merely served the most debased interests of social stability and material production, and in part because they posited the reconciliation of the irrational and rational in an expanded state of "surrationality" similar to the state of surrealism that reconciled the false opposition of dream and reality.[17] This appeal to the authority of Freud for verification of their theories of poetic creation was, of course, another example of the avant-garde's joining of the rational and irrational aspects of experience. It was also an expression of their frequent desire to give poetry a social function and to define and justify aesthetic experience in terms of a prevalent epistemology, while at the same time using rationality to critique itself and to expand the frame of conceptual reference. In fact, surrealism developed into the most programmatic avant-garde movement because of its extensive use of Freudian ideas and because of its later incorporation of the theories of Marxist and socialist activists. Only the Russian futurists, who also began to base their aesthetic programs on an extended interpretation of a Marxist theory of production, were able to nearly equal the systematic dimension of the surrealist movement.

Although the surrealists' understanding of Freud was not thorough and they tailored his ideas to their purposes (just as they were selective in their use of other psychologists, such as Janet and Jung), they turned primarily to Freud for an understanding of the relationship between repression and the maturation process, for his description of the insistence of the subconscious to break through into the conscious domain, and for an analysis of the similarities among dream, art, and play and their relationship to repression and sublimation. The focal point to which they most frequently returned was the concept of the unconscious.

The unconscious, as the surrealists understood it, posed an insurmountable challenge to the presumed authority of consciousness. For even though the conscious mind ceaselessly struggled to suppress or control desire and, under the agency of positivism, claimed to explain, classify, and manage all physical and mental phenomena, it could not account for a wide range of daily experiences that were neither logical nor apparently "significant," nor could it totally prevent subconscious emotions, responses, and desires from being expressed at unpredictable moments in jokes, slips of the tongue, a preconscious voice, unguarded perceptions, and fantasies, as well as in dreams. With the notable exception of Antonin Artaud, for the surrealists the unconscious, which kept alive modes of emotion and desire excluded from ordinary life, was essentially benign. Its visions held little terror, certainly nothing that would not ultimately be beneficial to personal and collective existence if liberated by the poet or a new social order. To the surrealists, repression was only an unnecessary social force which excluded apparently illogical, but not essentially destructive, desires and affective responses from consciousness.

In spite of repression, the surrealists maintained, the unconscious continued to live a life of its own to which the poet, scientist, and revolutionary could appeal. Unremarked by the conscious mind, the expansive impulse that the child once experienced, the impulse that responded immediately and uncritically to all phenomena, or that saw no contradiction in the possibility of several lives or several interpretations of an event coexisting, still responded to the individual's experiences.

> In spite of what we pretend, we see how little reality satisfies us; thus, beneath the pressure of our interior repressions, we create within ourselves a whole fantasy life which, by carrying out our desires, makes up for the insufficiencies of our actual existence.[18]

According to Breton, the war between this fantasy life and "real life" was continuous. Because most of us are weak and submit to the reality principle, for the most part our desires are channelled into fantasies and dreams; occasionally, they erupt into pathological and neurotic behavior in daily life. Sometimes, however, an "energetic" person "manages to turn these desire-fantasies into reality." At other times, for still other people, the desires are sublimated into artistic creations.[19] For the surrealists, sublimation both permitted the essential health of the artist and was a means of capturing or rediscovering the original impulse that was denied by reality. Ultimately, the surrealists based their model of social revolution on the belief that the artist, being most in touch with the unconscious and its expression, could help create a society of strong, "energetic" individuals who could make their desire-fantasies into reality. Thus, even though surrealist writing often seems hermetic and self-centered, its goal was to provide a model of self-exploration and recovery.

The paradigm that the surrealists offered was based simultaneously on self-doubt and affirmation. Sensing the power of subconscious desire, they argued that the ego was largely irrelevant to the existence of a hidden and truer self. Hence, *Nadja* opens with the question "Qui suis-je?"—*Who am I?*—and Breton confesses almost immediately that he does not really know. "What I regard as the objective, more or less deliberate manifestations of my existence are merely the premises, within the limits of this existence, of an activity whose true extent is quite unknown to me."[20] The primary surrealist effort was to identify this unknown activity, to explore it, and to allow it to be articulated. Each artwork represented a quest of sorts, a quest for an inner self and for the wisdom or quality of experience it could offer. Like Rimbaud making himself monstrous to plunge into the unknown, or Apollinaire, suffering as he entered a new world never entered by other humans, the surrealists aimed "quite simply at the total recovery of our psychic force by a means which is nothing other than the dizzying descent into ourselves, the systematic illumination of hidden places, and the progressive darkening of other places, the perpetual excursion into the midst of forbidden territory."[21]

Although this descent could be disorienting, and even maddening for some writers such as Artaud, for most of the surrealists it was not very threatening, for they strongly believed in the marvelous beauty to be found there and in the revolutionary benefits for the conscious mind and society that would result from making the unconscious conscious. The hidden places concealed no horror or perversion. Rather, the surrealist activity would cast "light upon the unrevealed and yet revealable portion of our being wherein all beauty, all love, all virtue that we scarcely recognize in ourselves, shine with great intensity."[22] Prior to surrealism, these writers maintained, this intensity was experienced infrequently only by mystics, mediums, and, of course, writers at moments of poetic inspiration. Indeed, the surrealist venture was systematically to provoke states of mind in which the individual was inspired, in which he or she was in profoundest union with the entire self—conscious and unconscious—and with the phenomenal world and other people. Inspiration, the state of mind that was the surrealist ideal, was

> that total possession of our mind which, at rare intervals, prevents our being, for every problem posed, the plaything of one rational solution rather than some other equally rational solution, by that sort of short circuit it creates between a given idea and a respondent idea. . . . In poetry and in painting, Surrealism has done everything it can and more to increase these short circuits.[23]

In this particular passage the essential dynamics and productive paradoxes of the surrealist program are touched upon. The surrealist poetic and social venture was, at every moment and specific activity, directed toward reconciling apparently contradictory, or at least opposing, elements of the aesthetic, psychological, and social life of the

individual. Inspiration, that total possession of self, for example, signified the optimum union of conscious and unconscious aspects of
the self and was to be achieved in the surrealist program by the ra-
tionally motivated attempt to undercut rationality. The ego accepted
the need to submit to the id; the active consciousness became the
passive observer of the interaction of ideas. The short circuit that
occurred when images interacted without the agency of the critical
consciousness was the surrealists' aesthetic focus—the creation of metaphor, and by extension, the process of associative cognition and perception. From the recognition of the power and significance of this
"short circuit" an activist program was designed to stimulate and use
this essentially independent and alogical process for rational purposes. The surrealists saw no paradox in these conflicting elements of
their poetics, for the oppositions and their resolution constituted the
surrealist state of mind that the writers and artists sought. For just as
Breton posited the resolution of dream and reality and the irrational
and the rational, the disparate elements of the artwork and creative
process thrust the artist and audience toward a new vision in which
what was disrputive proved unified. This apparent paradox was especially evident in four aspects of surrealist aesthetics: the imagery of
the surrealist work; the creation of the work; the aesthetic and cogni-
tive status of the work; and the social and aesthetic role of both the
work and the art process.

   In the first "Manifesto of Surrealism," Breton reveals that the discovery of the basis of the surrealist program was itself the result of
the fortuitous combination of scientific and intuitive concerns. He
traces the origin of the movement to a moment in 1919 when, just
prior to falling asleep, he heard a phrase, clearly articulated, to the
effect that "there is a man cut in two by the window," a phrase which
had no apparent connection to any conscious thought or remembered
event.[24] His desire to experience and understand the nature of the
preconscious voice which offered up images such as this led him and
the proto-surrealists to explore automatic writing and dream recitation, but for Breton the strange attraction of this image was given
particular significance by his scientific and aesthetic pursuits of the
time.

   During the pre-dada period of 1918–1919, Breton states, he was im-
mersed in Freud's ideas and was particularly influenced by the poetry
and observations of Pierre Reverdy, which, he admits, he did not
fully understand at the time. It was only later, when his fascination
with the imagery the preconscious voice presented him was viewed in
a Freudian light and began influencing his poetry, that the words of

Reverdy proved prophetic for the surrealist movement. In the manifesto, Breton cites Reverdy:

> The image is a pure creation of the mind.
> It cannot be born from a comparison but from a juxtaposition of two more or less distant realities.
> The more the relationship between the two juxtaposed realities is distant and true, the stronger the image will be—the greater its emotional power and poetic reality.[25]

These comments later became tenets of surrealist poetics, for they identified the results of the processes of unconscious or preconscious creation to which the surrealists turned.

Beyond the authority of personal experience, the surrealists found support in the work of Freud of this period. In his analysis of "the dream work," which appeared in the widely read *Introductory Lectures on Psychoanalysis* (first published in German in 1916 and in French translation in 1922), Freud states, for example,

> The "creative" imagination, indeed, is quite incapable of *inventing* anything; it can only combine components that are strange to one another. . . . The dream-work . . . tries to condense two different thoughts by seeking out (like a joke) an ambiguous word in which the two thoughts may come together.[26]

For Breton, the surrealist image was precisely the surprising juxtaposition of images of disparate realities initiated by unconscious processes. It was not in the individual's conscious power, Breton at first suggested, to effect as startling a juxtaposition as the unconscious could. Traditional poetic association of images, especially comparisons as Reverdy had noted, depended too much on logic. Breton sought instead the "spark" of illumination that resulted from the "activity I call Surrealist, reason's role being limited to taking note of, and appreciating, the luminous phenomenon."[27]

This activity was, in essence, the creation of metaphor, and it was to the idea of metaphor and alogical, associative thinking that surrealist discussions constantly returned. At first, during the pre- and early surrealist period, 1919–1925 (which Breton later called the *"intuitive* epoch"[28]), the surrealists were content to randomly record these images, as they gave themselves over to automatic writing and collaborative word games and poems. The activist side of the early surrealist passivity was their intention to place themselves in situations where the conscious mind would have little control over the

direction of their thoughts or sensations. To this end, the writers'
participation in the Paris dada movement taught them techniques to
disrupt consciousness and to enter or observe the products of their
subconscious. Very soon, however, the French writers' involvement
with dada activities went beyond Tzara's ironic love of the purely
gratuitous event. For example, whereas Tzara's random clipping of
words from newspapers to create poems was meant to demystify the
idea of poetry and poetic inspiration, for the writers who were soon
to form the surrealist movement, these random collations actually
renewed their inspiration. Here, passivity was therapeutic; inspiration came from the writer's unconscious response to fortuitous juxtapositions of images. The writer learned how to be receptive to the
preconscious activity. In the first "Manifesto of Surrealism," Breton
presented several examples of these surrealist collage "poems."

> Surveillez
> Le feu qui couve
> LA PRIÈRE
> Du beau temps

> *Watch out for*
> *the fire that covers*
> *THE PRAYER*
> *of fair weather*[29]

Another "dadaist" creative activity the proto-surrealists engaged in
was writing collaborative poems: one poet would write a line and another would write the next, not knowing the first line. However,
though these sometimes resulted in startling metaphors and extended
images, the writers soon preferred more active involvement in the
creative process than mere chance allowed.

Shortly after the surrealist movement officially began (during the
"reasoning" epoch of 1925 and after), the surrealists developed activist
aesthetic strategies which they believed emulated the unconscious
processes and "artificially" produced the "short circuits" between images.[30] Two such methods, to which Breton referred in his 1935 lecture "Surrealist Situation of the Object," were those of Salvador Dali
and Max Ernst. Dali's comments deserve noting since they introduce,
once again, the avant-garde effort to link irrationality with critical
reason. For Dali, this was accomplished by a paranoid, split perception. His "paranoiac-critical activity" was a "spontaneous method of
irrational knowledge based on the critical and systematic objectifica-

tion of delirious associations and interpretations" in which one obtained a "double Image," a "representation of an object which . . . is at the same time the representation of another object that is absolutely different."[31] Similarly, Ernst recalls Lautréamont's haunting phrase, "as beautiful as the fortuitous meeting of a sewing machine and an umbrella on an operating table," to invoke the power of surrealist juxtaposition, "or, to use a shorter term, *the cultivation of the effects of a systematic bewildering.*"[32] However, if the systematic aspects of the surrealist program emphasized bewildering the conscious mind and disrupting—or "derealizing"—usual perceptions and representations of the world, the goal of the artist was to force both the artist and audience into a new mode of perception from which a unified vision, encompassing the bewildering disparate elements, would emerge. Each surrealist artwork and text ideally entailed both a disruption and unification of images and concepts.

This dual process tended to result in poetry which displayed dramatic and sometimes polar oppositions among the work's themes. Thus, as several critics have noted, surrealist poetry is—in the words of Mary Ann Caws—"characterized by its basic double center—reality and dream, presence and absence, identity and distance, intimacy and loneliness, unity and multiplicity, continuity and discontinuity, language and silence, mobility and immobility, clarity and obscurity."[33] Nevertheless, in spite of these conceptual polarities, there are few polar oppositions among the specific images of surrealist poems. Surrealist oxymorons, in particular, are not usually constructed from diametrically opposed elements, probably because the principle of direct opposition itself is not alien to logic nor uncommon in traditional poetic language. Instead, surrealist poems bewilder by their fluid and incongruous associations of images, images that are frequently from sharply different contexts. For example, surrealist poems may bring together states of mind, absurd landscapes, physical sensations, and illogical arguments.

Paul Éluard's poem "Coeur à pic," for instance, combines images from a landscape with material objects alien to that environment, abstractions, such as language, and mental and physical reactions to the combined—and interacting—elements. A landscape at once mental and physical is evoked, suggesting the powers of the creative imagination not only to link subject and object, but to tranform the world and mind by a new vision. Significantly, there is no verb in this poem, only a series of static images whose occasional repetition in new contexts (lamps, bread, perfume) suggests an ongoing process of transformation. A unity of the world and also of the perceiving mind is implied, but neither the envisioned landscape nor the observing mind achieves a supremacy over the other. The last ten lines of this thirty-three-line poem are representative; twelve of the twenty-six nouns appear elsewhere in the poem.

> Lampes de pain enfants de feuilles
> Pain des enfants parfum des femmes
> Moulins des miroirs et des yeux
> Îles des seins sillons des mots
> Neige câline de la force
> Mares fanées de la fatigue
> Torrents d'animaux lourds de sang
> Travail secret miel noir des songes
> Trésors noués par des désastres
> Sang commun sur toute la terre

> *Lamps of bread children of leaves*
> *Bread of children perfume of women*
> *Windmills of mirrors and of eyes*
> *Islands of breasts furrows of words*
> *Caressing snow of strength*
> *Faded ponds of fatigue*
> *Torrents of animals heavy with blood*
> *Secret work black honey of dreams*
> *Treasures tied by disasters*
> *Universal blood over all the land*[34]

Éluard and the surrealists found great pleasure and freedom in the aesthetics of association, for they acted on the assumption that all relationships among objects, states of mind, and individuals were subject to poetic revision. Few aspects of reality were privileged or unquestioned, with the exception, perhaps, of woman, whom they saw as mediator between the alienated individual (male) and the world. Indeed, the surrealists and their poetry are obsessed with the image of women and with the theme and experience of love. Love evoked in the adult, conscious individual states of imaginative and sensual intensity usually found only in dream and fantasy. And woman, as a separate, mysterious being, could provide for the surrealist male, who longed for an integration with the "otherness" of the world, a direct response and accepting embrace. Thus, in many surrealist works, women not only mediate between the poet and the world, but the world is described in essentially feminine terms. Correspondingly, the women described often merge with the physical environment. Women were often described with outrageous metaphoric freedom, precisely because they served as the conductive element between the poetic mind and the world.

Throughout the surrealists' writings, we come across paeans to the poet's creative power that arise from analogic thinkin, and frequently the praises are invoked by the image of a woman. In Aragon's *Le Paysan de Paris,* for example, the poet, observing a coiffeur uncoiling a blond woman's hair, exclaims,

> et brusquement, pour la première fois de ma vie, j'étais saisi de cette idée que les hommes n'ont trouvé qu'un terme de comparaison à ce qui est blond: *comme les blés,* et l'on a cru tout dire. Les blés, malheureux, mais n'avez-vous jamais regardé le fougères? J'ai mordu tout un an des cheveux de fougère. J'ai connu des cheveux de résine, des cheveux de topaze, des cheveux d'hystérie. Blond comme l'hystérie, blond comme le ciel, blond comme la fatigue, blond comme le baiser. Sur la palette des blondeurs, je mettrai l'élégance des automobiles, l'odeur des sanfoins, le silence des matinées, les perplexités de l'attente, les ravages des frôlements. Qu'il est blond le bruit de la pluie, qu'il est blond le chant des miroirs!

> *and suddenly, for the first time, it struck me that men have found but one simile for blond,* blond like wheat, *satisfied that they have thus put it in a nutshell. Wheat, wretches, but have you never looked at ferns? For a whole year I bit fern hair. I have known resin hair, topaz hair, hysteria hair. Blond like hysteria, blond like the sky, blond like fatigue, blond like a kiss. On the palette of blondnesses, I shall include the elegance of automobiles, the odor of* sainfoin, *the silence of mornings, the complexities of waiting, the ravages of another body grazing mine. How blond the noise of rain, how blond the song of mirrors!*[35]

This passage, which begins with the poet's assertion of the blondness of other objects, quickly becomes a reverie on blondness in which Aragon is enthused by the images, sensations, and memories evoked by blondness. Thus, a single, initial image and comparison thrusts the poet into an imaginative ecstasy which sustains itself until the moment when the original perception is called to Aragon's mind as the hair-dresser begins to set the blond hair.

> Blond partout: je m'abandonne à ce pitchepin des sens, à ce concept de la blondeur qui n'est pas la couleur même, mais une sorte d'esprit de couleur, tout marié aux accents de l'amour. Du blanc au rouge par le jaune, le blond ne livre pas son mystère. . . . La mémoire: la mémoire

est blonde vraiment. A ses confins, là où le souvenir se marie au men-
songe, les jolies grappes de clarté! La chevelure morte eut tout à coup
un reflet de porto: le coiffeur commençait les ondulations Marcel.

*Blond as far as the eye can reach: I capitulate to this pitchpine of the
senses, to this concept of blondness which is not the color itself but (as
it were), a spirit of color inexplicably wed to the style of love. From
white to red by way of yellow, blond does not relinquish its mystery.
. . . Memory—memory is really blond. At its far reaches, where fact
weds fancy, what pretty clusters of light! Suddenly the dead head of
hair caught a glint of port: the coiffeur was beginning his Marcel
waves.*[36]

In Éluard's poem and Aragon's narrative, the analogies are significant for both the images that are created and the poetic state of mind
stimulated by—and, in turn, creating—those images. It can be argued,
in fact, that the best surrealist works are those which bear witness to
the "surrealist activity," which reveal the creative-receptive mind undergoing and directing the association of images. Conversely, the
weakest surrealist texts are those which merely compile analogies for
their descriptive uniqueness. One such poem is Breton's "L'Union
libre," which describes the parts of his lover's body in rather unin-
spired terms. Here, in the first few lines, fairly traditional images are
succeeded by banal, then startling images.

> My wife with hair of wood fire
> With thoughts like heat lightning
> With an hourglass waist
> My wife with the waist of an otter in the tiger's teeth[37]

"L'Union libre" ends with the lines

> My wife with savanna eyes
> My wife with eyes of water to drink in prison
> My wife with eyes of wood always under the ax
> With eyes of water level of level of air earth and fire

Like Éluard's "Coeur à pic," its last line evokes a vision of totality,
here in the association of the four elements with the lover, there with
the vision of universal blood.

Both poems suggest the dual aspects of the surrealist aesthetic: a
belief, on the one hand, in the poet's absolute freedom to link any
element of experience with any other in order to create a new reality

present to the mind; and a faith, on the other hand, that ultimately there is an essential unity to the world beyond whatever particular arrangements and interpretations our minds make of experience. This unity, into which the unconscious mind desires to merge, is denied by the habits of consciousness, but can be glimpsed in the surrealist work and state of mind via the agency of the image which mediates between consciousness and the world. (Again, significantly, in Breton's poem the mediating agent is a woman's body.) Thus, the surrealist image and text direct our attention alternately to the immediate experience of surprise and marvel evoked by the image and beyond it to the unarticulated universe of desire, phenomena, and experience from which it emerges, and from which further poems will emerge. In effect, the individual poem stands alone, self-sufficient as a record of a particular surrealist vision and, at the same time, intimates other combinations of images and experiences sharing the same source. Breton spoke at times of the "latent possibilities" of the surrealist object, as opposed to its "manifest existence," and at other times mentioned the latent and manifest content of life.[38] His transference of Freud's terms from the context of dream interpretation to the interpretation of life signalled his and the surrealists desire to find—or assert—their connection with the essential unity and meaningfulness of the world beyond its apparent, or manifest, meaning which has been created by the impoverished and alienated conscious mind. For the surrealists, the phenomenal world was thus analogous to the unconscious. Just as the conscious mind sought to understand the unconscious by interpreting the dream or artwork, it could find in the surrealist artwork an expression of the subconscious response to the phenomenal world, which intimated a union of self and world never consciously admitted, but often desired.

If the successful surrealist image represented the creative bonding of disparate images and momentarily reconciled conscious and unconscious mind, and self and phenomenal world, the surrealist processes of creation, which were based on associative thinking, revealed the same patterns of internal oppositions and contradictions. In the creative process, however, these conflicts were even more evident, for the surrealists attempted to develop systematic explanations and methodologies upon what was, in essence, an irrationalist theory of creativity. Throughout the history of the surrealist movement, the surrealist writers and artists experimented with different techniques of creation and various patterns of aesthetic structuration—from total automatism to the explicit crafting of self-reflexive artifices. Each strategy balanced, in differing proportions, oppositions between passivity and activism, aesthetic determinism and freedom, irrationality and rationality, and psychic reception and projection. All of the surrealist techniques sought to provoke the "surrealist state of mind," a mental condition in which each opposition would be reconciled.

The primary concern of surrealist aesthetic theory was the relationship of the activist creative consciousness to the source of inspiration and poetic imagery, the unconscious. In general, the surrealist writers and artists tried to develop new creative practices in one of three ways: (1) by disengaging conscious, critical judgment in order to allow the preconscious flow of images or the "inner voice" to be directly experienced; (2) by seeking to stimulate the unconscious processes of response and creation through unexpected, and frequently gratuitous events and situations; (3) by consciously emulating what the writers believed to be the unconscious processes in order to direct the expansion of mental experience and to create works which would unpredictably affect consciousness much as the unmediated works of the unconscious did.

The first two procedures were most prevalent during the early stages of the surrealist movement, during its "intuitive" epoch. However, even though Breton announced this epoch to have ended in 1925, the aesthetic strategies and assumptions that characterized it continued at least through 1929, for the automatic texts and recorded dreams were published until then in *la Révolution Surréaliste*. The earliest surrealist writing—Soupault's and Breton's collaborative automatic writing—and later, the trance recitation of Robert Desnos, René Crevel, Benjamin Péret, and others represent the least consciously controlled of the surrealist works. In each case, the writer or "dreamer" would passively allow an inner monologue to be "spoken as rapidly as possible without any intervention on the part of the critical faculties, a monologue consequently unencumbered by the slightest inhibition."[39] These writers and the painters who, like Andre Masson, created "automatic" paintings by allowing their pens and brushes to wander aimlessly across page or canvas, sought more than the unexpected marvelous surreal image. They were attempting to observe and learn from the creative processes which had been previously unconscious. Even more, by becoming the uncritical voice of these processes, they *became* those processes. The poetic ego could claim no credit, Breton argued; however, in their newfound humility, the poets did perform a significant function.

We, who have made no effort whatsoever to filter, who in our works have made ourselves into simple receptacles of so many echoes, modest *recording instruments* who are not mesmerized by the drawings we are making, perhaps we serve an even nobler cause. Thus do we render with integrity the "talent" which has been lent to us.[40]

In the automatic writings and, later, in the works stimulated by willfully chosen games of chance or gratuitous activities, poetic activism came into play only before and after the creative process: before, with the decision to seek out and explore or observe the unconscious process; after, with the recognition that this discovery might serve a function, a social cause. At the very least, the surrealists were arguing for a redefinition of aesthetics, one in which talent and formal artifice would have no role, although, as we shall see, the works had observable form. The immediate attraction of the automatic text, in addition to the creation of new images, was the sensation of freedom the creative process offered. The surrealists maintained that they were liberated from a false sense of logic and a narrow view of critical judgment. Their works were also freed from determination by the arbitrary and restrictive conventions of realism—in effect, freed from the external world.

Nor did the surrealists express any fear that they were escaping one form of determination to embrace another—that of submission to the obsessiveness of the primary processes. Rather, their assumption was that they were making contact with a repressed and, in an essential way, a truer self. The desires and obsessions released in the surrealist process were the product, indeed the record, of the hidden self's affective life. The surrealists believed that this repressed self had an unperceived continuity, a continuity that the conscious self, which had always to accommodate itself to the quotidian world, could not claim. Thus, the dada-surrealist random wanderings through the streets of Paris could provoke chance responses to objects, locales, or events which might call up unremarked past responses and, as a consequence, reunite the conscious self not only with the unconscious self, but with its/their past. In effect, the surrealists posited the existence of profound meaning and order within the apparently random flow of automatic images and tales.

The automatic texts are not without apparent order, either. For instance, they are perfectly grammatical. In spite of the surrealists' claim that they suspended their critical faculties and all inhibitions to become mere recording instruments, at some point the images spirited up from the unconscious entered linguistic form. What could be construed as the intrusion of the conscious mind was not a problem for the surrealists however, since, on the one hand, they were primarily interested in the power of the images and their surprising juxtapositions and, on the other hand, they were attempting to capture "the actual functioning of thought," which they equated with "psychic automatism in its pure state."[41] Furthermore, it may be argued, automatic writing represented not the submersion of consciousness into the subconscious, but the meeting of the two as subconscious images emerged into the field of cognition.[42] In fact, Breton admits that after the first automatic sentence is recorded, there is a tendency for the second sentence to show the influence of the conscious mind's response to the first.

This aspect of automatic writing is, perhaps, best noted in some of the works of Robert Desnos, the major "dreamer" of the early surrealist period. His sentences' constantly shifting subjects disrupt any sense of thematic continuity of the passage, but the syntactical structure of the individual sentence is perfectly coherent. For example:

> With a throbbing heart we storm the breach at the frontiers
> populous suburbs overflow with champions
> let us go up the stream of nocturnal channels
> to the impassive heart where our vows to asleep[43]

Even though Anna Balakian calls Breton's *Poisson Soluble* "the most authentically automatic writing, apparently free of any contrivance or artifice,"[44] these dream sequences which apparently were written without revision in a "feverish frenzy"[45] frequently are coherent narratives based on a single, sustained metaphoric displacement, such as in the sixth passage.

> La terre, sous mes pieds, n'est qu'un immense journal déplié. Parfois une photographie passe, c'est une curiosité quelconque et des fleurs monte uniformément l'odeur, la bonne odeur de l'encre d'imprimerie. J'ai entendu dire dans ma jeunesse que l'odeur du pain chaud est insupportable aux malades, mais je répète que les fleurs sentent l'encre d'imprimerie. Les arbres eux-mêmes ne sont que des faits-divers plus ou moins intéressants: un incendiaire ici, un déraillement là.

> *The ground beneath my feet is nothing but an enormous unfolded newspaper. Sometimes a photograph comes by; it is a nondescript curiosity, and from the flowers there uniformly rises the smell, the good smell, of printers' ink. I heard it said in my youth that the smell of hot bread is intolerable to sick people, but I repeat that the flowers smell of printers' ink. The trees themselves are only more or less interesting minor news items: a fire here, a derailment there.*[46]

The implicit collaboration in these texts between the unconscious creation and juxtaposition of imagery and the conscious—or at least unself-conscious—use of grammatical and narrative conventions signified for the early surrealists the promise of the creative interaction of the two aspects of the mind and the consequent overcoming of the narrow, positivist conception of reality. The automatic texts thus provided the writers with an immediate model of self-expansion and possession.

The surrealists, however, were soon anxious to pass beyond the purely passive role they first assumed and, once they had entered the "reasoning" stage of the movement, to make the creative processes more subject to conscious elaboration. From the mid-1920's on, the surrealist texts generally became more sophisticated. They continued to rely on the unpremeditated reception of the marvelous image, but concentrated more on the conscious mind's response to that image. The texts frequently sought to sustain the creative union between unconscious and conscious mind—to sustain the state of surreality—as the mind played with its conscious and unconscious creations, as in Aragon's musings on "blondness." In Desnos' *La Liberté ou l'amour!*, one passage, for example, shows the narrator's response to an initial metamorphosis of an image—from a leaf to a glove. The narrator continues the transformation, giving each leaf its own metamorphosis and each metamorphosis a history.

Le vent apportait des feuilles arrachées aux arbres des Tuileries et ces feuilles tombaient avec un bruit mou. C'étaient des gants; gants de toutes sortes, gants de peau, gants de Suède, gants de fil longs. C'est devant le bijoutier une femme qui se dégante pour essayer une bague et se faire baiser la main par le Corsaire Sanglot, c'st une chanteuse, au fond d'un théâtre houleux, venant avec des effluves de guillotine et des cris de Révolution, c'est le peu d'une main qu'on peut voir au niveau des boutons. De temps à autre, plus lourdement qu'un météore à fin de course, tombait un gant de boxe. . . . Parfois même je ramassais l'un d'eux. D'une étreinte douce il me remerciait. Je le sentais frémir dans la poche de mon pantalon. Ainsi sa maîtresse avait-elle dû frémir à l'instant fugitif de l'amour.

The wind carried the leaves pulled from the trees of the Tuileries and these leaves fell with a soft sound. They were gloves; gloves of all kinds, leather gloves, suede gloves, long formal gloves. A woman in front of a jeweller takes off her glove to try on a ring and allows her hand to be kissed by the Corsair Sanglot, she is a singer, in the depths of a turbulent theater, coming with the effluvium of the guillotine and the cries of Revolution, it is the glimpse of a hand one can see by the

buttons. From time to time, heavier than a meteor at the end of its
journey, a boxing glove falls. . . . Occasionally I picked up one of the
gloves. With a gentle grasp, it thanked me. I felt it tremble in my pants
pocket. Thus its mistress must have trembled in the fleeting moment
of love.[47]

A third type of surrealist text is even more self-consciously structured than these. It is similar in effect to the recorded dream sequences of *Poisson Soluble,* but is not the product of automatic dictation. Rather, it represents an effort to capture the sense of the uncanny
that Freud noted in dreams in which, through a simple substitution
of a plausible "real" event or object by an apparently incongruous
image or event, a normal scene which retains its logical coherence is
rendered absurd. This type of text, such as Aragon's "Les Frères la
Côte," is similar to the surrealist paintings of Dali, Delvaux, and
Magritte in which representational scenes or objects are radically
altered by the introduction of objects from entirely different contexts, even as the conventions of realism are maintained just enough
to create an unsettling sense of logical relationship.

> Le raz de marée entra dans la pièce
> Où toute la petite famille était réunie
> Il dit Salut la compagnie
> Et emporta la maman dans le placard
> Le plus jeune fils se mit à pousser de grands cris
> Il lui chanta une romance de son pays
> Qui parlait de bouts de bois
> Bouts de bois bouts de bois
> Comme ça
> Le Père lui dit Veuillez considérer
> Mais le raz refusa de se laisser emmerder

> *The tidal wave entered the room*
> *Where all the little family was gathered together*
> *He said Hello everybody*
> *And shut the mother up into the cupboard*
> *The youngest son began to howl*
> *He sang him a song of his country*
> *Which spoke of pieces of wood*
> *Pieces of wood pieces of wood*
> *Just like that*
> *The father said Please consider*
> *But the wave refused to be bothered*[48]

The effect of these surreal vignettes is to immerse the reader suddenly and totally into an already contained and existing situation.
We do not see the transformation of the original referent into surreality as we do, for instance, in Desnos' description of leaves or
Aragon's passage on blondness. These vignettes present a surrealist
state of mind that is structurally determined and internally dynamic.
Of all the surrealist writings, they make most explicit, and gain their
suggestiveness from, the oppositions between unconscious and conscious elements, and between disjunctive images and controlled form.

The creative tension between internal dynamics and aesthetic
structure in these works is related to a more common conflict within
surrealist aesthetics. On the one hand, the surrealist imaginative experience was presented as an unbroken flow of sensations, images,
and thoughts, a flow originating in, or emulating, the unconscious
processes to which the conscious mind responded. But on the other
hand, this experience was often declared to be a moment of abrupt
illumination, an arrested moment of intensity in which all elements,
conscious and unconscious, subjective and objective, were revealed to
be integral aspects of an absolute state of being—the surreal state.
The vision of this totality was the goal of many surrealist artworks.
Breton's cry at the end of *Nadja*, "La beauté sera CONVULSIVE ou
ne sera pas!"—*Beauty will be CONVULSIVE or will not be at all*[49]—
is preceded by an analogy that captures this tension of movement and
sudden suspension.

> [La beauté] est comme un train qui bondit sans cesse dans la gare de
> Lyon et dont je sais qu'il ne va jamais partir, qu'il n'est pas parti. Elle
> est faite de saccades, dont beaucoup n'ont guère d'importance, mais
> que nous savons destinées à amener une *Saccade,* qui en a.

> *Beauty is like a train that ceaselessly roars out of the Gare de Lyon and*
> *which I know will never leave, which has not left. It consists of jolts*
> *and shocks, many of which do not have much importance, but which*
> *we know are destined to produce one* Shock, *which does.*[50]

In effect, the surrealist writer describes a condition of awareness of
the ceaseless flow of images, words, and affective responses to phenomena and ideas, yet is in constant anticipation of the moment of
surprise in which the union of self and world will be unveiled. Such
a moment, like the surrealist text, is self-contained and static, yet
destined to be left behind in the necessary movement of time and experience. The surrealists believed that the union of self and world
was constant, but the moments of awareness—at least in the modern

age—were each unique. Breton's exclamation, "Toujours pour la première fois"—*Always for the first time*[51]—is itself a complete surrealist manifesto.

Given this glorification of the convulsive intensity of the moment, it is only natural that the surrealists proclaimed their medium to be poetry. In manifesto after manifesto, the surrealist revolution was declared to be a *poetic* revolution. Accordingly, the surrealists railed against prose, the prose of the world, the prosaic mentality that valued exposition over insight. True, the surrealists maintained that any medium—film, painting, even the novel—was poetry if it contained the "spark" of illumination, but they privileged written poetry, because it provided the greatest freedom of expression and potential transformation of language and vision. Breton, like many other avant-garde writers, insisted that a transformation in the means of expression would effect a transformation in perception and behavior and that such change could most directly occur within the language and form of poetry. The poet's entrance into the preconscious regions of mind and the subsequent alteration of both consciousness and poetic articulation freed the writer from any *a priori* relationship to the world. Since poetry had been traditionally more concerned with the poet's responses to the world and thus had focussed on states of mind and emotion rather than on the need to represent given reality, the poet was more able to distort language or disrupt referentiality than the prose writer. And for the surrealist, ultimately, the specific condition of the "real" world was of decidedly less importance than both the poet's own state of mind and his or her relationship to the process of seeing the self and world in their potentially new relationships.

> En ce qui me concerne, plus importantes encore que pour l'esprit la rencontre de certaines dispositions de choses m'apparaissent les dispositions d'un esprit à l'ègard de certaines choses, ces deux sortes de dispositions régissant à elles seules toutes formes de la sensibilité.
>
> *As far as I am concerned, a mind's arrangement with regard to certain objects is even more important than its regard for certain arrangements of objects, these two kinds of arrangement controlling between them all forms of sensibility.*[52]

Accordingly, the surrealist poet claimed the right—and the power—to dismiss any commonly accepted and logical relationships between the perceiving consciousness and the world in order to allow language to engage itself and, through its self-questioning and self-contradictory interplay, create images of both new mental states and potential realities. Thus the poem may focus, as we have seen, on either the process of mental exploration and creation, or the particular, sudden products of that process. The poem may present itself as a paradigm of perceptual and creative action or present a vision of totality.

However, precisely because the surrealists did claim such freedom for their essentially lyric poetry, it seems to me that the most interesting surrealist texts are the prose narratives, such as Breton's *Nadja* (1928), *Les Vases communicants* (1932), and *L'Amour fou* (1937), Desnos' *Le Liberté ou l'amour!* (1927), and Aragon's *Le Paysan de Paris* (1926). Each of these works achieves the surrealist poetic ideal in prose. Breton's and Aragon's works, in particular, succeed in transforming the record of the writers' personal experiences of daily life into magical tales of poetic perception and expression, while both retaining the dominant referential aspects of traditional prose and creating new narrative forms. Breton and the other surrealists dismissed the traditional novel and later condemned the strategies of socialist realism (although Aragon, after leaving the surrealist movement, wrote socialist realist books), as gross distortions of reality. Many of the great modernist novelists held that traditional realism's weakness was that it assumed a social, temporal continuity that obscured or ignored the private, idiosyncratic dynamics of the isolated individual's experience. The surrealists altered this argument, however, to suggest that the fault of realism was that it replicated the discontinuity of waking life, that it did not account for the continuity of unconscious and conscious self, which, admittedly, had to be uncovered.[53] Breton, for example, stated that he had no interest in the empty moments of his or anyone else's life, moments the realist felt compelled to describe in order to create the illusion of a three-dimensional character.[54]

The goal of the surrealist narrative was to testify to the true continuity of the individual's life, the continuity insured not by consciousness or social reality, but by the unconscious. As a consequence, works like *Nadja* and *Le Paysan de Paris* seem to wander as aimlessly as the surrealists (and Apollinaire before them) wandered the streets of Paris, ever receptive and ready to submit to any urging or outbreak of the unconscious. These works shift effortlessly from moments of reflection, to descriptions of the environment, to evocations of memory and emotional states, to eruptions of chance coincidences, mystery, and occasionally startling beauty.

The entire narratives display a quiet, sustained beauty, expressive of the generally reflective and vulnerable attitudes of the narrators who are receptive to the most mundane or odd incident and emotion. Since these texts are literary representations of the type of activity and state of mind that characterized the dada-surrealist strolls, they frequently call up intuitive responses that unite the writer with his past self. Many of the objects and locales described in Breton's and Aragon's books are associated with the past, not only of the individual writers but of Paris itself, the Paris of the Passage de l'Opéra described in *Le Paysan de Paris* and the Paris of the second-class theaters constantly closing down to be replaced by others, that Breton invokes in *Nadja*. Of course, these old objects or locales, which stood out in a city caught up in the changes of modernity, were more likely to catch the receptive viewer's eye and accent their estrangement from their environment. In addition, this estrangement and the frequently absurd juxtapositions it created further emphasized the passage of time and the surrealist sense of the inherent instability of experience. As a result, a spell of nostalgia is cast over these texts, a nostalgia that lends beauty to them but which curiously works against the surrealist spirit of openness to the future that they so often invoked.

Just as these narratives testify to the potential ambiguity of the individual's relationship to past and future moments, and just as the automatic text and some surrealist poems accent a tension between an undifferentiated flow of time and the arrested moment of convulsive revelation, both the surrealist narrative and automatic text have a severely ambiguous status in relation to their audience, especially the reader of the future. To the surrealists, for example, the automatic text was the product of an intensely personal process of self-exploration and articulation—engaging unconscious processes to create new and unforeseen images. But the actual significance of these images and the text as an imaginative experience for the reader is problematic, since the works are potentially only fossils of a once vital process. A passive reading of the work will not place the reader in touch with his or her own unconscious. If the poet's private images have the effect of stirring the reader's unconscious, it is more by chance than by the nature of the text. At most, as Fredric Jameson has noted, the automatic text serves as an *idea* of surrealism, as a model of an activity that the sympathetic reader might emulate in order to unveil the unconscious.[56] In effect, the automatic text-as-lesson provides support for the surrealists' frequent reference to Lautréamont's dictum, "poetry must be created by everyone."[57]

The evolution of surrealist aesthetics beyond the stage of intuitive, passive creation resulted in more self-consciously controlled literary works that had a more aggressive, direct effect. Nevertheless, the nature of the work and its effect were still ambiguous, for it had two meanings, one for the creator and one for the audience. The concept of systematic bewilderment, for example, like automatic writing, was a way for the writer or artist to break free of the restraints of logic and aesthetic convention to discover surreality. It was a means of stimulation which ultimately resulted in the artwork. But the product of the bewilderment, although it pointed back to its origin, acted on the reader in a different manner. Whether the artwork revealed the process of its creation (as did the automatic text and Aragon's and Desnos' metaphoric transformations), or presented itself as the self-contained result of the process (as did Aragon's *"Les Frères la Côte"* or Breton's *"L'Union libre"*), the work initiated a new process of systematic bewilderment in the audience, a bewilderment that took them beyond the text toward another, unknown perception of surreality.

For the surrealists, the surrealist object and text were to be experienced as products of a process of dream and liberation that had stimulated a vision of surreality. However, they were not the vision of surreality themselves. Surreality, in effect, could not be represented; it had to be sensed—not in the object, but in the conjunction of the object and the daily world. The work served primarily to "shake up [the audience's] settled ways of thinking," Breton asserted.[58] It did this by locating in the audience's perception a new reality that took its place among other real objects and demanded that the reader or observer expand his or her manner of perceiving the world to accommodate the new object. For example, in 1924 Breton proposed the manufacture of objects seen in dreams, which, when placed in circulation, would undermine the concept of usefulness by which the plethora of commodity objects in modern society were evaluated. Such an assault on the idea of function was

> a prerequisite for the unleashing of the powers of *invention*. . . . The aim I was pursuing went far beyond the mere creation of such objects: it entailed nothing less than the objectification of the very act of dreaming, its transformation into reality.[59]

This objectification of the surrealist's act of dreaming disoriented its perceiver, who was then inspired to see the world in a new manner, to recognize a realm of possibility heretofore ignored or repressed, and to unleash his or her own powers of invention.

The creation of surrealist objects was important to the surrealists because it represented a movement beyond the hermetic realm of art into daily life. It was an extension of the entire surrealist venture to unite art and life through the artwork or through the personal experience of the artist, such as that described in surrealist narratives like *Nadja* and *Le Paysan de Paris*. But these texts further accentuated the implicit tension between the private and public significance of the surrealist artwork. *Nadja,* for example, is even more problematic than the automatic texts. It is not the direct transmission of an aesthetic process, but the record of Breton's attempt to lead an automatic life. The chance occurrences that allowed him to discover his unknown self are *described,* hence, are even further removed from the reader than the images that emerged from automatic writing. Even the poet raises the question whether the text is necessary, for the experiences he has described, especially the relationship with Nadja, have, by their evocation of a sense of mystery, prepared him for the even more significant—and convulsive—discovery of both himself and love. Nadja disappears from the text; she wanders out of Breton's life, but she has also served a function for which he no longer has use. Addressing an unnamed *toi* whom he has discovered after Nadja has disappeared, Breton states,

> Je dis que tu me détournes pour toujours de l'énigme. Puisque tu existes, comme toi seule sais *exister,* il n'était peut-être pas très nécessaire que ce livre existât. J'ai cru pouvoir en décider autrement, en souvenir de la conclusion que je voulais lui donner avant de te connaître et que ton irruption dans ma vie n'a pas à mes yeux rendue vaine.

> *I say that you have turned me from enigmas forever. Since you exist, as you alone know how to* exist, *it was perhaps not so necessary that this book should exist. I have decided to write it nevertheless, in memory of the conclusion I wanted to give it before knowing you and which your explosion into my life has not rendered vain.*[60]

For Breton, the book is a memorial, a monument. Nevertheless, it is necessary, for he is not only testifying to the importance of Nadja, and not only addressing the *toi* who represents the possibility of living fully. He is also presenting the work as a model of surrealist life, that, if read correctly, might have an effect on the reader. At one point he hopes that the events he recounts will be of such a force

> à précipiter quelques hommes dans la rue, après leur avoir fait prendre conscience, sinon du néant, du moins de la grave insuffisance de tout calcul soi-disant rigoureux sur eux-mêmes, de toute action qui exige une application suivie, et qui a pu être préméditée.

to send some men rushing out into the street, after making them aware,
if not of the non-existence, at least of the crucial inadequacy of any so-
called categorical self-evaluation, of any action which requires a con-
tinuous application and which can be premeditated.[61]

If this effect is possible, it is, again, as with the automatic text, only
because Breton provides an example of self-discovery. Since the events
he describes are so removed from the reader's experience, their tran-
scription does not have the effect that other surrealist texts or objects
have of forcing the events' reality on the reader's consciousness.
Rather, it is the *idea* of the event that Breton has undergone, for
himself and for the reader, that has revolutionary potential.

Surrealist writing and art appear to shift their focus constantly
from the private significance of the process of creation and the artwork to their public role. The activist aesthetic model of surrealism
embraced both poles of the experience and implied that there was no
contradiction between them. The activity of the artist could be a
paradigm for others, the surrealists maintained. Similarly, their essentially private visions could change the public's perception and way
of responding and behaving in the world. This activist faith that art
could affect life moved the surrealists toward an alliance and conflict
with other forces that were attempting to change consciousness and
life, in particular, the Communist Party. The resulting struggle to
join aesthetic and political praxis called into question the surrealist
belief in the social and aesthetic role of both the artwork and the
creative process, and eventually led to the fragmentation of the surrealist movement.

Surrealism in the Service of the Revolution

La poésie et l'art garderont toujours un faible pour tout ce qui trans-
figure l'homme dans cette sommation désespérée, irréductible que de
loin en loin il prend la chance dérisoire de faire à la vie. C'est qu'au-
dessus de l'art, de la poésie, qu'on le veuille ou non, bat aussi un
drapeau tour à tour rouge et noir.

Poetry and art will always retain a preference for all which transfigures
man in this desperate, irreducible demand which, now and then, he
takes the derisory chance to make on life. The fact is that above art
and poetry also, whether one likes it or not, there beats a flag—in turn
red and black.[62]

Throughout the history of surrealism, and especially in the writings of Breton, a radical demand for the absolute liberation and trans-

formation of humanity was expressed. From Breton's statement in the first manifesto, "the mere word 'freedom' is the only one that still excites me. I deem it capable of indefinitely sustaining the old human fanaticism,"[63] to his invocation in *Arcane 17* (1945) of the abiding power of the black and red flags to inspire poetry, Breton championed the ideal of personal and collective freedom. However, the dual allegiances of surrealist poetry to the anarchist and communist flags revealed an inherent tension in the surrealist program concerning the nature and role of poetry's contribution to human liberation.

The historical and theoretical roots of surrealism were found in the anarchist attitudes of the poets associated with the dada movement. Early in the surrealist movement, several writers declared both their enthusiastic rebellion against bourgeois society and their disinclination to admit the authority of any specific political, revolutionary creed. From 1925 through World War II, however, many of these writers struggled to come to terms with the policies and example of the Communist Party, for the Party and the revolution in Russia provided the most promising context for the surrealists' increasing antagonism against the social conditions in the capitalist West in the period between the wars. By the end of the 1930's, some of the surrealists followed the red flag exclusively, while others carried the black.

Even though the early surrealists disaffiliated themselves from the dadaists' refusal to image the possibility of any significant change in society, they clearly sustained the bohemian, anarchist attitude of social provocation that characterized the Zurich and Paris dada movements. In the third issue of *la Révolution Surréaliste* (15 April, 1925), Robert Desnos proclaimed: "For a revolutionary, there is only one possible form of government: REVOLUTION means TERROR. . . . Assassins, bandits, pirates, you were the first rebels."[64] In the next issue (15 July), excerpts from a lecture Aragon delivered in Madrid in April, 1925 were printed. The tone of the lecture was particularly abusive to his audience of students and professors. Aragon declared his disdain for work and for all who submit to the god of the West— Labor. Like Desnos, he invoked the Great Terror and announced that surrealists would usher in the "new spirit of revolt, a spirit dedicated to attacking everything." But beyond mere rebellion and nihilism, these attacks and surrealism were based on a principle that was repressed and derided by modern society: "It is in love, it is in poetry, that rebellion is eternally born."[65] Out of the necessity of love, rebellion was fomented; out of destruction, love would be liberated, the surrealists maintained.

For Aragon and the other surrealists at this time, the surrealist revolution was solely of the spirit. It had little to do with the apparently petty questions of government structures, economic systems, or political praxis. Aragon, who left the surrealist movement in 1932 to become a Communist Party member (eventually rising to the position of a deputy member of the Central Committee of the French Communist Party), published in the second issue of *la Révolution Surréaliste* a reply to an attack on him by the communist editors of the journal *Clarté*.

> I have always placed, and place today, the spirit of revolt far above *any* politics. . . . The Russian Revolution? Forgive me for shrugging my shoulders. On the level of ideas, it is, at best, a vague ministerial crisis. . . . The problems raised by human existence do not derive from the miserable little revolutionary activity that has occurred in the East during the course of the last few years. I shall add that it is only by a real abuse of language that this latter activity can be characterized as revolutionary. . . . I will not accept from anyone, even yourself, a lesson in the name of some social dogma, even that of Marx.[66]

In effect, for the early surrealists the surrealist revolution took place "on the level of ideas," the only level which could be relevant to the creation of a new, absolute "state of mind."

By the end of 1925, however, the idealism of the first epoch of surrealism was tempered by the surrealists' efforts to expand the activist scope of the revolution of the spirit. The "reasoning" period of surrealism entailed a more problematic exploration of the consequences of surrealist activity, an exploration partially under the aegis of Freud and partially under the "social dogma" of Marx. Breton and the surrealists were especially angered by the outbreak of the French colonial war with Morocco in 1925 and by the willingness of a number of leading French intellectuals to defend the "Fatherland's" right to wage such a war. The surrealists' protest against the war drew them toward the primary opposition to the war, the Communist Party, and for a while, communist intellectuals and writers united with the surrealists to work in an unsteady alliance, neither group fully submitting to the other.

More important than this specific alliance, however, was the surrealists' growing interest in Marxist and dialectical theory. Breton, in particular, was greatly influenced by his reading of German dialectical thinkers and by Trotsky's work on Lenin.[67] The former provided the surrealists with a theoretical basis for their conception of both historical development and the processes of aesthetic and mental change, which, they asserted, involved the interaction of contradictory elements. For the surrealists, for example, the oppositions between the rational and the irrational, or between dream and reality, and their resolution by a third term—surreality—followed the general patterns of dialectics. As a consequence, they believed that the conflict of surrealist revolutionary desire and social reality would also exhibit a dialectical dimension by which new revolutionary conditions would be created.

Perhaps most significant was the surrealists' change of attitude toward the Russian Revolution. Breton's review of Trotsky's reminiscences of Lenin in *la Révolution Surréaliste*, #5, acclaims the grandeur and perfection of the two revolutionary leaders. Lenin and Trotsky are declared to be no mcrc statesmen, but men whose very names cause heads to turn and people to ponder the promise or threat these revolutionaries pose.[68] Breton exhibits a significant tendency to romanticize the revolution here and to treat the two leaders not as men, but as ideal revolutionaries. This tendency to elevate the individual into a type continued throughout Breton's life and it allowed him—and other surrealists—to refuse to compromise their ideal vision and absolute demands when confronted by Party policies delivered by Party bureau members whom the surrealists considered mere unimaginative functionaries.

The romance of the revolution was especially strong during the early 1920's, of course, and Breton and the surrealists were not alone in their self-elevation to the pantheon of revolutionary leaders. In the same issue in which Breton discussed Lenin and Trotsky, both the *Clarté* editors and the surrealists, including Aragon, along with other intellectuals such as Henri Lefebvre and Emil Benveniste, declared themselves "the revolt of the spirit," whose ancestors were the poets, philosophers, and political theorists who had announced the coming disaster in the bourgeois world—Blake, Hegel, Proudhon, Marx, Lautréamont, Rimbaud, and Nietzsche, among others.[69] For a brief time the writers and intellectuals associated with these two journals sustained their uneasy alliance, and the surrealists, as a group, were increasingly drawn toward the Communist Party itself. Once the surrealist dream of revolution projected itself into the political realm, it focused on the promise implicit in the communist revolution of a total transformation of society.

In January, 1927, Breton, Aragon, Éluard, and others joined the French Communist Party. In November, however, they resigned from it, a few days after Trotsky's expulsion from the Russian Communist

Party. The dismissal, exile, and eventual murder of Trotsky dramatically illustrated for many of the surrealists the failure of the Bolsheviks to sustain the ideal of revolution which the surrealists—and many other artists, intellectuals, and workers worldwide—believed the communists to embody. Trotsky, the internationalist, the believer in imminent world revolution, and the most literate member of the communist leadership, represented to the surrealists the radical, the utopic, aspect of political action. Following the soviet's rejection of Trotsky and the rise of Stalin, many of the surrealists found it increasingly difficult to maintain their faith in the political revolutionary promise. Only the concurrent rise of fascist states in Italy, Spain, and Germany, the growing political conservatism in France, and the worldwide economic depression forced most of the surrealists to continue struggling for practical political correlatives to their political vision.

During the 1930's the surrealists were engaged in a long and complex struggle with the Communist Party and each other. Over the decade, the movement disintegrated slowly and acrimoniously as the writers were torn between their poetic and political allegiances. As a coherent movement, surrealism broke apart by the eve of the war, when most of the still active surrealists chose to respond to the exigencies of the war and the Resistance, which was dominated by the communists. A few writers, such as Breton, who neither trusted the communists nor was trusted by them, chose exile. The extended battles the surrealists fought with the communists were similar to the conflict that wracked the Russian futurist movement in the 1920's, but because the artists and writers in France were not under the political control of the Communist Party, the struggle lasted longer, the issues were more developed, and the opposition between the contestants more dramatic. As a consequence, the surrealist movement made evident the inherent incompatibility of the avant-garde aesthetic and social vision and the policies of the political avant-garde which, in this century, has been dominated by the Russian Communist Party. For this party, the aesthetic avant-garde simply was not revolutionary; for the surrealists, and most avant-garde writers and artists, the Communist Party was misguided and repressive. Neither group could totally accept the premises and methodology of the other.

The surrealists' political program was a direct extension of their poetic assumptions. Their social and aesthetic ideal was freedom. Since their desire for freedom originated in their awareness of repression, and the sensation of freedom was a fleeting and occasional experience, they accepted no *a priori* limitations on the type of personal or collective freedom they sought. In effect, freedom could not be defined or determined; for the surrealists, it was pure potentiality. Glimpses of it were found in love (which pulled one out of the cage of alienation), in the moment of poetic creation (which led beyond itself toward a world of promise), and in the *idea* of revolution (which represented the desire to fight all restraints).

For the surrealists, if the terms of liberation and revolution could not be restricted, neither could revolutionary method. In *Donner à voir,* Éluard wrote, "There is no model for the one who searches for what he has never seen."[70] From their exploration of the unconscious to their search for surreality, the surrealists' quest was to discover the imaginative and creative potential of humankind. At times, they would follow what they believed was a Freudian model, at other times a Marxist, but because they refused to place limits on the conception of humanity that might emerge from the revolutionary period, they refused to privilege an economic, political, or psychological methodology or standard of judgment. Furthermore, they believed each successful revolutionary advance, whether political, psychological, or aesthetic, would open up further vistas of potential development and exploration, and at the same time would aid the revolutionary struggles in the other areas of human need. Thus, they countered the communists' charges that their indebtedness to Freud trapped them in the "idealist illusion" that psychological behavior was determined independently of social conditions, by arguing that insights into both the processes of repression and the generation of desire would illuminate the nature of revolutionary action.

Although they accepted a Marxist model of the relationship between the economic infrastructure of society and the cultural superstructure, of which poetry was a particularly "evolved" part, the surrealists asserted that changes in the superstructure could occur independently of the infrastructure and could also reinforce the changes occurring at the social base. It was on precisely this point that the surrealists were most adamant and for which they received the most criticism from the political activists. The surrealists insisted that the method and the goals of poetic creation could only be determined by poets. The discoveries and effects of the aesthetic works and strategies might prove important in other contexts, but the surrealists would adopt—or follow—directives from those contexts only to the extent that they furthered specifically surrealist action.

In the last issue of *la Révolution Surréaliste* (December, 1929), the "Second Manifesto of Surrealism" appeared which, in part, addressed some of the criticisms directed at the movement by the communists. In the manifesto, Breton stated simply,

> We would not want Surrealism to be at the mercy of the whims of this or that group of persons; if it declares that it is able, by its own means, to uproot thought from an increasingly cruel state of thralldom, to steer it back onto the path of total comprehension, return it to its original purity—that is enough for it to be judged only on what it has done and what it still has to do in order to keep its promises.[71]

At this point, the goal of the movement was the liberation of thought from repressive reality and the return of it to a state of original purity, presumably that of poetry, dream, and childhood. There was little desire to harness thought for another social group. Nevertheless, the manifesto also reaffirmed the surrealists' sympathy for the socialist cause, and seven months later the first issue of *Le Surréalisme au Service de la Révolution* appeared. The new journal signalled the surrealists' efforts to expand the political scope of their aesthetic and social revolution.

Throughout the following decade, the surrealists maintained that they served the revolution in three general ways, all of which were merely extensions of established surrealist practice: (1) the surrealist texts stimulated a desire for freedom and alternate life; (2) they increased the artists' and audience's awareness of the dimensions of possibility; and (3) they helped demystify the arbitrary and restrictive values of the bourgeois world. In themselves, these did not require three separate types of action. Any one surrealist work might do all three, but the specific focus of a surrealist text usually reflected one of them. In 1939, Éluard, who had already broken with Breton and was fast approaching the Communist Party again, published *Donner à voir,* a moving testament to surrealist desire and history. At one point, he refers to a conception of poetry he had in the 1920's, and only slightly qualifies it.

> The poem de-sensitizes the world for the profit of human faculties, permits man to see in another manner, to see other things. His old vision is dead, or false. He discovers a new world, he becomes a new man.[72]

By revisioning the world, the poem allowed a new person to be born. By itself, this statement could have been made by almost any avant-garde writer, from Rimbaud through the beats. In the context of the surrealist movement, it illuminated the core of their program.

During the 1930's, that program increasingly emphasized the de-

mystification of the bourgeois world, not, however, through dreams
or appeals to the irrational, but by assaults on bourgeois ideology.
The new journal differed significantly from *la Révolution Surréaliste*
in the number and the vehemence of the poets' attacks on bourgeois
patriotism, religion, philosophy, literature, conservative psychology,
politics, and sexual codes. In effect, the surrealist literary texts and
artworks were given a new context—they were surrounded by socio-
political tracts. Significantly, the surrealist revolution continued to
be fought on the level of ideas. The disparagement of bourgeois institutions and ideology allowed the development and expansion of
new, putatively revolutionary ideas. Phenomenologically, this aggressive negativism could be seen as another expression of avant-garde
nihilism, or, more immediately, the surrealists' indebtedness to their
dada origins. But this negativism, like the surrealist texts, was given
a new context: the surrealist revolution was, the surrealists believed,
serving the larger political revolution.

To their communist detractors, the surrealists admitted that they
were not proletarian revolutionaries; nor did they mimic proletarian
art. Rather, they proclaimed themselves "traitors to their class."
Working from within the bourgeoisie in order to destroy it, the surrealist artist remained a paradigm of activism. The artist illustrated
dialectical behavior, taking cognizance of his or her original class
position, then taking an opposing stand, so that a third and new class
might come to power.[73] Thus, although acting independently of political directives, the artist's work could serve a larger function. In
addition, the surrealists pointed out that their "irrational" artworks
could be interpreted, analyzed, and learned from, just as one could
profit from the interpretation of dreams. Furthermore, art itself was
an interpretive activity. Breton was particularly insistent on this
point. Partially in order to defend the free space of art, he argued
that, by probing the unconscious and imaginative desire, art uncovered aspects of human nature repressed and distorted in bourgeois
culture, aspects which were helpful to revolutionary action and which
had to be liberated if the socialist transformation of collective life
was to be healthy and successful.

> Our ambition is to unite . . . this activity of transformation with this
> activity of interpretation. . . . Every error in the interpretation of
> man gives rise to an error in the interpretation of the universe; it is,
> consequently, an obstacle to its transformation.[74]

In essence, Breton was not only offering the fruits of surrealist exploration to the service of the political revolution, he was also warn-

ing the communists that without the special insights into desire and creation that the poet possessed, the political transformation of society could not achieve its own potential.

For the communist political and aesthetic theorists of the Stalinist era, this position was mere bourgeois idealism. They were not interested in art as imaginative exploration, nor in art as an independent activity of the "evolved" superstructure. For the communists, art was a reflection of material conditions, conditions analyzed and affected by the scientific approach of historical materialism. Thus the artist followed the directives of party dogma, illustrating, not initiating, insights into contemporary conditions and future realities. Specifically, the surrealists were directed, as were all other Russian and European literary movements, to follow the aesthetic model of socialist realism, a style they claimed did not distort reality, but which directly addressed recognizable social conditions, in particular those of the proletariat.

The opposition of the aesthetic and political positions of the communists and the surrealists uncovered the most problematic aspects of the surrealist—indeed, the entire avant-garde—activist position. Even though the communists had an especially narrow understanding, even a fear, of aesthetic imagination, they recognized the implicit confusions and contradictions in the surrealist merger of social and aesthetic activism. They were particularly wary of the surrealists' ability simultaneously to link Marxist and Freudian thought with alchemy, mysticism, and poetic inspiration. For the surrealists, as for other avant-garde writers and the Romantic poets before them, art, politics, science, and magic were all means of transforming the world. Having identified the common aspect of desire in these categories of human action, the surrealists freely associated, merged, and blurred them, in part in their effort to achieve a surrealist synthesis of states of mind, in part to justify the various directions of their poetic explorations. Thus, when Breton at one point described the common properties of scientific and artistic thought, under whose observation—"the real, confused too long with given data, splinters in every direction possible and tends to become a component of the possible"—he might well have also been talking about the destructive and constructive components of politics or magic.[75] And J.-M. Monnerot, who later linked science, magic, and poetry,[76] argued in *Le Surréalisme au Service de la Révolution* #5 (15 May, 1933) that to serve the communist cause, the surrealists would dedicate a greater effort to the most regimented form of thought—revolutionary theory and propaganda. But the future role of the poet, after the success of the worldwide communist revolution, would be to draw upon the sources of poetry in dream and the unconscious to become the "liberating sorcerers of dream." Through this sorcery, the world would be transformed; the reality principle would unite with the pleasure principle, the rational with the real (the surreal).[77] Such a conflation of realms stimulated surrealist utopic visions, but also undermined their claim to be taken seriously as true political revolutionaries.

This tendency to link poetry and magic, and politics and utopia, was related to tensions already noted in surrealist poetics—between the moment of surrealist inspiration and the unmediated flow of experience, and between the apparent self-sufficiency, or self-reflexiveness, of the poetic experience and the unenlightened non-poetic realm. Avant-garde poetry, Michel Beaujour has argued, cannot be truly revolutionary precisely because of these tensions. Poetry can only promise, not act. It can present an image and experience of imaginative fulfillment, but in so doing, it steps out of time; it is incompatible with the political revolutionary's image of time as historical process. Radical poetry's real goal, Beaujour continues, is the recovery of an original, pure language, an edenic state—in short, its roots are in a religious and mythic impulse.[78] Indeed, as we have seen in the second manifesto, Breton explicitly contrasted the surrealists' desire to return thought to its "original purity" with their independence from political directives. And certainly, the poetic revolutionary cry, "Always for the first time!," did not provide a stable base upon which to develop political praxis. Furthermore, the surrealist and avant-garde poets' desire to make the creative moment a paradigm for revolutionary action was seen by Trotsky and others to reflect a desire for apocalypse, the instantaneous transcendence—and denial—of the historical reality in which political revolutionaries struggled.[79]

Finally, the surrealists' own efforts to overcome the tensions between their poetic and political visions were neither convincing nor acceptable to the French communists. On the one hand, the surrealists argued that their poetry could be interpreted and put to political use, but would be meanginful only if it was accepted on its own terms, terms which challenged the communists' understanding of art and praxis. On the other hand, when they admitted that the surrealist artwork was not self-sufficient, they maintained that it was only meaningful when it entered and disrupted the social world. But the resulting demystification of rationality and the revelation of a state of surreality, in which dream and reality would be achieved, undermined the "scientific" basis of communist dogma.

Although the surrealists were aware of the communist criticisms of their program, and although several of the surrealists went over to the communist side, those who remained in the movement felt justified by the excessive narrowness and rigidity of the communist policy. They thought it absurd to insist on a single model of proletarian literature that had been developed in post-revolutionary Russia, when political and class conditions in Europe were radically different. And whereas they criticized proletarian and socialist realist doctrines in order to justify their own position as bourgeois revolutionaries, they were even more concerned with the communists' tendency to restrict revolutionary praxis to a single model of acceptable action. Communist thought must not become codified, or it would die, Breton argued. Nor could a revolutionary leave to other individuals the decisions he or she should make.[80] The loyal party members' uncritical submission to party doctrine was proof that the party had betrayed the goals of true revolution. A movement should be judged according to its practice, not its stated goals, Breton later commented. "To my mind the aim of anything is less what it claims to be than what the means it uses make it."[81] To Breton, the Moscow trials revealed the horrifying aims of the established communist leadership. As a consequence, Breton condemned Stalin and his followers for their destruction of the revolution and its workers. He reaffirmed his belief in Trotsky and communist ideals, and though becoming an increasingly isolated voice in the late 1930's, he continued to articulate the surrealist position.

In 1938, Breton travelled to Mexico, met Trotsky, and worked with the Russian theorist and the Mexican artist Diego Rivera on a "Manifesto for an Independent Revolutionary Art." The document, a call for the creation of an artist's association independent of current political regimes, was unwittingly a memorial to avant-garde—and political—revolutionary hopes of the times. The new artists' association was short-lived; Breton returned to a surrealist movement that was on the verge of collapse; and Trotsky was murdered two years later. The manifesto affirmed Breton's belief that the artist was a "natural ally of revolution," and reasserted Trotsky's position from the early 1920's, that in the revolutionary state, the artist must have freedom to explore new ideas and desires.

If, for the better development of the forces of material production, the revolution must build a socialist regime with centralised control, to develop intellectual creation an anarchist regime of individual liberty should from the first be established.[82]

As Breton stated in *Arcane 17* seven years later, only the black flag of anarchism could make his pulse beat powerfully when he thought of poetry's—and his own—allegiance to the transfiguration of humanity.[83]

Trotsky's vision of a centralized socialist state and an intellectual and artistic anarchy was itself an idealization of the promise and the history of the Russian Revolution. For a brief period after that revolution such freedom did exist, partly by design, partly by default. For the avant-garde, however, the moment was particularly significant, for it gave activist writers and artists—in particular, Mayakovsky and the Russian futurists—the opportunity truly to place art at the service of the revolution.

Chapter

VI

The Avant-garde and Political Revolution: Mayakovsky and Russian Futurism

Although avant-garde writers and artists desire that aesthetic innovation not only provoke a radical alteration of art and consciousness but contribute to the political transformation of society as well, at only one historical moment has an avant-garde movement been able to join with a significant and effective political, economic, and social revolution. The outbreak of the 1917 Russian Revolution at the height of the Russian futurist movement suddenly placed the idealism, aestheticism, and bohemianism of these avant-garde artists in a new context. It enabled them to entertain dreams of aiding in the overthrow of the oppressive culture against which their pre-revolutionary manifestoes had railed and of assuming the position which they had always claimed as their right, as the vanguard in the creation of a new social and artistic order. But by associating directly with the Communist Party's efforts to alter the material bases of society, the futurists found it necessary to re-evaluate their assumptions about the nature of art, the artist and audience, to compete with opposing politically inspired literary movements, and, finally, to justify their innovative practices to men of politics who were suspicious of the indebtedness of their innovations to the modernist and avant-garde art of the discredited bourgeois culture.

The uneasy, and ultimately unsuccessful, efforts of these writers to link avant-garde formal innovation with political praxis in a revolu-

165

tionary society set an example for all avant-garde movements that followed. Chronologically, the Russian futurists were the first group to experience the conflict that developed between the avant-garde whose origins lay in the bourgeois tradition of art, and the program of proletarian literature and art that arose during the early years of the soviet state. Once codified in the doctrine of socialist realism in 1934, the proletarian program was imposed by the soviet Communist Party on all political activist writers who wished to ally themselves with the communist movement in their efforts to transform the artistic, social, and political life of their societies. Thus the conflicts experienced by the futurists in the 1920's would later resurface in the careers of the surrealists, Brecht, and the post-World War II vanguard writers and artists of Europe and North and South America. Perhaps no avant-garde figure struggled with the opposing demands of avant-garde vision and proletarian dogma as tragically as did Mayakovsky. And just as the fate of Russian futurism announced the dilemma of subsequent avant-garde movements, so Mayakovsky's life and works stand as a warning to writers who desire that political action be the equal of poetic vision.

Russian Futurism

Russian futurism, as a literary movement, originated in the participating writers' bohemian attitudes and their rejection of the spiritual, hermetic, and aristocratic tendencies of the turn-of-the-century Russian symbolist movement with which most of them had identified early in their careers. Futurism was most strongly influenced by the remarkable ferment in Russia's visual and performing arts caused by the sudden influx of Western European modernist art into the cultural centers of Moscow and St. Petersburg during the first fifteen years of the century. The excitement generated in the visual arts by the rapid and successive discoveries of impressionism, post-impressionism, cubism, orphism, the *Blaue Reiter,* and Italian futurism stimulated a remarkable development in the Russians' aesthetic sophistication. These discoveries soon led to a renewed identification with Western European culture, and eventually to the Russians' own distinctive contribution to that culture through Kandinsky, Chagall, and later the supremitists and constructivists. The excitement generated by Russian experimentation in painting soon spread to many other art forms, and eventually, through them, the effects returned to the European tradition in which Russian innovation had originated.

The first quarter of the twentieth century proved to be a period of unmatched creativity in Russian poetry, fiction, drama, criticism, music, dance, theater, and cinema. As in Europe, at the heart of this creative ferment was a heightened sense of *modernity,* expressed particularly in the writers' and artists' efforts to free themselves both from the provincialism and social themes of late-nineteenth-century realism (represented in art by the Wanderers movement), and from the otherworldliness of the symbolists. The compulsion to be modern was also a product of the rapid and fundamental changes occurring in the Russian urban and industrial environments, partly as a result of the instability of the Romanov dynasty, the nation's defeat in the Russo-Japanese war, and the abortive revolution of 1905. But until these social changes overwhelmed the new artists, the immediate, indeed the exclusive, focus of their literary and artistic innovation was aesthetic. Livshits, one of the founding futurists, was later to remark for all Russian modernists and avant-gardists alike that the new painting introduced from Europe fed "not only a new vision of the world in all its sensuous magnificence and staggering variety . . . it was also a new philosophy of art, a heroic aesthetics, which shattered all established canons and opened . . . breathtaking perspectives."[1]

The ideal of a *heroic* aesthetics suited the young futurist movement well. It fit their image of bohemian artists as daring radicals, strident in their criticism of the old forms of art and undaunted in their creation of the new. While this bohemianism did not require any external stimulus, the Russian futurists soon found a model and an ally in Italian futurism. Compared to other European art movements, Italian futurism was a relatively minor import, but it served in name and program as an important catalyst for the spirit of modernity and aesthetic heroism activating the Russian futurist movement. While there is a marked debate over the specific date and means of the Russians' discovery of the Italians, it is clear that Russian futurism came to embody many of the Italians' precepts, and the extreme antics of Khlebnikov, Burlyuk, Mayakovsky, Livshits, and the other futurists closely resembled the Italians' forms of self-promotion and aesthetic radicalism. Yet even though the Russians had possible knowledge of the Italian movement early in their career, the origins of Russian futurism appear to predate their interest in the Italians, and can be seen instead as an expression of the general spirit of modernity and avant-gardism of the period.

The first stirring of the Russian futurist movement was the appearance in 1910 of the not especially innovative, and barely distributed anthology *Sadok sudei* (*A Trap for Judges*), which brought together the early core of the movement—David Burlyuk, the prime mover of pre-revolutionary Russian futurism, his brother Nikolai, Vasily Kamensky, Victor Khlebnikov, and Elena Guro. While the anthology did not display much in the way of eventual futurist style, the group apparently was referring to its members by this time as *budetlyane*, ("men of the future"). The year 1912 was the true start of the movement as such. Nourished by the public exhibitions, lectures, and discussion of modern painting (including Italian futurism) which surrounded the "Jack of Diamonds" and the "Donkey's Tail" art shows (in which several of the *budetlyane* took part), and by meetings at the Burlyuk's country home, the proto-futurists, now joined by Livshits, Mayakovsky, and Kruchenykh, formed the Hylaean group. Their public debut as a fully declared vanguard movement was their late-1912 manifesto "A Slap in the Face of Public Taste" in which, among other things, they declared that in order to free modern writing from the "constricting past": "Puskin, Dostoevsky, Tolstoy, etc., etc., must be thrown overbroard from the Ship of Modernity." The Hylaeans, asserting that "we alone are the *face of our Time*," praised "Today's virile souls" and announced the "dawn of an unknown beauty."[2]

These polemics, which echo so many avant-garde manifestoes, have a purely aesthetic orientation. There are no references to the nature of the new age they envisioned, or to the essential modernity of the city, technology, or the new man that their works would eventually mention. Rather, the futurists expressed their need only to enlarge the poetic vocabulary by creating new words, and to be freed from the conventions of "good taste." Finally, as Vladimir Markov points out, there is little in this manifesto that identifies the basis of the new movement: rather, it contains only the group's defensive posturing against the past.[3] By it, however, the futurist movement was launched; in 1913 it began to call itself cubo-futurism to seize on the public's recognition of the term "futurism," which by then had been well-introduced from Italy, and to distinguish itself from a minor group, ego-futurism, which had been the first group in Russia to adopt the term.

The initial poetic goal of Russian futurism was to shift the creative focus of poetry from the polysemic imagery of symbolism—specifically, the symbolists' effort to suggest a multiplicity of meaning, symbolic essence, and ultimately a mystical reality in a highly ornate, if traditional, poetic language—toward the phonetic and syntactical interactions of the brute sounds and words themselves. In this manner, poetic activity would be reduced to an unembellished linguistic process from which new semantic and phonetic combinations might develop. Kruchonykh's sound poem[4] of 1913, for example, was composed entirely of apparently meaningless letter groupings and was as inscrutable as any dada chance creation.

	dyr	bul	scchyl
	ubeshshchur		
	skum		
vy	so	bu	
r	l	éz	

As Edward J. Brown points out, however, this experimental "poem" is constructed out of precisely those sounds characteristic of Russian speech which were commonly regarded as too harsh for poetry.[5] For the futurists, the poem represented a provocative attack on the conventions of poetry and thus initiated an innovative aesthetics based on the primary elements of language. Words by themselves, ripped free from traditional syntax and context, pure sounds, neologisms, archaisms, even nonsense words, were all experimented with in the Russians' search for a new literary language.

These experiments were similar to those of several avant-garde groups, but especially to the Italian futurists, whom the Russians always disparaged. Kruchonykh's "trans-rational language," known as *zaum,* recalls Marinetti's "words-in-freedom" and "imagination-without-strings" in its syntactical anarchism and its isolation of words or parts of words into self-sufficient agents of communication. Similarly, Livshits' "ferroconcrete poems," which depend on unusual typographical juxtapositions of letters, phonemes, word fragments, and lists of words which suggest a particular scene, invoke impressionistic collages of perceptions and emotions independent of grammar. These works bear great resemblance to some of the Italians' graphic poems, particularly Marinetti's *Zang-tumb-tumb,* and to the works of the futurist painters.

As similar as these innovations are to the work of the Italian futurists, however, the Russians' earliest work displays an analytical, almost scientific, approach to the operations of language which is absent from the Italians' efforts to create a primarily impressionistic language to communicate lived sensations and emotions. This analytic aspect is evident, for example, in Kruchonykh's sound poem and in Khlebnikov's manipulation of the forms of words in "Incantation by Laughter," or his improvisation on the roots of words in "Zangezi."[6] This analytical approach brought the futurists into a productive relationship with the group of formalist linguists, critics, and literary historians who formed the *Opoyaz* society in 1914—Viktor Shklovsky, Roman Jakobson, Osip Brik, and Boris Eykhenbaum, among others. These formalists were also exploring the operations of the constitutive elements and structures of literary and semiotic systems and were particularly interested in the nature of linguistic innovation and transformation. The two groups remained allied throughout the revolutionary period and the 1920's, and supported each other's efforts to develop a "scientific" theory of literary innovation and production in Marxist society. They were also to share the same fate during the Stalinist period.

The Russian futurists' early experiments in literary language were intended not merely to create an art illustrative of modern society—as they believed the Italians had done—but to generate both a new means of expression and a new reality itself. Throughout the history of the Russian futurist movement, one dictum was constantly repeated: new form creates new content. Whether that content be literary or political, the futurists believed that only by analyzing, deforming, and developing the means of articulation could a new aesthetic and social consciousness, hence a new reality, be created. Kruchonykh commented to Khlebnikov, for example, that the Italians only wrote about the theme of modernity, whereas the Russians *produced* modernity by their works.[7] The Russians thus envisioned greater powers in the artist who would create the "new man" and spiritual reality of the future, whereas they believed that the Italians only identified and joined with those forces already bringing the new world into existence. As Noemi Blumenkranz Onimus has phrased it, the Italians began with a new signified and sought new signifiers to denote it, while the Russians did the opposite.[8] They created new language and conventions in order to uncover or create a new reality. But as a result, their works, like many similar avant-garde creations, were frequently incomprehensible to their contemporary audience. The futurists' faith was, of course, not only that a new vision and reality would result from their work, but also that a new audience would develop which would understand the poems. The futurists would then be justified in their belief that their work altered the vision, language, and spiritual life of the Russian people.

The high points of cubo-futurism were the members' public antics and readings which began in Moscow and St. Petersburg in late 1913 and were followed, in early 1914, by the "futurist tour" of Mayakovsky, David Burlyuk, and Vassily Kamensky to seventeen Russian cities. Walking through the cities' streets, with their faces painted, radishes stuck in buttonholes, wearing gaudy clothes—Mayakovsky's yellow blouse was especially noted—then reciting their poems and manifestoes in the streets or public halls, and haranguing the audience, the futurists adopted the aggressive, insulting, and outrageous mannerisms so characteristic of most avant-garde self-promotion. These specific tactics also owe much to Italian futurism, though rather than attempting to stir their audiences out of a presumed state of personal and political lethargy, as did the Italians, they mainly followed the time-honored bohemian effort to "épater les bourgeois." With the exception of an emerging urbanism in Mayakovsky's poetry, his sentimental identification with the oppressed and the poor, and his increasing scorn for the rich and the bourgeoisie, the futurists at this stage were clearly apolitical. Their rebellion was only against the aesthetic and spiritual conditions of their society. In fact, they explicitly distinguished themselves from the Italians on this point. Whereas Marinetti and his followers sought to link art and politics, the Russians, Shershenevich stated in 1916, were "interested solely in art. Italian futurism is a social movement, the Russian is an artistic movement."[9]

The revolutions of 1917 suddenly forced the futurists to alter this attitude. By the beginning of World War I, the futurist movement had just about run the course of rebellion and subsequent acceptance typical of avant-garde movements. They were no longer the outrageous outsiders of the literary world. They read their works at the important literary cafes, were published regularly, and were the subject of frequent public discussions. Even if they had not succeeded in creating a new reality or in totally transforming the language of art, they had won their place within the established art world. But with the overthrow of the Romanov dynasty and the creation of the soviet state, a new dimension was added to the futurist bohemian utopianism. They encountered the social manifestation of the futurist dream, the destruction of the aristocratic and bourgeois order and the promised transformation of society.

The futurists' response to the February 1917 revolution was one of general support. Led by Mayakovsky, they welcomed the political change, but expressed the hope that are would remain free of direct political control. Soon after the November revolution, they declared their identification with the Bolsheviks since both could claim to be vanguard parties of their respective revolutions. But, again, though their aims were parallel, the futurists asserted that writers should not submit to direct state control, since, in their eyes, the futurists worked for a spiritual revolution, a third front to further the work of the Bolsheviks on the economic and political fronts.

Not all futurists rallied unhesitatingly to the imagined conjunction of poetic and social revolutions, however. The Burlyuk brothers, for example, had close ties to the old order and favored the White armies during the civil war. Nikolai Burlyuk evidently was killed by the Red army in 1920; David, after a short involvement with the post-revolutionary futurist movement, emigrated to the United States. Others wandered around the edge of the fighting and social tumult, slowly rejoining the now politically oriented futurist movement in 1920 once the new regime had clearly established itself.

In the immediate post-revolutionary period, futurism found itself faced with the task of re-evaluating its entire literary assumptions and program. This was not unique; all new and established writers and literary groups participated in an urgent critical discussion about the role of literature in the new society—its bases of production, its formal and thematic concerns, its economic determinants, its relation to the former bourgeois, educated audience, and to the potential audience of workers and peasants, and finally, its relationship with the Communist Party. For the allied and competing groups which strove to create a literature appropriate to the new society—the futurists, the late symbolists, the proletarian writers movements, and the interested Communist Party theorists—just what that society needed, what it would be like, and how it would be run were themselves the subjects of constant debate and polemics. During the first decade after the revolution, no one, neither writer nor party member, could unilaterally predict the nature and duty of artistic production in the new state.

In fact, during the first years of the revolution, the very existence of the state was extremely precarious. As a consequence, in the chaotic period of the civil war and "war communism," the literary world was in a state of upheaval. Paper and printer's ink were in desperately short supply (to mention nothing about the grievous shortages of food, fuel, and most necessities for life). Predictably, there was little opportunity to publish, and the futurists and other writers had to content themselves with meeting in literary cafes as they had before the revolution and simply declaiming their poetry, manifestoes, and programs for the future.

The futurists' initial plans after the revolution were extensions of their earlier demand: that the old literary order by demolished. Declaring that attachment to the literature and values of the past could only retard the aesthetic and spiritual growth of the "new man" that would emerge from the revolution, the futurists called for the rejection of pre-revolutionary academic, critical, and aesthetic practice.

These demands are not significantly different from those of any number of avant-garde groups in much less politicized situations. And, it may be argued, the futurists' own insistence on the coming *spiritual* revolution was essentially a continuation of a general aestheticist vision shared by many Russian writers in the pre-revolutionary period. As Bengt Jengfeldt has pointed out, for example, there is little mention in their early-post-revolutionary writings of the political or economic changes that were the focus of the real changes taking place in their society. Rather, their stated task was revolutionizing the arts so that the soul of the new man would be liberated from attachments to the past.[10]

In this respect, the futurists were not alone in anticipating a primarily spiritual revolution in the new society. As much as they believed their aesthetic program to be distinct from that of the symbolists, both groups hoped for the spiritual transformation of culture. Several of the late symbolists, most notably Blok and Biely, at first responded positively to the revolution, and predicted dramatic changes in the spiritual condition of the nation in highly charged religious imagery. Indeed, much of late symbolist literature, reflecting the declining days of the aristocratic society, had been imbued with a sense of fatalism and had envisioned in apocalyptic images the spiritual salvation of the decaying culture. But the religious revival that was latent in the revolution, or at least that Blok pictured in "The Twelve," or Biely hoped for in "Christ is Risen," was finally proven to be only the idealistic and nostalgic yearnings of men who soon withdrew from active alliance with the new order and came to be called "fellow travellers" of the revolution.

The futurists, on the other hand, quickly recognized the inappropriateness of their continued bohemian behavior and their spiritual-aestheticist vision. Since they sought public forums for their literary and personal activities, they were particularly attentive to their audience's response. Cafe disputes, outlandish costumes, the flaunting of literary conventions and their audience's sensibility, and their combative egotism might have seemed necessary when confronting bourgeois culture, but clearly served no purpose in the developing society. However, in spite of this re-evaluation of their literary programs, their past antics, combined with their continued friendship with members of the symbolist movement, condemned them, in the eyes of the writers and critics associated with the proletarian movement, to be forever associated with pure aestheticism. Nevertheless, the futurists sought to adapt their literary experimentation to the political needs of their culture, and by early 1918 they undertook to change their stance towards their audience from antagonism to solidarity. In 1918, for example, Mayakovsky stopped the publication of a collection of pre-revolutionary bohemian and romantic poems (though he did have himself photographed in early futurist garb).

Shortly after the revolution, the futurists began publishing a series of politically inspired newspapers. In March of 1918, Mayakovsky, Burlyuk and Kamensky published a single issue of *Gazeta futuristov* (*Futurists' Newspaper*), which claimed that the futurists were the true revolutionaries in art, attacked the continued dependence on classical literature, and issued the call for the spiritual revolution in the communist state. This was followed in December 1918 by a weekly paper *Iskusstvo Kommuny* (*The Art of the Commune*), edited by the futurists and published by the Fine Arts Section (IZO) of the People's Commissariat of Education. During its brief life of nineteen issues, it published poetry (Mayakovsky's "Orders for the Armies of the Arts" appeared here), discussions of the nature of revolutionary art, and numerous manifestoes declaring the uselessness of museums which enshrined past art.

> What we need is not a dead temple, where dead works of art can fossilize but a live factory of human spirit. We need raw art, raw words, raw deeds. . . . Art ought to assemble not in lifeless temple-museums but everywhere—in the streets, in streetcars, factories, laboratories, and in workers' districts.[11]

The futurists were able to gain control of *Iskusstvo Kommuny* because at the time of the revolution they were the best organized literary group, and they had quickly and stridently declared their solidarity with the Bolsheviks in their defeat of the old society. They were also helped by the Commissar of Education Anatoly Lunacharsky's initial sympathy for them and by his particular appreciation of Mayakovsky's talent. But he was soon distressed, as were many other party members and Russian writers, by the futurists' proclamation that they were the sole true artists of the revolution, and by their disdain for any but the most formally innovative literature. Lunacharsky, in the pages of the journal he sponsored and which the futurists edited, rebuked the futurists for their "youthful" attack on the art of the past and for their belief that only they spoke with authority for the art of the commune. Furthermore, the Communist Party viewed the futurists with distinct mistrust and rejected the application of *Kom-Fut* (the organization of communist futurists), for registration as a purely political party cell.

The futurists, however, encountered the greatest opposition to their early post-revolutionary programs from the writers associated with the developing proletarian literary movements, who labelled them bourgeois chameleons seeking to survive by disguising themselves as revolutionaries. These initial attacks were important because, although the proletarian movement went through several significant political changes during the 1920's, its principal concerns determined the later development of the soviet literary orthodoxy which plagued—and eventually destroyed—the futurist movement.

The most strident condemnation of the futurist program came from the Proletarian Cultural and Educational Organization (Proletkul't) which was organized shortly before the Bolshevik revolution by Aleksandr Bogdanov, a close friend of Lunacharsky's and a former associate—though they had become estranged—of Lenin's. The Proletkul't declared that the only true art of the revolution would be created by the proletariat and that culture had to be the product solely of the workers. Since the proletariat had no culture of its own, and bourgeois culture could not articulate the situation of the working class, an extensive organization for training the workers had to be developed. Bogdanov organized a network of "studios" throughout Russia to teach the workers to write. By 1920, the organization claimed four hundred thousand members, of whom eighty thousand were active in the literary centers. Even during the civil war period, Proletkul't boasted of publishing fifteen literary journals. Although the work produced by the new writers was held by most to be extremely poor and was usually modeled on the literary realism of the bourgeois culture they rejected, the members of the Proletkul't believed that the activity of writing and publishing served a greater purpose than merely describing scenes of the revolution; it actively helped sustain the revolution. Ironically, some of Bogdanov's ideas were similar to those of the futurists he criticized. According to Bogdanov, who earlier had been expelled from the Bolshevik party, there were three parallel roads to revolution. He believed that art was a primary means of organizing the proletariat and that although the cultural revolution served the same ends as the political and economic revolutions, it remained separate from the other two. Consequently, he established his training schools independently of the Communist Party. Doing so inevitably brought him into direct conflict with the Bolsheviks—especially Lenin—who insisted on the integral relationship of the three revolutions. Lenin also posited that a true proletarian culture would be attained only after a long process of development, which would itself depend on the prior success of the political and economic revolutions. As a consequence, Lenin strongly criticized the Proletkul't movement for trying to create such a culture immediately, "in a laboratory," rather than aiding its natural, and slow, development in the midst of class struggle. These attacks proved effective, and since the organization itself was unwieldy and subject to internal divisions, it rapidly disintegrated after 1920; Bogdanov retired from the cultural front in 1921. The ideas of the Proletkul't lived on, however, in a succession of movements— the Smithy, October, *Na postu,* VAPP, RAPP, and eventually, under Stalin, the Union of Soviet Writers, which transformed them into the doctrine of socialist realism. For all these groups, in opposition to the Proletkul't, the worker-artist unquestioningly followed the specific directives of the Communist Party.

The futurists suffered outrageous attacks from these groups in the mid- and late-1920's. But during the early part of the decade, no single literary group was strong enough to dominate the literary scene. Nor did the party, which had reservations about them all, directly control literary development. Lenin had even less personal sympathy for the futurists than for the Proletkul't, and he directly objected to Lunacharsky's allowing Mayakovsky's works to be published in what he considered to be large editions. But because the futurists were not as large and potentially as competitive a movement as the Proletkul't had been, initially they met with little direct pressure from the Communist Party. They managed to survive most of the first post-revolutionary decade partly because of the benign acceptance of Lunacharsky, and the Communist Party's refusal to dictate the direction of the arts. But perhaps most importantly, the futurists were aided by something which they strongly criticized as a defeat of the ideals of the revolution—the temporary retreat from communism under the NEP (New Economic Policy), instituted in 1921 by Lenin. Attempting to revitalize the war-torn economy, the Bolsheviks reluctantly agreed to the reinstatement of private capitalism in parts of the economy.

Under the NEP, private publishers, magazines, and literary patrons flourished. At the height of the NEP there were 220 private publishers in Moscow alone. This situation allowed the futurists greater access to print than they had enjoyed since the revolution. They were able to publish their works and theories in a series of independent magazines which, however, grew increasingly less viable over the course of the decade. They founded LEF (an abbreviation for the Left Front of the Arts) in 1923. It lasted until 1925. *Novyi LEF (New Left)* followed in 1927, to meet its demise in 1928. And ultimately REF (for the *Revolutionary Front of the Arts*) made a brief appearance from 1929–1930. During the NEP, the liberalization of soviet relationships with other countries also contributed to the writers' and artists' opportunities to publish their works abroad, as well as to travel and encounter the works of other avant-garde movements. Mayakovsky met members of the Berlin dada movement and was particularly impressed by Heartfield and Grosz. Later, he met the surrealists, and was responsive to their "temperament," though he expressed doubts about their politics. The period of liberalization and economic independence came to an end, however, as the soviet state became stronger. The NEP terminated in 1927; the next year the first five-year plan began. By 1930, there were only a few publishing concerns, and all were under the direct control of the Communist Party.

During the era of the NEP, the futurists enjoyed their most creative period. Ironically, however, although they profited from the liberalism of the NEP and from the party's initial non-interference in the arts, the specter of a re-emergence of elements of capitalism signified to the futurists a continuation of the life of the old order. Rather than maintaining its vanguard position, the communist leadership tolerated a renewed conservatism in social and cultural life, a conservatism that might have reflected the personal tastes of men such as Lenin, but which nevertheless strengthened the power of *byt*—the dreaded inertia of the routine of daily life that was the primary enemy of Mayakovsky and the futurists. To the futurists, the return of the old academics and critics of literature and the arts to positions of power in the new order, and the adoption of the aesthetic conventions of bourgeois realism as the basis of proletarian art, were signs of the victory of *byt* over the revolutionary potential of the new society. The futurists found themselves again attempting to sustain a vanguard position in a society increasingly antagonistic to their innovative efforts, a society they believed to be betrayed by the failure of the leadership of the Bolshevik party. They found themselves fighting the same aesthetic battles they had fought before the revolution, only now in the name of what they believed to be the interests of their communist society.

The primary article of faith of this politicized futurism was the traditional avant-garde belief that activist art should fundamentally alter social behavior and consciousness—in particular, the individual's manner of perceiving and expressing the new world. For the futurists, this necessitated formal innovation in art. Describing the art of the Proletkul't and its successors as merely the introduction of new content in old forms, they claimed that the workers who were the heroes of the realistic tales were, in effect, bourgeois characters in proletarian costume. Instead of individuals who exemplified the dialectics of the revolutionary struggle, futurists charged, the most popular creations of the proletarian writers' movement were idealized, quasi-allegorical figures who displayed a new set of "universals," the ahistorical traits of human behavior that were the basis of bourgeois fiction.

The pages of *LEF* constantly reaffirmed the futurists' belief that new forms of expression enabled new content to be expressed. Only through innovative language could the new content of revolutionary culture be liberated from the restraints and contamination of old ways of thinking. Rather than merely repeating the pre-revolutionary polemics against bourgeois literary practice, however, the futurists sought to root their innovation in the needs of the new society. They justified their experimentation as an outgrowth of the scientific and technical spirit of the workers' state. These concerns strengthened the futurists' alliance with the formalist critics, for both groups sought to justify their studies of literature and innovation in terms of a Marxist theory of production. *LEF* became the rallying point for their theories and poems, as well as for the work of artists in other fields, such as Eisenstein and Rodchenko, who designed many of the covers of *LEF* and *Novyi LEF* and collaborated with Mayakovsky on his advertising work and his most innovative books of poems. Such collaboration constituted the moment of the most fruitful conjunction between the two underlying rationales of avant-garde activism—scientific development and political praxis. The writers and artists called themselves the scientists, engineers, and workers of their particular fields, who studied the means of production of their arts, then attempted to alter the processes of the art activity in order to achieve their stated aims most efficiently. N. F. Chuzhak declared in the first issue of *LEF*, for example, that art was a "method of constructing life" which had to be seen as a part of "the series of other means of constructing life."[12] For Sergei Eisenstein, as for many contemporary and subsequent artists, the artist was to be regarded as a *producer* of life, not an imitator of something merely given and static. In *The Film Sense*, he noted,

> In the actual method of creating images, a work of art must reproduce that process whereby, *in life itself*, new images are built up in the human consciousness and feelings.[13]

These artists and critics paid particular attention to two primary determinants of literary production: the linguistic elements of the literary creation, and the situation of the audience. In order to expand the possibilities of expression, they analyzed the operations of all forms of discourse. Even though their primary concern was with literature, they insisted on the de-aesthetization of poetic language by stressing the continuity of all forms of linguistic activity—prose, poetry, journalism, and everyday speech.

> We are working for a phonetic organization of the language, for po-lyphony of rhythm, for the simplification of verbal construction, for the invention of new thematic devices. This work represents no purely aesthetic strivings, but rather a laboratory for the best rendition of contemporary facts. We are no pontificating creators, but master agents of the social order.[14]

The futurists maintained, however, that the formal concerns of art were never independent of the content. Instead of maintaining a concept of an illustrative, realistic content favored by the proletarian writers, however, they defined the work's content, or subject, as its destination—its goal and audience. In so doing, they emphasized that the work was a *process* designed to reach a particular destination. Consequently, formal and thematic concerns were secondary to the destination, but were, nonetheless, the essential means of achieving it. The futurist program elucidated in *New Left* was thus to study the actual social destination of the art object, the effect it should produce, then to analyze how such an effect could be achieved most completely and economically.[15] Their basic assumption was that the artwork was determined by the audience, but the audience itself was still undergoing change. Formal innovation which expanded the audience's receptive and expressive capabilities thus helped that audience achieve its destiny. The work submitted to the people's needs just as, in turn, the people would discover themselves through the formal processes of the work.

As the decade progressed, efforts to make futurism the paradigmatic art of the workers' state were increasingly criticized by party leaders, Trotsky and Lenin in particular, and by the proletarian writers. In what is perhaps the most insightful critique in pre- and post-revolutionary Russian literature, *Literature and Revolution,* Trotsky pointed out that the extremism of futurism revealed both its bourgeois-bohemian origins and its idealistic attempts to graft itself onto the workers' revolution. Not unsympathetic to them, Trotsky admitted that formalist innovation was a necessary rebellion against the literary traditions of the old order (a rebellion, however, that would have been recuperated into the literary hierarchy, as so many previous avant-garde rebellions had, had it not been for the Russian

Revolution), but that the conditions which provoked the rebellion no longer existed. Furthermore, the proletariat, lacking the futurists' ties to literary tradition, had little use for their battles. The fact that proletarian writers continued to use bourgeois forms of creation was, according to Trotsky, not a sign of the continuation of the old mentality, but the appropriation of an established artistic tool useful for the workers' efforts to develop their own culture. And while he agreed that significant lessons were to be learned from the linguistic investigation of the futurists and formalists, he cautioned against extrapolating from such experiments to project a utopic vision of the future. In his critique of the futurist program, Trotsky provided us with one of the most perceptive insights into the entire avant-garde venture.

> The problems raised by the theorists of the "Lef" group about art and a machine industry, about art which does not embellish life, but forms it, about conscious influence upon the development of language and systematic formation of words, about biomechanics as the education of the activities of man in the spirit of the greatest rationality, and therefore of the greatest beauty—are all problems which are extremely significant and interesting from the point of view of building a Socialist culture.
>
> Unfortunately, the "Lef" colors these problems by a Utopian sectarianism. Even when they mark out correctly the general trend of development in the field of art or life, the theorists of "Lef" anticipate history and contrast their scheme or their prescription with that which is. They thus have no bridge to the future. They remind one of anarchists who anticipate the absence of government in the future, and who contrast their scheme with the politics, parliaments and several other realities that the present ship of State must, in their imagination, of course, throw overboard. . . .
>
> To tear out of the future that which can only develop as an inseparable part of it, and to hurriedly materialize this partial anticipation in the present day dearth and before the cold footlights, is only to make an impression of provincial dilettantism.[16]

Trotsky continued by stating that this utopianism and dilettantism were the products of a pre-revolutionary bourgeois mind, critical of its class and society, and desperately trying to join itself to the revolution which it had the fortune to "fall into." Because the workers "stepped in the Revolution, while Futurism fell into it,"[17] the workers had a truer sense of history and evolution and realized that the future could only be the product of material change. Trotsky's criticism sought to develop a clearer idea of historical processes in the artists of his day—including the proletarian writing movement. He saw no particular need for the development of proletarian culture since he anticipated the success of the world-wide revolution and the inevitable development of a classless socialist society in which a workers' art would be irrelevant. As a consequence, he favored an open, but critical, competition among the various literary movements, none of which would be allowed to claim exclusive rights to represent the new culture.

Lenin also felt that proletarian culture was not an imminent reality, but only because the proletariat had been prevented from developing the capabilities necessary to create it. He hoped that through an extended period of training the workers would learn the craft to create their own art, a craft based on the highest products of existing—bourgeois—art. A fervent admirer of traditional art, Lenin had no patience with the avant-garde of literature, and claimed that it was unintelligible to the workers. Thus, he branded Mayakovsky's poem "150,000,000" an expression of "hooligan communism."[18]

Finally, the most strident, and ultimately destructive criticism originated not with the party leaders, but with the writers of the proletarian movement, specifically the Na Postu (On Guard) group. Denouncing the futurists and all formalism as vestiges of bourgeois art, they asserted that only those works which directly articulated the viewpoint of the proletariat and which were created by proletarian writers could advance the revolution. They declared that the fellow travellers (such as Pasternak, Babel, and the writers of the Serapion Brotherhood and Pereval group), and, by extension, the futurists, worked against the revolution and that any call for an open competition among writers that allowed such subversive groups to practice was itself an expression of "reactionary utopianism." Proletarian culture, they argued, would develop only under the direct guidance of the VAPP (the All-Russian Association of Proletarian Writers, which the Na Postu group dominated).

The stridency and the strength of this group eventually forced the Communist Party to take an official stand on the situation of literature in the new society. Though the party leaders, from Lenin on down, had generally rejected the idea of direct party control in cultural affairs and had doubted the possibility of immediately creating a viable proletarian culture, by 1925 when the Central Committee of the party issued its report, "On Party Policy in the Field of Imaginative Literature," the balance of power within the party and cultural organizations had changed. Lenin was dead; Trotsky was in growing disfavor. Lunacharsky and Voronsky, the liberal editor of

Red Virgin Soil (the primary party-sponsored literary journal, which gave substantial support to the fellow travellers), were both losing their previous positions of authority. Bukharin, then editor of *Pravda* and a leading theoretician of the party, wrote the document. A foe of Trotsky, and in direct opposition to the late Lenin, he favored the policies of the proletarian writers and believed, as Stalin would later, that the party should concern itself primarily with solidifying the revolution within the Soviet Union at the expense of the world-wide movement. This meant that in cultural matters proletarian arts should be directly stimulated by the party. The 1925 document, however, was the result of apparent compromise among the opposing factions. On the surface, it reiterated the party's policy of non-intervention and several times stated that the principle of free competition among all groups, including the fellow travellers, should be encouraged. In addition, it rebuked the proletarian writers' excessive claim to be the sole representatives of the new society. But, in effect, the document stated that the future of the Soviet Union's culture was proletarian literature and art, and that while other groups could now exist, it was because they might make valuable contributions to this privileged movement. Fellow travellers were to be won over to proletarian culture, not eliminated. The proletarian writers, on the other hand, were to be directly aided by the party, both morally and materially.

As a result of this party pronouncement and the growing strength of the VAPP, which became the RAPP (the Russian Association of Proletarian Writers) in 1928, the literary scene of the second half of the 1920's was dominated by the proletarian movement. Futurists, fellow travellers, and critics who supported them were viciously attacked and scorned as anti-revolutionary. Literary journals increasingly reflected the proletarian line, and with the emergence of Stalin, the unhappy future of non-proletarian realist writers was insured. The formalists and the futurists who grouped around the declining *Novyi Lef* and *REF* journals were divided among themselves over the degree of their political commitment and were especially vulnerable to the RAPP attacks. The end of the futurist movement was signalled first by Mayakovsky's and Osip Brik's breaking away from the non-political elements of the futurists in 1928 to form *REF*, then, in 1930, by Mayakovsky's joining RAPP in his effort to retain access to the masses for whom he wrote. This effort was not successful, however, and Mayakovsky's suicide shortly thereafter was only the most dramatic symbol of the end of futurism in Russia.

Vladimir Mayakovsky

Of all the futurist poets, Mayakovsky was the most politically committed. He devoted his poetic talents and social energy to what he saw as the interests of the masses and the new soviet state. Believing himself to be the revolutionary poet of the soviet people, he was extremely dependent upon their acceptance. Mayakovsky was, therefore, excessively pained by the proletarian writers' calumnious charges that he had betrayed the masses and the revolution he championed. Barely able to publish or read his poetry, subjected to constant condemnation or official disregard, and finally encountering unsympathetic and uncomprehending audiences schooled by the proletarian doctrines, Mayakovsky committed suicide in 1930 at the age of thirty-six, evidently believing that the future he had envisioned had foundered on the rocks of mediocrity and pettiness. To Mayakovsky, who had frequently depicted his poetic life as a tragedy, this last impasse must have confirmed his belief that only in future generations would his worth as a poet of the revolution be recognized and his deserved fame be accorded by the people and the state.

Ironically, Mayakovsky's official recognition came only five years later when Stalin stated (in words not without their own dark irony): "Mayakovsky was and is the most talented poet of the Socialist epoch, and indifference to his memory is a crime."[19] As a result of Stalin's declaration, Mayakovsky was rapidly acclaimed by the soviet literary bureaucracy, the same people who had hounded him in his last days. His works were published in bowdlerized editions of many thousands, his poetry was taught in schools throughout the Soviet Union, and his writings made the subject of a burgeoning critical industry. Furthermore, by 1950 "in the Soviet Union ten steamboats, three tanks, a bomber, a submarine, a subway station, a museum, a region in Georgia, a village in Armenia, a mountain in the Pamirs, various parks, theaters, and streets, as well as a major square in Moscow, [were] named for Mayakovsky."[20] But just as the society of which he was the poet laureate was radically different from the one he had envisioned, the Mayakovsky of the official editions, of the statues, of the pedestrian and regimented literary criticism, only obliquely resembles the futurist poet whose private and public life displayed a series of unresolved and perhaps unresolvable conflicts between avant-garde visionary aesthetics and political praxis.

For Mayakovsky, avant-garde art and the Bolshevik revolution together promised the emergence of a new social order, a new art and

role for the artist, and, most essentially, a new personal life. His work
is the expression of the dream and drama of a visionary ego attempting to overcome the personal alienation so endemic to modern culture. In Mayakovsky's case, this was to be achieved through personal
union with a vanguard poetic movement, a communist society, and,
always, women who provided personal acceptance and who represented new possibilities of liberated behavior. But Mayakovsky's life
and death also illustrate the vicissitudes of the constant battle between an idealized vision and actuality, between the demands of the
imagination and immediate political praxis, and between the avant-
garde venture and established aesthetic conventions, particularly in
a developing nation. For the poet, these battles always take place in
the present moment, and if Mayakovsky's whole life and poetry can
truly be called an expression of *futurism,* his personal and public
struggles dramatically reveal the problem of desiring to be in advance
of one's time.

Indeed, at the heart of Mayakovsky's life and work is a sense of
extreme ambivalence, of being caught between a negative present
moment and an ideal, yet unrealized, future. The pain of personal
and social unfulfillment moved him to alternate expressions of self-
pity and rebellion, and of lyricism and rage. His criticism of the
present and his invocation of a redemptive future were spoken in the
name of both himself and his fellow sufferers. The public roles of
spokesman, prophet, and rebel—and, after the October revolution, of
revolutionary worker—signified to him an immediate means of overcoming his alienation and gave him the strength to continue his
struggle into the future. Consequently, Mayakovsky's work, though
frequently intensely personal, always implied its social extension,
and, in effect, oscillated between an individualistic and collectivist
perspective. At times, the public's suffering, the revolution, and the
soviet promise seemed only the objectification and intensification of
Mayakovsky's magnificent ego. At others, his personal life appeared
to embody the voice of collective desires and labor. In fact, in Mayakovsky's poetry, it is difficult to distinguish between signs of the
inflation of his ego, and its submission to the whole. In both cases
Mayakovsky the poet becomes Mayakovsky the people. Their suc-
cesses were his and their failures diminished his own hopes. At the
same time, he ascribed his own weaknesses to those of his society, so
that when he doubted himself, he condemned the entire state. As a
consequence, when a wedge was driven between himself and his
audience, he lost both self-assurance and external encouragement
and, therefore, faith in his ideal of personal and collective destiny.

Remarkably early in his life, Mayakovsky felt the need for radical social change and identified with the forces that seemed to promise it. Born in Georgia in 1893, the son of a forest ranger of noble descent, Mayakovsky had already participated in a protest against the murder of a Bolshevik activist by the age of twelve. After his father's death, the family moved to Moscow and fell into grinding poverty. There, he readily took up political activities. He joined the Bolsheviks at age thirteen and was arrested at age fourteen for carrying illegally printed political pamphlets. He had been arrested twice more by age fifteen, serving seven months in jail, five of them in solitary confinement. During his imprisonment, he began writing poetry seriously (apparently having written some terrible political verses while in high school). Once released, he moved away from party politics and began studying art at Moscow's College of Painting and Fine Arts. There he met David Burlyuk in 1911 and became associated with the futurist movement. Declared by Burlyuk a poetic genius, Mayakovsky concentrated on writing poetry, contributing to the manifesto "A Slap in the Face of Public Taste" (1912) and publishing, in 1913, his first chap book—a cycle of four poems appropriately entitled "I." This was followed later that year by the performance of his verse play, *Vladimir Mayakovsky: A Tragedy*.

This play, a futurist drama (though quite similar to expressionist theater), introduced a series of images that would remain staple features in all his subsequent work. Its main theme is Mayakovsky the poet, the lyric voice of the suffering populace and the martyr for their pain. Surrounded by bizarre characters meant to be both representatives of the city's victims and extensions of the poet's soul—"the old man with scrawny black cats (several thousand years old)," "the man with one eye and one leg," "the man with one ear," "a man without a head," "a man with two kisses," "a woman with a tiny tear,"—the poet bears his soul on a platter "to be dined on by future years," and announces that he "may well be / the last poet there is."[21] This poet, the "king of lights," is both prophet and martyr, and, in the play's prologue, he offers to reveal new souls to those who "ripped the silence / you who howled / because the nooses of noon were too tight"; then the poet will hobble off to die.

This public expression of avant-garde agonism—the poet's simultaneous act of self-sacrifice and consecration, his acceptance of the necessity of martyrdom as the price of his gift of articulation and transformation of the people's pain—was repeated throughout Mayakovsky's poetic career. In the two acts of the play that follow the prologue, it dominates the symbolic action. Surrounded by the grotesques who suffer from love and the loss of love, from the oppressive rule of "things," and from poverty, the poet who identifies with them and embraces them declares:

> I'm a poet.
> I've wiped out the differences
> between faces like mine and those of strangers.
> I have sought out my sisters in the pus of morgues.
> I have kissed the sick most exquisitely.
> But today,
> on a bonfire's yellow flames,
> hiding more deeply the tears of the seas,
> I'll throw both the sisters' shame
> and the wrinkles of gray-haired mothers.
> On plates from fancy salons,
> we'll chomp at you, meat, for centuries!

(p. 27)

But this act of transforming pain into the substance of rebellion, while frightening to the representative of the established order ("the conventional young man"), inevitably leads more to self-sacrificial consumption than to active revolution. In Act II the poet soon recognizes that his identification with the people's pain brings him the excessive burden of anguish and lost love—tears and kisses—that he must carry for them. His heroic self, having adopted a toga and laurel wreath, must now stand up under the weight of carrying the tears to the far north, to the source of the sea of infinite anguish.

> I thought
> I'd be joyful:
> with eyes clear and bright,
> I would sit on the throne
> like a pampered Greek.
> But no!
> Never,
> dear roads,
> will I forget your thin legs
> and the gray hairs of the northern rivers.
> And so today
> I'll go out through the city,
> leaving

> shred after shred of my tattered soul
> on the spears of houses.
>
> (p. 36)

The new poet who comes down off Parnassus finds himself both one of the people and separate from them. To articulate their present pain and to be a prophet in advance of their transformation, the poet must ready himself to be both accepted and rejected in his time. And correspondingly, the trials he undergoes are agonizing realities and badges of distinction. This role is, of course, consciously chosen, and throughout Mayakovsky's poetry the poet is portrayed as a doomed prophet (John the Baptist is a recurring image), or, in a mixture of self-pity and egotism, as the self-sacrificial revolutionary leader. (Christ, the messiah, is another frequent image.)

Soon after *Vladimir Mayakovsky: A Tragedy* appeared, Mayakovsky took his futurist show on the road with a "futurist tour" of Russia in 1913–1914. For a vanguard poet seeking an audience and proclaiming his mission, each reading brought him proof of both his identification with the people and his isolation. He attacked and scandalized his primary audience, the bourgeoisie and traditional poets, and by their rejection, his avant-garde status was confirmed. But while he declared himself at one with the poor and the poor in spirit whose voices were silent and who were not a part of the literary tradition he disrupted, Mayakovsky was also aware that his poetry had yet to find an audience beyond his fellow futurists, and that in spite of his participation in a vanguard movement, he was essentially alone. This radical alienation from contemporary culture and the sensed isolation caused by being in advance of the future ideal are experienced to some degree by all avant-garde writers. But they dominate all of Mayakovsky's works. This condition was alternately regretted and brandished: it was experienced as an ever-present feeling of incompletion and as a mark of uniqueness.

Perhaps no other early work better illustrates these dynamics of desire and doubt than "A Cloud in Trousers" (1915). A four-part poem with a prologue, it describes the poet's state of intense personal anguish and his antagonistic relationship to his culture. In a preface to the second edition of the poem, published after the revolution, Mayakovsky asserted, perhaps hyperbolically, that the four parts of the poem represented the wholesale rejection of the pre-revolutionary society. The sections declare respectively: "Down with your love!"; "Down with your art!"; "Down with your social order!"; and "Down with your religion!"[22] Yet characteristically, while the poem ranges widely in its attacks on bourgeois society as a whole, the immediate source of the poet's despair and anger is not social, but personal—his rejection by two women, both named Maria. For Mayakovsky, the personal and social dimensions cannot be separated. Thus he takes the rejection of the first Maria as a sign of the corrupting values of bourgeois forms of love, and he reads the second Maria's rejection as the failure of a woman to provide protection from social persecution. The first leads to a general condemnation of society and transforms personal anguish into a poetics of emotional and social revolt. The second, however, leads from social to personal defeat and finally to a vision of the indifference of the cosmos to the poet's plight. In effect, the poem oscillates between expressions of pain and anger, rejection and rebellion.

Although the pain of rejection is antecedent to the rebellious response, the poem's prologue exhibits a spirit of dramatic aggression directed against its society, only then to shift in part one to a sense of frustration and despair. But in part two, the poet once more strikes a note of rebellion, and later falls again into doubt and rejection. This pattern occurs three times in the work, each time in response to a different personal or public event, each time shifting the focus of the poet's hopes and fears. In the midst of these conflicts and upheavals, the poet seeks to establish his identity as a poet, lover, and social activist.

These aesthetic, personal, and social challenges constitute the three main themes of the poem. The first is Mayakovsky's avant-garde stance toward poetry and the values of his society. The poem exhibits many of the traditional avant-garde posturings—praise of the new, of youth, of aggressive art, and scorn of the bourgeoisie, of traditional art, and of religion. Like so many avant-garde poets, Mayakovsky flaunts his self-proclaimed role of prophet, exhibiting in the process a striking blend of egotism, nihilism, and idealism. This poetic role, however, is developed in direct response to the other two foci of the poem, Mayakovsky's personal needs and social desires, the poet as lover and prophet.

The prologue of the poem[23] most clearly embodies avant-garde bombast. It begins with a direct and contemptuous address to the audience and asserts the poet's uniqueness and privileges.

> Your thoughts,
> dreaming on a softened brain,
> like an over-fed lackey on a greasy settee,

> with my heart's bloody tatters I'll mock again;
> impudent and caustic, I'll jeer to superfluity.
>
> Of grandfatherly gentleness I'm devoid,
> there's not a single grey hair in my soul!
> Thundering the world with the might of my voice,
> I go by—handsome,
> twenty-two-year-old.

But though these heart's tatters may mock, they also reveal the poet's tenderness, love, and pain. Ill-suited to traditional lyricism and refined feelings, the heart finds its direct expression as the poet turns himself inside out "and nothing but human lips become!" (p. 99). However raw, the lips can sing of tenderness as well as anger—a tenderness that reveals the poet to be "extraordinarily gentle, / not a man, but—a cloud in trousers!" (p. 99). An outsider, this new poet directs his gentleness to individuals formerly excluded from lyric poetry. Not to "flowery Nice," but to "men, bedridden as a hospital, / to women, worn-out as a proverb" (p. 99), will his song be addressed.

The first part of the tetraptych reveals that the origin of Mayakovsky's provocative stance was not any particular social critique, but merely having been stood up by a woman from four p.m. until midnight who, when she did appear, announced that she intended to marry another man—a decision Mayakovsky ascribes to her need for bourgeois financial and personal security. The first half of this section details the poet's growing anxiety and frustration as he awaits her and receives her message. In imagery as intense as anything he was ever to write again (equalled perhaps only by a similar description of the pain of isolation and jealousy in "About That" in 1922), the personal voice builds itself up into a state of extreme desperation, and eventually cries out like a vulnerable child for its mama. But with the pain grows anger, and his cries for help alternate with threats of imminent revenge as an uncontrollable emotion tries to burst from him. Too small to contain this inner power, his body and identity are rent as a new self and poetic voice simultaneously emerge.

> And I feel
> that "I"
> is for me too shallow.
> Someone bursts out of me and won't be smothered.
> . . . . .

> Every word,
> even platitudes,
> vomited by my reeking mouth-hell
> hurl themselves out, like naked prostitutes
> from a burning brothel.
>
> (pp. 103–104)

This threatened "I" realizes it is no longer in control of itself and at most can only shriek its pain. "Mother! / I can't sing. / In the church of my heart the choir is on fire!" (p. 105).

A few lines later, however, at the start of section two, the poet has gained control of his fire and language. Now, he channels them into activist discourse, damning the established order and lifting his voice for the silent ones, the common people he mentioned in the prologue. Once again, avant-garde bravado and nihilism reign:

> Glorify me!
> I and the great am no compare.
> I place "nihil"
> on everything that's been done before.
>
> (p. 105)

In this section Mayakovsky justifies his verse, his poetic subjects, and his prophecy. Recognizing that the masses have no voice of their own and no tradition of poetry sympathetic to them, he finds his calling: "the tongueless street twists and writhes,— / having nothing with which to talk or wail" (p. 106). When a sound does emerge from the street, like the poet's previous agony, it is barely articulate; at most a word or two like "bastard" or "borcht" is ejected. But instead of stating that these words are unsuitable to poetry, as bourgeois poets maintained, and trying to make the street speak in acceptable poetic language, Mayakovsky insists that a new poetry be built on them. The old poetry of Homer, Goethe, and Ovid is to be rejected, for they never created images of the common people and their experience; they never depicted the reality of misery compared to which their creations are mere fantasies. "I know— / a nail in my boot that's hurting / is nightmarish more than a fantasy of Goethe" (p. 108). Instead, poetry should be formed by and with the people. "We ourselves are the creators of blazing hymns— / in the roar of factories and laboratories" (p. 108).

This is a poetic manifesto, one that, however self-serving the personal pity and dramatization, was to remain the basis of all of Mayakovsky's later works. Here, the shift from personal concern to the

prophetic voice of the sacrificial, yet daring poet comes to a climax
in the last lines of section two.

> I,
> laughed at by tribal contemporaries,
> like a lanky
> joke obscene,
> see coming over time's mountain-peaks,
> one whom nobody sees.
>
> There, where man's bereft of vision,
> heading the hungry surging,
> in the thorny-crown of revolution
> nineteen-sixteen's emerging.
>
> And I amongst you—am its prophet;
> wherever pain is—there am I;
> on every single tear that's shed
> I myself have crucified.

(pp. 109–119)

Although this mixture of self-pity, agonism, and avant-garde predi-
lection for prophecy appears in many other avant-garde writers, they
are quintessential expressions of Mayakovsky's self-image. For this
willed identification with the people and with history, even in the
midst of his flagrantly bohemian futurist tours, denotes Mayakovsky's essential poetic and political effort.

   In the first section of the poem, the poet described his soul being
trampled on by others who oppressed him; in the second he has
turned his victimization into active rebellion, rending his own soul
for others. The third section develops more explicitly the political
dimension, though characteristically, Mayakovsky emerges larger
than life, embodying the masses' power. It opens with a personal
account of Mayakovsky's pleasure at his liberation from the ways and
the poetic practice of his society and depicts him strutting alone,
Napoleon tied on a leash in front of him, the earth submitting to
him. But suddenly, Mayakovsky intuits a brutal repression of this
freedom. Now he urges his fellow rebels:

> Hey, passers-by, take your hands from your pockets—
> pick up a bomb, a knife or a stone,
> and those without hands, or arms in their sockets—
> come and batter with bare brows alone!

(p. 113)

His images refer to the commune of 1871, and in naming his oppo-
nent as General Gallifet, who put down the commune, Mayakovsky
introduces an intimation of defeat. His calls to the crowd to defend
themselves—like his urging of an initial revolution—prove inadequate. He is not heeded, and the dream of change that dominates
sections two and three dissipates; he is forced to admit "Nothing will
happen" (p. 114), and to retire to a bar to huddle with the others.
Watched over by a third Maria—the Virgin—whose picture hangs on
the wall, he falls back upon biblical imagery, and admits that the
revolution he, as prophet-saviour, announced, has been rejected by
the masses, who have chosen a Barrabas of materialism instead. His
only remaining hope is that he may serve as an apostle of eventual
change.

Section four then shifts to the poet's demand that another woman,
the second Maria, allow him to come in off the streets which have
proven so inhospitable, streets now peopled by those who cannot
understand his words. But again, he is rejected by a woman, so he
withdraws into self-pity which, in turn, breeds defiance. Wounded
and dying, he approaches heaven and God, the Father, whom he
berates for creating the depraved love that now rules society, and
demands that creation be re-made, this time as a pleasurable, if
blasphemous place—a merry-go-round on the tree of good and evil,
St. Peter dancing the kikupu, beautiful girls on the boulevards. When
God declines the suggestion, Mayakovsky responds that he too is an
angel and pulls a knife, threatening to carve up this God and his
creation. But finally, Mayakovsky recognizes that this rebellion will
also be abortive, for like women and the people, God and the heavens
ignore him. At the end, the poet is left with a vision of the universe
sleeping on its tick-infected ear.

Mayakovsky was only too aware that although he spoke "at the top
of [his] voice," he would often remain unheard. The universe, the
masses, the state, and even more tragically, his loves, ignored or rejected him. Rarely did he seem to question the efficacy of his self-
inflation. Rather, he often simply spoke louder, attempting to project
himself in even more grandiose and seductive terms into the lives of
those around him. Nevertheless, acceptance or tolerance rarely
proved sufficient to satisfy his demands and Mayakovsky was left unfulfilled, doubting himself and his world, hoping only that the future
would justify his demands.

Initially, the Russian Revolution appeared to change this situation
radically. No longer did the agonistic self-consumption in the name
of the unrealized future seem necessary. The revolution promised a

collective action in which the poet could directly participate, that would bring about the idealized future. In fact, the immediate engagement in the process of social and individual transformation was extremely important for Mayakovsky, since in his earliest works he could offer no sustained depiction of the ideal world of the future, but could only appeal to the *act* of rebellion. The revolution thus provided a vehicle and a program of actual change. It offered a context for the poet's personal and aesthetic yearnings for a new order. No longer the embattled, isolated, and ultimately doomed prophet, Mayakovsky could project himself as a fellow worker and revolutionary, at one with the Bolshevik vanguard and the masses at large. No longer the defiant shouter of personal needs and collective pain, he was able to imagine his voice intensified as he submerged his ego into the spirit of the masses and became their voice. No longer the self-declared leader of the populace that couldn't hear, he saw himself as their follower, even as he strove to make his poetry a vanguard banner urging them on to further action.

While providing the opportunity for the resolution of many of Mayakovsky's personal conflicts, the revolution also demanded the transformation of the traditional image and role of the poet, the nature of poetry, and the composition of the audience. Mayakovsky's goal was to make his poetry and the futurist movement agents of that transformation. In the days immediately following the revolution Mayakovsky, like the other futurists, vaunted the futurist movement's unique relationship to the forces of change. After all, the futurists had been the major literary voice demanding the total rejection of the art and manners of the old culture. But even though for Mayakovsky the revolution primarily signified a transformation of the spiritual condition of his culture, unlike the other futurists and the fellow travellers, he recognized that poetry also had to work actively for the material alteration of society. He saw that if a spiritual development were to occur, it would depend on the success of the revolution in the material base of society, a society initially beset by civil war, foreign invasions, disease, famine, and severe economic disruption.

During the period of 1918 and 1919, Mayakovsky reconsidered his poetic program. He wrote few poems, and many of the ones he did write were direct agitational or editorial statements in *Iskusstvo Kommuny*, which addressed the needs of the new society. His major innovative work was the comic contemporary morality play *Mystery Bouffe,* a satiric allegory of the collapse of the bourgeois world and the coming of the universal revolution. Though produced by Meyerhold in 1918, it was only performed three times and to no great success.

Success would come in an entirely different genre. By 1920, Mayakovsky had decided to place his poetic and graphic talents at the service of ROSTA, the Russian Telegraphic Agency, which was the main internal propaganda organization of the new state. Working as a publicist for various political, military, economic, and health campaigns, Mayakovsky wrote jingles, slogans, and homiletic poems, as well as drawing posters and cartoons addressed to the workers and peasants. From October 1920 through February 1922, he drew two thousand drawings and 280 posters captioned with his short poems that became famous throughout Russia. To the horror of some of his fellow futurists and the fellow travellers, Mayakovsky declared that these creations constituted one of the high points of his art. The posters included such jingles as this advertisement for a department store:

> Arriving from dachas, towns and villages
> No need to wear out shoes searching—immediately
> In GUM you'll find everything,
> precisely, what you want quickly and cheaply.[24]

Mayakovsky believed that a socially committed poetics, which attempted to teach people the necessity of boiling water during health emergencies, and of freeing themselves from the teachings of the church, as well as the importance of buying state-produced products, had greater meaning than the lyric expressions of private sentiments. Thus, even though he continued to write personal poems, the major thrust of his poetic work during this period was the development of aesthetic activism in direct response to the social demands of the time.

Many of Mayakovsky's more substantive poems in the years immediately following the revolution were concerned with the role of poetry. They served as rallying cries or marches for the military, the workers, and the poets. The pre-revolutionary futurist demand for new forms in the arts became, in "Order No. 2 to the Army of the Arts" (1921), a rejection of all poetic styles—including that of "little futurists"—not commensurate with the advances in soviet industry. The poem announces that the creation of the new state and economic order needs new workers, and poets no longer can be "long haired preachers," but must become workers along with the coal miners, electrical workers, and mechanics. If the entire state calls out for necessary resources, the poets must evaluate their participation.

> While we dawdle and quarrel
> in search of fundamental answers,
> all things yell:
> "give us new forms!"
> There are no fools today
> to crowd, open-mouthed, round a "maestro"
> and await his pronouncement.
> Comrades,
> give us a new form of art—
> an art
> that will pull the republic out of the mud.[25]

Throughout the 1920s, Mayakovsky maintained that the futurist movement in poetry, along with the constructivists in art and the avant-garde in theater, music, and film, would provide those new forms. His sponsorship of *LEF* and his support for the less explicitly political members of the avant-garde earned him the distrust and condemnation of the proletarian writers and much of the Communist Party. But to a great extent Mayakovsky's own work became less dependent on the experimental techniques of his earlier futurist creations. There are fewer neologisms, strained metaphors, and syntactical disruptions in much of the work of the twenties (even though poems like "About That" are extremely complex and opaque to most readers unfamiliar with the details of his private life).

In general, the new forms Mayakovsky sought to create after the revolution were attempts to form and speak to a new audience. According to Mayakovsky, the avant-garde poet could no longer be content to sell the products of his alienated and aesthetically advanced sensibility to the bourgeoisie and nobility that he berated. Rather, the poet had to write to a mass audience of workers and peasants whose literacy was low and who had no familiarity with the poetic traditions that had been the basis of many of the literary battles and innovations before the revolution. This meant becoming as much an impersonal member of the working masses as a vanguard creator. It meant both seeking new forms and, as he stated several times, wilfully strangling part of the poetic talent that he had developed before the revolution. The futurist-as-ROSTA-functionary became the model of personal union with the creation of a new reality. In characteristically hyperbolic style—yet without frivolous intent—Mayakovsky wrote in his 1925 poem "Back Home!" that poetry should be judged in accordance with any other social activity.

I want
　　　　the Gosplan to sweat
　　　　　　　　　　in debate,
assigning me
　　　　　　goals a year ahead.
.　　.　　.　　.
I want
　　　　the factory committee
　　　　　　　　　　to lock
my lips
　　　　when the work is done.
I want
　　　　the pen to be on a par
　　　　　　　　　　with the bayonet;
and Stalin
　　　　　　to deliver his Politbureau
reports
　　　　about verse in the making
as he would about pig iron
　　　　　　　　　　and the smelting of steel.
　　　　　　　　　　　　(Blake, pp. 187, 189)

The desired union of personal and poetic identity with the collectivity was, however, no simple matter. Mayakovsky was well aware that both submission of his ego to an impersonal mass and the masses' acceptance of him and his poetry were problematic matters. The poem "Back Home!" is an intensely personal work chronicling Mayakovsky's lugubrious return from a depressing reading tour in the United States and Europe—a trip in which his money was stolen and his distaste for the bourgeois life intensified. In the poem he expresses his anticipation that by rejoining the soviet state the irrelevancy he feels as a poet and individual will be resolved. But the original ending of the poem[26] did not mention Stalin's recognition of the importance of his work. Instead, it stated:

I want to be understood by my native land,
but if I'm not understood—
　　　　　　　　　　well again,
over my native land
　　　　　　　　I'll pass on the slant
as passes
　　　　obliquely the rain.

It is a great leap from this expression of self-doubt to the demand that Stalin report to the Politbureau on Mayakovsky's work. On the one hand, the change signifies a self-curtailment. Mayakovsky stated that he had plucked from the "paradisical tail" of the first version of the poem all the beautiful feathers, wet with rain, in order to stress the depersonalization of his lyricism.[27] But on the other hand, his demand that he be judged on a par with the bayonet or steel production indicates his desire that his poetry achieve heroic proportions, and be seen as essential to the state. Once again, Mayakovsky's identification with the masses may be read, as his pre-revolutionary poems have been, as the attempt to incorporate the situation of the masses in his personal drama.

This was Trotsky's judgment, for example, of Mayakovsky's poetic venture, in general, and of his folk-epic poem "150,000,000," in particular. This work, published in 1921, depicted the "championship of the world's class-struggle" fought between Ivan, the collective embodiment of the 150,000,000 Soviet people, and Woodrow Wilson, who represented the capitalist world. Written in a broad humorous style, utilizing images from folk literature, it was published anonymously, stating self-contradictorily, "No one is the author of this poem of mine."[28] As Trotsky pointed out, it was not Mayakovsky's submission of self, but rather the inflation of his ego that was most apparent in this work. There was no question whose work it was, nor any doubt that the author "plays the strong man" Ivan. A perceptive critic of Mayakovsky, Trotsky recognized the importance of the revolution to the poet, but also saw that his essentially bohemian individualism poured itself into the proletarian revolution but "did not blend with it."

> Mayakovsky is closer to the dynamic quality of the Revolution and to its stern courage than to the mass character of its heroism, deeds and experiences. Just as the ancient Greek was an anthropomorphist and naively thought of the forces of nature as resembling himself, so our poet is a Mayako-morphist and fills the squares, the streets and fields of the Revolution with his own personality. True, extremes meet. The universalization of one's ego breaks down, to some extent, the limits of one's individuality, and brings one nearer to the collectivity— from the reverse end. But this is true only to a degree.[29]

Trotsky admitted the difficulty of overcoming one's background of bourgeois individualism in order to achieve solidarity with the proletariat. Furthermore, he believed that this was even harder for artists than for intellectuals (such as the leaders of the Bolsheviks, most of whom had bourgeois origins), because the intellectuals could scientifically analyze the objective material conditions upon which the "economic and historico-philosophic" doctrines of the proletarian revolution were based, and thus could act according to those doctrines. The poet, on the other hand, articulated the world of feelings, the inner record of lifelong personal and social experience. This inner life could not be easily re-made purely by scientific analysis, but only by extended personal experience of new conditions.[30] Consequently, Mayakovsky's and the futurists' poetic attempts to champion the revolution were more a bohemian effort to conquer the spiritual problems that shaped their personal and aesthetic past than a means of overcoming the problems which the proletariat and society as a whole faced.

Mayakovsky was fully aware of the party's distrust of him, and of the nature of his difference from the proletariat. Echoing Trotsky's words about futurism's "fall" into communism, he stated in "Back Home!"

> Proletarians
> > arrive at communism
> > > from below—
> by the low way of mines,
> > > sickles,
> > > > and pitchforks—
> but I,
> > from poetry's skies,
> > > plunge into communism.
> > > > (Blake, p. 185)

Though increasingly criticized by the party and the VAPP, Mayakovsky maintained that the revolution he was fighting for was not over and the future he envisioned for all of society would neither restrict the expression of one's ego, nor restrain imaginative and personal development. He saw a society in the midst of transforming itself, and felt that the process of change was still open-ended, for its strategies and goals were not determined in advance. But as the decade wore on, Mayakovsky found it increasingly necessary to fight against the premature closing of options. Nevertheless, revolutionary writing for him had to remain avant-garde writing, which created new images of potential self-creation. And even though one could claim that it was difficult, if not impossible, for avant-garde art to be a leader of proletarian culture, since its premises were so far removed from the indigenous traditions of worker and peasant poetry and songs, it was even more absurd, Mayakovsky believed, to model revolutionary art on the equally foreign tradition of conservative bourgeois realism, as the VAPP sought to do.

The revolutionary leader, whether political or poetic, had to be at one with the people, yet also in advance of them, leading them toward an unachieved, and perhaps as yet unknown future. In 1926, Mayakovsky wrote the humorous, yet serious poem "Conversation with a Tax Collector about Poetry" to justify "the place of the poet in the workers' ranks" (Blake, p. 191). Proclaiming the heavy toll that his search for words and inspiration takes in order for the poet to "move hearts for thousands of years," in this poem the poet states that he is to be judged like any other worker. But he is also a vanguard worker. He is

> simultaneously
> > a leader
> and a servant
> > of the people.
> The working class
> > speaks
> > > through my mouth,
> and we,
> > proletarians,
> > > are drivers of the pen.
>
> > > > (Blake, p. 201)

Though the proletariat was the driver of the pen, neither they nor their self-proclaimed representatives, the VAPP, were able to dictate what the poet should say. Mayakovsky refused merely to translate party doctrine into poetic images or to manipulate a standardized set of socialist-realist images. As he wrote in "To Sergey Esenin" (1925), the poet could not bear it "if a Party man / had been given the chore / Of watching / that your main stress / was on content."[31] Instead, he maintained, as all avant-garde writers have, that the poet must still be the searcher for new content, new images, and new forms. To the tax collector, he insisted: "Poetry— / —all of it!— / is a journey to the unknown" (Blake, p. 195).

Mayakovsky's poetry attempted to keep alive this adventurous spirit of avant-garde imagination. But such a vanguard mentality could be sustained only if the entire society continued in its revolutionary spirit or, as in bourgeois society, merely ignored it. Increasingly, however, Mayakovsky found the revolutionary promise fading. The party's need to solidify the base of the revolution, to improve economic conditions through the NEP and the five-year plan, to develop an orderly educational and cultural progression, and finally to build a stable social structure, all required a period of retrenchment. Mayakovsky's response was to doubt the immediate revolutionary potential of his society, art, and, eventually, himself.

The growth of this doubt is evident in Mayakovsky's post-revolutionary love poetry. As in the works written before the revolution, here he focuses most frequently on the anguish and loss of love, his jealousy and his rejection by women. And just as his earlier works link the personal drama with existing social values, his post-revolutionary lyrics reflect both a personal and political struggle. For example, Mayakovsky publicly held his passionate relationship with Lily Brik (the wife of his friend, collaborator, and publisher, Osip Brik), their ménage à trois, and their efforts to live an ideal love, to be as valid a subject for poetry as more specifically political topics. Mayakovsky's self-dramatization, glorification, and pity were as complexly developed in "About That" as in "A Cloud in Trousers." Whatever the actual story of his and Lily's breakup in 1922 (which was never definitive, since he continued to live with the Briks off and on until his death eight years later), Mayakovsky needed to make public this private drama in his poetry. For at the very least, his poetry was a means of self-criticism as well as social activism. Mayakovsky stated in "Back Home!" that without communism, he felt no love. Here, the failure of their love and life to rise above pre-revolutionary patterns of personal behavior signalled to Mayakovsky the defeat of both the personal and social hope of a new society. The vision of Lily and her *mondaine* salon was distressing, but even more so was Mayakovsky's recognition of his own jealousy, which he read as a sign of his failure to root out bourgeois morality and possessiveness. Unfortunately, the defeat he suffered in this relationship was only one in a series of similar failures.

Mayakovsky's life was marked by a number of failed love affairs, all of which seemed to exhibit the same pattern of a domineering possessiveness alternating with a willed submissiveness and sense of vulnerability. The man who described himself as a roaring lion in the poem "I Love," also pictured himself as a puppy dependent on his mistress in his correspondence with Lily Brik. But this puppy demanded that his lovers live up to his ideal of love. Love, for Mayakovsky, transcended sensual passion, security, marriage, child-rearing, and, theoretically, possessiveness, to become a barely controllable ex-

pression of self-aggrandisement. In the poem "Letter from Paris to
Comrade Kostrov on the Nature of Love," Mayakovsky declared:

> To love
> 　　　means this:
> 　　　　　　to run
> into the depths of a yard
> 　　　　　　　　and, till the rook-black night,
> chop wood
> 　　　with a shining axe,
> giving full play
> 　　　　　to one's strength.
> To love
> 　　　is to break away
> 　　　　　　from bedsheets
> torn by insomnia,
> 　　　　　jealous of Copernicus,
> because he,
> 　　　　rather than Maria Ivanna's husband
> is
> 　　the true
> 　　　　rival.
>
> 　　　　　　　　　　　(Blake, p. 213)

Such energy and ambition, however, could also oppress the object of
his passion if she did not manage to live up to Mayakovsky's desire.

Similar patterns of domination and dependence appear in Mayakovsky's relationship with the masses. His will to submerge himself
in the masses in order to achieve full identity with them and to become an anonymous tool of their destiny was, at the same time, an
attempt to achieve an intensification of self through that communion,
and in the process to receive recognition from the masses as their
voice and leader. The consistent failure of his lovers and the masses
to support this vision invariably plunged Mayakovsky back into self-
pity and depictions of himself as their unappreciated martyr and
prophet, living in advance of the eventual realization of his desire
and subsequent recognition. In "About That,"[32] Mayakovsky accepted his own weakness, but most of his sorrow and rage were directed at the woman who rejected him and at the people of Paris and
Moscow who did not understand him. He could only look toward the
future. He stood alone, yet was a representative of the world's un-
requited love.

I'll wait,
                together with the earth love-bereaved
with the whole human mass
                                    we'll achieve it.
Seven years I've stood,
                        two hundred I'll defy,
just for that waiting,
                    crucified.
On the bridge of the years,
                    derided,
                                scorned,
a redeemer of earthly love I'll be, alone,
I must stand,
                stand up for everyone born,
for everyone I'll moan,
                    for everyone atone.

Finally, at the end of the poem,[33] he appealed to scientists one thousand years hence to resurrect him so that his unfulfilled love might be requited and so that that society itself would be able to love.

Resurrect—
                I want to live out my life!
So that love won't be a lackey there
of livelihood,
                wedlock,
                        lust
                            or worse.
Decrying bed,
                forsaking the fireside chair,
so that love shall flood the universe.

Yet during the 1920's, that ideal future seemed increasingly distant, and, correspondingly, Mayakovsky became increasingly dependent upon it. In spite of his support of the principles of the revolution, he found himself frequently doing battle with the revolution's representatives, both in politics and the arts. The social antagonism and the aesthetic and political activism that had been the mark of his pre-revolutionary futurism now were expressed in his post-revolutionary verse. Soon after the revolution, Mayakovsky discovered that his agit-prop poems were needed for more than teaching and leading the proletariat and peasants to support the new society. They also had to be turned against the rapid growth of a conservative bureaucratic mentality in the new state, for many of the civil servants of the old regime scurried for secure places in the new. At first, Mayakovsky's satirical verses found favor in the party hierarchy. Even Lenin quoted one, "In Re Conferences," praising its social value, though he stated he knew nothing of its artistic merit. But as the decade progressed, first under the bureaucratic chaos of the NEP, then under the regime of Stalin and the first five-year plan, Mayakovsky's criticism of his society grew, while antagonism to his barbs became widespread. His last two efforts at play-writing, *The Bedbug* (1928) and *The Bath House* (1929), were primarily social satires, and though they are among Mayakovsky's most interesting and powerful works, they were almost universally condemned or ignored by the literary-cultural establishment. In fact, this establishment, dominated more and more by the VAPP, then the RAPP, was totally unsympathetic to Mayakovsky's work in general. It attacked his subject matter, his egotism, his style, his association with the futurists, formalists, constructivists, and fellow travellers, and constantly referred to his pre-revolutionary futurist works as if he had written nothing different from them. His work was called vulgar, incomprehensible, bohemian, and hooligan, and in the presses and literary organizations a campaign was mounted to prevent him access to the proletarians for whom, they claimed, he could have no beneficial effect. Mayakovsky found it difficult to publish or to get his plays produced, and he rarely received favorable notice of his work, when he received any notice at all. The 1930 special retrospective exhibition of twenty years of his work was virtually ignored or boycotted by the literary world.

In 1930, shortly after the exhibit opened, Mayakovsky joined the RAPP, an action which was taken by many of his associates as a sign of capitulation. Many of them broke with him, and Mayakovsky quickly discovered that, although the RAPP was happy to boast of his acceptance of their hegemony, they gave him a distrustful and cold reception. Mayakovsky joined the organization because it controlled the media, the major access to the proletariat which he sought to address. But if he continued to seek an identification and intimate union with the people, it was soon apparent that the RAPP would insist on being the mediator of that union, and that his work would be under constant pressure to conform to their literary and ideological dictates.

During the last months of his life, he worked on what would have been a major long poem in praise of the five-year plans. Only the beginning polemical fragment was written. It was to be followed by a lyrical section, but perhaps that lyrical voice only found expression in his suicide note. What remains of the long poem is the part called "At the Top of My Voice," an appeal to the future communist state to find in his works the utopic society's origins. Once again, Mayakovsky could only find sustenance for his effort by projecting a future which would prove his condemned efforts to be valid and in advance of their time. He declared himself a revolutionary worker and poet, participating in a revolution that he now recognized would take centuries to complete. The world he described to his "comrades of posterity" encompassed both the pre-revolutionary society and the dreadfully weakened new state. Referring to the "contemporary petrified shit" and the conditions of tuberculosis, prostitution, and blockades, of which he assumed the future would have no knowledge, he asserted that these were the material conditions that demanded that his poetry develop as it did. (The implied assumption that such conditions existed after the revolution and not solely before it shocked and angered his more righteously dogmatic communist critics.) The poem was Mayakovsky's literary testament. He cited the sacrifices he made when he became a propagandist for boiling water and sanitary practice.

                I,
                    a latrine cleaner
                                    and water carrier,
                by the revolution
                                    mobilized and drafted,
                went off to the front
                                    from the aristocratic gardens
                of poetry
                        the capricious wench. . . . .
                Agitprop
                        sticks
                            in my teeth too,
                and I'd rather
                            compose
                                    romances for you—
                more profit in it
                            and more charm.
                But I
                    subdued
                            myself,
                                setting my heel

> on the throat
>   of my own song.
>   (Blake, pp. 221, 223, 225)

His lyricism stifled, his fame rejected, his only audience in the future, he spoke "as one alive, / I'll address the living. / I'll join you / in the far communist future" (Blake, p. 225).

Mayakovsky, the martyr and prophetic poet, from his earliest writings to his last, reaffirmed his willingness—even his compulsion—to accomplish through the most extreme agonist act the desired union with the revolution, a revolution which only in the far future could transcend the personal and social failings of the present moment and fulfill the desires of the individual's and the collective's imagination. In lines that accept their own death, Mayakovsky prepared the way for his own self-sacrifice.

> Let fame
>   trudge
>   after genius
> like an inconsolable widow
>   to a funeral march—
> die, then, my verse,
>   die like a common soldier,
> like our men
>   who nameless died attacking!
> I don't care a spit
>   for slimy marble.
> We're men of a kind,
>   we'll come to terms about our fame;
> let our
>   common monument be
> socialism
>   built
>   in battle.
>   (Blake, p. 231)

Chapter

VII

Literature, Politics, and the Critical Spirit: Brecht

Bertolt Brecht's formative and most creative years coincided with the rise and decline of surrealism, and although they are different in significant ways, the aesthetic programs and social positions of Brecht and the surrealists shared several important traits. They were, first of all, both shaped by the cultural and political turmoil of Europe between the wars; both, therefore, indicate the difficulty of creating and sustaining an activist, innovative art in a changing political context. The works of Brecht and the surrealists also share a critical attitude toward capitalist society; and because both were allied with the communist movement, Brecht and the surrealists experienced, to varying degrees, the conflict between the avant-garde aesthetic vision and the rigid aesthetic doctrine the Communist Party held during the 1930's.

Although he was not an extreme innovator, Brecht was closer to the avant-garde than to the more traditional political writers of the period. Like the writers of the various avant-garde movements, Brecht believed his work to be an art of change which responded to developing social conditions and acted in concert with the historically progressive tendencies within his society, particularly political and scientific critical thought. He explicitly developed new forms of literary expression appropriate to these social changes. For his works were intended to alter the audience's customary patterns of experiencing both art and their world and to help, in the process, form a new "man," a new audience, and a new society. However, Brecht's work and career clearly distinguish themselves from the general practices—and fate—of the avant-garde. His work is rarely as extreme in its formal innovation, or as uncompromising in its aesthetic and social vision. While it strives to disorient the audience in order to teach them a new manner of perceiving the artwork in the world, Brecht's work generally lacks that aggression against the audience that characterizes most avant-garde programs. Nor did Brecht proclaim himself a prophet, a visionary poet in advance of his times; rather he explicitly located himself, his work, and his audience in the midst of a terribly complex, and not necessarily successful, struggle with the prevailing ideological and political conditions of his society, conditions which could not easily be transcended by an avant-garde appeal to a utopian future. Certainly, Brecht's literary and political struggles had a much more immediate and threatening context in Weimar and fascist Germany than did those of the surrealists in post-war France. Like the activities of the Berlin dada movement, Brecht's works responded to the immediate social struggle, but unlike most of the dadaists, Brecht did not retreat from creating a politically activist art when social conditions proved antagonistic to his aesthetic and political vision. Instead, the political terms he chose, the social focus he adopted, and the aesthetic methodology he used, all transformed characteristic avant-garde behavior and desires into strategies of aesthetic and social action appropriate to the political and cultural conflict during the rise and fall of fascism.

The primary difference between Brecht and his surrealist contemporaries can best be assessed by comparing their responses to the material conditions of their environment. Breton, as we have seen, asserted that "a mind's arrangement with regard to certain objects is even more important than its regard for certain arrangements of objects."[1] Brecht responded indirectly, however, by stating,

> the difference in our [we communists'] seeing validates things; it is concerned with things not with eyes. If we wish to teach that things should be seen differently, we must teach it to the things. And we want not only that things should be seen "differently," but that they should be seen in a certain way; not just differently from every other way, but correctly—that is, as fits the thing.[2]

Breton's statement speaks for most of the avant-garde, and the modernists as well. It originates in the fundamental alienation of the writer from the environment and suggests that that alienation can be resolved or transcended most effectively by transforming the writer's and culture's way of perceiving and conceptualizing the world, rather than by altering the objective, material conditions of their world.

For Brecht, the mind's new "arrangement with regard to objects" was merely a sign of a withdrawal from an unpleasant reality, unless that arrangement was part of a larger strategy to bring about a change in reality or evidence of an already achieved change. A purely formal innovation in art would only perpetuate the interests of the negative reality if it did not first attempt to reveal the world as it was and then act to change it. Brecht, the materialist, argued that the writer's delight and sense of freedom that came from the shock of the new and the resulting reorientation of personal perception were illusory. As aesthetic aspirations they were poor substitutes for discovering an innovative response "appropriate" to the given conditions. Indeed, they merely displaced the "correct" way of seeing.

Brecht's assumption that there was a *correct* way of seeing by which one's actions and art were shaped and judged signaled the radical difference between Brecht and most of the avant-garde. Brecht and many avant-garde writers asserted that they acted within socially progressive time and were allied with extra-aesthetic forces of change, but for most of the avant-garde, art remained an independent source of imaginative and behavioral transformation. Even writers and movements that consciously allied themselves with specific political ideologies or parties—Mayakovsky, Berlin dada, Italian futurism, surrealism—thought that the primary function of the aesthetic act was to explore the unknown, to invoke the unrealized potential of human life, to create new means of seeing, thinking, and acting, and only indirectly, or secondarily, to validate the political program it endorsed. For these writers, what was "correct" could be finally determined only by the success or failure of the literary experiment. As the record of the avant-garde's political alliances has shown, the greatest source of tension between aesthetic innovation and political action has been the avant-garde's rejection of any *a priori* determination of form or vision and its denial of the privileged status of any mode of thinking, especially rational and analytic thinking, that would claim authority over the artistic processes.

While Brecht was not subservient to political and aesthetic dogma—indeed, he struggled against and exposed the weaknesses and contradictions of socialist realism—he understood, nevertheless, that his work was only a particular part of and contribution to larger, shaping historical forces. Instead of merely invoking the radically new experience that art would stimulate or depict, Brecht attempted to identify the basic elements that art shared with the forces of significant historical change and to construct an aesthetic theory and method upon them so that the work would both aid the historical forces and be judged by them.

Brecht posited a complex, yet fundamental unity of the forces of change in his society and asserted that that unity could either be strengthened or manipulated into contradictory tendencies. Throughout Brecht's career—from his earliest apolitical writing, through his explicitly didactic marxist *lehrstücke,* his complex major plays written during his extended exile, and, finally, his work with the Berliner Ensemble in East Germany—he sought to understand and depict the specific conditions that determined the course of social change in the modern era. Before becoming a Marxist and achieving insight into the political dynamics and direction of change, he recognized that the world he lived in was in some ways fundamentally new, and that it presaged the birth of a "new man." Even though he was initially dismayed by some of the forms of that change, he knew that his art had to explore and illuminate that change. By the time he became a Marxist, he realized that his early ambivalence to social change was based on the intuitive recognition that all change in his society was not necessarily good, that, for example, certain political "developments" acted to abort necessary, progressive change, that scientific progress could either serve or be separated from significant social progress, and that innovative art could withdraw from and obscure real social developments already occurring. But it was also his firm belief that what the avant-garde asserted—the alliance of art, politics, and science—could become a productive reality. Ultimately, Brecht's efforts to understand his age and to create an art appropriate to it led him to create an art that shared the basic analytic impulse which he believed dominated the modern era's science, politics, and, potentially, its art.

For Brecht, the progressive dynamics of the modern age were rooted in the spirit of *Wissenschaft.* This analytic thinking, initially manifested in the physical sciences, developed under the revolutionary bourgeoisie as a means of mastering material conditions; it was later forced into specifically limited areas of investigation, however, once the bourgeoisie effectively dominated the economic and social structure. But *Wissenschaft* also included the development of rational social theory, particularly the scientific theories of Marx which struggled against the bourgeois distortion of the scientific spirit. Furthermore, this spirit could include an art dedicated to changing the conditions of life. Brecht recognized that the basis of the scientific spirit, whether in the science, politics, or art of the modern era, was a *criti-*

cal attitude. This attitude is implicit in all avant-garde movements, but it became the explicit and central premise of Brecht's work. According to Brecht, an art appropriate to its age, an art that sees "correctly," is one based on the critical spirit. This art's innovative methods teach one how to see the world and one's social experience critically, so that one can see them correctly and then act to change them. Consequently, the focus of Brecht's innovative art is not on the unknown whose glimpsed attractions would stimulate a desire for change, but on the given conditions of life that demand that one change them.

Brecht's identification of the necessity and basis of significant change and his creation of an aesthetic style responsive to his historical situation were not easily achieved. His theatrical theory and practice developed and were modified throughout his career in direct response to dramatically changing personal and historical conditions. If all avant-garde writers and movements are shaped by their immediate social context, Brecht's career is particularly noteworthy for his ability constantly to adapt to a variety of social situations and still retain the bases of his original innovative, critical drive. In contrast, the truly innovative work of most avant-garde movements and writers is limited to specific and brief historical moments. The avant-garde frequently suffers from the radical disparity between the demands of the utopian-aesthetic imagination and the rapidly changing social conditions to which that vision was originally a response. Movements such as Italian and Russian futurism, dada, and surrealism did not survive long after the promulgation of their original theses and actions, or, if they did, it was often merely as pale shadows of their original identity which could only struggle futilely to remain valid in new historical conditions. As the orginal stimulus—World War I, the early revolutionary period in Russia, the post-war chaos of Germany—changed, the art that arose out of it was suddenly found to be deracinated, caught in the paradox of not changing even as it proclaimed the need for change.

In effect, the avant-garde often falls victim to the dynamics of modernity it seeks to master. Its programs cannot validly exist independently of the conditions that give it birth since those programs implicitly ask that they be judged by their ability to affect the original conditions. Only writers or artists who split off from the original avant-garde movement either to identify with a subsequent avant-garde or aesthetic ideology—Tzara, Heartfield, Éluard, or Aragon, for instance—or who retained an individual style independent of any movement—Arp, Dali, Schwitters—managed to survive aesthetically

for any significant length of time. Others, such as Rimbaud, Apollinaire, and Mayakovsky, however, seem fated to retreat from their
original vision, die early, or be silenced prematurely.

Brecht, then, is a relatively unique figure within the history of the
avant-garde. From the very beginning of his career, his work represented a critical exploration of his world in an effort to depict it,
understand it, and eventually change it. Rooted in an awareness of
the changing patterns of individual behavior, his work responds to
the rapidly—and radically—changing conditions of Germany from
World War I through the 1950's. Specifically, Brecht's career was
shaped by the conclusion of the First World War, the abortive sparticist revolution, the weakness and contradictions of Weimar society,
the rise and conquest of fascism, his long period of exile in a succession of countries, and, finally, his return to the post-war communist
state in East Germany. Brecht's personal characteristics—especially
his wiliness, pragmatism, devotion to his close friends and to his
work—enabled him to adapt well to adverse conditions. In short, they
made him a survivor. His work reflects this sensibility. It is rarely as
extreme as that of most of the avant-garde, since he did not presume
to be in complete command of his fate or even his ideas. His plays
are not utopian because they were created in a threatening—and only
sometimes promising—social reality. Although Brecht's poetry and
fiction also articulate a political stance, Brecht, the poet, was essentially a private figure; and Brecht, the fiction writer, was never as
accomplished or innovative as the dramatist. Because his dramatic
theory and plays had the greatest influence on twentieth-century literature, and because they evidenced his major innovations, this chapter will focus on the dramatic works.

Although Brecht's literary experiments were not as formally disruptive as those of many avant-garde writers, from his first play, *Baal,*
through his last productions, his personal, innovative style was constantly developing and challenging theatrical conventions. This is
especially evident in his first three plays, *Baal, Drums in the Night,*
and *In the Jungle of the Cities,* all written before he read Marx in
late 1926. With these works, Brecht quickly established himself as a
unique voice in the German theater of the 1920's because he rejected
or distorted not only the reigning conventions of expressionism and
late naturalism, but also those of the bourgeois popular theater as
well. Each work introduced new language, characters, and dramatic
conflicts and demanded entirely different types of responses from its
audience. These are among his most difficult, most ambiguous plays,
for they exhibit a spirit of caustic social rebellion, even nihilim, yet

they do not make clear the basis or orientation of that revolt. Of all of Brecht's works, they are closest to the classic avant-garde mode of strident negativism, and, indeed, they suggest the influence of expressionism and Brecht's personal identification with the bohemianism of the earlier avant-garde.

As a young writer in his early twenties, Brecht played the role of the aggressive, egotistical bohemian and led an anti-social, amoral life, affecting an eclectic costume of leather jacket, silk shirt, and proletarian cap. In his journals of September, 1920, he exclaims:

> I stride along the curb, making faces, not caring a thing for people's reactions, sneering, so that they can see my rotting teeth. I could easily shatter a mirror. So much for refined people. Here I am, rejoice! Repulsive, impudent, newly born out of the egg. (With eggshell, muck, blood, for all that.)[3]

At this time, Brecht felt himself to be the outsider and he rejected the uneasy complacency of post-war bourgeois society. He identified briefly with the sparticist revolution in Bavaria, wrote theater reviews for a socialist newspaper in Augsburg, and suffered from hunger and poverty during the early instability of the Weimar republic and the great inflation crisis of 1921–1923.

As a young dramatist, following the general conventions of the reigning avant-garde movement of expressionism, Brecht centered his first three plays on the figures of bohemian poets and social misfits. However, even though both *Baal* and *In the Jungle of the Cities* rely heavily on the expressionist strategies of linking symbolic and abstract staging to events which present the irrational or subconscious motivations of poetic and socially displaced characters, Brecht rejected expressionism's general glorification of the poet's passionate soul and demystified the movement's unfettered romanticism. Against the idealism and abstraction of expressionism, Brecht presented a generally materialist perspective—an intensely physical evocation of the amoral natural forces that underlie all social conventions. Many critics have seen these plays as expressions of an essential nihilism. I believe, however, that they signal Brecht's efforts to depict both the individual and society in an entirely new manner. They indicate a radical questioning of the individual and culture that took nothing for granted and led the spectator to observe behavior which could not be explained by most conventional theories of motivation and dramatic figuration. A phenomenon was presented; that it was not explained in convenient terms was not necessarily a sign of nihilism.

True to his name, Baal is the most extreme of the characters of

Brecht's first three plays. He acts like the god of nature who rejected the social and religious morality created by the Judeo-Christian tradition which feared him. The poet Baal is, in essence, a natural force, a human identity reduced to the uncontrolled urges of physical existence, disregarding all social conventions and values, even the self-control that would protect him from himself. Ultimately, he is the inhuman, brute ryhthm of nature, the amoral life force out of which humanity arises and by which it is always threatened.

At first, Baal is romantically attractive to the bourgeoisie in the play, who see in him the poet who lives life more intensely than they permit themselves. But quickly he becomes hateful as he uses them indiscriminately for his own insatiable urges, seducing, abandoning, and killing those who come his way. Baal, finally, is least human, but most himself, when he follows the dominant ryhthms of nature which find their own completion in self-consumption and profligacy, decay, and death. Not even human enough to be pitiable, yet oddly threatening to the end, Baal crawls off into the wilderness to die. In his brief career, he has torn through human society, revealing how fragile, how inauthentic it is, breaking its codes, seducing its members; he finally leaves it unconvinced of its own authority. Baal, the destroyer of the social order, is unleashed by it. The bourgeoisie, which expresses that fascination with the irrational so prevalent in German culture during the turn of the century and war years, receives from Baal first a titillation, then a vision of its future. In ways of which Brecht was probably not fully aware, even as he sought to shed light on the changes in his time, the "new man" that Baal represented would soon find a different, but more terrifying historical figuration in Nazi culture.

In *Drums in the Night,* Kragler, the returned veteran, finds Berlin on the brink of the suppression of the spartacist revolution, and his fiancée pregnant and engaged to the capitalist Murk. Kragler serves at first to illuminate the wholesale corruption of his society. Beaten down, rootless, emaciated by the years of war and prison, he is both a product of the culture and excluded by it. In anger and self-loathing, he leans at first toward joining the doomed revolutionaries, but, offered the chance to reunite with his now discredited fiancée, he chooses to return to home and bed with her, saying, "I'm a pig and pigs go home." Later in his career, Brecht criticized the early version of the play for its lack of political wisdom and altered it to include a suggestion of the real heroism of the revolutionaries in order to more forcefully condemn Kragler's capitulation. But in the light of the society which had betrayed its revolutionary possibility and then lived in smug delusion about its secure future, the first version is a pitiless reflection of a debased culture and the quality of individual life within it. Here, instead of dying on his own terms outside society as Baal does, the outsider dies spiritually within it. Ironically, the play was a tremendous success, largely because of the popularity of the theme of the returned soldier in Germany, and it earned Brecht important recognition. Even more ironically, and significantly, it signalled the start of his efforts to distance the audience from their uncritical reception of drama. He hung signs in the theater—"Don't gape so romantically!" and "Each man feels comfortable inside his own skin"—the first intended to short-circuit the audience's identification with the veteran as victim and the second to raise the problem that obsessed Brecht throughout the 1920's: the nature and basis of individual identity. Kragler's own skin is a pigskin, a pitiful, abused identity in which he chooses to remain, though it is far different from the one he thought himself to have worn prior to the war.

If Baal is content to dismiss, then die outside the society, and Kragler finds only a questionable peace in its embrace, the characters of *In the Jungle of the Cities* discover, on the one hand, that the city is, in fact, a jungle where the laws of nature operate and, on the other hand, that once outside social bounds, poeple are forced to create their own social contract. In this disturbing and mysterious play, the Malay Shlink draws George Garga out of his naive well-being within society, first by destroying his job and family, then by challenging him to a struggle, "an inexplicable wrestling match," as Brecht termed it.[4] Once the match is accepted, Garga, initially the victim, soon reveals himself well able to live beyond all law and morality and comes to dominate Shlink. Garga discovers an intensity and strength, while Shlink becomes the passive member of an increasingly erotic, aggressive relationship. Their battle thrusts them beyond the social framework and becomes, for Shlink, at least, the minimal, but only valid form of social contract. Shlink has always known—more than he could admit—that there is no real human contact, certainly not in the midst of society. "If you cram a ship full to bursting with human bodies, they'll all freeze with loneliness. . . . So great is man's isolation that not even a fight is possible."[5] Unfortunately for him, he is right. The fight is a failure; Garga prefers to live in his newfound isolation and dismisses Shlink, who is, at the end, a dying man.

The prologue of this play instructs us: "Don't worry your heads about the motives for the fight, keep your minds on the stakes. Judge impartially the techniques of the contenders, and be prepared to concentrate on the finish."[6] These remarks are appropriate not only to this play, but to Brecht's two earlier works. Common to all three is an absence of clear motivation; instead, Brecht focuses on a dramatic conflict in which his characters rapidly find themselves playing for the highest of stakes—their identities and their lives—in a social context seen either as woefully inadequate to their needs or actually harmful to them. Brecht was intent on studying and depicting a phenomenon for which neither he nor his society had the appropriate means or understanding to explain. In his notebooks from this period, there is little comment on the meaning of the plays. Brecht was more concerned with finding the best form, the best *"gest,"* for the action. He reveals that he started from a character or a situation and only later developed the plot.[7] He was fully aware both that he was denying his audience the resolution they expected, and that they would be able neither to fully understand what was happening, nor to identify with the characters. Instead—and Brecht returned to this theme repeatedly—they were to be left in their "splendid isolation,"[8] finding comfort neither in the assuring completeness of the play nor in that ordinary manner of viewing their world which the plays undermined.

What Brecht denied his audience, he denied himself. The poet, he stated, cannot take the side of his character. If anything, the poet must take the side of nature, the situation, or the conflict the character confronts.[9] For it was clear to Brecht that the whole idea of individual character had to be rethought. Brecht found no convenient social formulae to explain his characters, nor, evidently, to explain the life he saw around him. He realized that, as a poet refusing to fulfill conventional expectations, he was denying society the assurance they needed that life was meaningful, and that their essential isolation could be overcome.[10] Brecht seemed intensely aware that his art had to respond accurately to—and depict—his time, but Brecht took no convention for granted. Nor did he allow himself an easy faith in some future utopic vision which, he felt, was the main limitation of the avant-garde. In an essay justifying his use of the metaphor of sport, Brecht described the importance of recognizing the true nature of the historical conditions affecting the writer.

I believe that an artist, even if he sits in strictest seclusion in the traditional garret working for future generations, is unlikely to produce anything without some wind in his sails. And this wind has to be the wind prevailing in his own period, and not some future wind. There is nothing to say that this wind must be used for travel in any particular direction (once one has a wind one can naturally sail against it; the only impossibility is to sail with no wind at all, or with tomorrow's wind), and no doubt an artist will fall far short of achieving his maximum effectiveness if he sails with today's wind.[11]

Throughout his career, Brecht insisted that his work respond to the winds of his time, that it learn to recognize the direction the winds were blowing and use them to illuminate the potential for progressive social development. But it was also his tendency to be constantly sailing against them.

The process by which Brecht arrived at an understanding of the meaning of his period and the fate of the individual within it can be followed in his notes on a character he struggled to create for more than half a decade. While he was working on his first three plays and an adaptation of Marlowe's *Edward II*, Brecht was fascinated with the figure of Joseph Galgei, who eventually became Galy Gay of *Man is Man*, a simple man stripped of his original identity and forced to take the place and identity of another man, a British soldier. As early as 1920, Brecht noted that the central conflict was between the citizen Galgei and "evil men" who stripped him of his name and skin. The implicit moral, similar to that of *Drums in the Night*, was that each person must watch out for his or her own skin.[12] Two months later, he referred to the work as a "rape-murder play" and stated that the only important questions were how long could the victim hold out, what were his resources, and how long could he actually remain himself?[13] But by the next year, Brecht indicated that Galgei had no autonomous resources. Instead, Brecht chose to focus on Galgei's participation in the transformation of self. Galgei's lack of center allowed him to undergo everything. His story revealed "the barbaric and shameless triumph of senseless life that grows in any direction, that uses every shape, that suffers from no reservations. Here lives the ass, who has been willed to continue living as a pig. The question is, Is he really living? He is lived."[14] We see here, and throughout Brecht's early writing, an oscillation between the poles of individual and social life, between social pressure and the individual's alienation from or compliance with that pressure. In these works the "senseless" life of the individual beyond or prior to social formation—the figures of Baal, Kragler, Garga, Galgei—has no positive value in itself except to the extent that it resists or unmasks social definition. And though Brecht would later cast this opposition in entirely different terms, the conflict between the individual and the social environment remained the constant theme of his works. It was a conflict that was never adequately resolved in any of Brecht's plays.

The story of Galgei went through several versions, nearing completion in late 1926 as *Mann ist Mann*. In April, 1927, a radio version of the play was broadcast; for this Brecht wrote an introduction in which he stated that even though Galy Gay, the packer who was forced to become the soldier Jeraiah Jip, appears weak, he is actually stronger than those who changed him. He loses his "precious ego," but "he becomes the strongest once he had ceased to be a private person; he only becomes strong in the mass." The man comes to no harm; he wins, Brecht continued. In fact, at the end of the play Gay/Jip is able to conquer a fortress which the others couldn't, "because in doing so he is apparently carrying out the unqualified wish of a great mass of people who want to get through the narrow pass that the fortress guards."[15]

This explanation satisfied few members of the play's audience. It was inappropriate to the characters and events of a play in which Galy Gay still seems closer to the ass becoming a pig than to a victorious embodiment of a previously unmentioned and unidentified mass, a mass which apparently can only be the imperialist British army. However, the radio speech did signal the great change in Brecht's thinking that occurred in late 1926 when he undertook a serious study of Marx. It was at this point that many of the social conflicts and unresolved problems he had been depicting in an uncompromising, if mystifying, manner were seen in a new light. Now, both the struggle of the ill-defined and malleable individual with the collective forces of society and the nature of that apparently unstable and even self-destructive society were to be understood in the context of social history. The unfamiliar aspects of the individual which Brecht had previously associated with the amoral forces of nature or with bohemian nihilism he now saw as signs of the growth of a still incompletely formed or understood new human type—mass man. Similarly, the contradictions of the social framework now revealed to Brecht both the decay of the bourgeois dominance and the uneven, and generally unrecognized emergence of mass culture. In the same radio speech in which Galy Gay was heralded as the embodiment of mass desire, Brecht stated: "What matters most is that a *new human type* should now be evolving, at this very moment, and that the entire interest of the world should be concentrated on his development."[16]

For the rest of his life, Brecht's work emphasized that development, as he sought both to create the means of depicting it and to influence its course. It is particularly significant, however, that while Brecht firmly believed that a new type of human was developing, he saw that this type was neither fully evolved, nor necessarily guaranteed a successful future. Although he adopted a Marxist perspective and envisioned the possibility, and certainly the desirability, of a communist future, Brecht was all too aware that the winds of his day, especially in Germany, were unpredictably turbulent and just then not blowing in the right direction. The society in which this new type was emerging was torn by class conflict, economic instability, and the competing forces of bourgeois reaction, communism, and the growing fascist movement. But the conflict itself indicated significant change, and potentially, historical progression. In the radio speech, Brecht asserted that he *believed* that this new human type would master the world, rather than be mastered by it, but Brecht also saw clearly that this would be a hard struggle, one in which the artist had to take an active part.

For the next fifteen years, Brecht worked to create the activist theatrical theory and practice necessary for his times. Rather than being products of a modernist, individualistic effort to effect a solely formal change in art, Brecht's works were consciously revolutionary, founded on a theory of historical change. In November, 1927, in his first discussion of "epic" theater, he stated, "It is understood that the *radical transformation of the theater* can't be the result of some artistic whim. It has simply to correspond to the whole radical transformation of the mentality of our time."[17] Two years later, it had become evident to Brecht that the literary works which required a new form to depict this new type of individual must themselves acknowledge a new function in their society. In an essay, "Über Stoffe und Formen," in which he reiterated that the investigative nature of his early plays did not concern itself with traditional views of character motivation but rather sought to depict accurately the new subject matter, Brecht stated that it was now necessary to place that subject in the context of new social relationships, and in the process, to transform the role of art in that context.

> Once we have begun to find our way about the subject-matter we can move on to the relationships, which at present are immensely complicated and can only be simplified by *formal* means. The form in question can however only be achieved by a complete change of the theatre's purpose. Only a new purpose can lead to a new art. The new purpose is called paedagogics.[18]

During the late 1920's and early 1930's Brecht began to create plays whose formal means would enable the audience to perceive in relatively simple terms the essential questions at the heart of contemporary complex social relationships. These works adopted a paedagogical stance by which the audience was taught to analyze and act upon its new knowledge. These didactic plays—the *lehrstücke*—were plays written for the modern, scientific age.

Designed for an audience that could be taught, rather than merely entertained, the *lehrstücke* were unadorned explorations of specific political themes, often through highly charged conflicts between individual and collective needs. They signal Brecht's most stringent efforts to develop an avowedly Marxist aesthetic, because they force the actor and audience to analyze critically the meaning and value of specific revolutionary actions within the dramatized situations. In this form, Brecht also found an opportunity for literary experimentation, for the *lehrstücke* were not encumbered by the economic, political, and institutional pressures that shaped theatrical production of the bourgeois theater's large stages. Most of the didactic plays were written to be presented over the radio or in schools or at Party and labor headquarters in the working-class sections of the major cities. Thus they allowed Brecht to join with the more than two hundred agit-prop groups in Germany which were part of the recently created working-class theater movement modelled on Soviet revolutionary theaters.[19]

Brecht's didactic plays were closely watched by the police, as well as by the fascists, who clearly felt threatened by their power and popularity. But Brecht also soon found himself in conflict with the communists, who consistently criticized Brecht's presentation of the proletariat and especially the Communist Party workers. They claimed that Brecht had no real understanding of revolutionary methods, but instead only a typically bourgeois emotional view of the demands of party discipline. Indeed, Brecht's *lehrstücke,* especially *Die Massnahme, Der Jasager*, and *Der Neinsager,* are stridently uncompromising and unsettling plays. These, and most of his other didactic plays of the period, are about either the problematic relationship between the individual and the masses or the collective needs of the masses; as a consequence, they do not present a doctrinaire picture of political action.

In *The Measures Taken (Die Massnahme)*, for example, a young, inexperienced Russian Party worker is sent with four other agitators in disguise to help organize the communist revolution in China. But his undisciplined, emotional, and empathetic responses to the workers' plight cause him to upset procedure, force the issue before it can be productively exploited, and ultimately harm the cause as well as costing many workers their lives. Exposed and threatened with ruin, the five agitators are forced to flee, only to find they must kill the youth, whom they will be unable to smuggle out of the country. The play is a staged report of the workers to their superiors, in which each member of the group alternately acts out the young comrade's sympathetic responses and his indiscretions—and his final acquiescence to his execution. At the end of the play, the four are told they acted correctly.

Communists at the time were offended that they had been portrayed as such brutal figures; the play served to support the anticommunist beliefs of fascists and liberals. For Brecht, however, who was revising the dominant concerns of his early plays, the conflict between individual and collectivity had to be posed in the most striking terms. For him, the most important question at this time was the degree to which the individual was to be transformed by the demands of the modern—and progressive— collectivity. The starkest message of the play is the shift from the traditional conception of individual worth to the individual's position within a new historical frame of value. In 1934, four years after *Die Massnahme,* Brecht wrote, "In modern society the notions of the individual psyche are utterly uninteresting; it was only in feudal times that a king's or a leader's passions meant anything. Today they don't."[20] Throughout Brecht's career, he continued to be primarily interested in tracing the limits, even the lack of validity, of the individual psyche within the processes of its historical transformations. This is true even of his major dramas of the late 1930's which center on the conflicts and contradictions of remarkable characters like Mother Courage, Galileo, Grusha, and Shen Te, the strengths of whom have led many critics to romanticize them. But in the early *lehrstücke,* Brecht took his denial of the importance of the individual psyche to its most extreme point to suggest that subjugation might be necessary and that the destruction of the psyche and life by a collectivity might allow a new type of person to emerge.

Yet in spite of the fact that the *lehrstücke* present specific resolutions to the dilemmas that the individuals encounter, their main concern was not the correctness of the particular solution, but the nature of the conflict. The solution in *Die Massnahme* is not offered as dogma or revolutionary strategy. Rather, the conflict was meant to engage the audience in the process of perceiving and resolving the demands of the dramatic situation. The *lehrstücke* called for an active, not a passive, audience; their function as entertainment was subsidiary to their role of forcing the audience into the posture of critical thinkers. Speaking of another *lehrstück, Der Flug des Lindberghs,* Brecht stated that it "is useless unless learned from. It has no value as art which would justify any performance not intended for learning. It is an *object of instruction*."[21]

This instruction applied to the writer as well as the audience. The plays were intended to initiate a discussion among the writer, actors, and audience that could result in revisions of the drama. This was the case with the two *lehrstücke* developed from Japanese Noh plays, *Der Jasager* and *Der Neinsager*. The first is the story of a man who accepts the necessity of his death when he falls ill on a mountain pass while on a mission to deliver desperately needed medicine. Rather than delaying or stopping the rescue party, he acquiesces to an old tradition of self-sacrifice. His plight reflects once again Brecht's inquiries into the submission of the individual to the collective needs. When the play was presented at the Karl Marx School in Berlin, however, the pupils objected that the death was not necessary and suggested that the man could demand that the tradition of self-sacrifice be changed. Consequently, Brecht wrote *Des Neinsager,* in which the principle character, as representative of the living generation, demands the freedom to challenge the authority of tradition and decide his own fate, a demand that is accepted by the group. Individually, and together, then, the two plays functioned to raise questions that had no simple solution, or, in fact, whose apparently simple answer would force the audience into a radical confrontation with their own assumptions about their dependence on the traditions of their society. As a group, the *lehrstücke* represent a significant stage in Brecht's exploration of an innovative drama—innovative in form and in practice.

At the same time that Brecht was writing these plays, he was both following his early critical success with the great popular success of *The Threepenny Opera* and developing his most important theoretical ideas for the theater he wished to create. But his increasingly political perspective soon led to his generally poor reception in the major theaters of his day, and his next works, *Happy End, The Rise and Fall of the City of Mahagonny,* as well as his revised film script for *The Threepenny Opera,* either folded quickly or met with a decidedly negative reception. Shortly thereafter, Brecht was forced into exile and found himself creating for the "bottom drawer," writing plays which had little chance of production. Furthermore, although during the late 1920's and throughout the 1930's, he made his major contribution to theater theory, he had almost no opportunity to test his ideas in actual productions. This was unfortunate because even while the basic import of Brecht's revolutionary ideas went far beyond the dramatic text, these ideas could only be tested or find fulfillment by being put into practice in the theater. Nevertheless, during these two decades Brecht developed a coherent conceptual framework which links the *lehrstücke,* his theoretical statements, and his major plays. All were expressions of his ongoing effort to found a theater on the critical spirit—political, scientific, and aesthetic—of the modern age.

The initial formulations of this theater are found in his comments in the mid-1920's about the need for an "epic" theater. The function of the epic theater—descended from Piscator's political, broad-scale epic productions on which Brecht worked—was, like the *lehrstücke,* paedagogic. Unlike the *lehrstücke,* however, which either presented a clear image of significant historical development or posed a direct question of interpretation and praxis to the audience, the epic theater was to be a theater of complexity and ambiguity, for by being confronted with the lived limitations of the characters in the dramatic world, the audience would be pushed to discern the complexity of their own lives. The epic theater would teach the audience how to see— to see the play, themselves, and, ultimately, their world—in a new manner. The dramatic text and its production were designed to appeal to the audience's critical reason, not merely its emotions. If the epic theater became successful, the theater would no longer be merely the locale of an escape into entertainment, into a realm set apart from the world in which the audience could briefly ignore, or temporarily resolve, the conflicts and tedium of quotidian social existence. No longer would the audience be able to be passive, to give up its identity, its troubles, its unanswered questions and unfulfilled desires, to merge with the seemingly magical, total world of the artwork. Rather, the epic theater Brecht proposed would force the audience to become conscious of its distance from the characters and the world they viewed. Brecht decried the uncritical empathy evoked between the audience and the dramatic character of the traditional theater—which he called, rather loosely, "Aristotelian" theater. In opposition to this, Brecht assigned the spectator the responsibility of recognizing the world presented in the epic theater not as a privileged world of lived totality, but rather as a world like his own, rife with contradictions, unnecessary mystification, and, potentially, subject to change—as his own world should be.

During the late 1930's, Brecht's theoretical writings focused increasingly on the concept of the *Verfremdungseffekt*—the alienation effect—which was his new term for the epic theater's major strategy of disrupting the audience's expectations. The *V-effekt* described the programmatic dissociation of the elements of the theatrical production from each other. The result was a thorough assault on the apparently seamless totality of the work of art and the world of the viewer. Brecht's use of didactic or ironic placards (first present in *Drums in the Night*), stage narrators, songs which commented on the play's action, and the deliberately unsettling collaboration of set design, lighting, music, and acting techniques revealed the theatrical creation—and, implicitly, the world of the spectator—as the sum of disparate, and frequently competing, if not contradictory, parts.

The result of this disjunction was a new activist aesthetic principle in which the artwork could no longer be transparent, the world could no longer be depicted as natural, and the audience could no longer remain passive consumers of aesthetic pleasures.

> Too much heightening of the illusion of the setting, together with a "magnetic" way of acting that gives the spectator the illusion of being present at a fleeting, accidental, "real" event, create such an impression of naturalness that one can no longer interpose one's judgment, imagination or reactions, and must simply conform by sharing in the experience and becoming one of "nature's" objects. The illusion created by the theatre must be a partial one, in order that it may always be recognized as an illusion. Reality, however complete, has to be altered by being turned into art, so that it can be seen to be alterable and treated as such.[22]

The basis of this disruption of naive realism is the "scientific" attitude of critical analysis which underlies all avant-garde and leftist political praxis. Ideally, the critical spectator sees the historical nature of the character's situation and limitations and learns to refute the patterns of delusion and avoidance which the characters adopt, even as the viewer has sympathy for their honest efforts to come to terms with their desires to do good in an evil world. But achieving a critical perpective on the characters' lives is only the initial step demanded by Brecht's activist art. Privileged in a perspective that the characters can't achieve, the spectators must learn to perceive themselves and their own historical conditions critically, to become alienated from themselves so that they may recognize just what they are a function of, and how they may act to change their historical situation.

Brecht's emphasis on the political significance of the formal disruption of literary realism's conventions placed him in the midst of the controversies about this subject which raged throughout the 1930's. Lukács and the Marxist theorists of social realism took one side, and numerous modernist and avant-garde writers and the critical sociologists of the Frankfurt School took the other. Brecht knew many of the participants in these debates, and recognized the similarity of his ideas to aspects of each of their positions. But even though he was attacked by some and prematurely claimed as an ally by others, he emerged with a unique form of aesthetic and political activism.

Like the Russian futurists, formalists, and surrealists, Brecht was placed on the defensive by the strident pronouncements of the proletarian writers' movement in the soviet cultural establishment. As an exile who travelled to Moscow several times during the 1930's from his bases in Scandinavia, Brecht was fully aware of the theories of socialist realism and the nature of the powers behind them. He was also aware of the probable liquidation of some of the writers he respected who did not parrot the Union of Soviet Writers' aesthetic line. And although he was a titular co-editor of the German exile literary magazine *Das Wort,* published in Moscow, he saw his own ideas and those of his friends attacked in its pages by Georg Lukács in a series of articles condemning expressionism, the avant-garde, and the work of Ernst Bloch and the Frankfurt School.

Brecht had no sympathy for the principles of socialist realism, which demanded that fully-drawn, recognizably traditional literary figures represent either the clearly negative aspects of capitalism or the positive forces of communism. Such characters, according to Brecht, simply did not represent the complexity of real people's experiences. Lukács's position was more sophisticated than that of the socialist realists with whom he was allied, but, in Brecht's eyes, he too was guilty of promulgating a static model of nineteenth-century bourgeois realism by which he judged all forms of modernist and avant-garde works. Brecht's literary career was the record of a search for a progressive model of realism that could depict the changing situation of the individual in advanced capitalist society. At times, that search entailed the creation of characters with distinctly limited or distorted perspectives; at other times, it resulted in barely human figures driven by subterranean, amoral urges. Lukács railed against such figures who, he believed, dominated both expressionist and surrealist writing and the works of such modernists as Joyce, Kafka, and Dos Passos. To Lukács, so restricting individual identity to subconscious impulses, or consciousness to subjective perspective, was both a distortion of true human capability and a submission to the irrelevant and delusive surface phenomena of capitalist culture. He argued that the reader should instead be shown fully integrated characters who confronted those social forces that revealed the underlying structure of society, characters such as ones found in the novels of Thomas Mann or Romain Rolland—or even John Galsworthy.

Brecht's response to Lukács took the form of four short essays which he intended to publish in *Das Wort,* but which finally did not appear until the 1950's. In them, Brecht deftly turned Lukács's charges about the formalism of modern literature against him, by asserting that to hold a single model of correct realism—that of the nineteenth-century bourgeois novel—and to apply it as the absolute standard of judgment was itself an example of excessive formalism. According to Brecht, not only did Lukács effectively ignore the changing forms of realism—that "realistic" does not mean the same thing in works by Cervantes and those of Balzac or Tolstoy—but he denied that the conditions of twentieth-century social organization were significantly different from those of the period of early revolutionary capitalism. As was his tendency, Brecht paid particular attention to the concept of character in modern society; in this society an individual was shaped by both the positive (socialist) and the negative (fascist) forces of collectivization. One could understand why a bourgeois critic would desire to applaud works with classically drawn individuals who seem in command of their social situation, Brecht commented, but a revolutionary critic should be willing to analyze the positive and negative implications of the altered shape of individual identity in a changing society. Twentieth century individuals simply did not act like nineteenth century literary characters. While Brecht agreed with Lukács that the goal of the literary work was to foster a critical awareness of contemporary society, he believed that it was naive and potentially mystifying to sustain a portrait of the world in which the representative figures were more critically aware and politically exemplary than the audience. The explicit burden of social analysis, which had to fall on the audience, could only be facilitated by the text's formal disruption of the audience's expectations.[23]

On theoretical grounds, there should have been no real basis for Brecht's critique of Lukács. If Brecht believed that the audience could achieve a critical perspective on their society, then it should have been possible to depict characters such as the audience in the literary work, as Lukács demanded. Brecht's insistence on formal innovation, however, signalled his concern that the audience had to be made active, and that the function of art had to be radically changed. It no longer seemed sufficient for the audience merely to view other people striving to come to terms with their social situation; the members of the audience had to do so themselves. Hence,

Brecht's innovations were more than reflections of changes in the modern world. They *produced* new ways of seeing that world. They were educative not because they illustrated an already formulated— and sanctified—theory of political necessity such as Lukács and the socialist realists privileged; rather, they taught the spectators to work to create their own response to an historical process that one could not assume was determined beforehand. Walter Benjamin succinctly described Brecht's mistrust of the cultural—and political—commissars of his time:

> "With these people," I said, referring to Lukács, Gabor, Kurella, "you just cannot build a state." Brecht: "Or *only* a state, but not a community. They are quite simply enemies of production. Production makes them uneasy. It can't be trusted. It is the unpredictable. You never know where it will end. And they themselves do not want to produce. They want to play the *apparatchik* and supervise others. Each of their criticisms contains a threat."[24]

Brecht's theory of the artwork as production brought him close to the ideas of the Russian formalists and the Frankfurt School, as well as to the avant-garde tradition of formalist activism. In fact, his first use of the term *V-effekt* occurred only after a trip to the Soviet Union. In the late 1920's, after reading Marx, Brecht had referred to *Entfremdung,* the traditional term for alienation, but *Ver*fremdung, a virtual neologism coined by Brecht for the process of *making strange,* entered his critical vocabulary after he saw the Chinese actor Mei Lan-fang in Moscow in 1935. Most likely, the term is a translation of Viktor Shklovskij's concept of *"Priem Ostrannenija"* which Brecht probably encountered during the soviet visit. However, unlike Shklovskij and the formalists, for whom the term described the process by which shifts in literary conventions occur over time—and thus, only secondarily, implied the corresponding shifts in historical consciousness—for Brecht, "making strange" meant consciously disrupting the literary presentation of reality so that one could learn to distance oneself from the false authority of given reality.

Brecht's elaboration of this view of alienation echoed the works of the Frankfurt School, particularly Benjamin's, with whom he shared his ideas during his exile in Denmark. In 1934, Benjamin had given Brecht his own essay, "The Writer as Producer," in which Brecht was discussed as an important writer who was creating a revolutionary form of art for the modern period. For Benjamin and the Frankfurt School, Brecht represented the great modernists who, whether politically conservative or progressive, expressed a self-conscious alienation from the dominant values of bourgeois culture; in their various strategies of formalist distancing, these modernists seemed to sustain the power of negative thinking so that the imaginative and critical faculties might project images of the desire for alternative modes of being. Ultimately, however, in their despair (Adorno) or severe doubt (Marcuse) about the possibilities of revolutionary action within late capitalist society (or, for that matter, in the soviet bloc), the critical sociologists desperately clung to *any* expression of negative thinking—modernist or avant-garde, Kafka and Beckett, or Rimbaud and surrealism.

Even though Brecht was also distressed about the historical situation of the proletariat in Europe, he had more faith in their revolutionary potential and in the Soviet Union than did the Frankfurt theorists. Furthermore, he did not believe that merely achieving a critical distance from bourgeois society was a sufficient response to the modern world. Commenting on the formal innovations of modernism and the avant-garde, Brecht once remarked that it was not enough to free oneself from the laws of grammar and thereby think oneself free of the laws of capitalism. Alienation and formal innovation had to provide the basis for specific action. Formal innovation must be *productive*.

His belief that the artwork must lead beyond itself toward action in the world connects Brecht to the tradition of the avant-garde—a tradition, of course, which he felt too narrowly focused. For the avant-garde, a disruptive, critical distance from society was the first step of an aesthetic activist program, and the formal innovations were meant to change consciousness and ultimately the world. As Brecht stated: "Reality, however complete, has to be altered by being turned into art, so that it can be seen to be alterable and treated as such."[25]

There is, of course, a great difference between altering the world in the artwork (or altering the conventions by which the world is turned into art), and altering the world itself. One must move beyond mere subjective perspectivism, however critical and scientific, to literally act in the world. This is something that the avant-garde occasionally attempted to do, but most often their activist programs were invocations of a utopic state. Brecht, as we have seen, demanded that the world be seen not only differently, but correctly. His belief in the primary importance of a specifically political perspective provided the necessary grounding of aesthetic activism in the real world. Instead of the open and abstract potential of most avant-garde utopias, the potential that Brecht worked for was what Lukács called concrete potentiality, a world of human dimensions based on actual

228 The Literary Avant-garde

human behavior and needs. "Truth is concrete," was written above the door to Brecht's workroom in Denmark. Brecht's innovative plays are not visionary artworks. There is rarely even a suggestion of what the future might be like. Instead, he placed his characters—and the audience—in the middle of terribly complex social situations which demanded concrete solutions—solutions that were not given by the artwork.

As a consequence, even though a critical perspective on social reality both generates Brecht's innovations and is the goal of his ideal audience, the actual achievement of that perspective by his real audiences has remained one of the most problematic aspects of his career. Brecht's plays have been subject to many interpretations—and many misinterpretations and distortions, most of which have arisen out of two main components of Brecht's critical theory: the complex portrayal of uncritical or incompletely self-conscious characters within ambiguous and often threatening social environments; and the ideological demands the *V-effekt* places on the producer, director, actors, and audience.

As we have noted, Brecht rarely depicted characters open to simple literary or political analysis; only slightly more often did he present them in easily definable ideological conflicts. In his major plays, when he did portray relatively simplistic characters (such as Grusha and Joan Dark), their relation to their social environment and the questions that relationship raises for them are disturbingly complex; and when a critical understanding of the environment is available to the audience (as in *Mother Courage, Galileo,* and *The Good Person of Setzuan*), the characters are placed in such a problematic relationship to that environment that it is difficult to judge them without a conscious critical distance.

In most of Brecht's major plays written during his exile—especially from 1937 to 1945—the central characters have an inadequate understanding of themselves and their social conditions. Their desires and actions, and their true needs and immediate goals are often contradictory, and although, at times, the characters may strive with apparent heroism toward apparently worthwhile ends, frequently that heroism is an expression of self-interest (as in the case of *Galileo*), cowardice, or avoidance of a greater problem (*Mother Courage*). Usually, these contradictions result from the characters' inability to perceive the true nature of their environment, or from deluded assumptions that they can act either independently or in spite of it. Few achieve the recognition that Brecht insists is the basis of his work and which it is the task of the audience to learn—that "man [is] a function of the environment and the environment [is] a function of man."[26] Characters who believe themselves integral, independent figures are blind to the forces influencing them. When they do achieve an insight into their personal condition, their responses are usually inadequate, since their perceptions are incomplete.

Mother Courage is a prime example of a figure who almost totally accepts as natural or necessary the conditions in which she finds herself. She struggles not merely to survive in them but to turn a profit from them, no matter what the cost to her family. A petit bourgeois woman scavenging the battlefields for opportunities to sell her wares, she watches her children die and her means of subsistence diminish, yet she barely questions herself or her surroundings. She sees that she is not in control of the forces around her, but seems to believe that she has control over her individual fate—even though her life is one long "song of capitulation," a giving-in to the horrors of the world. When she is briefly moved by the harm done to her family, she may, as she does after Kattrin's rape in scene six, curse the war; but, in her very next speech, which opens scene seven, she praises that war for the money it brings her. That she is damning herself is never evident to her; that her profit comes at the expense of her children is a fact she can't avoid, but invariably accepts.

Among Brecht's characters, Mother Courage is not unique. Like Mother Courage, other figures also lack control of their lives or social situation; like her, they are torn by contradictory personal desires or impulses. Only the strategies they adopt in these struggles vary. If Mother Courage manages to avoid the evident contradictions of her life, Galileo and Puntilla, by different means, repress that part of themselves which accents the contradictions; others, such as Grusha of *The Caucasian Chalk Circle*, or Shen Te/Shui Ta of *The Good Person of Setzuan*, consciously live the contradictions but are unable either to resolve them or to find personal unity. It is remarkable, in fact, how many of Brecht's central figures are divided against themselves. They are torn by contradictory impulses—to do good, yet be evil or weak; to act to change their conditions, yet acquiesce to them. Occasionally, the split takes the form of apparent schizophrenia, as in the case of Puntilla or Shen Te/Shui Ta. The former can only be warm-hearted, humane, and a rebel when he is drunk. Sober, he is almost a parody of the evil landowner that he actually is. Puntilla can never attain a coherent and consistent perspective on himself. Shen Te, driven to do good, recognizes the impossibility of doing so in an evil world and can protect herself only by becoming the hard-hearted Shui Ta, who subverts all the good begun by Shen Te even as s/he strives to protect the spirit of that good. Nor is there apparently any way out of these dilemmas. Brecht once noted that Grusha in *The Caucasian Chalk Circle* demonstrates that "the more she strives to do good, the more she endangers herself and the child she tries to help. . . . That is how things are, given the conditions of war, the law as it is, and her isolation and poverty."[27] Grusha, like so many of Brecht's characters, is nearly overwhelmed by the conditions of her environment. And even though she may struggle against them, the very form of that struggle is largely determined and rendered ineffectual by them. This is the situation that many of Brecht's figures from Kragler of *Drums* through the late plays find themselves in—to be a function of an environment which leads them to rebel or at least think themselves in command of themselves and at the same time to be defeated by that environment.

If this constant element of Brecht's plays is an extension of his effort to discern and depict the problematic relationship of the individual to modern society, it is significant that Brecht's attitude towards his characters appears to change with his personal experiences. The characters of his great plays written during exile—*Mother Courage, The Caucasian Chalk Circle, The Good Person of Setzuan, Galileo,* along with many of the lesser works of this period—are rarely presented so starkly or harshly as Baal, Kragler, Garga and Shlink; nor do these plays exhibit the ideological clarity of the *lehrstücke*. Rather, Brecht presents his heroes and heroines, as well as his villains, rather sympathetically. There are no unproblematic heroes in these plays, and neither are there pure villains. Many critics have noted Brecht's sentimentality in this respect. In spite of his renowned toughness, vulgarity, and egotism, his writing reveals a touching sympathy for individuals in their struggles with a threatening social and political environment. Brecht was a survivor, and in the hardest times of his exile, he expressed an appreciation of the innate strengths of individuals who survived harsh circumstances. He was especially drawn to characters who resorted to ruses, contradictory actions, and individual wiliness to get along—the Schweik's of the world, or the Azdak's, the "disappointed revolutionaries"[28] who found themselves inevitably doing good in spite of their self-interest. Brecht was also sentimental about his vulnerable characters who were instinctively good in a world that denied, if not destroyed them—Grusha, St. Joan, Shen Te—and yet he also enjoyed the spectacle of evil or destructive figures who exhibited a weakness for pleasure, sympathy, or even personal affection—Puntilla, Pierpont Mauler of *St. Joan of the Stockyards,* even the absurd character Arturo Ui.

This sympathy, however, did not prevent Brecht from insisting that these figures be seen in their historical specificity and be judged according to the significance of their actions within these social contexts. Indeed, the weaknesses of the heroes and heroines must cast their victimization into a complex perspective for the audience. Similarly, the humane impulses of his villains, or the stirrings of motherly affection within a battlefield scavenger, should increase the viewer's awareness that these figures are monsters. Mother Courage is, as Brecht declared, a woman of irresolvable and destructive contradictions given her particular milieu. She is a mother and a businesswoman, and the latter necessarily destroys the former. If one sees the play as a tragedy, the tragedy is that something "timeless"—"motherhood"—is broken down by the specific conditions of her age—war and the woman's profession. This "tragedy" is historically conditioned, and, Brecht insisted, to see Courage's final acceptance of her isolated struggle as an expression of innate human courage is to universalize a particular situation. The war is not fate: neither is her profession. It is up to the audience to achieve an historical perspective on her situation; this is something Mother Courage might glimpse, but she studiously avoids the implications of that knowledge.

Only a few characters in Brecht's minor plays, such as Pelagea Vlassova in *Die Mutter,* the widow Carrar in *Die Gewehre der Frau Carrar,* and Simone Machard in *Die Gesichte der Simone Machard,* consciously act within an historical context. Some others, Kragler, Galileo, the commune leaders in *The Last Days of the Commune,* are aware, to varying degrees, of their historical opportunity and responsibility, but they fail to achieve what might be possible. They cannot be seen as models of action, and they would certainly fail to qualify as heroes of socialist realism. Rather, they are subjects for the audience's and producers' critical focus. Their mistakes and weaknesses are to be learned from. For example, Galileo is more self-conscious than most of Brecht's characters. He understands the nature of the conflict between himself and his society, specifically between himself and the church. He also knows his own weaknesses and despairs of being able to effect change without losing his life. As a result, he can neither act nor transmit his knowledge to others, and through this failure of courage—in the revised version of the play, a failure of historical faith—he retreats into his private life and becomes a figure of contradictions to his friends. When Brecht revised the play in 1945, he had Galileo criticize himself and his failure to sustain faith in the historical movement to which he could have contributed. In a manner of speaking, Galileo thus became the only

Brechtian character to achieve a total perspective upon himself and his environment. He is the only character to be alienated from himself. The final lesson he learns and teaches his assistant—and the audience—returns us to the second half of Brecht's individual/environment equation: the environment is a function of the individual. The environment can be subject to individual action when it is understood through an historical perspective. But while Galileo's self-critique and admission of failure may provide an inspiring moral, the didactic lesson which seems to have been merely tacked on is an unsatisfactory ending for the play. Brecht's greatest works are powerful precisely because they depict the problematic relationship of the character to the environment and force upon the audience the responsibility of making sense of the characters' confused and confusing lives.

Just as the audience must achieve the perspective that the characters lack, the play's producers have the responsibility of enhancing the audience's critical distance so that they may fully perceive the contradictions in the characters' lives and not believe these contradictions to be inescapable or absolute. If the characters on the stage are ultimately passive or ineffectual, the producers cannot allow the audience to accept passively the characters' point of view, nor, finally, to be passive about their own historical situation.

Finally, for the play to be successful, the audience must be willing to adopt an ideological stance, to see itself and its world politically. Even more important, the producers, especially the director and the actors, must also achieve that critical distance from both the work and their own lives; their work, in short, must be explicitly revolutionary. The frequent failure of directors, actors, musicians, and designers to do this in contemporary productions of Brecht's plays is the second major reason Brecht's work is constantly distorted and misinterpreted.

The theoretical and political demands Brecht places on his producers make his works especially vulnerable to the producers' failures. According to Brecht's alienation theories, the success of the play results from the collective effects of the various elements of production—not only the text, but also the setting, staging, directing, music, and acting. This is the case, of course, with any theater piece, but given Brecht's emphasis on the alienation effect, especially in the actor's relation to the character, the full meaning of the character in his or her world cannot be found in the literary text alone. In fact, the text, read by itself, is potentially distorting if it is privileged by the reader or audience, since there the characters speak within a closed context that must be rendered strange by the non-textual world of the production itself. Consequently, unless the actor is able to achieve a critical distance from the character and unless the director and staff share Brecht's commitment to making the ideological components of the work evident, the text itself can easily be used to justify an interpretation antithetical to the writer's intentions. Problematic and paradoxical elements in the characters' lives can be taken as expressions of tragic depth; what is ambiguous can be rendered simplistic—all according to the intention, intelligence, and politics of the producers. This is especially apparent in postmodern productions of Brecht. For if one of the aspects of the contemporary period is a lack of faith in radical historical change, particularly change predicted by Marxist theory, the theater of learning that Brecht sought to develop becomes merely a theater of entertainment or one more expression of theater of the absurd.

Brecht anticipated these difficulties. In 1948, after fifteen years in exile, Brecht was finally given the opportunity to mount productions of his plays as he desired. Accepting the directorship of the Theatre am Schiffbauerdamm in East Berlin, he attempted to solve all the problems he had observed or heard about in productions of his work in Scandinavia, New York, Hollywood, and Zurich during his exile. From his position as an outsider, an author with the customary lack of control over the production of his text, Brecht now moved to a position of relative control; he was given his own theater by the state and enabled to create a working ensemble in accordance with his theatrical and political vision. It is particularly significant that he concentrated mainly on mounting his past plays, works that he had been unable to see produced, and not on writing new pieces for his theater. For, far from being a sign of artistic cowardice or an effort to avoid having to write socially progressive works for the German Democratic Republic, this signalled Brecht's effort to test and develop his theories through practice. Significantly, his theoretical writings of this period, in particular "A Short Organum for the Theatre," markedly qualify some of the more extreme theoretical statements of his exile writings.

Much controversy remains over the extent of Brecht's identification with East Germany. (After all, he fought to receive an Austrian passport and made sure that all his works would be published in West Germany.) Nevertheless, he chose to work in a Germany that was attempting to build a socialist state, a nation that offered him the possibility that the political vision which had informed his work for over twenty years might become material reality. In this context, so radically different from those in which he had written his plays, mounting his productions was a form of activist labor and not merely an alienated literary critique of society.

> Now I live in a state where a vast effort is being made to transform society. You may not approve of the means used—I hope, by the way, that you are really acquainted with them, and not just from the papers; you may not accept this particular ideal of a new world—I hope you are acquainted with this too; but you can hardly doubt that in the state where I live the transformation of the world, of men's life together, is being worked at. And you may perhaps agree with me that the present-day world can do with transforming.[29]

Once the plays were produced as he wished, Brecht was concerned that the activist, and difficult blend of entertainment and instruction, of empathy and critical distance be given a stability and authority that would guide later productions of the same plays not controlled by Brecht. To this end, he developed "Model Books" of his productions, designs, photographs, and descriptions of the sets, staging, methods of acting, and analyses of the processes of production development, and interpretation. These were a form of activist archive, a text that would stand between the dramatic text and the future production.

Nevertheless, these books did not fully accomplish their mission. In spite of frequent denials, many Eastern European productions of Brecht reduce the tensions, contradictions, and critical distance which Brecht's theories demand to relatively simplistic levels of ideological interpretation and entertainment. Similarly, many Western productions oscillate between traditional, empathetic, and tragic interpretations of the individual's conflicts and flashy productions which transform the alienation effect into cheap dazzle.

In spite of this, the theories remain; the texts await committed producers and audiences. Almost unique among avant-garde writers, Brecht has provided a personal and aesthetic model of an artist able to work over a long period of time, constantly developing, revising, and reviving the spirit of an activist art. Alone or with collaborators, in exile or with state acceptance, Brecht was one of few activist writers who produced major activist and innovative work during the period 1930 through 1955, an era during which the entire avant-garde movement was in retreat in fascist, socialist, and capitalist societies alike. His plays adopted the main tendency of avant-garde art of the first half-century—critical distance—and joined it with a faith in historical change. In the postwar period, a time when late modernist writing was characterized by existential alienation and absurdity—the despairing forms of critical distance and solipsistic social critique—Brecht suggested the potential of a continuing avant-garde tradition.

Chapter

VIII

Postmodernism
and the Neo-avant-garde

Is there an avant-garde today? Is avant-garde an appropriate term to describe aesthetic activity within this period increasingly known as the postmodern? Certainly, for the past two decades, much of the serious literature in the United States, Europe, and South America has been marked by frequent self-reflexive formal innovation, while at the same time new theater, poetry, music, visual art, performance art, and dance have been characterized by a spirit of constant experimentation. Nevertheless, this wave of self-conscious innovation in the arts displays an ambiguous relationship to the stylistic inventiveness that shaped the traditions of both modernism and the avant-garde before World War II. Contemporary critics ask, for example, if recent fiction's and criticism's explicit focus on textuality—on the function, structure, limits, and possibilities inherent in literary and social discourse—exhibits that analytical, critical, and essentially antagonistic attitude toward culture which defined avant-garde aesthetic innovation. Is postmodern experimentation an expression of the contemporary writer's attempt to alter, expand, or liberate consciousness from a repressive and exploitative society? Or is the recent flowering of innovative texts merely a manifestation of a by now well-established, if marginal, tradition of individual stylistic signatures, a sign of the serious writer's seemingly unresolvable, but no longer threatening, alienation from the prevailing literary tastes of the majority culture?

Is postmodernism, in effect, only a continuation of the ironic self-consciousness of modernism?

The current debate over the terminology of period styles represents an effort by contemporary critics to identify the social and aesthetic concepts of recent writing that might distinguish it from the literature of high modernism. Continental criticism, which is more firmly based in a political context and more directly familiar with the history of indigenous avant-garde movements than English and American criticism, has increasingly referred to the "neo-avant-garde" and to the "embourgeoisement of the avant-garde," when it has noted the economic success and the public acclaim of much of post-war art and literature.[1] These critics have argued that the avant-garde, instead of sustaining an alienated and socially antagonistic posture, has allowed itself to be "recuperated" within the mechanisms of the bourgeois culture industry. In turn, the avant-garde seems to repay the art market with largely self-reflexive, formalist works dedicated more to the tradition of artistic and literary innovation than to social change.

In the United States and England, which have enjoyed a generally apolitical critical tradition—a tradition strongly influenced by the precepts of high modernism—and within which there has been little significant avant-garde activity, the term postmodernism is more in vogue.[2] British and American critics have focused primarily on the strategies of literary experimentation and their indebtedness to modernist aestheticism. To these critics, the term *post*modernism is particularly significant because it indicates the contemporary writer's rejection of modernism, even while the premises of modernist innovation still serve as a foil to the new creations. Similarly, in Europe, the concept of the *neo*-avant-garde identifies aesthetic behavior which turns back toward the past to situate the contemporary work. What is interesting to note is that both groups of critics sense that there is something qualitatively different about contemporary art, but there is no consensus about what constitutes that difference. All that can be determined is that the new works break off from some of the principles that guided the creations of the period of high modernism and the avant-garde, even if, in fact, the felt need to reject the past in the name of the new present is the essential feature of the modernist and avant-garde aesthetic. The fact that there is much terminological confusion and unease is itself a sign that there is little assurance on the part of contemporary critics and artists about the nature and significance of art in our society. To be able to achieve such an assurance, of course, would require that the artists, writers, and critics have a clear conception of the nature of the society as a whole, while all that they share presently is an inquiry into the struggles of an age apparently attempting to give birth to itself with no definite vision of what it might bring into existence, certainly with no image of, or even faith in, the future.

In this book, I have argued that the term modernism can be used both as a general period term and to refer to a particular literary sensibility shared by a diverse group of writers, and I have discussed the avant-garde as a subsidiary movement of writers and artists within the culture of modernism. Similarly, I believe it most practical to take the concept of postmodernism as the temporary but necessary period term of our times, and to see within this contemporary sensibility the vestiges of an avant-garde spirit. Yet to the extent that there is a contemporary avant-garde—even a neo-avant-garde—the dominant aesthetic principles of the period make it at best a tentative and self-critical venture. For while much of the serious art and literature of our times continues to manifest an aggressive innovative stance toward aesthetic language and social ideology, this art also threatens to undermine any principle upon which a significantly different art or social vision might be created.

As we have seen, the tradition of the avant-garde has four defining characteristics: (1) temporal dynamism—the avant-garde writer is self-consciously situated in a culture perceived as constantly changing, one which implicitly demands new forms of art to reflect those changes; (2) social antagonism—the writer is self-consciously alienated from and critical of the dominant aesthetic, ethical, and spiritual values of modern culture; (3) the historical possibilities of art and society—the avant-garde writer presages some idealized future which his or her work acts to bring into existence, often in alliance with other presumably progressive or revolutionary forces in contemporary society; (4) aesthetic activism—literary or artistic innovation is held to be an agent of the transformation of consciousness, articulation, and behavior in art, life, and society. In the post-war period, each of these concepts has been affected by changes within Western society and by the corresponding alteration of the writers' and artists' social position. Contemporary bourgeois society has apparently limited and defused the writer's antagonism and the visionary expectations which previously generated avant-garde behavior.

During the four decades since World War II, Western European and American societies have undergone significant changes which have altered cultural production. The social and economic situation of the writer and artist has not fundamentally changed: for the most part, there is still a sensed opposition between aesthetic concerns and social values, and the artist is still compelled to offer up the artwork as a commodity to a generally anonymous public of consumers. However, shifts within the society's power structure and ideology have changed much of daily life within contemporary society and, to a certain extent, have obscured the degree and critical significance of an aesthetically—or politically—based opposition. Sociological critics of the left and the right have directed our attention to some important tendencies of what is variously called late-capitalist or post-industrial society, and on occasion, the "bureaucratic society of consumption."[3] During the period of economic recovery following the war, the increasing prosperity of the general populace, the shift of the productive center of society from an industrial base toward the service sector, and the development of a state-modulated, monopoly economy have altered the face of the capitalist system. Of particular interest to the aesthetic and social critical impulse which governed avant-garde art is the proliferation of mass culture and the resulting blurring of both aggressive individualism and class lines. Class antagonisms may remain unresolved, as some leftist critics maintain, but they are submerged in the mass, pluralistic society that also threatens the concept of distinct individual identity. Hence, both the strident indvidualism and a sense of collective identity which was evident in most avant-garde writers is largely missing from our culture.

Furthermore, contemporary society exhibits a series of internal oppositions and contradictions which find direct expression in recent innovative literature, while at the same time challenging the critical perspective and assumptions of that writing. If the avant-garde always signalled a protest against its society, yet could be read as a direct expression of that society, in the contemporary period, this paradoxical situation is more extreme. For example, with the growth of mass, pluralistic society, we both encounter a heightened sense of individual freedom (at its most extreme, expressed in anarchic tendencies), and simultaneously observe signs of a pervasive, social uniformity and control. Individual innovation, style, and desire are accented, but they lose their distinctiveness—their multi-dimensionality—in a homogenizing pluralism that obscures personal originality. Constant change, either the product of personal effort or corporate plan, is experienced, but the society as a whole seems oppressively static. Within this context, the disruptiveness, absurdity, and radical experimentation of contemporary avant-garde literature and art appear to be merely the most visible expressions of a generally accepted stylistic flux, particularly within the art "scene." As such, innovative works, losing their element of social or aesthetic protest, are capitalized upon as manifestations of fashionable style or as products suitable for financial speculation. In the process, the aesthetic culture becomes, as Lucien Goldmann has argued, truly ahistorical,[4] and innovation within the most narrow terms of art history is reduced to an expression of heightened modernity.

At the same time that internal change loses its sharp definition and class or social antagonisms are apparently defused, the external model of social revolution to which the earlier avant-garde frequently turned—the Russian revolution—has been largely discredited. Neither the Stalinist regime nor the post-Stalin "thaw" proved hospitable to avant-garde art. Nor have they been attractive alternatives to the labor movement or to many leftist intellectuals in the West. As a consequence, socially critical writers, artists, and intellectuals have either adopted a leftist-utopian and anti-soviet stance, as did the Frankfurt School, for example, or they have turned for inspiration to more recent socialist revolutions in the third world—China, Cuba, Vietnam, Nicaragua—none of which, however, is close enough to Western conditions to offer more than a romantic appeal, and none of which has proven sympathetic for more than a brief time to the type of aesthetic experimentation that characterizes the avant-garde.

To a certain extent, traditional oppositional politics have influenced some of the literary and art forms of certain subgroups within society, particularly in the United States. The political and cultural struggles of blacks, chicanos, native Americans, and women, have engendered various forms of innovative writing. However, much of the tendentious writing that has come from these movements is traditionally representational in form, or, if innovative, often finds its sources not in the artist's and writer's freedom to create *sui generis* aesthetic forms, but in popular, folk, and oral traditions indigenous to the particular group. Thus the works of Ron Arias, Ishmael Reed, or Leslie Silko, for example, are as strikingly innovative as that of any postmodern Euro-American writer, but much of their stylistic vitality turns back toward an earlier and largely ignored narrative tradition rather than toward a rootless future. To the extent that the political aspirations of these groups can reach beyond their immediate populace, the social changes demanded by minorities or women might revive a broader cultural faith in socio-historic movement. But if they remain the circumscribed programs of the individual subcultures, the success or failure of the political vision will remain functions of the all-embracing and enervating cultural pluralism that dominates contemporary society.

If a new model of significant social change has emerged in recent innovative works, it is what Ihab Hassan has called a techno-arcadian belief.[5] Expressed most fully by the peripatetic avant-garde composer, visual artist, and writer John Cage, it is an idealization of the transforming powers of science and technology to bring modern society into tune with the natural rhythms and sustaining virtues of the ecosphere. As such, it is a contemporary expression of the traditional avant-garde faith in the progressive powers of science. For by the inherent rationality of science, Cage and Buckminster Fuller have informed us, technology will master its current masters; the principles of greed and exploitation that govern business will be shown to be inefficient and self-destructive. This utopic vision is closely related to Cage's anarchic vision, a vision he shares with many other contemporary innovative writers and artists, for at the heart of his social hopes is a belief in a fortuitous balance between individual liberty and a benign social engineering that must evolve from the internal principles of the economic and political order that currently exists. Traditional oppositional politics, in fact, will restrict the individual to a rigid and inadequate concept of authenticity, and will, furthermore, retard the necessary evolution of the social system. Thus, in Cage's book *A Year from Monday,* we note that his diary passages are entitled "How to Improve the World (You Will Only Make Matters Worse)."[6] The aesthetic implications of these assumptions will be discussed later in this chapter; here, we need only mark the shift away from the traditional avant-garde faith in aggressive individualism striking against a reactionary political structure.

Finally, if writers and artists continue to feel alienated from the values, if not the political structure, of their society, nevertheless they frequently find themselves in significantly more comfortable conditions than did their predecessors. For the visual artists, elaborate support systems of galleries, museums, critics, and investors keyed to every stylistic innovation have arisen in Europe and the United States. Innovative writers, on the other hand, have had an increasingly difficult time getting published by the large trade presses which, in the United States at least, have been taken over by corporate conglomerates that expect literature to turn a profit equal to any other commodity. However, the recent increase in the number of small magazines, independent presses, and writers' collectives in England and the United States, coupled with the domination by writers of small but influential presses in France, has enabled many experimental writers to be published.

More important, perhaps, is the widespread incorporation of the tradition of literary modernism, and to a lesser extent a depoliticized avant-garde, into the university curriculum. In the United States especially, post-war literary criticism has been dominated by the New Critics, whose formalist values are clearly tied to the premises of literary modernism. Even the current post-structuralist critical methodologies, while undercutting the idealist bases of New Criticism, accent the non-directional rupture of shifting discourse. Thus, formal innovation, rather than being seen as the result of individualistic action on language and aesthetic tradition, is taken for the necessary and depersonalized play of semiotic elements within any discourse. As a result, the academy has looked favorably upon literary works that accent stylistic disruption, and has created an educated, middle-class audience for contemporary innovative writing, but in most cases has ignored the social and political aspirations of much of that work. In addition, a significant number of postmodern innovative writers hold positions within the universities. This cultural recuperation of writers and artists tends to blunt even further any residual avant-garde social antagonism and contributes to the academicism that makes aesthetic innovation merely an expression of formalist dynamics.

Nevertheless, although models of social opposition and historical possibility have weakened, for the past three decades, artists, writers, and distinct portions of the general populace of our culture have responded to sporadic, if frequent signs of social ferment and potential change within our culture. For example, it can be argued that the nineteen-fifties saw a fully constituted avant-garde movement in the Beats, and that the numerous socially and aesthetically radical movements of the sixties—Fluxus, Happenings, the *Umbra* group, Concrete Poetry, and the Black Arts movements, among many others— sustained the avant-garde sensibility in the post-war period. The Beats represented the latest in a long line of bohemian protests against an oppressively smug, materialist middle-class society and an effort to revive the image of the artist as outsider, rebel, and visionary. During the nineteen-sixties, the political and moral challenges to the dominant culture that came from the civil rights, black power, and countercultural movements, as well as from the international attack on Western economic and military hegemony by growing opposition in the third world, helped provoke self-consciously avant-garde behavior among writers and artists. Once the culturally and politically volatile period passed, however, the writers, artists, intellectuals, and many other cultural critics proved incapable of or uninterested in sustaining an aesthetic activism that extended far beyond the immediate realm of art. And even within the innovative movements of the sixties lay the seeds of what by the nineteen-seventies and eighties would appear as the culture of postmodernism, which to a large extent undermines the values and goals of the avant-garde.

The emergence of postmodernism may be most clearly traced in the changing assumptions about the nature and significance of individual identity and autonomy, specifically the value accorded the individual to create new meaning in his or her world and to struggle against social determinism. This change can be noted especially in the opposition between the early post-war existentialist elaboration of modernist and avant-garde questions—of which the Beat movement was an expression—and the generally anti-humanist and anti-individualist writing first announced in France by the *nouveau roman,* and which has come to dominate innovative writing of the last two decades. This opposition between an aesthetics based on a defensive, but affirmative humanism and an aesthetics that undermines humanist assumptions occurs in practically all literatures of Europe and the Americas.

In post-war France, the literature of the absurd, the engaged writing that Sartre championed, and Camus's personal version of socially affirmative absurdism were, in effect, all continuations of the modernist tradition. For even though committed literature argued for the return to a social perspective and an aesthetic realism renounced by many literary modernists, the point of departure of both absurdism and committed literature was the existentially isolated individual who attempted—as did the modernists—to assert a coherent system of value or meaning in an essentially meaningless world. On the one hand, the absurd writer—Ionesco, Adamov, Beckett—took an ironic approach to such efforts and revealed the inevitable collapse of any meaning system. On the other hand, both Sartre and Camus, despite their personal differences (not the least of which was Sartre's Marxism and Camus's apology for the bourgeois order), affirmed the inescapable freedom of the self-conscious creation of meaning in a world of no *a priori* foundations. For Camus, the absurd was precisely the rational individual's knowledge that all human creations were gratuitous in an apparently irrational cosmos, but that those creations could—and must—be defended as valid expressions of human desire. Nevertheless, both the bathos of Beckett's creatures and the heroism of Camus's rebels were expressions of the last gasp of a modernist defensive humanism, the end products of the steady diminishment of the realm of individual authority in modern society.

In other countries after the war similar literary explorations of the nature and relationship of individual and social behavior were evident. In Germany, for example, Böll, Grass, Johnson, Lind, and Nossack had both to create a literature without immediate tradition, since all modernist and avant-garde writing had been suppressed during the Nazi era, and also to investigate the question of individual and collective moral and philosophic responsibility in a world in which no value could be taken for granted. In England, where a fetish is made out of class structure, there has never been a fully developed avant-garde movement. The only gesture in that direction—Vorticism—rapidly veered toward a fascist sensibility. After World War II, English fiction sought to investigate the damage done to the social and moral order by which the individual defined him- or herself. The novels of Murdoch, Spark, Lessing, and Golding were explorations of psychological and social anxiety rooted in an existentialist vision, as was the brief moment of the personal and social aggression represented by the "Angry Young Men."

Similarly, in the United States, the literature of the late nineteen-forties and the fifties was dominated by an individualistic and generally existentialist perspective. On the one hand were moral investigations of individual action, such as those of Bellow, Updike, Wright, Salinger, and Ellison, and on the other hand were the intense works of Mailer and the Beats, which glorified personal passion and self-expression. Were we to study the Beats as an example of the avant-garde, we would observe many of the aesthetic and social attitudes associated with prior avant-garde movements: the writers' self-projection as a socially disaffected minority group; their belief in the imminent appearance of a new social type of which they were the model and precursors; a programmatic self-deformation and expansion of consciousness through various ecstatic experiences found in sex, jazz, drugs, and alcohol; the idealization of spontaneous, impassioned behavior as an end in itself or as a means to achieve mystical visions of timelessness and universality; an attraction toward non-Western religious or symbolic systems; and an identification with social outsiders, such as the hipsters, and with oppressed minorities, such as the blacks.

During the nineteen-sixties in the United States, Afro-Americans also provided a model for a number of countercultural and politically motivated arts groups. Indeed, the decade's general social unrest, manifested in the civil rights movements, the urban rebellions, the anti-war movement, and the explosion of the youth culture, fostered avant-garde movements in the literary and art worlds, for example the Black Arts movements in Newark, Harlem, Detroit, and Chicago, the Happenings and E.A.T. groups in the arts, and the various theater collectives associated with the Living Theater, the Performance Group, the Open Theater, the San Francisco Mime Troup, the Bodacious Buggerilla, *El Teatro Campesino,* and many of the spontaneously appearing street theater groups. In fact, the sixties literary avant-garde was strongest in the performing arts which united radical studies of the actor's physical and psychological capacities with the collective experience of political and aesthetic activism, both under the twin spirits of the former avant-garde represented by the theories of Artaud and Brecht. However, if we were to inquire closely into the dynamics of postmodern theater, we would observe, as we will notice throughout postmodern aesthetics, a broad-based rejection of this emphasis on the centrality of the individual performer and the activist extensions of his or her self-transformation. Throughout Europe and the Americas, the culture of postmodernism redefines the terrain and significance of an activist aesthetics.

With few exceptions, postmodern writing is much less anguished and is narrower in scope than its antecedents. Rare are the heroic modernist efforts to conceive metaphoric or mythic systems which encompass and transcend social reality. Similarly, the bravado of the earlier avant-garde assault on culture is curiously lacking. This quiescence may indicate both an accommodation—or recuperation—of the avant-garde in its society and a failure to discern in this culture significant forces of social change, but at the heart of postmodern innovative writing is a troubled and problematic creative sensibility. The writer's analytical stance still fosters a critical response to culture, but there is clearly less faith in one's assumptions of self-knowledge and mastery, in one's perception and knowledge of the external world, and even more importantly, in the writer's very means of expression.

Gone are the modernist and avant-garde premises of the privileged nature of the artist's perspective and language. No longer does the feeling of alienation suggest a compensating critical vantage point from which the artist can declare his or her independence from the dominant culture. Instead, the essential dynamics of postmodernism indicate a major re-evaluation of the nature of the individual's relationship to society, and specifically to society's semiotic codes of behavior, value, and discourse. The postmodern individual, the writer, and the text now experience and articulate themselves self-consciously from *within* the social context from which, nevertheless, they may still feel alienated and of which they may still be critical. But postmodern literature recognizes that all perception, cognition, action, and articulation are shaped, if not determined, by the social domain. There can be no simple opposition to culture, no transcendent perspective or language, no secure singular self-definition, for all find their meaning only within a social framework.

The subject matter of postmodern literature is at once the complex interactions of four parallel sets of oppositions: individual and culture; personal speech and collective discourse; specific text and literary conventions; and literature and society's semiotic codes. Each pairing reveals the ambiguous status of individual creator or creation in a society which seems alternately to control or prefigure individual expression and yet to allow substantial personal freedom. Whereas the practices of modernism and the early avant-garde emphasized the relative independence and privileged perspective of the first term of each of these sets in its opposition to the second term which it sought to transcend or transform, postmodern thought recognizes the effective primacy of the latter terms out of which, against which, but always within which individual subjects, voices, texts, or codes must articulate themselves. As a result, Rimbaud's playful pun in his letter to Izambard—*On me pense* (I am thought, or one thinks me) and *on me panse* (I am groomed)[7]—now takes on more disturbing resonances, for by our actions within discourse we are thought *and* groomed. Even more disturbingly, whereas for Rimbaud the impersonal *on* represented universal reason speaking through the passive seer, for the postmodern writer, that *on* signifies social discourse, and in particular, social ideology, the structure and terms of which compromise individual self-discovery, articulation, and liberation.

The individual activist subjectivity, then, whether that of the person, voice, or text, knows itself as the product of the inherent dynamics of established meaning systems. The new is created against existent meaning, but through the informing processes of social systems. Consequently, an avant-garde work within the postmodern context must make evident the troubling ambiguities, paradoxes, and contradictions of innovations within language and culture. It reveals itself at every turn to be a manifestation of the society it sets itself against and which it would change, and by necessity must meet within itself the very factors which would limit or deny its activist desire. Thus, if sociological critics of the avant-garde tended to divide along two lines—those like Lukàcs, who saw the literary work as a direct expression of bourgeois culture, and those, like Adorno and Marcuse, who considered the avant-garde work a significant critique of that culture—contemporary critics and writers must, in effect, adopt both these positions simultaneously.[8]

The postmodern work, then, embodies a dual vision of possibility and limitation. It announces the liberating awareness that comes from denying aesthetic and philosophic concepts which are felt to be inadequate or delusive, yet the principles of that liberation apparently preclude forming any alternative systems of value and meaning. In this way, the postmodern vision is similar to many aspects of the traditional avant-garde, especially the dada movement which found essential freedom in its negative spirit, but was unable to sustain any positive principle of creation and vision. The "negative speed" of postmodern literature, and its critical arm post-structuralism, is expressed in a series of terms which signify critical assaults on all principles of essentialist value, order, meaning, control, and identity: deconstruction, demystification, de-centering. These concepts criticize the premises of the Western philosophic tradition, but undermine, in particular, the foundations of the modern bourgeois world's humanist presumptions. The glorification of "man" and the assumed sanctity of individual identity, which have been under attack throughout this century, but which have been defended by the modernist and, to a lesser extent, by the avant-garde movements, now are attacked as untenable ideological strictures. Individual identity is shown to be a fiction, having no center, no clear boundaries. Instead, we are found to be constructs of discrete elements of social discourse, the shifting locus of apparent meaning created by the confluence of political, sexual, perceptual, and philosophic codes experienced by "creatures of biology and chance." The concept of the integral self, struggling against the oppressive embrace of the social realm by falling back upon a cherished sense of personal authenticity, is swept aside as a delusive fiction which ensured the legitimacy of the social opposition against which it fought. In the process, the rigidity of both social and individual definition is lost. Society is perceived as a fictive framework of ideological codes which, like all semiotic systems, are grounded in nothing more than human desire and fear but which appear to have the authority of essential truth. As such, social values and systems of order are subject to critical demystification and deconstruction, through which the embattled individual may perceive his or her conceptual freedom.

Postmodern thought thus positions us within society's semiotic codes; it figures us as elements of social language. Identity is recast in terms of the essential workings of language, especially of the play of variance and difference, and the shifting grounds of all discourse. The change is radical, for it signals a re-conceptualization of being from an ideal of possible and desired ontological presence to a semiotic system which denies presence and completion. Being, known through and as discourse, is experienced as the field of free play, the "field of infinite substitutions in the closure of a finite ensemble," to use Derrida's terms.[9] Substitutions of the terms for identity and social meaning are infinite, for although we and any semiotic system are finite, we have no absolute center or grounding, so the game of meaning and consciousness must continue unabated. For Derrida and many of the postmodern writers, this recognition of the groundlessness of all once-threatening or restrictive orders, as well as limited identity, is immensely liberating. It represents a mode of thinking and interpretation which "affirms freeplay and tries to pass beyond man and humanism, the name man being the name of that being, who throughout the history of metaphysics or of ontotheology—in other words, through the history of all of his history—has dreamed of full presence, the reassuring foundation, the origin and end of the game."[10]

The terms free play and game call our attention to the frequency with which metaphors of game and play appear in contemporary aesthetics. There is a delightful, playful, and rather gratuitous aspect to much of contemporary writing and art. The affirmative side of postmodern creation is expressed in the acceptance, even glorification, of play, chance, indeterminancy, and self-conscious performance.[11] Again, John Cage is an exemplary figure, gently revelling in the groundlessness, hence the sense of an absolute freedom, of all his creations. He asks rhetorically, "And what is the beginning of no middles meanings and endings? And what is the ending of no beginnings middles and meanings? If you let it it supports itself. Each something is a celebration of the nothing that supports it."[12] This ludic spirit, however, is as double-edged as any aspect of postmodern creation. For some writers, it signals a creative freedom that allows writers to demystify society's codes of meaning and value in order to rip free for their personal use the images and linguistic styles out of which new creations will be made. For others, there is something demonic and restrictive about the forced constraints of game. It suggests that art can be no more than self-reflexive entertainment, and that the anarchic spirit manifest in this belief that the individual can truly achieve a state of creative independence may, in spite of its deconstructive sophistication, belie the degree of our shaping by social codes.

A slightly different variation on this opposition is manifest in the argument that postmodernism contains within itself two general tendencies which replicate the earlier opposition and similarity between the twin movements of modernism and the avant-garde. One might read the legacy of a modernist position in the self-reflexive investigation of the nature and properties of literary language that dominates the inherently hermetic novels of John Barth, William Gass, Vladimir Nabokov, and Jean Ricardou. In these works the social context is only a backdrop to the foregrounded play of an explicit linguistic game. Like the modernist work, which led Ortega y Gasset to proclaim that "art is a thing of no consequence," these postmodern artifices suggest that the construction and playing of the game of self-creation lead to a state of aesthetic self-sufficiency. Unlike the modernists, however, who held that even if the artwork was not immediately functional in social terms it still provided a refuge from society and an evaluative perspective of it, these postmodern fabulators insist on the gratuitous nature of any meaning system, including their own. Thus, their works can only engage the process of creation for its own sake. The writers and their works concentrate on the self-reflexive generative aspects of the literary code, in effect to create uni-dimensional works whose signifier and signified are identical. Implicitly, their art is tautological. It can only make statements about itself and about the language that determines it.[13]

However, there are a number of postmodern writers who adopt these same premises to develop what may be considered an avant-garde stance toward literature and society. The works of such diverse writers as Philippe Sollers, William Burroughs, Thomas Pynchon, Ronald Sukenick, Monique Wittig, and the poets of the L=A=N=G=U=A=G=E group, for example, are based on the concurrent beliefs in the arbitrariness of all language systems and in the connections among all semiotic systems. Thus, the self-reflexive deconstruction of the literary work, which occurs simultaneously with that work's creation, allows a similar critical assault on the literary code in general and on the dominant social discourses of which literature is one manifestation. This exploration of the literary text points, on the one hand, to the freedom—and limits—of individual action within language and society and, on the other hand, to the internal contradictions, weaknesses, and dynamics of all social codes.

This postmodernist self-reflexive writing, in both its "modernist" and "avant-garde" forms, has become a major element of the writing, art, and criticism of Europe and North and South America, although it seems to be most extensively developed in France and the United States. In all cases, it emerged in distinct opposition to the defensive humanist writing that dominated the literature of the nineteen-fifties and early sixties. One of the earliest signs of the appearance of post-modernism was the concurrent development in France of the *nouveau roman* and structuralist criticism which represented direct attacks on existential literature and the philosophy of phenomenology. Robbe-Grillet's aggressive manifesto, *Pour un nouveau roman* (1963) and his early novels, *Les gommes* (1953), *Le voyeur* (1955), *La jalousie* (1957), and *Dans le labyrinthe* (1959), provided the focal points for the new novelists' and critics' attacks on the modernist tradition of existential humanism.

Robbe-Grillet's first four novels parodied the phenomenological intentionality of the traditional literary character, and in particular, the effort by the individual to project or find a world of inherently personal meaning. These novels revealed the unperceived, yet obsessively troubling contradictions, fixations, and unbridgeable gaps in the character's perception of a world which refused to fall into manageable order. It is even more significant, however, that Robbe-Grillet's writing in the nineteen-sixties paralleled developments in semiological analysis and, later, post-structuralist thought. He and the writers associated with *Tel Quel*—Philippe Sollers, Maurice Roche, Jean Ricardou, and Denis Roche—investigated not only the limits of the individual's projection of meaning, but the mechanics of that projection and the processes by which the individual user of language becomes a function of the particular linguistic system. Thus, the original focus on the demystification of ego and meaning shifted to the submission of ego and interpretation to the collective operation of society's semiotic systems. Among the more programmatically political of the French writers, such as Sollers, this shift of focus brings the reader and writer to a confrontation with the ideological codes of collective discourse. In the case of Robbe-Grillet's later novels and films, from *Project pour une révolution à New York* on, the narrative voice is trapped within his society's popular media obsessions, particularly pornography, sadism, and political and religious violence. Robbe-Grillet's disruption of a sustained narration, his breaking apart and refolding all images into each other to prevent any single scene from reaching its anticipated climax, is held by the writer to be an act of politically significant play, since it distances the reader or viewer from the seductive attraction of the popular images. The ability of the creator to play with these deracinated images represents to Robbe-Grillet a critical distance from, and an activist stance within, the charged semiotic field that is our culture. "Our ludic language is not created in order to protect us, to place us in a refuge from the world, but, on the contrary, to place ourselves and this world in question, and consequently to transform it by what you would call the imagination."[14] However, the fact that Robbe-Grillet seems incapable of freeing himself from the images of pornography or clichéd soft core titillation, represented for example by his adulatory descriptions of David Hamilton's photographs of pre-pubescent nude girls, suggests that the author may have neither the freedom nor the desire to transform himself or society by the clinically precise and sensual images he creates in these ludic works.

Nonetheless, this effort to establish a space of critical distance and freedom, if not activist intention, by disrupting language represents the major point of contention in all avant-garde postmodern efforts. It lies at the heart of recent French feminist fiction and criticism which struggles to determine if it is possible to create a new language or to discover and truly image oneself if one is a woman writer caught within male, phallo-centric language. The efforts of critics such as Luce Irigaray and novelists such as Monique Wittig and Françoise Collin to disrupt conventional, hence oppressive, language replay many of the earlier avant-garde writers' expressions of faith and despair over the ability of an individual or group to alter consciousness and language from within established discourse. And as with much avant-garde writing, the idea of the project is more exciting than the actual results, which may, as in the case of *Les guérillères* appear mostly to rewrite inherited myths in feminist form. But if as yet, as Julia Kristeva has observed, these "feminine attempts . . . have no stylistic and thus no literary novelty,"[15] the radical feminist investigations of literary form and social discourse have the potential to be the most significant expression of a revitalized avant-garde sensibility in the postmodern era, precisely because they bring together an aggressive aesthetic activism and a social collectivity that sees itself acting in society and its history.

In other countries of Europe as well as in South and North America, an oscillation between "modernist" and "avant-garde" tendencies within postmodernism are also to be observed. Usually, however, the postmodern investigations of language are rarely so explicitly linked to the patterns of cultural ideology as they are in France. Indeed, in Europe, much of the innovative writing which disrupts literary conventions and social discourse appears to stay more on the level of linguistic experiments, as does, for example, the work of the "Wiener Gruppe," in particular Ernst Jandl and Friederike Mayröcker, and the writing of Helmut Heissenbüttel, Jürgen Becker, and the concrete poets, such as Gerhard Rühm and Eugen Gomringer in Germany and Austria. In Italy and other East and West European nations, the *Poesia Visiva* movement has extended concrete poetry's graphic games to incorporate visual images with the linguistic elements of the poem and at times presents pure, aesthetically self-contained texts, while at other times, especially in the works of Paul de Vree and Lucia Marcucci, the poets create politically charged works. In South America, the fictions of Jorge Luis Borges established a pattern for North and South American postmodern writers by their playful presentation as self-reflexive artifices. Borges's writing ranges from the self-contained fabulations of his *Labyrinths* to his apparently artless and transparent evocations of the most basic *patterns* of story-telling in *Dr. Brodie's Report*. Other South American novelists— Carlos Fuentes, Julio Cortazar, Cabrera Infante, Manuel Puig, and Gabriel Garcia Marquez, among others—combine an appreciation of European modernist and avant-garde techniques with an indigenous mythic and historical approach to their cultures to create some of the most innovative fiction being written today. However, the work of only a few—Cortazar and Severo Sarduy, for example—extends aggressive formal innovation to an explicitly political or cultural criticism.[16]

Postmodern literary invention in the United States is extremely diverse, ranging from a variety of experiments in poetry—including the L=A=N=G=U=A=G=E group of poets who offer the most extensive and consistent series of poetic manifestoes and collections of poetry,[17] visual poetry, "sound" poetry, and recently feminist explorations of the lessons of late modernist poetry grouped around the small journal *HOW(ever)*—to performance art and video art, which, though centered in the visual art world of the galleries and museums, create new visions of narrative possibiilty, finally to the self-reflexive novel. The novel, in fact, appears to be the genre in which the most significant postmodern innovations have occurred, in the United States as well as in France and South America. This is, I believe, because the novel allows the most extended elaboration of the interpenetration of personal, literary, and social discourses. It illustrates the determination of the individual subject or literary text by the various meaning systems of the society and, conversely, can chart the gambits of demystification directed against those codes by the individual and text.

The range of postmodern fiction in the United States is broad and, like almost all postmodern phenomena, includes an hermetic—or "modernist"—strain represented by the tautological fabulists, such as Barth, Gass, and Walter Abish, who display an ironic attitude toward previous modernist assumptions. Similarly, postmodern American fiction is produced by an "avant-garde" group of writers whose texts chronicle the severely problematic interaction of personal and collective reality and implicitly work to discover within literature and society the basis of an activist aesthetics. However, the scope of this activism is largely limited to personal creativity and self-knowledge, and few of these writers would call themselves avant-garde or would even agree that the avant-garde in the traditional sense could still exist. Nevertheless, when we study the novels of William Burroughs, Thomas Pynchon, Ronald Sukenick, or Robert Coover, to mention just a few of the writers whose books adopt various avant-garde strategies of aesthetic disruption, we notice that their formal innovation explores literary and social discourse, and that they shift the previous social context of rebellion to the social text of ideology. To a significant extent the innovative writers Donald Barthelme, Ishmael Reed, Raymond Federman, Clarence Major, Kathy Acker, Kurt Vonnegut, Richard Brautigan, Steve Katz, William Demby, and Ursule Molinaro, as well as those mentioned above, all develop self-reflexive experimental texts which illuminate the conflicts and paradoxes inherent in the individual's discovery of the nature and limits of identity and expression in this society. In fact, if there is a dominant focus to postmodern American fiction, it is the problematical nature of subjective presence.

Whether subjectivity is seen in terms of character, writer, or the voice of the text and language, it is rarely able to achieve clear definition and stable identity. Characteristically, in contemporary fiction individual characters are presented as fragmentary, barely self-conscious creatures subject to constantly changing conditions. Indeed, the concept of integral identity is willfully abandoned. Instead, characters are depicted as epistemological processes in flux—as transitory loci of shifting, incompatible, and incompletely known desires, fears, events, external forces, and systems over which the individual consciousness has little control and scarcely more knowledge, but to which it attempts to give temporary, self-consciously improvisational order.

To separate oneself from the distortions of the ego may open the writer and the reader to their activist participation in, as well as their determination by, what Lucien Goldmann has called the trans-individual realm of collective identity.[18] But if the loss of the subject—the death of "man"—appears to be a denial of bourgeois mystification, for many writers and critics it does not necessarily signify an overcoming of ideology. For certainly within contemporary society, there are many signs that the idea of integral identity has only vestigial authority and that individuals commonly experience a sense of diminishing significance in mass, pluralistic culture. Whether the trans-individual dimension promises self-conscious collective identity and activism or anonymous collective manipulation is the latent question in almost all postmodern texts.

In contemporary American fiction, the challenges for subjective identity in mass culture, and for literary innovation in social discourse, are for the individual and the text to discern and operate within the imprecise boundaries between themselves and their particular context. And in a culture apparently threatening to completely reshape the possibilities of individual identity and expression, the most frequent theme in this fiction is that of pervasive paranoia. It has become both the primary psychological state of the literary character and a literary motif embraced by the self-reflexive text. Both the writer and character realize that successful self-definition or creation depends on developing techniques of constant testing and interpretation of self and the encroaching world. They devise strategies of retreat and antagonism, of formal hermeticism and aesthetic disruption. If a political vision is implicit in both the social and aesthetic dimensions of postmodernism, it is that of anarchism— the expression of a defensive rage and creative idealism.

William Burroughs's novels are the most graphic and extreme expression of anarchic rage in contemporary literature. His characters are incessantly beset by forces of exploitation which push them into lives of addiction, self-destruction, and progressive dehumanization. Rarely do they perceive either what is happening to them or their own participation in their degradation. Most accept uncritically the propaganda broadcast by the media, the institutions of social control, the "Time, Life, Fortune Monopoly," the "reality studios," or the political groups of *Naked Lunch*—the Liquifactionists, Divisionists, and Senders, all of which are intent on replicating themselves through their victims or dominating people's thoughts by instilling a single pattern of cognition and expression in society. We are born into an exploitative culture, Burroughs argues, and from childhood on we model ourselves on destructive forms of behavior by which we come to know ourselves and the world, but which ensure our dependency on and submission to that world. In response, Burroughs counsels rebellion, an active, disruptive campaign against corporate and political means of control and against the established social codes of meaning and value.

But like John Cage, Burroughs also recognizes that to struggle against social control means to battle against one's prior identification with it; and even more distressing is that actively to oppose the enemy condemns one to being defined by them—for as long as one is fixated on fighting the opposition, one is not free of it. In Burroughs's novels, the greatest danger is to allow oneself to become rigidly defined, even in antagonism, for then one's identity is restricted and ever more vulnerable. Consequently, the individual must not only disrupt the "reality studios," but continuously disorient him- or herself and language to prevent personal life from being controlled by anything except immediate, personal action. Against the institutions of control, Burroughs sends his anarchists, terrorists, and the "Nova Police" who expose what is believed to be reality for the grotesque horror it is. Against the three political parties in *Naked Lunch,* he pits a fourth, the Factualists, whose job it is to reveal in the most brutal—and often pornographic—terms the truth of our daily lives. But the Factualists cannot substitute an alternative vision, for Burroughs trusts no codified message or program. All they can do is disrupt, and expose and force people to recognize themselves for what they are, both before and after they accept a version of the "reality film." The images we are offered are distinctly unpleasant in both cases. "You will readily understand why people will go to any lengths to get in the film to cover themselves with any old film scrap . . junky . . narcotics agent . . thief . . informer . . anything to avoid the hopeless dead-end horror of being just who and where you all are: dying animals on a doomed planet."[19] Precisely what sends people into addiction—their fear of chaos or pain, their sense of personal fragmentation and insignificance—becomes the only means and basis of their cure. Disruption, chaos, violence, and exposure are what one must learn to live in. Only those strong enough to exist without external support and without a rigid identity will survive in Burroughs's brutal cosmos.

The literary techniques and concerns of Ronald Sukenick's novels and stories exemplify the work of a large number of contemporary innovative writers who share with Burroughs a sense of the unreliable nature of personal identity and social stability, yet whose works are not as obsessively violent or pained as are Burroughs's. While Sukenick's books have not achieved the following of Brautigan, Vonnegut, Barthelme, Coover, or Reed, the self-reflexive nature of his works makes clear the aesthetic strategies, dilemmas, and limitations that these writers, along with a host of other authors—such as Major, Federman, Demby, Katz, Molinaro—face. In Sukenick's and these writers' works, neither the social environment nor the characters' identities are stable. Everything in Sukenick's books, for example, is in a state of flux and fission. The half-lives of characters and their surroundings often last no longer than a few pages, at times a few sentences. Both external reality and identity are perceived to be fictions, subject to revision as the shifting situation warrants. As in so many postmodern novels, the causes of these revisions are unclear. At times, changes in the characters' identities seem to be unconscious effects of the alterations in their environment; at others, they appear to be creative or defensive responses to environmental changes; and at still others, their surroundings modulate in tune with the characters' willed mutations; and finally, at times all of these possibilities seem to occur at once. The result is a vision of complex and ill-defined connections between individuals and their world, leading alternately to conditions of extreme paranoia and exhilarating creative freedom. Characters are able to synthesize alternative versions of themselves out of their dreams, memories, subconscious desires, social roles, and fantasies, while at the same time remaining almost totally dependent upon the vagaries of experience. The only adequate response, Sukenick suggests, is to accept identity as merely a transitory locus of consciousness and experience. One must embrace and live within the flow of events, creating one's identity and assuring one's freedom from external control by improvising with the fragments of self and the stimuli thrust at one from the environment.

In *98.6,* the Children of Frankenstein, members of a doomed commune, declare that they are creatures of "biology and chance," shaped by determinants over which they have no control, but in response to which they depend on the creative imagination.

> Enough imagination to deal with your particular allotment of biology and chance that would be their standard if they were to imagine a standard. They think that Lance doesn't have enough imagination he has so little imagination they can't even tell where he's at. Where he's at is he has so little imagination he's completely at the mercy of what happens to him that's where Lance is at. Wind thinks that Lance is like a force of nature he thinks that's terrific but Cloud understands that a force of nature is simply the product of every other force of nature in the Great Computer in the Sky and Cloud thinks it far better to program than be programmed. The only way to program rather than be programmed in Cloud's opinion is to gather new data to expose oneself to the unknown to increase one's allotment of biology and chance.[20]

Especially chance: for by increasing the arbitrary, the unexpected, the gratuitous in one's life, one diminishes the power of established social conventions, concepts, and literary practice over the self. In response to the supposed authority of common experience and tradition, Sukenick creates self-consciously transitory fictions, momentary projections that demystify the oppressive "real" and recognize their own suggestive, if synthetic, power.

> Psychosynthesis is the opposite of psychoanalysis but apart from that Cloud refuses to define it. Cloud feels that life is a lot like a novel you have to make it up. That's the point of psychosynthesis in his opinion to pick up the pieces and make something of them. Psychosynthesis is based on The Mosaic Law. The Mosaic Law is the law of mosaics a way of dealing with parts in the absence of wholes.[21]

Such improvisation allows an activist stance through the manipulation and temporary coordination of fragments of experience, yet also expresses one's fundamental dependency upon the conditions in which one lives.

Improvisation may be, in fact, the most characteristic postmodern creative strategy, not only in literature, but in music, dance, performance art, and the visual arts as well. Within a general passivity to the larger context of given experience, an activist locus of personal creativity is accented. The results of an essentially anarchic impulse, the pleasures of postmodern works seem to come as much from the disruption of the pervasive, distrusted order of reality and interpretation as from the playfulness of gratuitous and undirected creation. The implicit ideal of postmodernism is a state of pure presentness. More directed against the constraints of the past than positing an ideal future of significant difference, the postmodern work is rarely concerned with an aesthetics of sustained development. In fact, it is unable to foster such an aesthetics, since any rigorously ordered work must be subject to the same processes of demystification of established meaning that generated the original creative impulse. Only in works which announce the gratuitous nature of their creation, which make of the work a self-conscious game, do we encounter fanciful artifices which glory in their elaboration, such as in the works of Barth, Nabokov, and Gass. For the postmodern writers and artists who struggle against their determination by social or linguistic order, however, the work can be neither a self-sufficient game unto itself nor an unself-conscious creation providing the traditional satisfactions of orderly narrative development and conclusion. If the "Mosaic Law" ordains that creation must take place in the absence of wholes, postmodern works cannot themselves presume to be whole.

There are troubling aspects to this anarchic playfulness, however. If the theorists of gratuitous, self-reflexive innovation assert that there is no legitimate alternative to a state of pure presentness, and that all systems of presumed totalization are mystifications, postmodern creations appear never to be free from the pressures of those false beliefs. The absence of the whole, which the Mosaic Law and all varieties of post-structuralist theory announce, seems to signal the inability of the contemporary writer to conceive of the possibility that any principle of totalization can be justified, while at the same time, writers, artists, and critics are aware of the imposing force of a society which appears to operate in the smug certitude that there are such assured principles of action and belief. Furthermore, if the contemporary character—and author—is the product of biology and chance, one's ability to reveal the fictional nature of identity and to improvise a new self is ceaselessly placed in doubt by the struggles of the postmodern character to free him- or herself from the embrace of the past. These two concerns—the resistances of the past and of social totalization to the premises of postmodern creative freedom—surface in almost all contemporary innovative works.

The pleasures and promises of creative improvisation are the generative bases of all of Raymond Federman's fiction, for example. Federman, like Sukenick, is fascinated by the willed permutations of identity, but he is less concerned with the active creation of alternative present and future selves than with recounting and revising the dynamics of past experience and identity that are responsible for his present state of being. His fictions, *Double or Nothing, Take It or Leave It, The Voice in the Closet,* and *The Twofold Vibration,* are joyous accounts of the pleasures of personal and textual improvisation. But all of them are based on the obsessive need of the author to return to the past, to the sense of origin out of which, against which, indeed, away from which, the spirit of play and creation are propelled. Yet as much as one appreciates Federman's fictive energy, one experiences a sense of biographical and aesthetic claustrophobia as the texts return again and again to the Ur-text, his fortuitous escape from the horror of the holocaust which destroyed his family. The tale of his escape and the stories of his subsequent creation—improvisation—of a new self are repeated in varying forms throughout his works. But instead of diminishing the literary effect, this repetition contributes to the substantial power of his books, for it illuminates the tension between the desires of creative freedom and the resistance of personal and collective reality. In Federman's personal tale and his literary philosophy, an entire struggle of postmodern aesthetics is played out, yet remains unresolved.

If all of Federman's work posits its beginning in the need of a deracinated youth to improvise a new life, the present teller of these tales asserts his equal freedom to recreate his past since that past was largely the conscious creation of his former self. In all his current improvisations, the given experience—fictive or not, past or present— sets the terms against which the self-reflexive play engages itself, while the authority of the past is mediated by a series of fictive projections and recountings. Federman's works find their greatest sense of personal and aesthetic freedom in the author's willingness to play with both the details of any past experience and the linguistic form of that retelling. The text itself becomes the space of the play of freedom and constraint as Federman shifts from French into English, plays with typography, and slips among the various voices of author, narrator, character, and text, all in an effort to proclaim a formal and personal control or at least ironic distance from the tale that insists on being told, a tale which may reveal how little personal and creative freedom we actually have. As a consequence, the present author and text are more likely to tell what the past has come to mean than what it actually was. To Federman, the concept of the self is a fiction, but for that matter, all life, insofar as it *means* something is a fiction as well. Federman correctly places these personal concerns at the heart of much of contemporary writing. Focusing on the mediation of experience by language, postmodern literature—which Federman here calls *Surfiction*—does not try to imitate reality, but instead

> exposes the fictionality of reality. . . . Therefore, there is some truth in that cliché which says that "life is fiction," but not because it happens in the streets, but because reality as such does not exist, or rather exists only in its fictionalized version. The experience of life gains meaning only in its recounted form, in its verbalized version, or, as Céline said, some years ago, in answer to those who claimed that his novels were merely autobiographical: "Life, also, is fiction . . . and a biography is something one invents afterwards.[22]

Federman's personal bias is also clearly autobiographical, and his autobiography as fiction becomes the principle of his postmodern aesthetics. In this, he is not alone. The creative freedom to improvise a self and to demystify, or appear to free oneself from, the constraints of past and present experience is the ideal of a large number of contemporary works which are manifestly based in their authors' autobiographies. For example, Burroughs, Sukenick, Kosinski, Vonnegut, Major, Demby, Katz, and Baraka all create self-conscious fictions which not only transpose factual elements into fictional terms, but offer themselves as paradigms for the struggle between imaginative

freedom and social and textual restriction. In effect, the autobiographical mode in postmodern fiction investigates the relationship
of one form of fictive discourse, self-creation, to the numerous public
systems of meaning which constitute "reality." And since the individual is seen as one element of those public discourses which threaten
to determine how the individual subject can "mean" or act in society,
successful self-creation depends on the ability to recognize both that
the social environment is a fictive system that can be demystified and
that the individual must improvise new patterns of self-knowledge
out of the fragments of personal and social discourses.

In the works of Pynchon, Coover, Barthelme, Brautigan, Reed,
Vonnegut, Sukenick, and Federman, for example, the environment
the characters struggle with is often only a series of patent fictions,
sign systems, hidden messages, obscure codes, familiar myths, pop
images, and most frequently what Barthelme has called *dreck*, the
detritus of popular culture, deracinated images of mass media in
pluralistic society. Barthelme's ironic and witty collages of high and
popular culture rituals, Reed's adaption of folk narrative and popular media, Coover's grand orchestration of myths, cartoon images, and
historical dramas, Brautigan's and Vonnegut's wry explorations of
American myths and popular and minor literary genres all testify to
the individual writer's and character's entanglements in the web of
meaning systems that make up mass culture.

But the meaning of these meaning systems is rarely very clear; the
environment is never neutral, and is frequently threatening. Correct
interpretation of the environment—even before its demystification—
thus becomes the initial step of self-definition. Of all postmodern
American works, Thomas Pynchon's novels, especially *Gravity's Rainbow,* illustrate the paranoid obsessions and anxieties associated with
the search for an adequate interpretation of one's world.

> The rest of us, not chosen for enlightenment, left on the outside of
> Earth, at the mercy of a Gravity we have only begun to learn how to
> detect and measure, must go on blundering inside our front-brain faith
> in Kute Korrespondences, hoping that for each psi-synthetic taken
> from Earth's soul there is a molecule, secular, more or less ordinary
> and named, over here—kicking endlessly among the plastic trivia, find-
> ing in each Deeper Significance and trying to string them all together
> like terms of a power series to zero in on the tremendous and secret
> Function whose name, like the permuted names of God, cannot be
> spoken . . . plastic saxophone reed *sounds of unnatural timbre,* sham-
> poo bottle *ego-image,* Cracker Jack prize *one-shot amusement,* home
> appliance casing *fairing for winds of cognition,* baby bottles *tranquil-*

ization, meat packages *disguise of slaughter,* dry-cleaning bags *infant strangulation,* garden hoses *feeding endlessly the desert* . . . but to bring them together, in their slick persistence and our preterition . . . to make sense out of, to find the meanest sharp sliver of truth in so much replication, so much waste.[23]

Such a truth is not to be found, though it is hinted at. Pynchon's characters consequently find themselves hopelessly caught between the apparent chaos of this world of replication and waste and suggestions of an omnipresent malevolent order, hidden behind but directing the chaos and the characters' lives. And if Pynchon is the best chronicler of paranoia in postmodern fiction, his creation Tyrone Slothrop is the emblematic postmodern character as he approaches the frightening realization that if there is a coherence to his identity, it is not something over which he has much control. Initially the product of the System's malign manipulation of his life, then the quester for the origin of that manipulation—his surrogate father, Lazlo Jamf—Slothrop finally enters a state of extreme fragmentation in which he loses the ability to intrepret reality and to perceive the grand design behind experience and his life. "Slothrop perceives that he is losing his mind. If there is something comforting—religious, if you want—about paranoia, there is still also anti-paranoia, where nothing is connected to anything, a condition not many of us can bear too long. Well right now Slothrop feels himself sliding onto the anti-paranoid part of his cycle. . . . Either They have put him here for a reason, or he's just here. He isn't sure that he wouldn't, actually, rather have that *reason.*"[24]

Slothrop's fate is an enigma. He is progressively dismantled, scattered across the Zone, apparently freed of the System's control and interest; he enters a state of silence where he appears to merge with nature. Whether this escape from the world of human meaning and language represents a victory or a defeat is a subject of debate among his friends and fellow victims of the System. Rather than the passivity of anti-paranoia as a means of "defeating" the System's influence, they champion "Creative paranoia," which "means developing at least as thorough a We-system as a They-system."[25] This "We-system"— the Counterforce—is self-consciously alogical, disorganized, and anarchic. Rather than proposing an alternative order, the Counterforce, like Burroughs's characters, turns willed fragmentation against the established order in an effort to disrupt and demystify it. But again, as Roger Mexico realizes, to define themselves as a system against the They-system, the Counterforce must play "their" game; it must remain a subsidiary system within the larger one. Furthermore, even though they sing "It isn't a resistance, it's a war," Mexico foresees that they have no real hope of dismantling the System. At most, they will only be able to carve out relatively small areas of personal satisfaction, and, being no significant threat, they will be condemned to "living on as Their pet." Recuperated within the System, they may achieve a certain romantic notoriety as "the glamorous ex-rebels, half-suspected but still enjoying official immunity and sly love, camera-worthy wherever they carry on . . . doomed pet freaks."[26] But the greatest anguish will come from their own awareness of how deeply implicated they are in the System as it stands, how their personal identities, desires, and expectations are the products of the very world they seek to interpret and demystify.

> Well, if the Counterforce knew better what those categories concealed, they might be in a better position to disarm, de-penis and dismantle the Man. But they don't. Actually they do, but they don't admit it. Sad but true. They are as schizoid, as double-minded in the massive presence of money, as any of the rest of us, and that's the hard fact. The Man has a branch office in each of our brains, his corporate emblem is a white albatross, each local rep has a cover known as the Ego, and their mission in this world is Bad Shit. We know what's going on, and we let it go on.[27]

This self-judgment can apply equally well to most contemporary literary characters, and is a succinct expression of the paradoxes confronting the self-conscious individual in mass culture. Of particular importance to postmodern fiction, however, is that this problem of the integrity of the individual subject is not limited to the characters created by the writers, but also dominates the self-reflexive text's relationship to established codes of literary and social language. Burroughs once wrote: "To speak is to lie—To live is to collaborate,"[28] and although he later qualified the extremism of this statement, such a sentiment indicates the ultimate limits of avant-garde writing in postmodern culture. The avant-garde literary sensibility must confront, as does the Counterforce, the ambiguous placement of the writer in society and its discourse. Indeed, the characteristic strategies of postmodern innovative writing—the aggressive disruption of language and the literary text through fragmentation, aleatory structures, strained metaphors, collage, "cut-ups," self-reflexively arbitrary formal structuration—adopt avant-garde techniques to alter the writer's and reader's literary expectations; but just as the fragmentation of the literary character suggests a diminishment of individual possibility within an increased anarchic freedom, the obverse side of the aggressive demystification of language and its concurrent search for a more personal and vital expression is a disheartening or resigned sense of linguistic restriction and individual creative inconsequence.

Postmodern literature's focus on language reflects the analysis of the individual's relationship to society's semiotic codes that is the subject of contemporary semiological, and especially post-structuralist, criticism. Both the literature and criticism conclude that: (1) there are no privileged codes of discourse, that literature is not qualitatively different from other modes of signification; (2) no particular code exists independently of all other semiotic systems in its culture; (3) the terms of the individual work, no matter how innovative, are always determined by the conventions of the established literary tradition; (4) the writer, working inevitably from within a specific tradition— and its parent culture—, cannot be considered the sole author of the particular text.

The latter two lessons dominate most self-reflexive literary works because they refer most directly to the possibilities inherent in literary innovation, for, as the semioticians inform us, meaning is the product of the interactions among linguistic elements of a specific discourse. Consequently, any statement or work has meaning only in reference to the particular linguistic framework in which it is placed, so that any innovative text, although struggling to transform that framework, is necessarily dependent on it, and at the same time legitimizes it. The literary work can never claim complete originality, and plagiarizes—or "playgiarizes," to use Federman's term—prior discourse, thus receiving life and meaning from what it defines itself against. Like the fictional character who reveals that personality is only the locus of individual and social determinants, the author and text disclose that they are spoken by the language which they give speech to. And even though the writer gives speech its reality by speaking, he or she in turn only exists as a speaker because of the patterns of existent discourse.

Such an awareness can lead to a sense of entrapment, if not exhaustion, since the writer's freedom and originality are limited by the discourse which shapes the stories he or she would tell. Barth's expression "the literature of exhaustion" aptly names a significant dimension of contemporary fiction. Some of the finest stylists and self-reflexive explorers of the medium—Nabokov, Barth, Gass, and Borges—have lovingly testified to the pleasures and frustrations of their encapsulation within literary discourse. There is little effort in their works to address or directly describe—to re-present—reality, for these postmodernists emphasize that reality, known only through language, is to be meaningfully experienced only as a fictive structure. The writer's primary allegiance, then, is to the demands of literary language. And while these writers' fictions frequently center on the absurd consequences of their characters' confusion of their representations of reality for reality itself, the novels fold back upon themselves to establish new forms of hermetic play. The works become self-reflexive games of internal wit and coherence, illuminating their constitutive rules and ultimately displaying the delights and consternation of articulation.

However, unlike the modernist attitude that such hermeticism provides a dimension of pleasure, insight, and value transcending daily language and materialism, these postmodern works claim a privileged status only by their self-reflexive undermining of all presumptions of linguistic authority, whether literary or social. For just as post-structuralist criticism, in its emphasis on the nature of discourse, can be seen as the direct descendant of modernist formalism yet betrays its predecessor's assumptions by stressing the limits of language through the constant deconstruction of texts, this type of postmodern fiction similarly represents the nether side of the modernist vision. The contemporary work's fascination with silence and with the intractability of discourse suggests an implicitly nihilistic stance. Rather than positing the value of the literary work against the threat of silence and meaninglessnesss, these postmodernists express an ironic acceptance of the inevitability of the limits of meaning, the necessary silence at the heart of speech, and the free play of language suspended in the void—a language that knows no essential beginning, end, or foundation. The irony that the great modernists relied on to balance the social insignificance of their works has become the protective irony that allows the postmodernists simultaneously to create their works and to participate in the artifact's necessary undermining.

These concerns about the relationship of author to language and of text to literary discourse are evident not only in the works of these particular writers, but throughout postmodern writing. However, the other two lessons of postmodern criticism—the loss of the privileged status of literature, and its relation to other social codes of discourse—are the particular foci of those writers who most suggest the survival of an avant-garde spirit in postmodern American fiction: Pynchon, Burroughs, Sukenick, Federman, Brautigan, Major, Katz, and Barthelme. They recall the avant-garde sensibility by their insistence on innovative writing which both focuses on the restrictive or deadening workings of the social organization, described in their works in terms of various semiotic codes—functionalism, bureaucratese, cybernetics, political jargon, sexual and racial innuendo, or ideological formulations—and offers by its self-reflexive formal disruption a paradigm for analysis, demystification, and personal liberation within those codes. These postmodern writers, rather than being obsessed with the silence of an apparently meaningless world, recognize that the world they inhabit is surfeited with meaning systems from which they must wrench their own language. For just as their characters sense the mutually supportive operation of the various social systems which shape their lives for ill or for good, the writers realize that literature is embraced by other social languages and has a role in legitimizing the ways people perceive, think, and speak in this culture. If, furthermore, the characters achieve a precise delineation of neither identity nor surrounding phenomena, then neither can the writer ever be sure of the ideological components and extensions of the work. Consequently, many contemporary avant-garde writers devise strategies of distrust and disruption, not only of society's semiotic codes, but of literature and their own texts.

Displaying the writer's paranoia, Burroughs states: "The writer sees himself reading to the mirror as always. . . . He must check now and again to reassure himself that The Crime of Separate Action has not, is not, cannot occur. . . . Anyone who has ever looked into a mirror knows what this crime is and what it means in terms of lost control when the reflection no longer obeys."[29] His response, however, reveals one of the paradoxes confronting the postmodern writer, for ultimately Burroughs must accept the necessity of that "crime." Unsure both of language and of his control over it, more precisely, of his dependence on it, Burroughs radically disrupts the text's continuity and constructs collage novels made up of fragmentary moments of new texts and cut-up and rearranged pieces of works by other writers and himself in order to force him and the reader to experience language and the literary text in a new manner. He is concerned with neither narrative unity nor conventional grammatical sequence, hence predictable meaning, but rather attempts to think in "association blocks," groups of random images which by their juxtaposition to each other suggest meanings beyond the writer's and traditional language's control. But here, Burroughs, ever distrustful of language, allows himself to be governed by the random images and unpredictable workings of language; indeed, he demonstrates that to speak *is* to lie and to live *is* to collaborate. As a result, the writer must willfully immerse him- or herself in the collective language in order to speak, for it is a greater delusion to assume that one's ego is integral or that it is in absolute control of its articulation. The only option is to admit the ambiguity of subjective placement in language and to highlight the struggle between individual expression and cultural system. Thus one testifies to a dependence on established discourse, yet can hope to purify it, nonetheless, by stressing the moment of surprise at the new creation's appearance.

Valuing the surprising and the new is, of course, one of the primary tenets of the traditional avant-garde, for the experience of the new thrusts one free of the fetters of the past and presages the hoped-for future. However, in postmodernism there is no strong invocation of an anticipated future, but rather, a preference for immediacy, for the intensity of experience found in the flow of constantly changing present moments. The focus of postmodern fiction is thus on the process of meaning-making which highlights the continuous deconstruction of established meaning and the projection of the new. Sukenick's character in *Out,* who says, "I want to write a book like a cloud that changes as it goes,"[30] exemplifies this position. And though few writers follow this desire to the extent that Sukenick has, the sense of the mutability of meaning and of the writer's freedom to create new images through literary disruption and innovation is the basis of many postmodern works.

Significantly, the primary focus of postmodern innovation is, as it has been throughout the history of the avant-garde, on metaphor. The creation of metaphor and of larger constructs, such as Burroughs's "association blocks" or the collage text, illustrates the diacritical workings of language, the joining of disparate elements from within established meanings to create new meaning. Metaphor is seen as the foundation of both the literary text and all cultural semiological systems. It is the "Great Lie," Pynchon's Fausto Maijstral declares in *V.,* but without it, he continues, society could not exist, for metaphor cloaks the "innate mindlessness" of things to provide a delusive security.[31] It is only a partial truth—a "thrust at truth and a lie"— Oedipa Maas learns in *The Crying of Lot 49,*[32] a convenient fiction which has the potential to become deadly. It is the poet's responsibility, Pynchon implies, to ensure that the system of metaphors that make up the Great Lie that is "the System" doesn't gain complete ascendency. For even though meaning systems give order to life, they inevitably become increasingly oppressive, exploitative, and finally entropic. The writer must reveal the lie of literature and culture, as well as their truth.

Pynchon's method is not to dismantle his text, as does Burroughs, but to parody excessively the rage for order in society to the point that his metaphors become grossly exaggerated and strained. Making ridiculous and grotesque the complex of social, political, sexual, cinematic, technological, and pop-cultural meaning systems that envelop us, Pynchon's metaphors proliferate freely to reveal both how meaning systems *do* interpenetrate and tend toward aggressive totalization, and yet how no system can bear too much input before it starts to fall apart under its own weight. His novels, especially *Gravity's Rainbow,* work by a principle of comic and surreal overdetermination, themselves nearly falling apart as their many narrative lines dissipate or their characters are either left in a state of unresolvable inertia or disappear into the complex of conflicting subplots. Thus *Gravity's Rainbow,* which initially appears to be another example of the modernist novel's effort to project a totalizing vision, is really a parody of modernism and is the fitting expression of a deconstructive postmodern work. The book recalls a sentence from Sukenick's *Out,* "Connection develops, meaning falls away."[33]

Such a pattern of the absence or ambiguity of meaning in the midst of surreal connections of images is common to the work of many postmodernists, such as Reed, Barthelme, Wurlitzer, Katz, Coover, Sorrentino, Charles Wright, Brautigan, and Vonnegut. But this neo-surrealism does not represent a search for a primal super-reality which might resolve contradictions; rather, it adapts the surrealists' love of absurd juxtaposition and the free play of the imagination. This new surrealism signals both the fragmenting madness of the System and, at the same time, the liberating imaginative vision one may find within the System. In *Gravity's Rainbow,* for example, Roger Mexico hears a German Renaissance hymn sung by a black, Jamaican soldier during a cold Christmas service in England. The singer's voice infuses the church with visions of brown girls sashaying among the Protestants. "These are not heresies so much as imperial outcomes, necessary as the black man's presence, from acts of minor surrealism—which, taken in the mass, are an act of suicide, but which in its pathology, in its dreamless version of the real, the Empire commits by the thousands every day, completely unaware of what it's doing."[34]

The antagonistic impulse of the postmodern avant-garde is to make this inherent surrealism evident to aid in the fragmentation of the Empire. Here again, we encounter the paradox of literary fragmentation which both describes a problematic situation for the individual and the text and is itself a means of achieving a degree of anarchic freedom. The writer might instinctively protest against the plethora of conflicting images and meaning systems which creates a confusing and oppressive environment, but he or she can only find

a degree of personal freedom by disrupting those systems and creating new, fragmentary, and often obscure images. Such a freedom,
Pynchon has shown, is both attractive and ultimately delusive, for
the improvisation of personal identity and meaning within the strictures of collective discourse can be seen as both an antagonistic response to an oppressive society and an expression of it. We *are* both
rebels and pets.

This paradoxical situation defines the postmodern arts. It is evident in the four related premises of postmodern criticism and literature: the confusing multiplicity of meaning systems and the apparent
devaluation of specific meaning; the focus on the structure of discourse as opposed to its operative function; the loss of subjective
definition in culture and discourse; the denial of historicity in social
and linguistic change. Each of these premises serves to radically qualify, if not deny, the resurgence of the avant-garde spirit.

The totalization of meaning systems is described by many postmodern writers, primarily as a confusing growth of competing and
entwining sign systems in which no clear hierarchy is discernible, no
infrastructure suggested, nor any undisputed meaning achieved. Literature recognizes its involvement in this web of meaning, but beyond its epistemological questioning it is unsure of its social function
and meaning. No longer able to present itself as a separate form of
meaning and value either within society or in opposition to it, postmodern literature offers itself as a paradigm of a questioning process
without answers, an agent of demystification that undermines itself.

The reduction of all experience and phenomena to elements of
sign systems which can be "demystified" as arbitrary, fictive constructs
implies a political response to culture, but the strategies of demystification, disruption, and improvisation are techniques played out solely
within the formal dynamics of the various semiotic systems and are
consequently of questionable efficacy in any activist political context.
The essential formalism—or idealism—of postmodern thought, its
belief that meaning is primarily a function of the diacritical workings
of discourse, not that the structure of the code is a response to material conditions, gives more significance to the mechanics of the
semiotic system than to its function, as if the latter were entirely a
product of the former. Thus no system of political interpretation,
whether of the left or the right, escapes this critique of language as
arbitrary fiction. And in the absence of any appealing and developed
political movement within contemporary society, the political dimension of the avant-garde can only remain an affirmation of its withdrawal of allegiance from any overt ideology. However, the ideo-

logical implications of this stance are rarely explored. And even the presumed anarchic freedom of the individual to withhold assent while attempting to play with and alter the established forms, values, and traditions of the culture suggests that significant changes are not the result of alterations of the world to which language refers and to which it attempts to give meaning, but are rather inevitable products of the normal dynamics of linguistic usage.

The goal of individual action in and on any language system is twofold: to find those areas of free play that suggest self-creation and freedom, and to disrupt if not change the totalizing impetus of the system as a whole. This ideal is anarchic, as has been the goal of much avant-garde activity in the past. But, as we have seen, the very notion of individual freedom is problematic precisely because each action within collective discourse reveals the unsure status of individualism in this society. Defined in terms of the system of discourse, the individual can find freedom only by submitting to the code, even as he or she tries to subvert it.

The resulting changes of self and system may, therefore, be no more than the formal dislocations of the system in which nothing substantial is altered. If the agent of change, self-reflexive innovation, is seen only as one element in a set of possible operations inherent in language, then one must ask what is the nature of the change which one can desire? Can postmodern innovation reflect an avant-garde belief in historical possibility? To be *in advance* of change would merely place one in a state of premature semiological shift. And finally, can an historical perspective be easily sustained in a society which seems both to inspire constant formal change and to remain singularly static?

The literary innovation that characterizes postmodern fiction provides no easy answers to these concerns, for it is an expression of a troubled exploration of the relation of ill-defined individuals to an ambiguous social framework. The postmodern focus on the mediation of self and others through literary language and society's semiotic codes reveals a constant doubt about the nature of the collectivity of which the writer is a member. Writing self-consciously from within the social context and the "social text," the contemporary writer can offer no modernist or avant-garde privileged and idealist perspective. The writer can only ask him- or herself and the audience whether social discourse, behavior, and ideology are manifestations of a growing collective consciousness in which it might be possible for them to act—to speak—together to create a new future, or whether they are signs of an increasing corporate, bureaucratic cybernetic control of collective experience and thought, as so many contemporary novelists seem to fear.

The innovative sensibility of much of postmodern fiction suggests a guarded avant-garde response nonetheless. It sustains the earlier avant-garde's faith that discourse, become self-conscious and self-reflexive, can raise the writer's and reader's awareness of the properties and operations of language and social discourse, as well as of their own problematic placement within those languages. Unable as yet, however, to locate within this society signs of imminent and significant change not compromised by the culture in general, or the prevailing philosophies of meaning and language, innovative writing remains primarily a personal and idealistic activity, as are the immediate, if limited and perhaps compromised rewards it offers: free play, improvisation, and temporary self-creation. Perhaps more cannot be expected, at least not until the social and historical conditions of the culture that postmodern literature responds to, and is an expression of, change. As much as postmodern avant-gardism is antagonistic to the given terms of social reality, it is implicated in the society it rebels against. Instead of being *in advance* of its time, it is a direct expression of this era.

Notes

Chapter I

1. Arthur Rimbaud, in a letter to Paul Demeny, 15 May, 1871. *Complete Works, Selected Letters*, trans. Wallace Fowlie (Chicago: University of Chicago Press, 1966), p. 309.
2. Umberto Boccioni, Carlo Carra, Luigi Russolo, *et al.* "The Exhibitors to the Public 1912," in *Futurist Manifestos*, ed. Umbro Apollonio (New York: The Viking Press, 1973), p. 45.
3. Charles Bernstein, in "The Pacifica Interview" (March, 1979), in *L=A=N=G=U=A=G=E*, Supplement No. 3, October, 1981, n.p.
4. Lucien Goldmann, *Pour une sociologie du roman* (Paris: Gallimard, Collection Idées, c. 1964), p. 55.
5. Charles Baudelaire, "Le Peintre de la vie moderne," in *Oèuvres Complètes* (Paris: Gallimard, Bibliotheque de la Pléiade, 1961), p. 1163.
6. Arthur Rimbaud, *Une Saison en enfer,* in *Oeuvres,* ed. Suzanne Bernard (Paris: Garnier Frères, 1960), p. 241.
7. Ezra Pound, "A Retrospect," in *Pavannes and Divisions* (New York: Knopf, 1918), reprinted in *Ezra Pound, A Critical Anthology,* ed. J. P. Sullivan (Baltimore: Penguin, 1970), p. 85.
8. Goldmann, p. 55.
9. T. S. Eliot, "Ulysses, Order, and Myth," *The Dial,* November, 1923, reprinted in *James Joyce: Two Decades of Criticism,* ed. Sean Givens (New York: Vanguard, 1948), pp. 201–202.

10. Richard Gilman, "The Idea of the Avant-Garde," *Partisan Review,* 39, 3 (Summer, 1972), p. 390.

11. See the discussion of the temporal sensibilities and aesthetic strategies of various modernist writers in Octavio Paz, *Children of the Mire,* trans. Rachel Phillips (Cambridge: Harvard University Press, 1974), p. 110, and Georges Poulet, *Le Point de départ* (Paris: Plon, 1964), pp. 740.

12. Lionel Trilling, *Sincerity and Authenticity* (Cambridge: Harvard University Press, 1971), pp. 99–100.

13. George T. Noszlopy, "The Embourgeoisement of Avant-garde Art," *Diogenes,* 67 (Fall, 1969), pp. 94–95.

14. See the discussion of the development of avant-garde terminology and thought in Matei Calinescu, *Faces of Modernity* (Bloomington: Indiana University Press, 1977), pp. 107 ff, and Robert Estivals, *et al., L'Avant-Garde: Etude historique et sociologique des publications périodiques ayant pour titre "L'Avant-garde"* (Paris: Bibliothèque Nationale, 1968).

15. Claude Henri de Saint-Simon, *De l'organization sociale,* quoted in Calinescu, pp. 102–103.

16. Olinde Rodrigues, "L'Artiste, le savant et l'industriel," in Saint-Simon, *Opinions littéraires, philosophiques et industrielles* (Paris: Galérie de Bossange Père, 1825), pp. 331 ff, quoted in Calinescu, p. 103.

17. Calinescu, pp. 103–106.

18. Donald Drew Egbert, *Social Radicalism and the Arts* (New York: Knopf, 1970), pp. 20 ff.

19. Charles Baudelaire, "Mon Coeur mis à nu," in *Oeuvres Complètes,* ed. Claude Pichois (Paris: Gallimard, Bibliothèque de la Pléiade, 1961), p. 1285.

20. Arthur Rimbaud, letter to Paul Demeny, 15 May, 1871, in Bernard, p. 348.

21. Peter Bürger, *Theorie der Avantgarde* (Frankfurt am Main: Suhrkamp Verlag, 1974), pp. 26–35.

22. See, for example, Calinescu, pp. 105–106.

23. Percy Bysshe Shelley, "A Defence of Poetry," in *Shelley's Poetry and Prose,* ed. Donald H. Reiman and Sharon B. Powers (New York: W. W. Norton, 1977), p. 508.

24. Raymond Williams, *Culture and Society* (New York: Harper and Row Torchbook, 1966), p. 47.

25. Williams, p. 43.

26. Fredric Jameson, *Fables of Aggression* (Berkeley: University of California Press, 1979), p. 14.

27. Adrian Marino, " 'Modernity' and the Evolution of Literary Consciousness," *Diogenes,* 77 (Spring, 1972), p. 116.

28. Paz, p. 26.

29. Noszlopy, p. 95.

30. Paz, p. 9.
31. André Breton, "Political Position of Today's Art," in *Manifestoes of Surrealism,* trans. Richard Seaver and Helen R. Lane (Ann Arbor: University of Michigan Press, Ann Arbor Paperback, 1972), p. 220.
32. Breton, "Speech to the Congress of Writers," *Manifestoes of Surrealism,* p. 241.
33. Herbert Read, *The Forms of Things Unknown* (New York: World, 1963), pp. 146–150.
34. Miklos Szabolsci, "Avant-Garde, Neo-Avant-Garde, Modernism: Questions and Suggestions," *New Literary History,* III, 1 (Autumn, 1971), p. 58.
35. Rimbaud, letter to Georges Izambard, 13 May, 1871, in Fowlie, p. 303.
36. See, for example, the well-documented PEN American Center Report, *The Campaign Against the Underground Press,* by Geoffrey Rips (San Francisco: City Lights, 1981).
37. Paz, p. 107.
38. See especially Michel Beaujour's discussion of these conflicts between poetics and revolutionary goals in "Flight out of Time: Poetic Language and the Revolution," *Yale French Studies,* 39 (1967), pp. 29–49.
39. Guillaume Apollinaire, "The New Spirit and the Poets," in *Selected Writings,* ed. and trans. Roger Shattuck (New York: New Directions, 1971), p. 235.
40. Baudelaire, "Mon Coeur mis à nu," in *Oeuvres Complètes,* p. 1285.
41. Rimbaud, *ibid.,* p. 309.
42. Beaujour, p. 39.
43. Renato Poggioli, *The Theory of the Avant-Garde,* trans. Gerald Fitzgerald (New York: Harper and Row, Icon Edition, 1971), pp. 65–68.
44. Antonin Artaud, *The Theater and Its Double,* trans. Mary C. Richards (New York: Grove Press, 1958), p. 74.

Chapter II

1. Rick Osmond, ed., *Rimbaud's Illuminations* (London: The Athlone Press, University of London, 1976); W. Frohock, *Rimbaud's Poetic Practice* (Cambridge: Harvard University Press, 1963); John Porter Houston, *The Design of Rimbaud's Poetry* (New Haven: Yale University Press, 1963); Robert Greer Cohn, *The Poetry of Rimbaud* (Princeton: Princeton University Press, 1973); Wallace Fowlie, *Rimbaud's Illuminations* (London: Hawill Press, 1953).
2. Cf., Henri Guillemin, *À Vrai dire* (Paris: Gallimard, 1956), 174 ff.
3. Letter to Georges Izambard, May 13, 1871, in Rimbaud, *Oeuvres,* ed. Suzanne Bernard (Paris: Garnier Frères, 1960), p. 343.
4. Cf. the discussion of this possibility in Suzanne Bernard's introduction to Rimbaud's *Oeuvres* (Paris: Garnier Frères, 1960), pp. xxxvii–xxix. See also pp. 492–494.

5. Rimbaud, *Oeuvres*, p. 171; *Complete Works, Selected Letters*, trans. and ed. Wallace Fowlie (Chicago: University of Chicago Press, 1966), pp. 125, 127. Subsequent references will be indicated in the text.

6. Vladimir Mayakovsky, "A Cloud in Trousers," in *The Bedbug and Selected Poetry*, ed. Patricia Blake (Bloomington: Indiana University, 1975), p. 61; F. T. Marinetti, "The Founding and Manifesto of Futurism 1909," in *Futurist Manifestos*, ed. Umbro Apollonio (New York: Viking, 1973), p. 23.

7. Valéry, in a letter to J.-M. Carré, published in *Autour de Verlaine et de Rimbaud* (1949), mentioned in Bernard, p. 526.

8. On this point, see the excellent discussion by Michel Beaujour, "Flight out of time: Poetic Language and the Revolution," *Yale French Studies* 39 (1967), pp. 29–49.

Chapter III

1. Guillaume Apollinaire, "La Phalange Nouvelle," in *La Poésie Symboliste: Trois Entretiens sur les Temps Héroiques* (Paris: L'Édition, 1908), p. 171.

2. A somewhat similar interpretation of Apollinaire's "perpetual effort of self-identification" is briefly discussed in Roger Shattuck's introduction to his edition of Apollinaire's selected works, *Selected Writings of Guillaume Apollinaire* (New York: New Directions, 1971), pp. 37–47. Shattuck also mentions that Marcel Raymond has arrived at this view too.

3. Apollinaire, "Merveilles de la Guerre," in *Oeuvres Poétiques,* ed. Marcel Adéma and Michel Décaudin (Paris: Gallimard, Pléiade, 1959), p. 272. Translation by Roger Shattuck in *Selected Writings of Guillaume Apollinaire*, p. 185. Further quotations and translations will be marked in the text.

4. In Shattuck's discussion of this threat to the lyric self, he refers to the same two passages of "Merveilles de la Guerre" and "Cortège." But his interpretation of the passages is opposite to mine. He sees the assertive tone of "Merveilles de la Guerre" as signaling a "positive conviction of identity" so that the statement "there is only I who am myself" announces a successful union of the I and the not-I. This reading, however, ignores the poet's recognition that he would prefer that the "not-I" would be in himself as well. In "Cortège" Shattuck sees the reconstruction of self as a tenuous affair (which it may be) made possible only by Apollinaire's friends coming to surround him and give him security. I prefer to read the passage as referring to more than a personal social problem, but as casting doubt on his whole poetic venture. Shattuck, "Introduction: Apollinaire, Hero-Poet," in *Selected Writings*, p. 39.

5. Apollinaire, "The New Spirit and the Poets," in Shattuck, p. 227. Further references to this essay will be noted in the text.

6. "Les Collines" in Adéma and Décaudin, p. 172; first stanza translation in Shattuck, p. 145; the rest of the translation is mine.

7. Apollinaire, letter to André Billy, quoted in *Oeuvres Poétiques,* pp. 1077–1078.

8. Georges Schmits, "Le Simulacre de la Voyance," in *Apollinaire inventeur de langages,* ed. Michel Décaudin (Paris: Lettres Modernes Minard, 1973), p. 56.

9. See, for example, Apollinaire's comments on futurism in "Nos amis les futuristes," in *Oeuvres Complètes* (Paris: Ballard et Lecat, 1966), v. I, pp. 883–884; also see the various articles Apollinaire wrote on the futurist painters which have been translated in *Apollinaire on Art,* ed. LeRoy C. Breunig (New York: Viking, 1972), especially pp. 199–205 and pp. 255–256.

10. Apollinaire, "The New Painting: Art Notes," in *Apollinaire on Art,* pp. 222–223. See also p. 255. Apollinaire wrote numerous articles on cubism and cubist painters which further developed these ideas. See both this book and *Les Peintres Cubistes,* ed. L. C. Breunig and J. C. Chevalier (Paris: Hermann, 1965).

11. "Reality, Pure Painting," in *Apollinaire on Art,* p. 265.

12. "The Salon d'Automne," in *Apollinaire on Art,* p. 335.

13. For a fascinating and illuminating transcript of twenty-two eminent German and American scholars' attempt to explicate "Arbre," with only decidedly limited success, see "Group Interpretation of Apollinaire's *Arbre,*" in *New Perspectives in German Literary Criticism,* ed. Richard E. Amacher and Victor Lange (Princeton: Princeton University Press, 1980), pp. 182–207.

14. "La Vie: Réponse à une enquête," *Oeuvres Complètes,* v. III (Paris: Ballard et Lecat, 1966), pp. 892–893.

15. Filippo Marinetti, "Portrait of Mussolini" (1929), in *Selected Writings,* ed. R. W. Flint (New York: Farrar, Straus & Giroux, 1972), p. 159.

16. Marinetti, "The Founding and Manifesto of Futurism," in *Selected Writings,* pp. 41–42.

17. Francesco Cangiullo, "La Battaglia de Firenze," Siparo (December, 1967), p. 29. Quoted in Michael Kirby, *Futurist Performance* (New York: Dutton, 1971), pp. 14–15.

18. Marinetti, "Beyond Communism," (1920), in *Selected Writings,* pp. 148–157.

19. Marinetti, "The Founding and Manifesto of Futurism," in *Selected Writings,* p. 42.

20. Cf. Michael Kirby, *Futurist Performance,* for a collection of these and other futurist theater pieces.

21. Marinetti, "Destruction of Syntax—Imagination without Strings—Words-in-Freedom," (1913), in *Futurist Manifestos,* ed. Umbro Apollonio (New York: Viking, 1973), pp. 98, 104.

22. *Ibid.,* p. 100.

23. *Ibid.,* p. 98.
24. Boccioni, in *Futurist Manifestos,* pp. 150–154.
25. Joshua C. Taylor, *Futurism* (New York: Museum of Modern Art, 1961), p. 48.
26. Boccioni, *et al.,* "Futurist Painting: Technical Manifesto 1910," in *Futurist Manifestos,* p. 29.
27. Marinetti, quoted in R. W. Flint's "Introduction" to *Selected Writings,* p. 35.
28. Marinetti, "Portrait of Mussolini," in *Selected Writings,* pp. 158–159.

Chapter IV,

1. Marcel Janco, "Dada at Two Speeds," in *Dadas on Art,* ed. Lucy Lippard (Englewood Cliffs: Prentice-Hall, 1971), pp. 36–37.
2. Francis Picabia, "Manifeste Cannibale Dada," *Bulletin Dada,* 7 (March, 1920).
3. Jean Arp, "Dadaland," in Lippard, p. 26.
4. Hugo Ball, *Flight Out of Time* (New York: Viking, 1974), p. 67.
5. Arp, "Dadaland," in Lippard, pp. 28–29.
6. Tristan Tzara, "Dada Manifesto 1918," in Lippard, p. 18.
7. Richard Huelsenbeck, "Dada and Existentialism," in *Memoirs of a Dada Drummer* (New York: Viking, 1974), pp. 142–148.
8. Tzara, in Lippard, p. 17.
9. *Ibid.,* p. 19.
10. *Ibid.,* p. 20.
11. *Ibid.,* p. 18
12. Mary Ann Caws, *The Poetry of Dada and Surrealism* (Princeton: Princeton University Press, 1970), p. 98.
13. Arp, "Dadaland," in Lippard, p. 23.
14. *Ibid.,* p. 24.
15. *Ibid.,* pp. 29–30.
16. *Ibid.,* p. 26.
17. *Ibid.,* p. 18.
18. Arp, "Dadaland," in *Arp on Arp* (New York: Viking, 1972), p. 232.
19. *Ibid.*
20. Ball, pp. 59–60.
21. *Ibid.,* p. 43.
22. *Ibid.,* p. 71.
23. *Ibid.,* pp. 58–59.
24. *Ibid.,* p. 100.
25. *Ibid.,* p. 117
26. Huelsenbeck, "The Dada Drummer," p. 63.
27. Huelsenbeck, "Dada Forward," in Lippard, pp. 45–46.
28. Huelsenbeck, "The Dada Drummer," p. 52.
29. Georg Grosz and Wieland Herzfelde, "Dadaism," in Lippard, p. 86. See also "Interview with Hannah Höch," in Lippard, pp. 70–73.

30. Grosz and Herzfelde, in Lippard, pp. 83, 84.
31. *Ibid.*, p. 81.
32. Huelsenbeck, in Lippard, pp. 48–49.
33. Tzara, "Lecture on Dada," in *Theories of Modern Art,* ed. Herschel B. Chipp (Berkeley: University of California Press, 1968), pp. 388–389.

Chapter V

1. André Breton, "Speech to the Congress of Writers," in *Manifestoes of Surrealism,* trans. Richard Seaver and Helen R. Lane (Ann Arbor: University of Michigan Press, Ann Arbor Paperback, 1972), p. 241.
2. Maurice Nadeau, *Histoire du surréalisme* (Paris: Seuil, 1964), p. 23.
3. Tristan Tzara, "Dada Manifesto 1918," in *Dadas on Art,* ed. Lucy Lippard (Englewood Cliffs, N.J.: Prentice-Hall, 1971), p. 19.
4. Anna Balakian, *André Breton* (New York: Oxford University Press, 1971), pp. 28–33.
5. Tzara, *ibid.,* pp. 17, 19.
6. Breton, "Deux Manifestes Dada," in *Les Pas perdus* (Paris: Gallimard, 1924), p. 74. Translation mine.
7. Breton, "Pour Dada," in *Les Pas perdus,* p. 90, trans. Ralph Mannheim, in Franklin Rosemont, ed., *What is Surrealism?* (n.p.: 1978), p. 5.
8. Breton, "Entrée des médiums," in *Les Pas perdus,* p. 150.
9. Breton, "Manifesto of Surrealism," in *Manifestoes,* p. 47.
10. Rimbaud, "A Season in Hell," in *Complete Works, Selected Letters,* trans. and ed. Wallace Fowlie (Chicago: University of Chicago Press, 1966), p. 187.
11. Baudelaire's phrase, in "Le Spleen de Paris," *Oeuvres complètes* (Paris: Gallimard, Pléiade, 1961), p. 303.
12. Apollinaire, "The New Spirit and the Poets," in *Selected Writings,* trans. Roger Shattuck (New York: New Directions, 1971), p. 233.
13. Breton, "Manifesto of Surrealism," p. 14.
14. Rimbaud, "Season," p. 201.
15. Breton, "Caractères de l'évolution moderne et ce qui en participe," in *Les Pas perdus,* p. 192.
16. Breton, "Manifesto of Surrealism," p. 14; further references will be cited in the text.
17. Breton, "Crisis of the Object," in *Surrealism and Painting,* trans. Simon W. Taylor (New York: Harper and Row, 1972), p. 276.
18. Breton, "Second Manifesto of Surrealism," in *Manifestos,* p. 160.
19. *Ibid.*
20. Breton, *Nadja* (Paris: Gallimard, 1928), pp. 7–8, trans. Richard Howard (New York: Grove, 1960).
21. Breton, "Second Manifesto," pp. 136–37.
22. *Ibid.,* p. 162.

23. *Ibid.*, p. 161.

24. Breton, "Manifesto of Surrealism," p. 21.

25. *Ibid.*, p. 20. Reverdy's statement originally appeared in *Nord-Sud*, March, 1918.

26. Sigmund Freud, *Introductory Lectures on Psychoanalysis,* trans. James Strachey (New York: Norton, 1966), pp. 172–73.

27. Breton, "Manifesto of Surrealism," p. 37.

28. Breton, "What is Surrealism?", in Rosemont, p. 116.

29. Breton, *Manifeste de Surréalisme,* nouvelle édition (Paris: Kra, 1929), p. 71, trans. "Manifesto of Surrealism," p. 43.

30. Breton, "Second Manifesto," p. 161.

31. Salvador Dali, quoted in Breton, "Surrealist Situation of the Object," in *Manifestoes,* p. 274.

32. Max Ernst, quoted in "Surrealist Situation of the Object," p. 275.

33. Mary Ann Caws, *The Poetry of Dada and Surrealism* (Princeton: Princeton University Press, 1970), p. 19.

34. Paul Éluard, "Coeur à Pic," *Oeuvres complètes* (Paris: Gallimard, Pléiade, 1968), pp. 802–803. Partial translation in Caws, p. 142; partial translation mine.

35. Louis Aragon, *Le Paysan de Paris* (Paris: Gallimard, 1926), p. 49, trans. Frederick Brown, *Nightwalker* (Englewood Cliffs, N.J.: Prentice-Hall, 1970), pp. 30–31.

36. *Ibid. Paysan,* pp. 50–51; *Nightwalker,* 31.

37. Breton, "L'Union libre," *The Autobiography of Surrealism,* ed. Marcel Jean (New York: Viking, 1980), pp. 187, 189.

38. Breton, "Crisis of the Object," p. 279.

39. Breton, "Manifesto of Surrealism," p. 23.

40. Ibid., pp. 27–28.

41. *Ibid.,* p. 26. On this point, Balakian notes that for Janet also automatic dictation was grammatical and that he, too, was primarily interested in the power of the image; p. 36.

42. This point was suggested by Ferdinand Alquié in *The Philosophy of Surrealism,* trans. Bernard Waldrop (Ann Arbor: University of Michigan Press, 1965), p. 141.

43. Robert Desnos, poem from *Littérature,* no. 6, in *Autobiography of Surrealism,* p. 103.

44. Balakian, p. 65.

45. *Ibid.,* p. 64.

46. Breton, *Poisson soluble,* in *Manifeste,* p. 110; trans. in *Manifestoes,* p. 60.

47. Desnos, *La Liberté ou l'amour!* (Paris: Gallimard, 1962), p. 21, translation mine.

48. Aragon, "Les Frères la côte," *la Révolution Surréaliste,* 4 (15 July, 1925), p. 4; trans. in *Autobiography of Surrealism,* pp. 175–76.

49. Breton, *Nadja,* French, p. 215; English, p. 160.

50. *Ibid.,* French, p. 214; English, pp. 159–60.

51. Breton, in *Clair de terre* (Paris: Gallimard Poésie, 1966), p. 181.
52. Breton, *Nadja,* French, p. 15; English, p. 16.
53. Fredric Jameson, *Marxism and Form* (Princeton: Princeton University Press, 1971), p. 97.
54. Breton, "Manifesto of Surrealism," p. 8.
55. Jameson points to this aspect of the fading environment in order to make a different point, pp. 103–105.
56. Jameson, p. 101.
57. Breton's paraphrase of Lautréamont, in "Surrealist Situation of the Object," p. 262.
58. Breton, "Second Manifesto," p. 152.
59. Breton, "Crisis of the Object," p. 277.
60. Breton, *Nadja,* French, p. 211; English, p. 158.
61. *Ibid.,* French, p. 73; English, p. 59.
62. Breton, *Arcane 17* (New York: Brentano's, 1945), pp. 25–26; trans. in Rosemont, p. 249.
63. Breton, "Manifesto of Surrealism," p. 4.
64. Desnos, "Description d'une Révolte prochaine," *la Révolution Surréaliste,* 3 (15 April, 1925), p. 26.
65. Aragon, "Fragments d'une Conférence," *la Révolution Surréaliste,* 4 (15 July, 1925), p. 25.
66. Aragon, "Communisme et Révolution," *la Révolution Surréaliste,* 2 (15 January, 1925), p. 32.
67. Balakian, p. 162.
68. Breton, "Leon Trotsky: Lénine," *la Révolution Surréaliste,* 5 (15 October, 1925), p. 29.
69. "La Révolution d'Abord et Toujours!", *la Révolution Surréaliste,* 5 (15 October, 1925), pp. 31–32.
70. Éluard, *Donner à voir,* in *Oeuvres,* p. 983.
71. Breton, "Second Manifesto," p. 124.
72. Éluard, *Donner à voir,* p. 980.
73. Aragon, "Le Surréalisme et le Devenir Révolutionnaire," *Le Surréalisme au Service de la Révolution,* 3 (December, 1931), p. 5.
74. Breton, "Political Position of Today's Art," in *Manifestoes,* p. 225.
75. Breton, "Crisis of the Object," p. 276.
76. J.-M. Monnerot, *La Poésie moderne et le sacré* (Paris: Gallimard, 1945), pp. 17–18, quoted in Alquié, pp. 27–28.
77. J.-M. Monnerot, "À Partir de Quelques Traits Particuliers à la Mentalité Civilisée," *Le Surréalisme au Service de la Révolution,* 5 (15 May, 1933), p. 37.
78. Michel Beaujour, "Flight out of time: Poetic Language and the Revolution," *Yale French Studies,* 39 (1967), pp. 29–49.
79. Leon Trotsky, *Literature and Revolution,* trans. Rose Strunsky (Ann Arbor: University of Michigan Press, 1960), pp. 128–32.
80. Breton, "Manifesto of Surrealism," pp. 208–209.
81. Breton, quoted in Alquié, p. 56.

82. Breton and Diego Rivera, "Manifesto for an Independent Revolutionary Art," in Rosemont, p. 185.
83. Breton, *Arcane 17*, p. 22.

Chapter VI

1. Benedict Livshits, quoted in Vladimir Markov, *Russian Futurism* (Berkeley: University of California Press, 1968), p. 3.
2. "A Slap in the Face of Public Taste," in *Russian Futurism*, ed. Ellendea Proffer and Carl Proffer (Ann Arbor: Ardis, 1980), p. 179.
3. Markov, p. 47.
4. Alexi Kruchonykh, quoted in Edward J. Brown, *Mayakovsky: A Poet of the Revolution* (Princeton: Princeton University Press, 1973), p. 58.
5. Brown, *ibid.*
6. Velimir Khlebnikov's two poems are excerpted in Proffer and Proffer, pp. 21–27.
7. Alexi Kruchonykh, quoted in Agnes Sola, "Futurisme russe et révolution," *Europe*, 552, (April, 1975), p. 163.
8. Noemi Blumenkranz Onimus, "Futurisme italien et futurisme russe," *Europe*, 552, (April, 1975), pp. 8–28.
9. Shershenevich, quoted in Onimus, p. 21.
10. Bengt Jengfeldt, *Majakovskij and Futurism, 1917–1921* (Stockholm: Almquist & Wiksell International, 1976), p. 66.
11. "Temple of Factory," *Iskusstvo Kommuny*, #1, December 7, 1918, quoted in Wiktor Woroszylski, *The Life of Mayakovsky*, trans. Baleslaw Taborski (New York: Orion Press, 1970), p. 246.
12. N. F. Chuzhak, quoted in Sola, p. 120.
13. Sergei Eisenstein, *Film Form and Film Sense*, ed. and trans. Jay Leyda (New York: World, 1957), p. 18. This passage first came to my attention in Stanley Aronowitz's article "Film—The Art Form of Capitalism," *Social Text*, 1 (Winter, 1979), p. 110.
14. A 1923 LEF declaration, quoted in Marc Slonim, *Soviet Russian Literature* (New York: Oxford University Press, 1977), p. 22. No author or title was mentioned.
15. Sola, p. 169.
16. Leon Trotsky, *Literature and Revolution*, trans. Rose Strunsky (Ann Arbor: University of Michigan Press, Ann Arbor paperback, 1960), pp. 134–35.
17. *Ibid.,* p. 132.
18. V. I. Lenin, quoted in Michael Holquist, "The Mayakovsky Problem," *Yale French Studies*, 39 (1967), p. 128.
19. Josef Stalin, quoted in Herbert Marshall, *Mayakovsky and His Poetry* (London: The Pilot Press, 1945), p. 13.
20. Ivan Bunin, *Vospominanija* (Paris, 1950), cited in Holquist, p. 134.
21. Vladimir Mayakovsky, "Vladimir Mayakovsky: A Tragedy," in *The Complete Plays of Vladimir Mayakovsky*, trans. Guy Daniels (New

York: Washington Square Press, 1968), p. 21. Other references to this play will be made in the text.

22. Mayakovsky, quoted in Herbert Marshall, *Mayakovsky* (New York: Hill and Wang, 1965), p. 98.

23. Mayakovsky, "A Cloud in Trousers," in Marshall, *Mayakovsky*, p. 99. Other references to this poem will be made in the text.

24. Mayakovsky, cited in Alexander Rodchenko, "V Mire Knig," No. 6, Moscow, 1973, translated and printed in David Elliott, *Rodchenko and the Arts of Revolutionary Russia* (New York: Pantheon, 1979), p. 102.

25. Mayakovsky, "Order No. 2 to the Army of the Arts," in *The Bedbug and Selected Poetry*, ed. Patricia Blake, trans. Max Hayward and George Reavey (Bloomington: Indiana University Press, Midland Edition, 1975), p. 149. Further references to this poem or edition will be made in the text.

26. Mayakovsky, "Back Home!" quoted in Marshall, *Mayakovsky*, p. 344.

27. Mayakovsky, cited in Brown, p. 302.

28. Trotsky, p. 152.

29. *Ibid.,* p. 149.

30. *Ibid.,* pp. 146–47.

31. Mayakovsky, "To Sergey Esenin," in Mayakovsky, *How are Verses Made?,* trans. G. M. Hyde (London: Jonathan Cape, 1970), p. 62.

32. Mayakovsky, "About That," in Marshall, *Mayakovsky*, pp. 200–201.

33. *Ibid.,* p. 214.

Chapter VII

1. André Breton, *Nadja,* trans. Richard Howard (New York: Grove Press, 1960), p. 16.

2. Bertolt Brecht, "On Non-objective Painting," in *Marxism and Art,* ed. Berel Lang and Forrest Williams (New York: David McKay, 1972), p. 424.

3. Brecht, *Tagebücher,* 1920–1922 (Frankfurt: Suhrkamp, 1975), p. 55. "ich laufe wieder auf dem Randstein, schneide Grimassen, pfeife auf die Wirkung, grinse, dass man die faulen Zahne sieht. Ich werde den Spiegel bald kaputtmachen konnen. Das ist was für feine Leute. So bin ich, freut euch! Hasslich, frech, neugeboren, aus dem Ei." (Mit Eihauten, Kot, Blut, immerhin.) (September 7, 1920).

4. Brecht, *In the Jungle of Cities,* trans. Gerhard Nellhaus, in *Collected Plays, Vol. I* (New York: Pantheon, 1970), p. 108.

5. *Ibid.,* p. 157.

6. *Ibid.,* p. 108.

7. Brecht, *Tagebücher,* pp. 48 and 147 (September 4, 1920; September 16, 1921).

8. *Ibid.,* p. 187 (February 10, 1922).

9. *Ibid.,* p. 187 (February 11, 1922).

10. *Ibid.*, p. 154 (September 28, 1921).
11. Brecht, "Emphasis on Sport," in *Brecht on Theatre,* ed. and trans. John Willett (New York: Hill and Wang, 1964), p. 7.
12. Brecht, *Tagebücher,* p. 16 (June 7, 1920).
13. *Ibid.*, pp. 38–39 (August 28, 1920).
14. *Ibid.*, p. 132 (May 28, 1921).
15. Brecht, "A Radio Speech," in *Brecht on Theatre,* p. 19.
16. *Ibid.*, p. 18.
17. Brecht, "The Epic Theatre and Its Difficulties," *Brecht on Theatre,* p. 23.
18. Brecht, "On Form and Subject-Matter," *Brecht on Theatre,* p. 30.
19. Werner Hecht, "Brecht's Weg zum epischen Theater," noted in *Brecht on Theatre,* p. 62.
20. Brecht, "Interview with an Exile," *Brecht on Theatre,* p. 66.
21. Brecht, "An Example of Paedogogics," *Brecht on Theatre,* p. 31.
22. Brecht, "From the Mother Courage Model," *Brecht on Theater,* p. 219.
23. See *Aesthetics and Politics,* translation ed. Ronald Taylor (London: New Left Books, 1977), for the series of articles by Bloch, Lukács, Brecht, and members of the Frankfurt School in which these ideas were elaborated.
24. Walter Benjamin, "Conversations with Brecht," in *Reflections,* trans. Edmund Jephcott, ed. Peter Demetz (New York: Harcourt Brace Jovanovich, 1978), p. 216.
25. Brecht, "From the Mother Courage Model," *Brecht on Theater,* p. 219.
26. Brecht, "Alienation Effects in Chinese Acting," *Brecht on Theater,* p. 97.
27. Brecht, "Contradiction in *The Caucasian Chalk Circle,*" *Collected Plays, Vol. VII,* ed. Ralph Mannheim and John Willett (New York: Pantheon, 1975), p. 301.
28. Brecht, "Casting of Azdak," in *Collected Plays, Vol. VII,* pp. 298–299.
29. Brecht, "Can the Present-day World Be Reproduced by Means of Theatre?" *Brecht on Theatre,* p. 275.

Chapter VIII

1. See, for example, Peter Bürger, *Theorie der Avantgarde* (Frankfurt am Main: Suhrkamp Verlag, 1974), or George T. Noszlopy, "The Embourgeoisement of Avant-Garde Art," *Diogenes,* 67 (Fall, 1969), pp. 83–109.
2. See, for example, Ihab Hassan, *Paracriticisms* (Urbana: University of Illinois Press, 1975), Frank Kermode, *Continuities* (New York: Random House, 1968), and Richard Poirier, *The Performing Self* (New York: Oxford University Press, 1971).
3. See, for example, Daniel Bell, *The Cultural Contradictions of Capi-*

talism (New York: Basic Books, 1976), Lucien Goldmann, *Pour une sociologie du roman* (Paris: Gallimard, 1964), Max Horkheimer, *Critical Theory*, trans. Matthew J. O'Connell et al., Jürgen Habermas, *Legitimationsprobleme im Spätkapitalismus* (Frankfurt am Main: Suhrkamp Verlag, 1973), as well as Habermas, "Modernity versus Postmodernity," *New German Critique*, 22 (Winter, 1981), pp. 3–14, and Henri Lefebvre, *La Vie quotidienne dans le monde moderne* (Paris: Gallimard, 1968), and *Au-delà du structuralisme* (Paris: Editions Anthropos, 1971).

4. Goldmann, p. 55.

5. Ihab Hassan, *Paracriticisms*, pp. 121–147.

6. John Cage, *A Year from Monday* (Middletown: Wesleyan University Press, 1967), *passim*.

7. Rimbaud, letter of 13 May, 1871 to George Izambard, in *Complete Works, Selected Letters*, trans. and ed. Wallace Fowlie (Chicago: University of Chicago Press, 1966), p. 303.

8. For a concise presentation of these two positions, see the essays of Lukács and the Frankfurt School collected in *Aesthetics and Politics*, trans. Ronald Taylor (London: New Left Books, 1977). Recent critics who have addressed the ambiguity of the contemporary avant-garde, and who locate this development in the premises of the earlier avant-garde and modernist movements, include Fredric Jameson, *Fables of Aggression* (Berkeley: University of California Press, 1979), Hans Magnus Enzensberger, "Die Aporien der Avantgarde," *Einzelheiten II*, 3d printing (Frankfurt am Main: Suhrkamp Verlag, 1970), pp. 50–80, and Peter Bürger, *Theorie der Avantgarde*.

9. Jacques Derrida, "Structure, Sign, and Play in the Discourse of the Human Sciences," *The Structuralist Controversy*, ed. Richard Macksey and Eugenio Donato (Baltimore: Johns Hopkins University Press, 1972), p. 260.

10. Derrida, pp. 264–65.

11. Ihab Hassan has written extensively on the various aspects of postmodern creative strategies. See, for example, "The Question of Postmodernism" in *Romanticism, Modernism, Postmodernism*, ed. Harry T. Garvin, *Bucknell Review*, 25, 2 (1980), pp. 117–126.

12. John Cage, *Silence* (Middletown: Wesleyan University Press, 1961), p. 139.

13. For a further discussion of literature and art as tautological constructs, see my article, "Toward Tautology: The *nouveau roman* and Conceptual Art," *Modern Language Notes*, 91, 5 (October, 1976), pp. 1044–60.

14. Alain Robbe-Grillet, "Discussion," of a talk by Michel Mansuy, "L'Imagination dans le nouveau roman," *Nouveau Roman: hier, aujourd'hui*, vol. I (Paris: 10/18, 1972), p. 97.

15. Julia Kristeva, "Postmodernism?" in Harry T. Garvin, p. 140.

16. A more extended discussion of the varieties of avant-garde writing in

Europe, Japan, and North and South America can be found, along
with examples of representative avant-garde works, in *The Avant-
garde Today,* ed. Charles Russell (Urbana: University of Illinois
Press, 1981).

17. See the collected texts of the journal L=A=N=G=U=A=G=E in
The L=A=N=G=U=A=G=E Book, ed. Bruce Andrews and Charles
Bernstein (Carbondale: Southern Illinois University Press, 1984).

18. Goldmann, p. 55.

19. William Burroughs, *The Ticket That Exploded* (New York: Grove
Press, 1967), p. 151.

20. Ronald Sukenick, *98.6* (New York: Fiction Collective, 1975), pp. 123–
124.

21. *ibid.,* p. 122.

22. Raymond Federman, ed., *Surfiction* (Chicago: Swallow Press, 1975),
pp. 7–8.

23. Thomas Pynchon, *Gravity's Rainbow* (New York: Viking Press,
1973), p. 590.

24. *ibid.,* p. 434.

25. *ibid.,* p. 638.

26. *ibid.,* p. 713.

27. *ibid.,* pp. 712–713.

28. William Burroughs, *Nova Express* (New York: Grove Press, 1964),
p. 15.

29. William Burroughs, *Naked Lunch* (New York: Grove Press, 1959),
p. 223.

30. Ronald Sukenick, *Out* (Chicago: Swallow Press, 1973), p. 136.

31. Thomas Pynchon, *V.* (New York: Bantam Books, c. 1963), p. 304.

32. Thomas Pynchon, *The Crying of Lot 49* (New York: Bantam Books,
c. 1966), p. 95.

33. Sukenick, *Out,* p. 128.

34. Pynchon, *Gravity's Rainbow,* p. 129.

Selected Bibliography

The Theory and History of the Avant-garde

Arendt, Hannah. *Between Past and Future.* Cleveland: World Publishing Co., Meridian Book, 1963.

Bathrick, David. "Affirmative and Negative Culture: Technology and the Left Avant-Garde," *The Technological Imagination,* ed. Teresa De Lauretis, Andreas Huyssen, Kathleen Woodward. Madison: Coda Press, 1980.

Baudelaire, Charles. *Oeuvres Complètes,* ed. Claude Pichois. Paris: Gallimard, Pléiade, 1961.

Beaujour, Michel. "Flight out of time: Poetic Language and the Revolution." *Yale French Studies* 39 (1967): 29–49.

Bell, Daniel. *The Cultural Contradictions of Capitalism.* New York: Basic Books, 1976.

Benda, Julien. *La Trahison des clercs.* Édition révue et augmentée. Paris: Grasset, 1946.

Benjamin, Walter. *Reflections,* ed. Peter Demetz. New York: Harcourt Brace Jovanovich, 1978.

Bergonzi, Bernard, ed. *Innovations: Essays on Art and Ideas.* London: Macmillan, 1968.

Bradbury, Malcolm and McFarlane, James, eds. *Modernism.* Hammondsworth: Penguin, 1976.

Bürger, Peter. *Theorie der Avantgarde.* Frankfurt am Main: Suhrkamp, 1974.

Calinescu, Matei. *Faces of Modernity.* Bloomington: University of Indiana Press, 1977.

Craig, David, ed. *Marxists on Literature.* Baltimore: Penguin, 1975.

DeMan, Paul. *Blindness and Insight.* New York: Oxford University Press, 1971.

Demetz, Peter. *Marx, Engels und die Dichter.* Frankfurt am Main: Ullstein, 1969.

Egbert, Donald Drew. *Social Radicalism and the Arts.* New York: Knopf, 1970.

Enzensberger, Hans Magnus. *Einzelheiten II.* 3d printing. Frankfurt am Main: Suhrkamp, 1970.

Estivals, Robert, Gaudy, Jean-Charles, and Vergez, Gabrielle. *L'Avant-Garde: Étude historique et sociologique des publications périodiques ayant pour titre 'L'avant-garde.'* Paris: Bibliothèque Nationale, 1968.

Fischer, Ernst. *Art against Ideology,* trans. Anna Bostock. London: Allen Lane, The Penguin Press, 1969.

Fischer, Ernst. *The Necessity of Art,* trans. Anna Bostock. Baltimore: Penguin, 1963.

Flaker, Aleksandar. "Notes sur l'étude de l'avant-garde." *Revue de Littérature Comparée* 56,2 (Avril–Juin, 1982).

Freud, Sigmund. *Introductory Lectures on Psychoanalysis,* trans. James Strachey. New York: Norton, 1966.

Gilman, Richard. "The Idea of the Avant-garde." *Partisan Review* 39, 3 (Summer, 1972): 382–396.

Goldmann, Lucien. *Pour une sociologie du roman.* Paris: Gallimard, 1964.

Graña, César. *Fact and Symbol.* New York: Oxford University Press, 1971.

Greenberg, Clement. *Art and Culture.* Boston: Beacon, 1961.

Hassan, Ihab. *The Dismemberment of Orpheus.* New York: Oxford University Press, 1971.

Hassan, Ihab. *Paracriticisms.* Urbana: University of Illinois Press, 1975.

Hess, Thomas B. and Ashbery, John, eds. *Avant-Garde Art.* New York: Macmillan, Collier Books, 1967.

Hinz, Berthold. *Art in the Third Reich,* trans. Robert and Rita Kimber. New York: Pantheon, 1979.

Holthusen, Hans. *Avantgardismus und die Zukunft der modernen Kunst.* Munich: R. Piper Verlag, 1964.

Howe, Irving, ed. *Literary Modernism.* Greenwich, Ct.: Fawcett Publications, 1967.

Jameson, Fredric. *Fables of Aggression.* Berkeley: University of California Press, 1979.

Jameson, Fredric. *Marxism and Form.* Princeton: Princeton University Press, 1971.

Jameson, Fredric. *The Prison-House of Language.* Princeton: Princeton University Press, 1972.

Josipovici, Gabriel. *The Lessons of Modernism*. Totowa, N.J.: Rowman and Littlefield, 1977.

Kampf, Louis. *On Modernism*. Cambridge: MIT Press, 1967.

Kateb, George. "Politics and Modernity: The Strategies of Desperation." *New Literary History* 3, 1 (Autumn, 1971): 93–112.

Kermode, Frank. *Modern Essays*. London: Collins, 1971.

Kirby, Michael. *The Art of Time*. New York: Dutton, 1969.

Kristeva, Julia. *La Révolution du langage poétique*. Paris: Seuil, 1974.

Lang, Berel and Williams, Forrest. *Marxism and Art*. New York: David McKay, 1972.

Lefebvre, Henri. *Au-delà du structuralisme*. Paris: Éditions Anthropos, 1971.

Lefebvre, Henri. *Introduction à la modernité*. Paris: Minuit, 1962.

Lefebvre, Henri. *La Vie quotidienne dans le monde moderne*. Paris: Gallimard, 1968.

Levin, Harry. *Refractions*. New York: Oxford University Press, 1966.

Lüdke, W. Martin. *"Theorie der Avantgarde," Antworten auf Peter Bürgers Bestimmung von Kunst und bürgerlicher Gesellschaft*. Frankfurt am Main: Suhrkamp, 1976.

Luft, David. *Robert Musil and the Crisis of European Culture 1880–1942*. Berkeley: University of California Press, 1980.

Lukács, Georg. *History and Class Consciousness*, trans. Rodney Livingstone. Cambridge: MIT Press, 1971.

Lukács, Georg. *Realism in Our Time*, trans. John and Necke Mander. New York: Harper and Row, Torchbook Edition, 1971.

Lukács, Georg. *The Theory of the Novel*, trans. Anna Bostock. Cambridge: MIT Press, 1971.

Lukács, Georg. *Writer and Critic*, ed. and trans. Arthur Kahn. New York: Grosset and Dunlap, 1971.

Mannheim, Karl. *Ideology and Utopia*, trans. Louis Wirth and Edward Shils. New York: Harcourt, Brace and World, Harvest Book, c. 1936.

Marcuse, Herbert. *Counterrevolution and Revolt*. Boston: Beacon, 1972.

Marcuse, Herbert. *Eros and Civilization*. Boston: Beacon, 1955.

Marcuse, Herbert. *An Essay on Liberation*. Boston: Beacon, 1969.

Marcuse, Herbert. *One-Dimensional Man*. Boston: Beacon, 1964.

Marino, Adrian. "Essai d'une définition de l'avant-garde." *Revue de l'Université de Bruxelles* 1 (1975): 64–120.

Marino, Adrian. " 'Modernity' and the Evolution of Literary Consciousness." *Diogenes* 77 (1972): 110–37.

Mayer, Hans. *Steppenwolf and Everyman*, trans. Jack D. Zipes. New York: Thomas Crowell, 1971.

Mumford, Louis. *Art and Technics*. New York: Columbia University Press, 1960.

Munro, Thomas. *Evolution in the Arts*. Cleveland: Cleveland Museum of Art, n.d.

Mukařovský, Jan. *Structure, Sign, and Function.* trans. John Burbank and Peter Skinner. New Haven: Yale University Press, 1978.

Noszlopy, George T. "The Embourgeoisment of Avant-garde Art." *Diogenes* 67 (Fall, 1969), 83–109.

Ortega y Gasset, José. *The Dehumanization of Art,* trans. Helene Weyl. Princeton: Princeton University Press, 1968.

Paz, Octavio. *Children of the Mire,* trans. Rachel Phillips. Cambridge: Harvard University Press, 1974.

Pleynet, Marcelin. "Les problèmes de l'avant-garde." *Tel Quel* 25 (Spring, 1966): 77–86.

Plumb, J. H. *The Death of the Past.* Boston: Houghton Mifflin, 1970.

Poggioli, Renato. *The Theory of the Avant-Garde,* trans. Gerald Fitzgerald. New York: Harper and Row, Icon Editions, 1971.

Poulet, Georges. *Le Point de départ.* Paris: Plon, 1964.

Read, Herbert. *Art and Alienation.* New York: Viking Compass, 1969.

Read, Herbert. *The Forms of Things Unknown.* New York: World, 1963.

Read, Herbert. *The Origins of Form in Art.* New York: Horizon Press, 1965.

Reszler, André. "Bakunin, Marx and the Aesthetic Heritage of Socialism." *Yearbook of Comparative and General Literature* 22 (1973): 42–50.

Reszler, André. *L'Esthétique anarchiste.* Paris: Presses Universitaires de France, 1973.

Rochberg, George. "The Avant-Garde and the Aesthetics of Survival." *New Literary History* 3, 1 (Autumn, 1971): 71–92.

Rosenberg, Harold. *The Anxious Object.* New York: Macmillan, Collier Books, 1973.

Rosenberg, Harold. *The De-definition of Art.* New York: Macmillan, Collier Books, 1973.

Sanguineti, Edoardo. "Pour une avant-garde révolutionnaire." *Tel Quel* 29 (1967): 76–95.

Shapiro, Meyer. "The Liberating Quality of Avant-garde Art." *Art News* 56, 4 (1957): 36–42.

Sokel, Walter. *The Writer in Extremis.* Stanford: Stanford University Press, 1959.

Sollers, Philippe. *L'Écriture et l'expérience des limites.* Paris: Seuil, Collection Points, 1971.

Spender, Stephen. *The Struggle of the Modern.* London: Hamilton, 1963.

Steiner, George. "The Writer as Remembrancer: A Note on Poetics." *Yearbook of Comparative and General Literature* 22 (1973): 51–57.

Sullivan, J. P., ed. *Ezra Pound, A Critical Anthology.* Baltimore: Penguin, 1970.

Szabolcsi, Miklos. "Avant-Garde, Neo-Avant-Garde, Modernism: Questions and Suggestions." *New Literary History* 3, 1 (Autumn, 1971): 49–70.

Taylor, Ronald, trans. *Aesthetics and Politics*. London: New Left Books, 1977.

Trilling, Lionel. *Beyond Culture*. New York: Viking, 1961.

Trilling, Lionel. *Sincerity and Authenticity*. Cambridge: Harvard University Press, 1972.

Trotsky, Leon. *Literature and Revolution,* trans. Rose Strunsky. Ann Arbor: University of Michigan, 1960.

Weisgerber, Jean. "Mines et contre-mines aux avant-postes." *Revue de l'Université de Bruxelles* 1 (1975): 3–9.

Weisstein, Ulrich. "Le terme et le concept d'avant-garde en Allemagne." *Revue de l'Université de Bruxelles* 1 (1975): 10–37.

Willett, John. *Art and Politics in the Weimar Period*. New York: Pantheon, 1978.

Williams, Raymond. *Culture and Society*. New York: Harper and Row, 1966.

Williams, Raymond. *Marxism and Literature*. New York: Oxford University Press, 1977.

Wilner, Eleanor. *Gathering the Winds*. Baltimore: Johns Hopkins University Press, 1975.

Individual Writers and Movements

Abrams, M. H. "Coleridge, Baudelaire, and Modernist Poetics." In *New Perspectives in German Literary Criticism,* ed. Richard Amacher and Victor Lange. pp. 150–181. Princeton: Princeton University Press, 1979.

Adéma, Marcel. *Apollinaire*. New York: Grove Press, 1955.

Ades, Dawn. *Dada and Surrealism Reviewed*. Arts Council of Great Britain, 1978.

Alquié, Ferdinand. *The Philosophy of Surrealism,* trans. Bernard Waldrop. Ann Arbor: University of Michigan Press, 1965.

Andrews, Bruce and Bernstein, Charles. *The L=A=N=G=U=A=G=E Book*. Carbondale: Southern Illinois Press, 1984.

Antin, David. *Talking at the Boundaries*. New York: New Directions, 1976.

Apollinaire, Guillaume. *Oeuvres Complètes*. 4 vols. Paris: Ballard et Lecat, 1966.

Apollinaire, Guillaume. *Oeuvres Poétiques,* ed. Marcel Adéma and Michel Décaudin. Paris: Gallimard, Pléiade, 1959.

Apollinaire, Guillaume. *Les Peintres Cubistes,* ed. L. C. Breunig and J. C. Chevalier. Paris: Hermann, 1965.

Apollinaire, Guillaume. *Selected Writings,* trans. Roger Shattuck. New York: New Directions, 1971.

Apollonio, Umbro. *Futurist Manifestos*. New York: Viking, 1973.

Aragon, Louis. *Chroniques du Bel Canto*. Geneva: Albert Skira, 1947.

Aragon, Louis. *Nightwalker,* trans. Frederick Brown. Englewood Cliffs, N.J.: Prentice-Hall, 1970.

Aragon, Louis. *Le Paysan de Paris.* Paris: Gallimard, 1926.

Arnaud, Noel. "Les Metamorphoses historiques en Dada," *Critique* 134 (July, 1958), 579–604.

Arp, Jean. *Arp on Arp,* ed. Marcel Jean. New York: Viking, 1972.

Artaud, Antonin. *Oeuvres Complètes,* vols. II, IV, and V. Paris: Gallimard, 1964.

Balakian, Anna. *André Breton.* New York: Oxford University Press, 1971.

Balakian, Anna. "Dada-Surrealism: Fundamental Differences." *Proceedings of the Comparative Literature Symposium,* vol. III, ed. Wolodymyr T. Zyla. Lubbock, Texas: Texas Technical University, 1970.

Balakian, Anna. *Literary Origins of Surrealism.* New York: King's Crown Press, 1947.

Ball, Hugo. *Flight Out of Time,* ed. John Elderfield. New York: Viking, 1974.

Banham, Reyner. *Theory and Design in the First Machine Age.* New York: Praeger, 1960.

Bann, Stephen. *The Tradition of Constructivism.* New York: Viking, 1974.

Beaujour, Michel. "Is Less More?" *Intertextuality: New Perspectives in Criticism,* ed. Jeanine Plottel and Hanna Charney. *New York Literary Forum* 2 (1978): 237–243.

Bonnefoy, Yves. *Rimbaud par lui-même.* Paris: Seuil, 1961.

Benamou, Michel and Caramello, Charles, eds. *Performance in Postmodern Culture.* Madison: Coda Press, 1977.

Berckman, Edward. "The Function of Hope in Brecht's Pre-Revolutionary Theater." *Brecht Heute* I, ed. John Fuegi, pp. 11–26. Frankfurt: Athenäum Verlag, 1971.

Bohn, Willard, "La Quatrième dimension chez Apollinaire." In *Guillaume Apollinaire 14,* ed. Michel Décaudin. *Le Revue des Lettres Modernes,* n.d., 93–103.

Bonnet, Marguerite. "Aux sources du surréalisme: place d'Apollinaire." In *Guillaume Apollinaire 3,* ed. Michel Décaudin. *La Revue des Lettres Modernes* 104–107 (1964): 4.

Bowie, Malcolm. "Paul Éluard." In *Sensibility and Creation,* ed. Roger Cardinal. 149–176. London: Croom Helm, 1977.

Brecht, Bertolt. *Collected Plays, Vols. 1, 2, 5, 6,* ed. Ralph Mannheim and John Willett. New York: Pantheon, 1970–1977.

Brecht, Bertolt. *Gesammelte Werke,* 20 vols., Frankfurt: Suhrkamp, 1967.

Brecht, Bertolt. *Tagebücher, 1920–1922,* ed. Herta Ramthun. Frankfurt: Suhrkamp, 1975.

Breton, André. *L'Amour Fou.* Paris: Gallimard, 1937.

Breton, André. *Arcane 17.* New York: Brentano's, 1945.

Breton André. *Entretiens.* Paris: Gallimard, 1952.

Breton André. *Manifeste du Surrealisme.* nouvelle edition. Paris: Kra, 1929.

Breton, André. *Manifestoes of Surrealism,* trans. Richard Seaver and Helen Lane. Ann Arbor: University of Michigan Press, Ann Arbor Paperback, 1972.

Breton, André. *Nadja.* 2d edition. Paris: Gallimard, 1928.

Breton, André. *Nadja,* trans. Richard Howard. New York: Grove Press, 1960.

Breton, André. *Les Pas perdus.* Paris: Gallimard, 1924.

Breton, André. *Point du Jour.* Paris: Gallimard, collection idées, 1970.

Breton, André. *Surrealism and Painting,* trans. Simon W. Taylor. New York: Harper and Row, 1972.

Breton, André. *Les vases communicants.* Paris: Gallimard, 1955.

Breton, André. *What is Surrealism?,* ed. Franklin Rosemont. n.p.: Monad, 1978.

Brion-Guerry, L., ed., *L'Année 1913.* 2 vols. Paris: Klinksieck, 1971.

Brown, Edward J. *Mayakovsky: A Poet of the Revolution.* Princeton: Princeton University Press, 1973.

Breunig, Leroy, ed. *Apollinaire on Art.* New York: Viking, 1972.

Brüggemann, H. *Literarische Technik und soziale Revalation.* Hamburg: Reinbek, 1973.

Butler, Christopher. *After the Wake.* New York: Oxford University Press, 1980.

Bürger, Peter. "Avant-Garde and Contemporary Aesthetics." *New German Critique* 22 (Winter, 1981): 19–22.

Cabanne, Pierre, ed. *Dialogues with Marcel Duchamp.* New York: Viking, 1971.

Carmody, Francis. *The Evolution of Apollinaire's Poetics.* Berkeley: University of California Press, 1963.

Carrouges, Michel. *André Breton et les données fondamentales du surréalisme.* Paris: Gallimard, collection idées, 1950.

Caws, Mary Ann. *The Poetry of Dada and Surrealism.* Princeton: Princeton University Press, 1970.

Chipp, Herschel, ed., *Theories of Modern Art.* Berkeley: University of California Press, 1968.

Cohn, Robert Greer. *The Poetry of Rimbaud.* Princeton: Princeton University Press, 1973.

Deleuze, Gilles. "Politics." *Semiotexte* 3, 2 (1978): 154–163.

Desnos, Robert. *La liberté ou l'amour!* Paris: Gallimard, 1962.

Dickson, Keith. *Towards Utopia.* Oxford: Clarendon Press, 1978.

Eisenstein, Sergei. *Film Form and Film Sense,* ed. and trans. Jay Leyda. New York: World, 1957.

Éluard, Paul. *Oeuvres complètes.* Paris: Gallimard, Pléiade, 1968.

Elliott, David. *Rodchenko and the Arts of Revolutionary Russia.* New York: Pantheon, 1979.

Entretiens sur le surréalisme. Paris: Mouton, 1968.

Ermolaev, Herman. *Soviet Literary Theories 1917–1934*. Berkeley: University of California Press, 1963.

Ewen, Frederic. *Bertolt Brecht*. New York: Citadel, 1967.

Federman, Raymond, ed., *Surfiction*. Chicago: Swallow Press, 1975.

Fennell, John, ed., *Nineteenth Century Russian Literature*. Berkeley: University of California Press, 1973.

Foster, Leonard. *Poetry of Significant Nonsense*. Cambridge: Cambridge University Press, 1962.

Foster, Stephen and Kuenzli, Rudolf, eds., *Dada Spectrum*. Madison: Coda Press, 1979.

Fowlie, Wallace. *Rimbaud's Illuminations*. London: Harvill Press, 1953.

Frisch, Werner and Obermeier, K. W. *Brecht in Augsburg*. Frankfurt: Suhrkamp, 1976.

Frioux, Claude. "Maïakovski est mort futuriste." *Europe* 552 (1975): 75–87.

Frohock, W. *Rimbaud's Poetic Practice*. Cambridge: Harvard University Press, 1963.

Garvin, Harry R., ed. *Romanticism, Modernism, Postmodernism*. Lewisburg, Pennsylvania: Bucknell University Press, 1980.

Gass, William H. *The World within the Word*. New York: Knopf, 1978.

Gauthier, Xavière. *Surréalisme et Sexualité*. Paris: Gallimard, 1971.

Gershman, Herbert. *The Surrealist Revolution in France*. Ann Arbor: University of Michigan Press, 1969.

Giddens, Anthony. "Modernism and Postmodernism." *New German Critique* 22 (Winter, 1981): 15–18.

Giust, Jean-Pierre. *Rimbaud Créateur*. Paris: Presses Universitaires de France, 1980.

Grossman, Manuel. *Dada: Paradox, Mystification and Ambiguity*. New York: Bobbs-Merrill, 1971.

Guillaume, Henri. *À Vrai Dire*. Paris: Gallimard, 1956.

Haas, Willy. *Bert Brecht,* trans. Max Knight. New York: Ungar, 1970.

Habermas, Jurgen. "Modernity versus Postmodernity." *New German Critique* 22 (Winter, 1981): 3–14.

Habermas, Jürgen. *Toward a Rational Society,* trans. Jeremy Shapiro. Boston: Beacon, 1970.

Hassan, Ihab and Hassan Sally. *Innovation/Renovation*. Madison: University of Wisconsin Press, 1983.

Hassan, Ihab. *The Right Promethean Fire*. Urbana: University of Illinois Press, 1980.

Heller, P. "Nihilist into Activist." *Gemanic Review* 28 (1953): 144–55.

Herbert, Robert, ed., *Modern Artists on Art*. Englewood Cliffs, N.J.: Prentice-Hall, 1964.

Hofmann, Werner. *Turning Points in Twentieth Century Art*. New York: Braziller, n.d.

Houston, John Porter. *The Design of Rimbaud's Poetry*. New Haven: Yale University Press, 1963.

Hubert, Renée Riese. "The Fabulous Fiction of Two Surrealist Artists." *New Literary History* 4, 1 (Autumn, 1972): 151–166.

Hubert, Renée Riese. "Nadja depuis le mort de Breton." *Oeuvres et Critiques* 2, 1 (Spring, 1977): 92–102.

Huelsenbeck, Richard. *Memoirs of a Dada Drummer*, ed. Hans J. Kleinschmidt. New York: Viking, 1974.

Hugnet, Georges. *L'Aventure Dada*. Paris: Galérie de l'Institut, 1957.

Huyssen, Andreas. "The Search for Tradition: Avant-Garde and Postmodernism in the 1970s." *New German Critique* 22 (Winter, 1981): 23–40.

Kostelanetz, Richard. *The Avant-Garde Tradition in Literature*. Buffalo: Prometheus Books, 1982.

Kostelanetz, Richard. *Visual Literature Criticism*. Carbondale: Southern Illinois Press, 1979.

Jakobson, Roman. "Fragments de la nouvelle poétique russe. *Poétique* 7 (1971): 287–298.

Jauss, Hans Robert. "Group Interpretation of Apollinaire's *Arbre*." In *New Perspectives in German Literary Criticism*, ed. Richard Amacher and Victor Lange. pp. 187–207. Princeton: Princeton University Press, 1979.

Jean, Marcel, ed., *The Autobiography of Surrealism*. New York: Viking Press, 1980.

Jengfeldt, Bengt. *Majakovskij and Futurism, 1917–1921*. Stockholm: Almquist and Wiskell International, 1976.

Joll, James. *Three Intellectuals in Politics*. New York: Pantheon, 1960.

Kirby, Michael, ed., *Futurist Performance*. New York: Dutton, 1971.

Kirby, Michael, ed., *Happenings*. New York: Dutton, 1966.

Kittang, Atele. *Discours et Jeu*. Bergen, Norway: Universitetsforlaget, 1975.

Last, Rex. *German Dadaist Literature*. New York: Twayne, 1973.

Last, R. W. *Hans Arp: The Poet of Dadaism*. Chester Springs, Pennsylvania: Dufour, 1969.

Lebel, Robert, ed., *Marcel Duchamp*. New York: Grossman, 1959.

Lippard, Lucy, ed., *Dadas on Art*. Englewood Cliffs, N.J.: Prentice-Hall, 1971.

Little, Roger. *Guillaume Apollinaire*. London: The Athlone Press, 1976.

Lyons, Charles. *Bertolt Brecht*. Carbondale: Southern Illinois University Press, 1968.

Lyotard, Jean-François. *La Condition Postmoderne*. Paris: Minuit, 1979.

Lyotard, Jean-François. "On the Strength of the Weak." *Semiotexte* 3, 2 (1978): 204–214.

Marinetti, Filippo. *Selected Writings*, ed. and trans. R. W. Flint. New York: Farrar, Straus & Giroux, 1971.

Marinetti, Filippo. "Zang Tumb Tuuum." Adrianopoli. October 1912. Milano, Edizioni futuriste di "poesia," 1919.

Markov, Vladimir. *Russian Futurism*. Berkeley: University of California Press, 1968.

Marshall, Herbert, trans. *Mayakovsky*. New York: Hill and Wang, 1965.

Marshall, Herbert. *Mayakovsky and His Poetry*. London: The Pilot Press, 1945.

Matthews, J. H. "Appollinaire devant les surréalistes." In *Apollinaire 3*, ed. Michel Décaudin. *La Revue des Lettres Modernes* 104–107 (1964): 4.

Matthews, J. H. *An Introduction to Surrealism*. University Park, Pennsylvania: Pennsylvania State University Press, 1965.

Matthews, J. H. *Surrealist Poetry in France*. Syracuse: Syracuse University Press, 1969.

Mayakovsky, Vladimir. *The Bedbug and Selected Poetry*, ed. Patricia Blake. Bloomington: Indiana University Press, 1975.

Mayakovsky, Vladimir. *The Complete Plays*, trans. Guy Daniels. New York: Washington Square Press, 1968.

Mayakovsky, Vladimir. *How are Verses Made?*, trans. G. M. Hyde. London: Jonathan Cape, 1970.

Melzer, Annabelle. *Latest Rage the Big Drum*. Ann Arbor: University of Michigan Research, 1980.

Middleton, J. C. "Bolshevism in Art: Dada and Politics." *Texas Studies in Literature and Language* 4, 3 (Autumn, 1962): 408–430.

Middleton, J. C. "The Rise of Primitivism and Its Relevance to the Poetry of Expressionism and Dada." In *The Discontinuous Tradition*, ed. P. F. Ganz. 182–203. Oxford: Clarendon, 1971.

Morawski, Stefan. "Challenge and Paradox of The Recent Avant-garde." *Arts in Society* 12, 2 (1975): 226–229.

Morley, Michael. *Brecht: A Study*. London: Heineman, 1977.

Motherwell, Robert. *The Dada Painters and Poets*. New York: Wittenborn, 1951.

Nadeau, Maurice. *Histoire du surréalisme*. Paris: Seuil, 1964.

Onimus, Noemi Blumenkranz. "Futurisme italien et futurisme russe." *Europe* 552 (April, 1975): 8–27.

Osmond, Rick, ed., *Rimbaud's Illuminations*. London: The Athlone Press, 1976.

Perloff, Marjorie. *The Poetics of Indeterminacy*. Princeton: Princeton University Press, 1981.

Peschel, Enid. *Flux and Reflux: Ambivalence in the Poems of Arthur Rimbaud*. Geneva: Librarie Droz, 1977.

Prawer, S. S. "Dada Dances: Hugo Ball's Tenderenda der Phantast." In *The Discontinuous Tradition*, ed. P. F. Ganz, 209–223. Oxford: Clarendon, 1971.

Proffer, Ellendea and Proffer, Carl, eds. *Russian Futurism*. Ann Arbor: Ardis, 1980.

Pütz, Manfred. *The Story of Identity: American Fiction of the Sixties.* Stuttgart: J. B. Metzlersche, 1979.

Raymond, Marcel. *De Baudelaire au Surréalisme.* Édition nouvelle revue et remaniée. Paris: José Corti, 1969.

la Révolution Surréaliste. New York: Arno Press, n.d.

Rimbaud, Arthur. *Complete Works, Selected Letters,* trans and ed. Wallace Fowlie. Chicago: University of Chicago Press, 1966.

Rimbaud, Arthur. *Lettre du voyant,* ed. Gerald Schaeffer. Geneva: Droz, 1975.

Rimbaud, Arthur. *Oeuvres,* ed. Suzanne Bernard. Paris: Garnier Frères, 1960.

Said, Edward. "Reflections on Recent American 'Left' Literary Criticism." *Boundary II* 8, 1 (1979): 11–30.

St. Aubyn, F. C. *Arthur Rimbaud.* Boston: G. K. Hall, Twayne, 1975.

Sanouillet, Michel. *Dada à Paris.* Paris: Pauvert, 1965.

Schifferli, Peter, ed., *Als Dada Begann.* Zurich. Im Verlag der Arche, 1957.

Schmits, Georges. "Le Simulacre de la Voyance." *Apollinaire inventeur de langages,* ed. Michel Décaudin. Paris: Lettres Modernes Minaud, 1973.

Sheringham, Michel. "From the Labyrinth of Language to the Language of the Senses." In *Sensibility and Creation,* ed. Roger Cardinal. 72–102. London: Croom Helm, 1977.

Shlovsky, Viktor. *Mayakovsky and His Circle,* trans. Lily Feiler. New York: Dodd, Mead, 1972.

Shattuck, Roger. *The Banquet Years.* Garden City, New York: Doubleday Anchor, 1961.

Shattuck, Roger. "The Nadja File." *Cahiers DADA surréalisme.* 1, 1966, 49–56.

Sinn und Form: Zweites Sonderheft Bertolt Brecht. Berlin: Rütten and Loenig, 1957.

Slonim, Marc. *Soviet Russian Literature 1917–1977.* New York: Oxford University Press, 1977.

Sola, Agnes. "Futurisme russe et révolution." *Europe* 552 (April, 1975): 159–171.

Sollers, Philippe. *Logiques.* Paris: Seuil, 1968.

Stahlberger, Lawrence. *The Symbolic System of Mayakovsky.* The Hague: Mouton, 1964.

Steegmuller, Francis. *Apollinaire, Poet among Painters.* New York: Farrar, Straus & Giroux, 1963.

Le Surréalisme au Service de la Révolution. New York: Arno Press, n.d.

Steinweig, R. *Das Lehrstück: Brecht's Theorie einer politisch-ästhetischen Erziehung.* Stuttgart: J. B. Metzlersche, 1972.

Striedter, Jurij. "The 'New Myth' of Revolution—A Study of Mayakovsky's Early Poetry." In *New Perspectives in German Literary Criticism,* ed. Richard Amacher and Victor Lange. 357–385. Princeton: Princeton University Press, 1979.

Taylor, Joshua. *Futurism*. New York: Museum of Modern Art, 1961.

Tytell, John. "Epiphany in Chaos: Fragmentation in Modernism." *Fragments: Incompletion and Discontinuity*, ed. Lawrence Kritzman. *New York Literary Forum* 8–9 (1981): 3–16.

Tzara, Tristan. *Approximate Man and Other Writings*, trans. and ed. Mary Ann Caws. Detroit: Wayne State University Press, 1973.

Tzara, Tristan. *L'homme approximatif*. Paris: Gallimard, 1968.

Tzara, Tristan. *Seven Dada Manifestoes and Lampisteries*. London: Calder, 1977.

Tzara, Tristan. *Le Surréalisme et L'Après-guerre*. Paris: Nagel, 1948.

Verkauf, Willy, ed. *Dada: Monograph of a Movement*. New York: Wittenborn, 1957.

Völker, Klaus. *Brecht Chronik*. Regensburg: Carl Hanser Verlag, 1971.

Weisman, John. *Guerrilla Theater*. Garden City: Doubleday, 1973.

Werdeli, Walter. *The Art of Bertolt Brecht*, trans. Daniel Russell. New York: New York University Press, 1963.

White, Alfred. *Bertolt Brecht's Great Plays*. London: Macmillan, 1978.

Wilde, Alan. *Horizons of Assent*. Baltimore: Johns Hopkins University Press, 1981.

Willett, John, ed. *Brecht on Theatre*. New York: Hill and Wang, 1964.

Willett, John. *The Theatre of Bertolt Brecht*. New York: New Directions, 1959.

Woodward, Kathleen, ed. *The Myths of Transformation: Technology and Postindustrial Culture*. Madison: Coda Press, 1980.

Woroszylski, Wiktor. *The Life of Mayakovsky*, trans. Baleslaw Taborski. New York: Orion Press, 1970.

Index

"A Slap in the Face of Public Taste," 168, 185
Abish, Walter, 252
Absurdity as an aesthetic act, 32, 88, 97, 98, 102, 103, 108, 116, 119–120, 125, 239
Acker, Kathy, 253
Adamov, A, 243
Adorno, Theodor, 227, 246–247
Aesthetic activism, 4, 24, 33–37, 96, 238
Aesthetic acts, gratuitous, 26, 34, 97, 105, 121, 248, 257
Aestheticism, 8, 15, 18, 20, 24, 26, 33, 39, 165, 237
Agonism, 38, 55, 86, 185, 191–192, 205
Alienation of writers, 5, 7, 8, 9, 10, 14, 20, 21, 22, 37, 39, 41, 54, 57, 69, 94, 122, 129, 184, 187, 195, 207, 226–227, 236–238, 241, 244–246
Anarchism, 29, 38, 42, 100, 102, 110, 112, 115, 118, 154, 239, 241, 248, 254, 257–258, 262–263, 269
Apollinaire, Guillaume, 4, 7, 25, 26, 27, 29, 35, 36, 37, 61–86, 94, 111, 119, 123–129, 133, 149, 211
  Alcools, 78
  Arbre, 82, 83
  Calligrammes, 80, 82
  Cors de Chasse, 77
  Cortège, 67, 69, 76–77
  La Jolie Rousse, 78–79
  L'Antitradition futuriste, 78
  Le Poete Assassiné, 80
  Le Pont Mirabeau, 77–78
  Les Collines, 69, 71–76
  Les Fenêtres, 69, 82
  Les Mamelles de Tiresias, 80, 128
  Liens, 82
  Lundi rue Christine, 82
  Merveilles de la Guerre, 66–67, 69
  Oneirocriticism, 80, 127
  "The New Spirit and the Poets," 69, 70, 71, 84
  Toujours, 70–71, 72
  Visée, 82–83
Aragon, Louis, 124–125, 139–140, 145–147, 149–152, 154–156, 210
  Le Paysan de Paris, 139–140, 145, 147, 149–152
  Les Frères la Côte, 146–147, 151
Arias, Ron, 240
Arp, Jean, 26, 35, 99, 101, 102, 105–108, 118, 210
Artaud, Antonin, 38, 131, 133, 245
Audience, avant-garde attitude toward, 34, 35, 36, 88, 89, 96–97, 102, 112, 120, 125, 151, 170–171, 173–174, 187, 206–207, 215, 221–223, 225–226, 232, 239

Automatic writing, 125–127, 134–136, 141–
    145, 150–153
Autonomy of artwork, 13, 18, 21, 33

Baader, Johannes, 116
Baargeld, Johannes, 117
Babel, Issac, 181
Ball, Hugo, 25, 35, 99, 100, 101, 108–112,
    113, 118, 126
Balla, Giacomo, 87, 91, 92, 93
Balzac, Honoré de, 225
Baraka, Amiri, 31, 259
Barrès, Maurice, 120
Barth, John, 249, 252, 257, 263
Barthelme, Donald, 253, 255, 260, 264, 267
Baudelaire, Charles, 7, 8, 9, 18, 35, 45, 58,
    119, 124
Beat movement, 40, 159, 242–244
Becker, Jürgen, 251
Beckett, Samuel, 10, 12, 14, 227, 243–244
Bellow, Saul, 244
Benjamin, Walter, 226–227
Benveniste, Emil, 156
Bernstein, Charles, 3
Biely, Andrey, 173
Black Arts Movement, 242, 245
Blake, William, 129, 156
Blaue Reiter, der, 62, 63, 166
Bloch, Ernst, 224
Blok, Aleksandr, 173
Boccioni, Umberto, 86, 87, 91, 92–93
Bodacious Buggerilla Theater, 245
Bogdanov, Aleksandr, 175–176
Bohemianism, 34, 39, 41, 97, 120, 154, 165–
    167, 171, 173–174, 179, 191, 198, 212,
    217, 242–243
Böll, Heinrich, 244
Borges, Jorge Luis, 252, 263
Bragaglia, Anton, 87
Brautigan, Richard, 253, 255, 260, 264, 267
Brecht, Bertolt, 4, 7, 29, 30, 35, 40, 62, 111,
    123, 166, 206–235, 245
    Arturo Ui, 230
    Baal, 211–215
    Der Flug des Lindberghs, 220–221
    Der Jasager, 219, 221
    Der Neinsager, 219, 221
    Die Gesichte der Simone Machard, 231
    Die Gewehre der Frau Carrar, 231
    Die Mutter, 231
    Drums in the Night, 211, 213–216, 223,
        230
    Edward II, 216
    Galileo, 228–232
    Happy End, 221
    In the Jungle of the Cities, 211–212,
        214–215, 230
    Journals, 212, 216–217
    lehrstücke, 209, 218–222, 230
    Man is Man, 216–217
    Mother Courage, 228–231
    Puntilla, 229–230
    St. Joan of the Stockyards, 230
    The Caucasian Chalk Circle, 228–230
    The Good Person of Setzuan, 228–230
    The Last Days of the Commune, 231
    The Measures Taken, 219–220
    The Rise and Fall of the City of
        Mahagonny, 221
    The Threepenny Opera, 221
Breton André, 23, 25, 118–121, 123–136,
    140–164, 207–208
    Arcane 17, 153–154, 164
    Deux Manifestes Dada, 126
    L'Amour fou, 149
    Les Champs magnetiques, 126
    Les vases communicants, 149
    L'Union libre, 140–141, 151
    "Manifesto for an Independent Revo-
        lutionary Art," 163
    Manifestoes of Surrealism, 124, 127, 129–
        135, 154, 158–159, 162
    Nadja, 132, 147–150, 152–153
    Poisson Soluble, 144–146
    Pour Dada, 126
    "Surrealist Situation of the Object," 136
Brik, Lilly, 201
Brik, Osip, 170, 182, 201
Brücke, die, 62, 63
Bukharin, Nikolai, 182
Bürger, Peter, 20
Burlyuk, David, 167–168, 170, 172, 174, 185
Burlyuk, Nikolai, 168, 172
Burroughs, William, 249, 253–255, 259,
    262, 264–266

Cabaret Voltaire, 101
Cage, John, 241, 248, 254
Calinescu, Matei, 17
Camus, Albert, 243–244
Carli, Mario, 91
Carra, Carlo, 87, 91
Cervantes, Miguel de, 225
Chagall, Marc, 166
Chance, as aesthetic element, 32, 35, 49,
    99, 143, 256–257

Chirico, Giorgio de, 128
Chiti, Remo, 91
Chuzak, N. F., 178
Clarté, 155–156
Collin, Françoise, 251
Communism, 99, 218
Communist Party, 29, 30, 31, 32, 94, 115–
    118, 122, 123, 153–164, 165–166, 170–
    171, 174–177, 179, 181–182, 185, 195,
    198, 200, 206, 219–220
Concrete Poetry, 36, 242
Constructivism, 62, 111, 166, 195, 203
Coover, Robert, 253, 255, 260, 267
Corra, Bruno, 87
Cortazar, Julio, 252
Crèvel, René, 142
Critical thought, 4, 19, 21, 22, 23, 26, 33,
    209–210, 223–228, 232–233, 236, 239,
    245, 251
Cubism, 62, 63, 80, 81, 82, 101, 124, 126,
    128, 166

Dada, 4, 7, 25, 26, 27, 29, 34, 35, 36, 40,
    49, 62, 76, 80, 88, 90, 94, 96–121, 123–
    129, 134, 136, 143, 150, 153, 160, 177,
    207–208, 210, 247
Dada, 125
Dali, Salvador, 136–137, 146, 210
Das neue Leben, 99, 113
Delaunay, Robert, 80, 81
Delvaux, Paul, 146
Demby, William, 253, 255, 259
Derrida, Jacques, 248
Desnos, Robert, 142, 144–147, 149, 151, 154
    La Liberté ou l'amour!, 145–147, 148
Dessy, Mario, 91
de Sade, Marquis, 124
de stijl, 62
de Vree, Paul, 252
Discovery, theme of, 46, 63, 70
Doolittle, Hilda, (H.D.), 10
Dos Passos, John, 224
Duchamp, Marcel, 99, 107, 108, 118, 119

Eisenstein, Sergei, 178
Eliot, T. S., 8, 10, 11, 12, 23, 24, 62
Ellison, Ralph, 244
El Teatro Campesino, 245
Éluard, Paul, 31, 118, 119, 124–125, 137–
    138, 140, 156, 158–159, 210
    Coeur à pic, 137–138, 140
    Donner à voir, 158–159

Enlightenment, 6, 22
Ernst, Max, 118, 136–137
Experimentalism, literary, 15, 24, 48, 70,
    80, 92, 101, 169–170, 178–180, 195, 208,
    211, 218–220, 236, 239–240, 253
Expressionism, 27, 28, 40, 62, 63, 87, 101,
    211–212, 224
Eykhenbaum, Boris, 170

Fascism, 10, 29, 30, 31, 90, 94–95, 157, 207,
    211–212, 218–219, 234, 244
Faulkner, 12
Fauvism, 62, 63
Federman, Raymond, 253, 255, 257–260,
    263–264
Flaubert, Gustave, 8, 14
Fluxus, 242
Formalists, Russian, 21, 169–170, 178–180,
    203, 224, 226
Forster, E. M., 10
Fourier, Charles, 16, 18
Frankfurt School of Criticism, 21, 223–227,
    240
Freud, Sigmund, 27, 29, 125–127, 129–130,
    134–135, 141, 146, 155, 158, 161
    Introductory Lectures on Psychoanalysis,
    135
Fuentes, Carlos, 252
Fuller, Buckminster, 241
Futurism, Italian, 3, 4, 7, 25, 27, 29, 30, 34,
    36, 37, 44, 62–65, 76, 80–81, 101, 102,
    104, 108, 111, 123, 128–129, 166–171,
    208, 210
Futurism, Russian, 4, 7, 27, 29, 36, 37, 40,
    48, 88, 90, 94, 111, 123, 131, 157, 164,
    165–205, 210, 224

Galsworthy, John, 225
Gass, William, 249, 252, 257, 263
Gaugin, Paul, 112
Gautier, Théophile, 8, 18
Gazeta futuristov, 174
Gide, André, 7, 10, 12, 14, 124
Gilman, Richard, 12
Golding, William, 244
Goldmann, Lucien, 6, 10, 240, 253
Gomringer, Eugen, 251
Grass, Günter, 244
Grosz, George, 114–118, 177
Guro, Elena, 168

Happenings, 90, 242, 245
Hamilton, David, 251
Hassan, Ihab, 241
Hausmann, Raoul, 114–117
Heartfield, John, 31, 115, 117–118, 177, 210
Hegel, G. W. F., 156
Heissenbüttel, Helmut, 251
Hemingway, Ernest, 7, 9, 10, 12, 14
Herzfelde, Wieland, 31, 115, 117–118
Höch, Hannah, 114, 115
HOW(ever), 252
Huelsenbeck, Richard, 25, 99, 100–101,
    103, 112–117, 126

Impressionism, 166
Improvisation, as aesthetic strategy, 255–
    259, 268
Infante, Cabrera, 252
Innovator, poet as, 39, 48, 62, 63, 65, 80,
    83, 92, 178, 210, 251, 269
Inventor, poet as, 64, 70
Ionesco, Eugène, 243
Irigaray, Luce, 251
Irrationalism, aesthetic, 28, 32, 34, 37, 48,
    52, 53, 99, 105, 121, 122, 125–127, 129–
    130, 140–141, 160
Iskusstvo Kommuny, 174, 193

Jakobson, Roman, 170
Jameson, Fredric, 20–21, 150
Janco, Marcel, 96–97, 98, 99, 101, 107,
    108, 113
Jandl, Ernst, 251
Janet, Pierre, 125, 127, 131
Jarry, Alfred, 119, 123, 130
Johnson, Uwe, 244
Joyce, James, 7, 10, 11, 12, 14, 38, 62, 224
    Ulysses, 11
Jung, Carl, 131

Kafka, Franz, 12, 224, 227
Kamensky, Vasily, 168, 170, 174
Kandinsky, Wassily, 166
Katz, Steve, 253, 255, 259, 264, 267
Khlebnikov, Victor, 167–170
Kitsch, 5
Kollwitz, Käthe, 118
Kosinski, Jerzy, 259
Kristéva, Julia, 251
Kruchonykh, Aleksey, 168–70

L=A=N=G=U=A=G=E, 3, 36, 249,
    252
la Révolution Surréaliste, 142, 154–156,
    158–160
Lautréamont, 36, 49, 58, 119, 123, 124,
    130, 136, 150, 156
Lawrence, D. H., 10, 11, 14
LEF, 176, 178, 180, 195
Lefebvre, Henri, 156
Lenin, V. I., 111, 155–156, 175–177, 179,
    181–182, 203
Lessing, Doris, 244
Le Surréalisme au Service de la Révolu-
    tion, 159, 161–162
Lind, Jakov, 244
Littérature, 119, 124–126
Living Theater, 245
Livshits, J., 167, 169
Lukàcs, Georg, 223–227, 246
Lunacharsky, Anatoly, 174–176, 181
Lyric, modern, 66, 67, 76, 83, 91

Magritte, René, 146
Mailer, Norman, 244
Major, Clarence, 253, 255, 259, 264
Mallarmé, Stéphane, 8, 10, 11, 13, 14, 81
Mann, Thomas, 12, 38, 225
Marcucci, Lucia, 252
Marcuse, Herbert, 246–247
Marinetti, Filippo, 37, 63, 64, 81, 87–92,
    95, 169, 171
Marino, Adrian, 22
Marx, Karl, 25, 29, 122–123, 124, 155–156,
    161, 209, 211, 217, 226
Marxism, 10, 32, 131, 155–158, 209, 217–218
Marquez, Gabriel Garcia, 252
Masson, André, 142
Mayakovsky, Vladimir, 4, 25, 26, 29, 30,
    35, 37, 44, 94, 123, 164, 166–168, 170–
    171, 174, 176–177, 181–205, 208, 211
    "About That," 189, 195, 200–202
    "A Cloud in Trousers," 187–192, 200
    "At the Top of My Voice," 204–205
    "Back Home!", 195–198, 200
    "Conversation with a Tax Collector
        about Poetry," 199
    "I," 185
    "I Love," 200
    "In Re Conferences," 203
    "Letter from Paris to Comrade Kostrov
        on the Nature of Love," 201
    Mystery Bouffe, 193

"150,000,000," 181, 197
"Orders for the Armies of the Arts,"
    174, 194–195
The Bath House, 203
The Bedbug, 203
"To Sergey Esenin," 199
Vladimir Mayakovsky: A Tragedy, 185–
    187
Mayröcker, Friederike, 251
Metaphysical yearnings of writers, 28, 32
Meyerhold, Vsevolod, 193–194
Miller, Henry, 11, 40
Modernism, as an aesthetic movement, 5,
    6, 7, 9–16, 18, 19, 23, 31, 33, 62, 63, 65,
    84, 94, 120, 124, 149, 165–167, 207, 218,
    223–227, 236–238, 242–246, 248–250,
    252, 264
Modernity, 4, 5, 7, 8, 9, 22, 23, 33, 60, 62–
    66, 69, 81, 86, 91, 121, 167–168, 170,
    210, 239
Molinaro, Ursule, 253, 255
Monnerot, J. M., 161–162
Murdoch, Iris, 244
Musil, Robert, 10, 12, 14, 62
Mussolini, Benito, 87, 95

Nabokov, Vladimir, 249, 257, 263
Naturalism, 211
Negation, as poetic strategy, 76, 96–99,
    247
Nerval, Gérard de, 119, 124, 130
New Criticism, 21, 24, 242
Nietzsche, Friedrich, 156
Nihilism, 15, 28, 34, 58, 64, 86, 96–98, 108,
    113, 115, 120, 125, 160, 188, 190, 211–
    212, 217, 264
Nonsense poetry, 112, 116, 120
Nord-Sud, 124
Nossack, Hans, 244
Noszlopy, George T., 15, 20, 21, 22
Nouveau roman, 243, 250
Novyi LEF, 176, 178–179, 182

Open Theater, 245
Opoyaz society, 170
Orphism, 63, 166
Ortega y Gasset, José, 249

Parnassian poets, 44
Pasternak, Boris, 181
Paz, Octavio, 15, 22–23, 32

Peret, Benjamin, 142
Pereval writers, 181
Picabia, Francis, 98, 99, 103, 113, 118, 119,
    120
Picasso, Pablo, 81
Piscator, Edwin, 222
Play in art, 26, 32, 99, 102, 120, 122, 248,
    257–259, 264, 269
Poésia Visiva, 252
Poggioli, Renato, 15, 38
Political vision of writers, 10, 15, 20, 24,
    25, 26, 28–31, 32, 34, 37, 63, 87, 89–
    90, 96, 100, 108, 122, 178
Post-impressionism, 166
Postmodernism, 4, 7, 26, 27, 29, 36, 37,
    223, 236–270
Post-structuralism, 21, 27, 37, 247–248,
    262–263
Pound, Ezra, 7, 9, 23, 24, 62
Priest, writer as, 97
Primitivism in poetry, 92–93, 97–99, 102,
    104, 105, 108, 115, 121
Proletarian writers movements, 166, 172–
    173, 175–177, 180–183, 198–199, 203
Proletkul't, 175–177
Prophet, writer as, 4, 37, 39, 64, 71, 72,
    80, 84, 86, 87, 97, 184, 187–188, 190,
    192
Proust, Marcel, 7, 9, 10, 12, 38
Proudhon, Pierre, 156
Puig, Manuel, 252
Pynchon, Thomas, 249, 253, 260–262, 264,
    266–268

Randomness in poetry, 82, 99, 105, 106,
    108, 120
Ray, Man, 118
Read, Herbert, 27
Reed, Ishmael, 240, 253, 255, 260, 267
REF, 176–177, 182
Reverdy, Pierre, 124, 134–135
Revolutionaries, writers as, 4, 29, 37, 39,
    184
Ribemont-Dessaignes, Georges, 118–119
Ricardou, Jean, 249–250
Richter, Hans, 107, 113
Rilke, Rainer Maria, 9, 11, 12, 13, 62
Rimbaud, Arthur, 3, 4, 7, 9, 18, 24, 25,
    28, 29, 35, 36, 37, 39–61, 70, 75, 76,
    80, 81, 86, 104, 106, 108, 112, 119,
    122–123, 124, 127–130, 133, 156, 158,
    211, 227, 246
Après le déluge, 55

Rimbaud, Arthur (*Cont.*)
  Aube, 55
  À Une Raison, 52–53
  Bruxelles, 46
  Chant de guerre parisien, 42
  Conte, 55
  Départ, 55
  Fête d'hiver, 46
  Fleurs, 46
  Génie, 59
  Le Bateau ivre, 55, 56–57, 59
  L'Éclatante Victoire de Sarrebruck, 42
  Le Mal, 42
  Les Illuminations, 36, 40, 50, 53, 61
  Les Mains de Jeanne-Marie, 42
  Les Poetes de sept ans, 5
  Les Ponts, 46
  L'Orgie parisienne, 42
  "lettres du voyant," 40, 47–48, 51–52, 54, 55
  Marine, 46
  Matinée d'Ivresse, 55–56, 59
  Mouvement, 47
  Mystique, 46
  Promontoire, 46
  Qu'est-ce pour nous?, 42–43, 55
  Rages de Césars, 42
  Scenes, 46–47
  Solde, 40
  Soleil et Chair, 45–46, 52
  Une Saison en Enfer, 40, 44, 47, 50, 56, 57–61, 127
  Veillées, 46
  Villes I, 49–51, 55
  Voyelles, 49
Rivera, Diego, 163
Robbe-Grillet, Alain, 250–251
Roche, Denis, 251
Roche, Maurice, 251
Rodchenko, Alexander, 178
Rodrigues, Olinde, 17
Rolland, Romain, 225
Romanticism, 6, 7, 13, 17, 18, 19, 22, 44, 49, 50, 130
Rühm, Gerhard, 251
Russolo, Luigi, 87

Sadok sudei, 167–168
Saint-Simon, Henri de, 16, 17, 18, 19
San Francisco Mime Troup, 245
Sarduy, Severo, 252
Sartre, Jean Paul, 243

Schwitters, Kurt, 99, 107, 108, 118, 210
Science and art, 26, 27–28, 31, 36, 37, 60, 62–64, 69, 122, 130, 134, 178, 209, 241
Seer, poet as, 7, 15, 25, 39, 47, 50, 54, 57, 66, 73–74, 97
Serapion Brotherhood, 181
Severini, Gino, 87
Shelley, Percy Bysshe, 13, 19
Shklovsky, Viktor, 170, 226
Sic, 124
Silko, Leslie, 240
Social activism of writers, 16
Social antagonism of writers, 4, 5, 10, 28, 41, 64, 238
Socialism, 16, 17, 41, 42, 58, 109, 110–111, 235
Socialist Realism, 163, 166, 208, 223–225
Sollers, Philippe, 249–250
Sorrentino, Gilbert, 267
Soupault, Philippe, 119, 124–127, 142
Spark, Muriel, 244
Spiritual aspirations of writers, 6, 11, 16, 25, 97–99, 109, 112, 116, 118, 170–173
Stalin, Joseph, 123, 157, 161, 163, 170, 176, 182–183, 196–197, 203, 240
Stein, Gertrude, 13
Stevens, Wallace, 10, 12
Subconscious, 24–25, 32, 35–36, 37, 49, 99, 103, 108, 109, 122, 125–127, 130–136, 141–145, 150, 212
Sukenick, Ronald, 249, 253, 255–260, 264, 266–267
Supremitism, 166
Surrealism, 4, 7, 24, 25, 26, 27, 28, 29, 30, 36, 37, 40, 49, 80, 88, 90, 105, 111, 121, 122–164, 166, 177, 206–208, 210, 224, 227, 267
Symbolism, Russian, 168, 173

Tel Quel, 250
Tolstoy, Leo, 225
Trakl, Georg, 10, 62
Trilling, Lionel, 13, 21
Trotsky, Leon, 155–157, 162–164, 179–182, 197–198
  Literature and Revolution, 179–181
Tzara, Tristan, 100, 101, 103–105, 107, 109, 110, 112, 116, 118–121, 125–126, 136, 210

Umbra group, 242
Universal order, ideal of, 48, 51, 108

Unknown, poetic search for, 48, 70, 76
Updike, John, 244
Utopianism, 17, 24, 25, 26, 27, 28, 32, 33,
    34, 44, 95, 106, 121, 171, 180–181,
    211, 215–216, 240

Valéry, Paul, 8, 10, 12, 13, 14, 53, 124
Verlaine, Paul, 41, 50, 58
Visionary impulse in art, 33, 37, 48, 51,
    80, 97
Vonnegut, Kurt, 253, 255, 259–260, 267
Vorticism, 88, 244

Williams, Raymond, 19, 20
Wittig, Monique, 249, 251
Woolf, Virginia, 7, 12
Worker, poet as, 87
Wright, Charles, 267
Wright, Richard, 244
Wurlitzer, Rudolph, 267

Yeats, William, 8, 11, 12, 13, 62

Zelle, Heinrich, 118